Also by Rak Razam

The Ayahuasca Sessions: Conversations with Amazonian Curanderos and Western Shamans

Aya Awakenings

A Shamanic Odyssey

Rak Razam

Foreword by Dennis J. McKenna

North Atlantic Books
Berkeley, California

Published by
North Atlantic Books
P.O. Box 12327
Berkeley, California 94712

Cover photo montage by Oli Dunlop and Vance Gellert
Aya Awakenings title logo by Tim Parish and Rak Razam
Interior book design by Brad Greene
Printed in the United States of America

Aya Awakenings: A Shamanic Odyssey is sponsored by the Society for the Study of Native Arts and Sciences, a nonprofit educational corporation whose goals are to develop an educational and cross-cultural perspective linking various scientific, social, and artistic fields; to nurture a holistic view of arts, sciences, humanities, and healing; and to publish and distribute literature on the relationship of mind, body, and nature.

North Atlantic Books' publications are available through most bookstores. For further information, visit our website at www.northatlanticbooks.com or call 800-733-3000.

Library of Congress Cataloging-in-Publication Data is available from the printer upon request.

ISBN 978-1-58394-800-2

1 2 3 4 5 6 7 8 9   SHERIDAN   18 17 16 15 14 13
Printed on recycled paper

For all those seeds the vine has touched
and for those yet to sprout . . .

Our vision will become clear
Only when you look inside your heart
Who looks outside dreams
Who looks inside awakens

—C. G. JUNG

RETURN

FOREWORD

Introduction to
Aya Awakenings

1971 was a pivotal and transformative year in the evolving social and cultural lurch that has characterized the progress of the human species in the latter half of the twentieth century and beyond. Then, as now, the times were turbulent; the war in Vietnam raged on, protesters were in the streets, the counterculture probed ever more edgy avenues of personal self-expression; then, as now, the nation as well as the world was riven with terrorism and conflict; then, as now, gigantic tornadoes, massive earthquakes and snowstorms were the environmental news of the day; then, as now, the ongoing spectacle of human folly and foibles ground on, with most of the world's people too distracted to notice or care about the fate of the planet or the meaning of human destiny.

1971 marked the real close of the 1960s, a crossing of a certain threshold that left society to sort out the consequences of the forces unleashed in that decade, a task with which we have been preoccupied ever since, and one far from finished. Among the many cultural, political, technological, and spiritual influences that surfaced in the sixties that continue to shape our collective worldview, one—the rediscovery of the psychedelic experience and its emergence in modern consciousness—is quite unlike anything that has happened before in human history.

The 1960s was the decade that psychedelics, largely in the form of LSD, erupted into modern society, and by 1971 the genie was thoroughly out of the bottle. I say "rediscovery" because of course there is nothing new about psychedelics; they have formed the foundations of indigenous shamanism worldwide for millennia; in modern times, perhaps the last 150 years, they have been curiosities attracting the interest of a few intelligentsia, psychologists, anthropologists, artists, writers, and "beatniks"; outside of these circles, they were hardly known, not much talked about. All that changed in the sixties, and the genesis of that change can probably be traced to a very specific event that occurred in 1957: the publication, in the May 13 issue of *LIFE* magazine, of R. Gordon Wasson's first public description of his quest for "magic mushrooms" in the mountains of Oaxaca.★

It was there that Wasson attended a mushroom *velada,* a vigil, with the *curandera* Maria Sabina, who subsequently became perhaps the most famous shaman of all time (to her regret). Wasson, on the other hand, became the first non-Indian to consume the sacred fungi in a ceremonial setting and was more than happy to make the most of it. His fantastic account of that magical night in a hut clinging to a Mexican mountainside was tinged with awe and wonder, like the tale of a long-lost traveler who has returned from lands beyond the edge of the known world; as indeed, Wasson had done. And there it was in *LIFE* magazine, with color photos and beautiful watercolor paintings of the several species of Oaxacan magic mushrooms; there it was, sitting on practically every coffee or kitchen table in sleepy 1950s America.

I was but a lad of six when that article was published; I could comprehend what it was about, within my limited reading skills at the time, but I didn't pay it much attention. Older brother Terence, who was ten at the time, paid it a lot of attention. In fact, he was so excited about it that I can remember one occasion when he followed our mother through the house, waving the magazine and demanding to know what it was all about! Well, if Terence was excited about it, I figured, it must be cool (to a six-year old, anything your ten-year-old brother does is cool, by definition) so I took an interest too. Thus began an obsession, or at least a passionate interest, that has consumed both of our lives.

And like a nanomolecular virus plopped into the quiet pond of Meme, the ripples generated by that article were the catalyst that

★R.G. Wasson, "Seeking the Magic Mushroom," *LIFE* magazine, May 13, 1957.

initiated the change in mass consciousness with respect to psychedelics. All subsequent events, from the rise of Leary to the eventual banning of LSD and ultimately all psychedelics (many in the UN Convention on Psychotropic Substances signed in Vienna in 1971) can be linked to that single publication. It brought psychedelics front and center for a brief time, and the American imagination, and fascination with the exotic and bizarre, kept it there for over a decade. The armies of hippies that descended on the tiny village of Huautla de Jiménez in the latter sixties in search of Wasson's treasure became the first, but not the last, instance of psychedelic tourism.

Flash forward to 1971. Terence was hiding out from Interpol in Vancouver, while I was a second-year undergrad at the University of Colorado in Boulder. Though immersed in the political and counter-cultural ferment of our times, our time on the barricades was limited. We were instead preoccupied with DMT, a rare and almost legendary psychedelic that occasionally surfaced in the underground. The sloppy bathtub syntheses that came our way were anything but pure, but they did the job. We had become utterly convinced that in this substance, and perhaps only in it, lay the salvation of humanity and perhaps the key that could unlock portals to other dimensions. So when we stumbled across a paper by R. E. Schultes, the famous Harvard ethnobotanist, about an obscure DMT-based hallucinogen used by the Witoto people of the upper Amazon, we knew we had to go after it.

We departed on our quest in late January 1971, determined to uncover a secret that would change us, and everything, forever. The secret we uncovered was something far stranger than the one we had set out to find; and it did change everything, though not in the ways we had envisioned.

Thus, unwittingly, Terence and I enscribed the first lines of a script that would play out over the next forty years in our own lives and in the culture at large. Those familiar with our myth have already heard the story of our misadventures at the mission village of La Chorrera in the Colombian Amazon in February and March of 1971.[2] Ten years later, as a graduate student in ethnobotany I returned to the Amazon, to Peru, to carry out fieldwork on ayahuasca and *oo-koo-hey,* the mysterious orally active Witoto preparation that had lured us to the Amazon in '71.

My objective, this time, was not to disrupt the fabric of reality but simply to carry out a comparative ethnobotanical investigation of the plants, active constituents, and pharmacological actions of these two similar-yet-different Amazonian psychedelics. Terence joined me for part of that journey, but it was my show this time. Eventually I completed my doctorate and published the results of my research in several peer-reviewed papers. Other than a few specialists, no one paid much attention; but gradually, interest was growing. I made another brief collecting trip to Peru in 1985 and after that did not visit Iquitos for another thirteen years. Thus played out the next few lines in the unfolding script.

What brought me back in January of 1998 was an ayahuasca retreat that had been organized by Jonathan "Sparrow" Miller Weisberger at Jardín Etnobotánico Sachamama, a retreat center and ethnobotanical garden established by one of my previous informants, Francisco Montes. Francisco's cousin, Pablo Amaringo, a former *ayahuasquero,* had attracted worldwide attention with his publication of a series of visionary paintings depicting his ayahuasca experiences in vivid, luminous detail. A few years previously, in collaboration with my colleague anthropologist Luis Eduardo Luna, Pablo had published a collection of his beautiful paintings+ that opened a window into indigenous Amazonian cosmology and the tradition of *"vegetalismo,"* the set of shamanic and ethnomedical practices that formed the basis of Mestizo folk medicine in the Peruvian Amazon.

The workshop at Sachamama brought together Francisco, Amaringo, Luna, myself, and about fifteen "ayahuasca pilgrims" to share ten

---

★Terence K. McKenna, *True Hallucinations: Being an Account of the Author's Extraordinary Adventures in the Devil's Paradise* (San Francisco: HarperSanFrancisco, 1993).

+Pablo Amaringo and L. E. Luna, *Ayahuasca Visions: The Religious Iconography of a Peruvian Shaman* (Berkeley, CA: North Atlantic Books, 1993).

days of encounters with the brew interspersed with lectures, seminars, and yoga sessions. Jonathan's retreat event was not the first ayahuasca retreat in Iquitos, nor was Sachamama the only retreat center in town, but it was among the earliest. Several other centers around Iquitos were just getting started and all were offering similar programs, and all were designed to be attractive to itinerate, foreign travelers with money to burn and a taste for exotic experience.

So by the time of my return to Iquitos after a thirteen-year absence, the seeds of the current ayahuasca tourism movement had firmly taken root, but was still a bit under the radar. By the time I visited again, six years later in 2004, the number of centers were proliferating, and there were plenty of dreadlocked gringos hanging out at the Yellow Rose and other watering holes.

Around this time Alan Shoemaker, a gringo expat who had married a local girl and settled in Iquitos, saw an entrepreneurial opportunity and began to organize annual summer conferences focused on the topic of shamanism, ayahuasca, and traditional *vegetalismo*. This brought the emerging ayahuasca tourism phenomenon to the attention of still more traveling seekers, and by the Second International Amazonian Shaman-ism Conference in July 2006, it was in full swing and had begun to take on a nearly circus-like atmosphere. People poured into town from all parts of the world; a nice conference venue was rented at the Hotel Parthenon, and local shamans printed business cards and set up shop at the periphery of the open-air auditorium. If you had the stomach for it (and many did) you could go off to drink with a different shaman every night, a phenomenon that I couldn't resist dubbing "shopping for shamans." But it was not a bad thing; if a particular shaman didn't suit your tastes, you were free to try another one the next night.

And this time, the ayahuasca tourist movement had its own chronicler in the person of gonzo journalist Rak Razam, the author of the book you hold in your hands. Rak makes no pretense of objectivity; he's very much a part of this new international tribe of archaic revivalists; but he also brings a certain bemused perspective to the whole colorful pageant, and he comes by his creds honestly. He's been an astute observer and participant in this melding, and inevitable transmogrification, of traditional Amazonian shamanism with global techno-tribalism. He's been telling the story of this social phenomenon for some years now, and has shared the brew with the best, and the worst, of the lot. The book he has created out of his experiences and the soon to be released documentary by the same name, *Aya: Awakenings,* offer an essential glimpse into the genesis and background of this social, spiritual, and cultural global movement.

What is clear from his account is that this movement has legs. Unlike the casual mushroom tourism of the late sixties, which quickly died out, the globalization of ayahuasca, sustained by the Internet and easy access to international travel, is not driven by a desire for cheap thrills, but by a deep longing on the part of many people, particularly young people, for a renewed connection to nature and genuine, meaningful spiritual experiences. In the process, this movement is both reviving and transforming, not always in good ways, a shamanic tradition that was endangered, and is slowly disappearing from Amazonian culture.

But traditions that never change, that do not adapt, do not last. Surely what is happening now to ayahuasca as it spreads its tendrils around the planet is better than the alternative: the slow decay, dissolution, and disappearance of an ancient healing tradition. The gnosis currently being bestowed on our species and spreading on the wings of the Internet comes directly from the plant teachers. In this moment of planetary crisis it is our task to accept it, understand it, and act on it. Indeed, failure to step up to this challenge may mean not only the end of our species but the death of Nature itself.

Dennis J. McKenna
Marine on St. Croix
May 2013

PREFACE

The Shaman's Path

Terence McKenna was one of the foremost proponents of the need for an "Archaic Revival" of culture. In his 1989 book *Food of the Gods,* he wrote: "Psychedelic shamans now constitute a worldwide and growing subculture of hyperdimensional explorers, many of whom are scientifically sophisticated. A landscape is coming into focus, a region still glimpsed only dimly, but emerging, claiming the attention of rational discourse—and possibly threatening to confound it. We may yet remember how to behave, how to take our correct place in the connecting pattern, the seamless web of all things."

As I write this introduction in 2013, twenty-four years after Terence first wrote his manifesto, the global shamanic resurgence, spearheaded by the ayahuasca movement worldwide, is seeing a critical mass of individuals exposed to the shamanic realms and the healing the great medicine ayahuasca—and a multitude of other entheogenic plants—can provide.

Now not everyone is yet "remember[ing] how to behave"—indeed, on many levels the evidence on the ground and in the jungle is that the West is commercializing and commodifying the ayahuasca experience. The lodge system in Peru has metastasized, with dozens of ayahausca retreats opening up to cater to the ever-increasing influx of seekers, and the number of curanderos has also mysteriously increased to cater to the demand.

The energy around ayahuasca is not always as pure as we would hope, and there have been many unfortunate reports of Westerners who have been abused, even a few very rare cases in which the duty of care was not present in ceremony, and people have died. Women especially, need to be aware that some curanderos have been said to prey sexually upon women during or after ceremony, betraying the trust that is put in them in this most vulnerable of intimacies. When this happens in the West with doctors, there is a legal system to disbar them; yet the shamanic safety net is still evolving—and we are the generation that must do the work to create it with this, and the wider issues the medicine work brings us as it integrates into the modern world.

Brujeria—negative intent—is also on the rise, and not just in the jungle, as the money and power ayahuasca tourism brings causes ripples within the culture in the old world and the new. Any genuine seekers wishing to explore ayahausca are advised to research well, and check out sites like the forums on Ayahuasca.com, where peer review and community moderation reports the latest news and developments from the front edge of consciousness. Reputations come and go, and even people documented in this book have sides to them I did not experience, nor document herein, in my own travels. So *caveat lector*—let the reader beware.

But also remember—all of this shadow work is coming to the fore as we are asked to deal with the reality of ayahuasca in the twenty-first century, and how to integrate this most potent of visionary medicines into our culture in a meaningful way. For while ayahuasca is being explored by science and academia worldwide, and acceptance of its healing properties is being documented on the medical level, this is still the tip of the spiritual iceberg. Biochemical evidence gives foundational credence to religious groups and those wishing to integrate ayahausca into existing healing and cultural modalities; yet it is my intuition that the vine—and the planetary intelligence that nurtures it—goes a whole lot deeper, and what it promises is a shamanic transformation of global culture itself.

Yes, ayahuasca has hit the mainstream, and the cultural inflection point shows no signs of slowing. The list of Hollywood celebrities who have drunk ayahuasca are many—even James Cameron is said to have been inspired by the "vine of souls" to communicate his experiences in his 3D blockbuster *Avatar.* Ayahuasca peaked most noticeably in Jennifer Aniston's 2011 Hollywood rom-com *Wanderlust,* in which in an unlikely script development she ends up in a tree thinking she could fly, as the disinformation used to say about LSD back in the sixties and in every acid-cliché since then.

This is the "horizontal" spread of the ayahuasca meme, and the deep experience under it, but there's another way to look—vertical. The vertical penetration of ayahuasca and plant entheogens goes as deep as horizontal goes wide, and that depth goes beyond popular culture, beyond tourism and commodification, beyond even us humans—and right to the soul.

Because, as Terence also hoped, a critical mass of people are also being initiated into a spiritual awakening that is larger than the plants themselves, and goes straight to the core of the human experience. The medicine is rebalancing the human species, the arrogant children who have trashed the planet, and it is doing so in a viral way. She's spreading fast now because the times we live in have never been more urgent, as the ecological emergency escalates around us. The planet is crying out for us humans to *come back to the garden,* back to that interdependent awareness of the web of life, the cause and effect that these entheogens can assist in revealing within us.

Things have evolved rapidly from the book you are about to read, which documents my first, archetypal journey into the Amazon in search of the mythic archetype of the shaman and the reasons why so many Westerners were setting out on this "gringo trail of the soul." Though I have been back to Peru three times since that virgin journey in 2006, none have equaled the depth of the experience chronicled herein, nor could they, as not only the circumstances were different— so was I.

This book was a labor of love—my "love song" back to Madre Ayahuasca and all that she showed me, and all that was revealed within me all along, just waiting to bloom. It was a leap of faith and an act of trust that the story I lived, and wrote, and knew I had to transmit to the world, was a story worth telling. I self-published it in 2009 under the banner of Icaro Publishing, which has now evolved into the Icaro Foundation (www.icarofoundation.org), which helps educate and make positive media about the shamanic experience, and to reconnect to the sacred in this changing world.

It was also on that first book tour in California with friends and media-makers Tim Parish and Lulu Madill, the seed for the film adaption of the book was born. That film, *Aya: Awakenings,* captures a wide-screen, broadstrokes slice of this book's themes, and matches it with hypnotic visuals, sensual soundscapes, and mind-blowing videography that transmits the raw experiences channelled herein directly to the visual cortex of the viewer in an immediate way. Like the book, the film is a "shamanic artifact," something that, once experienced, will transmit its energy into you as it communicates its message. My words are my medicine, and I hope they serve you well on your own voyages of discovery.

Ayahuasca has been part of my life now for the last seven years—a full human life-cycle—and in that time, many people in the burgeoning global medicine community have become my dear friends, colleagues, and companions on a collective journey of discovery. The vine really *has* reached out to embrace the world, and I have witnessed the organic, human embrace of ayahausca and the spirit worlds it opens up, as well as the repopulation on the world stage of *the medicine people for the global village.*

I say that the first wave of Westerners' involvement in ayahuasca shamanism can be marked from Richard Spruce's discovery of it with the Tokanan indians in 1851, all the way up to 1990, when Sachamama—one of the first ayahuasca lodges—was opened for Westerners outside Iquitos by Don Francisco Montes Shuna. Things speeded up over a generation from 1990 to 2012, when the tragedy of Kyle Nolan's death at the Shimbre lodge in Puerto Maldonardo closed the door on another epoch, and the "dark side of ayahuasca" started to see the light.

I feel a third wave of ayahuasca shamanism, as she reaches out to the world and those in search of healing, is this time, now, from 2013 on. You and I are the ones Madre works through, and we are the bridges from the old world to the new. And once the grand job of physical healing and energetic realignment is done, well, what awaits then?

As you will discover in the pages of this book, all those seeds that have heard the call of spirit are now on the shaman's path. Where does it lead? Join us, and we'll find out together.

Rak Razam
Mullumbimby, Australia
June 16, 2013

Part I
DEPARTURE

"The answer is never the answer. What's really interesting is the mystery. If you seek the mystery instead of the answer, you'll always be seeking. I've never seen anybody really find the answer—they think they have, so they stop thinking. But the job is to seek mystery, evoke mystery, plant a garden in which strange plants grow and mysteries bloom. The need for mystery is greater than the need for an answer."

—KEN KESEY

1

Seekers of the Mystery

Lima Airport, Peru
WEDNESDAY JUNE 28, 2006

The clean white walls of the stall are tagged with graffiti: "We who solve mystery, become mystery," alchemical wisdom handed down through the ages and now in the sterile men's toilets at the Lima airport departure lounge. Scrawled, no doubt, by one of the tourists waiting out in the food court.

Outside, milling under the ubiquitous gaze of security cameras, are bright splashes of colorful souls wearing crystals, beads, and Native American Indian paraphernalia; middle-aged academics with "Erowid" drug website t-shirts; and passengers that give you that odd conspiratorial smile that says, "yes, we are here for the conference." And here we are chowing down on McDonalds and Donut King, getting our last hits of civilization before hitting the jungle city of Iquitos and shamanic boot camp.

It feels like some whacked-out reality TV show, a generational snapshot of a new psychedelic wave just before it breaks. Bright-eyed Westerners about to die and be reborn in the humid jungles of Peru, drinking the hallucinogenic brew *ayahuasca*...

Ayahuasca is a plant medicine that has been used by the indigenous people of South America for millennia to heal physical ailments—and, they claim, to cleanse and purify the spirit. It was discovered by the West in 1851 when the legendary British botanist Richard Spruce explored the Rio Negro Basin and was introduced to the vine by the Tokanoan Indians. Spruce gave the vine its scientific name, *Banisteriopsis caapi;* in

3

different areas of South America it is also known as *yagé* or *hoasca*. For a while in the mid-twentieth-century chemists who isolated the active properties of the vine called their compound *"telepathine."*

Research showed it contained various *harmala* alkaloids, which are boiled up in a brew (also called ayahuasca) with a multitude of other plants, one being the leafy *Psychotria viridis,* which contains the powerful hallucinogenic chemical Dimethyltryptamine, also known as DMT. On its own the vine is only orally active at very high doses, but it also contains potent MAO *(mono-amine oxidase)* inhibitors that overpower the body's own enzymes and allow the DMT to potentiate.

Science has made cautious forays into the jungle to study the vine in its native setting or, as with the "Hoasca Project" in the 1990s, to study church members of groups like União do Vegetal (UDV) who drink ayahuasca as part of their syncretic Christian-jungle religion. What they found was that regular ayahuasca use flushed the brain clean and improved receptor sites, suggesting the vine could be a medicinal goldmine.

But what science cannot explain is the psychic effect of this "mother of all plants," the sense of the numinous and the spiritual world it reportedly opens up. Those who drink say that each ayahuasca journey is unique. They say that the spirit of the vine comes alive, it guides and teaches, and on the other side nothing is ever the same. Or so they say.

The native men and women who safeguard the knowledge of the vine and of the spirits it is said to reveal are the *curanderos* and *curanderas*—or, as the West would call them, shamans. Their role has been that of healer, priest, and traveler between worlds, acting as intermediaries between the spiritual dimension and this world on behalf of their patients.

Yet the demands of the work and the rise of Western materialism throughout South America have seen a fall in prestige—and customers— for the *curanderos.* The profession, usually hereditary, was in danger of extinction before an unprecedented wave of Western gringos started coming in search of ayahuasca and the healing it can provide.

Over the last twenty years or so a new gringo trail—this one a *journey of the soul*—has been blossoming in the jungles of South America. Seekers and thrillseekers alike have been coming from the West for a reconnection to the deeper reality shamanism connects one to—and bringing back amazing stories of hallucinogenic trips, healing, and enlightenment.

Indigenous shamanism has quickly become the most profitable business in town and numerous jungle lodges and retreats have sprung up across South America to cater to the influx of rich tourists. This has spilled over onto the internet as hundreds of ayahuasca websites, chat rooms, and forums have emerged to crystallize a global subculture engaging with an indigenous spiritual practice and seeding it back into the Western world.

As well as being used by hundreds of thousands, perhaps millions of indigenous peoples throughout South America, ayahuasca has also become one of the world's fastest growing religions, with branches of Brazilian churches like Santo Daime and União do Vegetal springing up in Europe, Britain, Australasia, America, Japan, and elsewhere. In January 2006, the U.S. Supreme Court ruled in favor of a New Mexico branch of the UDV, saying they had a constitutional right to be allowed to legally practice their ayahuasca ceremonies under the freedom of religion law. The U.S. government immediately appealed, but the genie was out of the bottle.

The mystery of ayahuasca had left the jungle and entered the cities, via religion, media, and the web. And here I was, a thirty-six-year-old freelance journalist, a gonzo reporter in the time-honored Hunter S. Thomson and Tom Wolfe style, freelancing for *Australian Penthouse* on an academic-style conference with a pronounced twist: it was all about Amazonian shamanism, with a hands-on component.

Strange, to think that in the first decade of the twenty-first century I would be heading to the Peruvian jungles in search of a connection to the primal consciousness that indigenous wisdom revealed. Yet in a world of global warming and environmental collapse it seemed all the more urgent to reconnect with the planet in a visceral way. And in this age of reality television, blogging, and urban surveillance, being an embedded journalist was par for the course. Nowadays we're all part of the story—and getting down-and-dirty in the far crevasses of consciousness was a prospect I was relishing.

Despite cultural diffidence back in the baseline world of war, mortgages, and climate change, *Australian Penthouse* was willing to have a peek under the covers of reality and embrace the story I was chasing—to understand the mythic pull of shamanism, one of the last global archetypes that connects to a numinous "Other." Yet at the same time it's also one of the most appropriated, glorified, and repackaged brands embedded in the global consciousness. So much so that it now attracts thousands of Westerners each year back to the disappearing jungles and the plant medicines they provide.

But what was the business of spirituality doing to all these backpacking ayahuasca tourists that dared to journey into the mysteries of creation? And what did it say about the growing Western need for an authentic reconnection to the planet?

"Margaret... Shane?" I spot a couple of familiar faces sitting at a table in the McDonalds food court, surrounded by their luggage and that homogenized glaze global travelers give off when they've been in airport departure lounges for too long and their internal body clocks have gone haywire. Margaret's furiously loading digital photos from their camera onto a MacBook while Shane pauses over the keyboard and looks up with a smile. With his stocky broad shoulders and close-shaven head he looks like a cop, but nothing could be further from the truth.

"Dr. Razam, I presume," Shane jokes, shaking my hand and grinning broadly. "I'm glad you could make it."

"Drinking hallucinogenic brews with the shamans of the Amazon? I wouldn't miss this for the world."

"Rak? How are you darling?" Margaret cries, standing up and giving me a hug full of unconditional love. She's a strong, confident woman with big brown eyes and shoulder-length brown hair, an earth mother from way back.

They both stare at me with a good-natured energy, like somebody's parents that also happen to be psychedelic trippers. I'd drunk ayahuasca with them in Australia a few months previously and wasn't surprised to see them here now, smack dab in the Lima airport food court, along with all the other ayahuasca tourists waiting for the early morning flight to Iquitos.

The first time I'd had "the medicine," as ayahuasca is called, was back in Australia after an outdoor electronic music festival in northern New South Wales, a few hours west of the hippie mecca of Byron Bay. Theo Valis, a rogue psychonaut chemist, had brewed up an ayahuasca analogue—often called "pharmauasca," or "Aussiehuasca"—using extracts from *Acacia maidenii* and *Syrian rue* for thirty participants to be initiated into the ways of the spirit world. But after downing the bitter brown liquid and chasing it with a hit of DMT crystal wrapped in tissue paper, I'd had no real psychedelic effect. The same had been true for my other three encounters with the vine, leaving me to wonder at the reports of otherworldly contact, overwhelming beauty, and a deep connection to the spirit that runs through all living things.

Ayahuasca was a mystery to me, and despite some people returning from last year's shaman conference, I got the feeling that many of the ayahuasca tourists here in the food court were in the same boat. We were all chasing the root of the vine, eager for the secrets she might provide, but like children in the ways of the spirit.

In the hours before the plane leaves the ayahuasca seekers magnetize together, gently feeling each other out and swapping stories. Two big ladies from the States in Native American–inspired tribal wear come over and introduce themselves, as does a bald-headed guy from L.A. and a young backpacker from Europe wearing a "Treehugger" t-shirt.

As we finally board the early morning flight to Iquitos, filing down the departure gate aisle, it strikes me how different we all are. A few obvious "New Agers" for sure, but the vast majority of seekers here are remarkable for only one thing: their conformity.

The ayahuasca network appears to cut across race, social class, and gender, a secret society of plant worshippers all united by the common experience of this potent hallucinogenic. And through them, the aya-huasca vine was spreading her tendrils across the world and a genuine "archaic revival" was underway.

My bags were packed, the jungle beckoned, and the ancient mystery of the rainforest awaited . . .

I wanted in on it.

As the plane nears Iquitos it lowers through the cloudbank and I can see flashes of vibrant green down below, an endless expanse of jungle with trees bunched up together into a dense viridian canopy and rolling out onto the horizon in an unbroken thread.

Some people call the Amazon the lungs of the earth, but here now, seeing the endless green of the rainforest, it looks more like the skin of an immense organism, a living creature made up of interlocking eco-systems. The jungle appears to have no end, and, seemingly, no clearings or signs of human settlement. It is a great green wonderland that hints at times long past when plants ruled the earth, and snaking through this primeval emerald forest are the muddy twists and turns of the mighty Amazon River.

A surge of adrenalin hits me as I realize I am finally in South America after living in airports and on planes for the last day—in that no man's land between departures and arrivals, stuck in a limbo of ticketing hierarchies and boarding passes. And now the forest spreads out underneath me, beckoning me into its embrace. As we bank lower, the dense foliage of the jungle gives way to large tracts of cleared land and the criss-cross circuitry grid of civilization begins. Huts become villages and before long a city appears on the horizon.

As I exit the plane I'm bathed in an intense humidity. It feels like I've arrived at the edge of the world and that Iquitos is a forerunner of things to come. There among the lush, verdant green surrounding the airport are the rusting hulks of two giant 727 passenger planes parked to the side of the runway, like props from some disaster movie. It's like looking at the West after peak oil, when the grid has gone down. *The jungle will conquer all the civilization you throw at it,* the hulks scream.

Iquitos is the end of the line and the beginning of the adventure. It's the largest city in the world not accessible by road, fed only by air or the Amazon River, with just a lone highway connecting it to the town of Nauta some hundred kilometers away. It lies almost four degrees south of the equator and is located in the northeastern Amazon plain in the Peruvian department of Loreto, over 1,000 kilometers from the national capital of Lima.

Officially founded in 1864 by the Peruvian government as a strategic base for navy ships, Iquitos (named after the Iquito Indians who lived here) has been dealing with the influx of *conquistadores,* missionaries, and tourists since Francisco de Orellana first "discovered" the Amazon River in 1542, ten years after the Incas were defeated.

The city itself rests on the banks of the Amazon and is considered one of the most important river ports in all of Peru. Virtually all consumable goods and machinery on sale throughout the region come through the busy ports of Iquitos, and much of the timber stripped from the jungle passes through here on its way to Brazil.

According to the scuttlebutt, nearly all the coca paste grown in Peru also comes from these parts and is transported upriver to Colombia for processing and export to the world. If the Americans really wanted to shut down the cocaine trade—and rumor also says there's a plethora of undercover American DEA and FBI agents operating out of Iquitos—then all they'd have to do is blockade the Amazon River above the city. But without coca Peru would go broke, and a whole wave of socialist revolution might swamp the country, like it has nearby Bolivia and Venezuela. Or so the rumor goes.

The ayahuasca tourists are standing around the lone baggage carousel with the other travelers, waiting for their luggage in the sparse, faded arrivals lounge of the Aeropuerto Coronel Francisco Secada. Tourism in Iquitos is like the jungle—whole belief systems must eat or be eaten, fed by a steady stream of true believers from both sides.

Travelers here are usually split between adventurous Westerners intent on braving the jungle at one of the many lodges that have little sales booths surrounding the walls of the arrivals lounge, staffed by bored Indians hustling their pamphlets and wares, or missionaries who have come to the jungle in large packs—many of them young church group members—to bring the good word to the Indians, just as their ancestors have done for hundreds of years. And now there's the new breed—the ayahuasca tourists, here to sample indigenous spirituality, and their number is booming.

Shane, Margaret, and I push through the departure lounge gates and are surrounded by a cloud of taxi hawkers all offering their services, at least two dozen of them that swoop down like vultures on fresh prey. We load our gear into one of the quaint three-wheeled *motorcarros* that are so abundant here, converted motorbikes with a covered carriage on the back like a rickshaw, and speed noisily into town.

The motorbike taxis are adorned with logos: Honda, Nike, Rolling Stones lips, and names like *Alfredo, Tupac,* and *Paradiso.* The drivers honk endlessly to communicate their moves, swerving in and out of each other's paths with the carefree nonchalance of those who are unafraid to die and are quite aware how to live. Thousands—literally thousands—of these noisy beasts roar through the streets of Iquitos, a constant rumble in the concrete jungle, a force of nature unto themselves, with nary a car in sight.

It's different here, you can feel it, and it's not just the heat—it's the vibe. Whole families four or five strong balance themselves calmly on motorbikes, grandmothers sitting side-saddle, feet dangling above the speeding ground, kids hanging onto their parents backs without even the rumor of a helmet. A five-year-old girl sits crouching on her knees and hangs onto her mother's shoulders as they speed down the road on their motorbike, and as our taxi draws parallel she shoots me a smile: See? *We are free here.*

We head towards the Hobo Hideout, one of the cheaper alternatives in the *Lonely Planet,* but also a hostel likely to have some beds free this early in the morning. Our taxi driver takes us around the rumbling one-way streets, clogged by currents of colorful transit buses with wooden frames and Jesus stickers, motorbikes, and three-wheeled *motorcarros,* exhaust fumes trailing behind them like hungry ghosts and gathering in foggy clouds when they stop at the traffic lights. My throat is itchy from all the fumes but the delirious otherness of being here makes me feel light.

We pass the center of Iquitos—the Plaza de Armas, an open square with a large fountain and a central obelisk memorial flanked by flagpoles that bear red and white Peruvian flags. A large billboard mural on the corner behind the plaza shows the shadows of a man and a girl, with the slogan "*No Al Tourismo Sexual Infantil,*" a stark reminder that Iquitos has had to cope with many different types of tourism, and that not all of them are welcome.

It also reminds me of William Burroughs and his encounters. Burroughs came through Peru in the early 1950s in search of ayahuasca, or *yagé* as it was also known then—an exotic jungle drug that was near impossible to find. When he drank the brew he described it in letters to poet Alan Ginsberg (later collected as *The Yagé Letters*) as "seeing or feeling what I thought was a Great Being, or some sense of it, approaching my mind like a big wet vagina ... a big black hole of God-Nose through which I peered into a mystery—the black hole surrounded by all creation." Fifty years later ayahuasca is now a booming international business, drawing up to a third of all Western tourists to this city.

Our *motorcarro* finally deposits us at the Hobo Hideout a few blocks from the plaza on Calle Putamayo, and we peer through the metal-grilled veranda into the dark and musty interior. Johnny—the gringo owner—is a hardened survivor, an ex-military man in his late thirties or early forties (I never muster the courage to ask) adorned with tattoos and exuding machismo, the quintessential archetype of the American expatriate in this frontier city. He's the one who killed all the animals we can see on the walls surrounding the reception area, I find out later: the anaconda, the bear, the jaguar, and the turtle, mixed among shots of him out hunting and leading tour groups into the jungle.

He flatly refuses to lift a finger around the hostel—"ask my wife about that" he says to all inquiries, or "I don't have no fucking change of *soles*," is his constant grumble from the back room. His wife is a gorgeous *mestizo* Indian with long black hair and wicked lips who fixes us up with room keys and fresh sheets.

As well as Shane and Margaret I soon find that the Hideout is playing home to another couple from Down Under—Marty, a dreadlocked dude, and his girlfriend Rachel, both of whom are here for the conference and to drink ayahuasca with the shamans. I'd first met Marty earlier in the year in Basel, Switzerland, at the one-hundredth birthday party symposium for Albert Hofmann—the chemist who invented LSD. Being an *Australian Penthouse* freelancer didn't quite pay the rent, but it definitely broadened my horizons.

I had heard that the practice of shamanism in Peru was changing rapidly as Western tourists like us arrived in search of spiritual knowledge. For many generations an entrenched yet unofficial "caste system" effectively ensured that jungle laborers stayed in the jungle, or worked shitty jobs in the city. The jungle Indians never intermingled with Indians from the higher castes, and so never got a chance at any action outside their proscribed communities. The *castellos,* the white *mestizo* half-breeds in their city clothes and cultured attitudes, had all the respect and the wealth.

But a curious thing has happened in Iquitos in the last twenty years—a surge of interest in shamanism that has upset the social apple cart and catapulted the jungle-dwelling *curanderos* to the top of the heap. They alone have the indigenous medical knowledge of the healing plants and the spiritual dimensions, the good juju that the rich gringos pay so handsomely for.

Some locals fear that the West is changing the nature of indigenous shamanism. Where once local youth wanted nothing to do with the old ways, now they're seeing a lucrative career path out of poverty, if not necessarily towards true spiritual practice. Pedro (not his real name), a local businessman who lectures on such matters, and is regularly attending international conferences and charging through the nose, used to be a fruit peddler ten years ago, I'm told, near the main square on Calle Putamayo, hustling oranges for a *sole*.

But knowledge is power and as the spiritually bereft West seeks to rebalance itself and comes in search of indigenous healing, those with the knowledge can name their price—and they do. One of the cheaper rates for a six-week intensive shamanistic initiation retreat is U.S. $1,900, or around U.S. $100 a day for single ceremonies. Spending U.S. $3,000 for two weeks on an ayahuasca jungle retreat is not unheard of. And in a country where the average weekly wage is ten *soles,* or around U.S. $30, the shamans are the new rich.

This dichotomy that spiritual tourism brings underscores the second "Amazonian Shaman Conference" I'm here for, organized by local businessman and onetime *curandero,* Alan Shoemaker. After getting settled at the Hideout I'd registered for the conference at Chinchilejo [Dragonfly] Tours in the heart of the city, where I met Alan and his wife, Mariella Noriega de Shoemaker.

Shoemaker is a slim man with glasses and a graying moustache, wearing a pink La Coste shirt and white pants, like an accountant about to head out for a day on the golf links. He chain-smokes incessantly and like Johnny, the owner of the Hobo Hideout before him, he's married to a stunning *mestizo* Peruvian with supermodel looks.

"When I met Mariella she was chubby and poor," he explains to me in the cool, air-conditioned front office of his home, anticipating any questions on that front. Now she's a trained travel agent and equal partner in their business and they have two beautiful children together.

Like the banker in *Monopoly,* Shoemaker seems to have bought up almost all the utilities, the railroad, and Park Lane. Let's see, he started off running a gift shop in town while exploring indigenous spirituality and drinking ayahuasca with local *curanderos.* That morphed into a successful travel agency, which also specializes in ayahuasca tourism, which is where the momentum for the Shaman Conference has come. Last year almost two hundred seekers came from all over the world in search of indigenous enlightenment, at U.S. $500 a pop for seven days, accommodation and frills extra. Alan also runs Soga del Alma—*The Vine of the Soul*—a church he founded in 2001 to nurture ayahuasca usage by the West.

The church currently has over 600 members and rising, and as a legally instituted religion there have to be some good tax breaks accompanying it, or at least a veneer of legal protection if the authorities were ever to crack down on the nascent ayahuasca tourism scene. Not that it should be a problem—ayahuasca is legal in South America, protected as an indigenous medicine.

In many places around the world the brew enjoys a gray area of legal usage—only when the psychoactive ingredients like *N,N-dimethyl-tryptamine* (DMT) are extracted from admixture plants added to the vine itself does the concoction become considered a chemical, and subject to the law. That law, by the way, was imposed on the U.N. and its signatory nations by America at the outset of the War on Drugs in 1971, by Richard Nixon. It takes no notice of local custom or the unbroken thread of indigenous use of sacramental plants across the world.

Shoemaker would know all this because he's personally been on the wrong side of the American *fatwa* on hallucinogens, targeted and arrested by the American DEA (Drug Enforcement Administration) in 2000 for a shipment of medicinal plants that contained the ingredients of ayahuasca. Approximately 600 pounds of ayahuasca vine and 220 pounds of *huambisa* leaves were seized by the government officials because they contained the hallucinogen DMT. Not synthetic DMT, but natural plant material that should be outside the definition of Schedule-1 "drugs."

Shoemaker's attorney, Mark Sallee, claims that the charges were reportedly a front to create a test case to deturn the burgeoning popularity of ayahuasca as a religious sacrament. Due to legal machinations compounded after he left America, Shoemaker took up Peruvian citizenship and is still awaiting resolution of his case.

He's been doing pretty well here in Iquitos, though, and his business interests are booming. Perhaps most lucratively in the long-term, Shoemaker is the sole owner and runs Gracia Ethnobotanicals, a lab licensed by the government of Peru to extract chemicals from native plants and explore remedies for diseases like Type II Diabetes, Parkinson's, and cancer. At the moment its planned business thrust is marketing a range of all-natural soaps, creams, and toothpastes.

The point is that in this new Wild West opportunities are up for grabs, and Shoemaker has been the right man in the right place at the right time to take advantage of them. Still, as he confides to me across his office desk while giving me my conference pass and information pack, "I'm still paying my rent month to month and trying to feed and raise my kids."

As an apparently rich gringo in town, he says he's always getting hit on for money—from friends, relations, and anyone who thinks he's good for it—and to his credit, he says he often obliges. All in all, this successful businessman epitomizes the turbulent power dynamic between the local Indians and the gringos, and this carries over to the conference that he hosts.

With its entrepreneurial blend of spirituality and capitalism, the "Second Amazonian Shaman Conference" promises to be the perfect mix of paradigms. It bills itself as a gathering of *curanderos,* scientists, and interested members of the public who have a yearning for indigenous spirituality.

It feels weird to be going all the way to Peru and the frontier city of Iquitos to sit around a hotel and listen to shamans and scientists *talk* about ayahuasca and the spirit world. But the conference also offers an immediate snapshot of the culture and the issues involved. And there will be three ceremonies drinking the vine in the jungle with *curanderos* at their lodges—like a good package tour, the conference promises a little bit of everything.

After registering I head back downtown to the Plaza de Armas. Despite my jetlag and lack of sleep, I want to check out a well-known gringo hangout, a restaurant bar called the *Yellow Rose of Texas,* to see what's going down in this roaring urban archipelago.

"Welcome to Texas," says Gerald Mayeaux as I reach gringo central in the heart of downtown Iquitos. Expats and tourists are lounging in cane chairs outside the bar and grill and hoeing into their breakfasts. Beautiful Peruvian girls with smooth caramel skin zoom by, bringing out the deep-fried Texan tucker. They're dressed in 1950s Americana waitress outfits with white straw cowboy hats and miniskirts, emblazoned with a bull's head logo and tassels.

Gerald is the heavyset, amiable proprietor of the Yellow Rose, voted "best sports bar in Peru, 2004" and longtime haunt of virtually every gringo this side of the Andes. The giant plasma TV out the back draws in the crowds to watch the *futbol* and the ice-cold beer keeps them there, surrounded by the stuffed bodies of native animals, giant turtle shells, anaconda skins, and Tex-Mex memorabilia. Iquitos is a small city—approximately 400,000 locals and maybe a few hundred semi-permanent gringos, and the Wild West ambience of the Yellow Rose meshes perfectly with the frontier atmosphere, giving it an archetypal cowboys-and-Indians undertone.

"If you got any problems at all, I can help, I used to work for the government," Gerald offers in his thick Texan showman drawl, handing out business cards to the gringos and taking off his glasses to wipe the sweat from his face with a small towel. He starred in the movie *The Motorcycle Diaries,* he soon tells me, as the big gambler that gets conned by Che Guevara's friend. It's perfect casting as Gerald is larger than life and twice as loud, but always the consummate host.

Local merchants, many of them young boys, cluster round attempting to sell cigarettes, bags, t-shirts, animal fangs, and other *tourista* handicrafts and are periodically shooed off by Gerald and his staff. "The little kids are the ones you have to watch out for," Gerald warns. "They steal your coins as they hug you."

I sit down next to four *eurofutbol* fans from Lima who are dressed in sports t-shirts and Hollywood sunglasses, global metro-chic. They're here for a long weekend and have already started drinking Pilsner—minus six degrees, the coldest beer in town—at 9:30 in the morning. They haven't a clue what ayahuasca is, of course, and as they head out the back to watch the World Cup on the big plasma TV screen I order a papaya juice and try to get my bearings.

With so many people in town for the conference I know that many of the tourists here are also probably ayahuasca drinkers, so I settle into some light conversation and try to scope out who's who. The other gringos are mainly older men and women in their thirties to fifties with a smattering of new age travelers and spiritual seekers, interspersed by guys who have the edge of Vietnam vets or down-and-out drifters culled from the trailer parks of the American dream and living the good life in Iquitos, the end of the line.

Two seats down from me is Ron Wheelock, a weathered gringo in his early fifties with a red Rio Amazonia tourist t-shirt and an Aztec bandana on. He's an old-time boy from Kansas who's been "living here off and on for almost ten years. It's kind of like the Wild West," he says good-naturedly.

Ron's been looking after his three-year-old son Queto, a beautiful little half-Indian boy with long black hair and gaps where his front teeth are still growing through. Queto fidgets around his dad at the table, picking at the finger food and radiating pure kid energy, free and inquisitive. He looks like a little Tarzan, Lord of the Jungle, and as if to confirm that this is his domain he stands in the gutter between the café and a row of motorbikes and urinates freely. Nobody bats an eyelid.

"I came from Leticia, Colombia, by boat yesterday," Ron says, and when he smiles he reveals a gold tooth right up front as plain as you please. Most of the American gringos who stay here for the three months allowed do a day trip up the Amazon to the tri-border of Peru, Colombia, and Brazil where they can get their visa renewed before heading back down to Iquitos.

"By the time I got to town and checked my email I reached for my cellphone and it was gone. I remember someone bumping me on the riverboat—it happens that quick, y'know." Ron, despite his down-to-earth trappings, says he is a shaman who has been working with ayahuasca during his time here, training with the native *curanderos,* but shamanism won't stop your phone being stolen, it seems.

Across from him is Bob, from Detroit. He's a small man in his forties with short buzz-cut hair, glasses, and three-day-old stubble. He seems like a nice guy, but he radiates a wounded kind of energy, like he's been really hurt by someone in his life and he's never really bounced back from it.

Bob says he's been into ayahuasca for two years, since his mother died. She was a "bible-basher," he tells me, one of the many strong women in his family. It's largely because of her and his problems relating to women that he's come here to Iquitos and the Shaman Conference to drink with Norma Panduro—perhaps the most famous female *curandera* in the area—to be healed.

Going down the table I meet Eric, a mature, bearded professor from Denver who grows san pedro cactus—the psychedelic kind—in his apartment back home, and Frank Echenhofer, a tall, gray-haired hippie who is also a professor and lecturer in spiritual traditions at the Californian Institute of Integral Studies.

Next to him is Elias Mamallacta, a short, broad-faced Ecuadorian shaman who's come to speak at the conference. He's dressed in a blue t-shirt, navy pants, and black sneakers and he sits here amiably with a big Buddha smile, smoking his cigarette and enjoying a papaya juice in the early morning sun. After a few minutes chatting with the tourists he dips into his black daypack and brings out a CD with recordings of him singing *icaros*—sacred shaman songs. On the cover of the CD he's dressed in ceremonial gear with a feathered headband and streaks of war paint.

To his right is Hal, is a retired Swedish psychologist in his fifties with short white-blond hair and glasses and an uncanny resemblance to Steven King. He's never taken ayahuasca but has studied it for years, he says. There's something in his eyes . . . in the way he sits . . . that makes me feel he's holding back something that threatens to cut loose.

It's the same with many of the ayahuasca tourists—they stand out with an energy that's hard to put into words, but is quantifiable nonetheless. Some might call them freaks, weirdos, or just plain crazy, but that wouldn't be fair or accurate. Still, there is something different about them, and after a while I develop a sixth sense that lets me read a crowd and pick the ayahuasca drinker, the radiant black sheep among the flock of white lambs.

"The locals think that we're crazy, coming to the doctor to take medicine when we're not sick, and they're right, 'cause it ain't fun," says Brian, a French-speaking Australian in his mid-twenties. "When I drank ayahuasca I could feel the sickness in my body all the way through the muscles and down to the bones, where there was this black tar-like residue binding together and I was confronted with my own sickness and mortality."

Brian's a cool dude with short, punky hair with an echo of a mohawk. He's into snowboarding, studies Chinese medicine, and he used to be a DJ in the trance music scene. If he and other cultural catalysts like him were here then it was just as I suspected—ayahuasca had penetrated the trendsetters of the global village, and its popularity would only rise. But you won't see it in the clubs or at parties where Western-style drugs are consumed with hedonistic abandon; instead, the spiritual vibe of this sacred South American plant is wiping clean the consumption habits of this new generation of seekers and tuning them into the one thing Western altered states has often lacked—respect.

"I could feel all the life I had left in me like a burning fuse and all that was dead was degraded. Then I remembered that this is really strong medicine and should really be respected. It isn't fun seeing that much of yourself and experiencing it come out of you when you purge," Brian tells me.

The other thing ayahuasca seems to do is invoke an almost religious fervor in those who have felt its power and a desire to share the understanding of the experience, which is often notoriously difficult to put into words. Not that it stops the ayahuasca tourists from trying.

"Most people choose to ignore the sickness in their bodies, just like they do with the knowledge of death, and aya brings it right up and slaps you in the face till your head is spinning," Brian says animatedly. "When you're going through these overwhelming experiences all you can really do is let go and experience it fully without judgment. It's not painful or scary—it's just our experience of life in the biology of the universe from the point where there is no judgment, no polarity, no life and death. Just life is death, so let it flow . . ."

Mariana, one of the waitresses, brings me my juice just then and looks at me suggestively with a smile. The women here are gorgeous—light-brown skin and eyes, jet-black hair, curves and bumps in all the right places, and a subliminal sexual frisson that threatens to erupt at any moment.

Shane and Margaret arrive, having settled in at the Hideout; Marty and Rachel pile into the backroom to check out the *futbol* and sink a few beers in traditional Aussie style; and even Jimmy, the Hideout owner, is here, all of us under the one street tarp. At *El Gringo Bar* next door with its loud lime-green walls, a few *normal* tourists look on at the colorful scene we all make, as our loud, wild conversation escalates.

A teenage street hustler with a goatee beard, "Guns'N'Roses" tattoos up one arm, and baggy hip-hop style pants tries to peddle his jewelry to the gringos. Within seconds he's joined by half a dozen native women dressed in colored tops and white skirts from the Shipibo-Conibos tribe which populate the river down near Pucallpa, several hundred kilometers away. They come in packs to hunt the tourists and sell them their wares, materializing out of thin air to besiege us with beautiful, dyed fabrics with intricate tribal patterns on them. They look like they've just stepped out of a postcard and as they hold up their handicrafts in the early morning light I am struck by the beauty of their work and the steady desperation of their sales pitch.

The Yellow Rose is a magnet for the tourists and the hustlers, and like a constant tide they are shooed away by Gerald or his Peruvian wife, Pamela, only to return again minutes later, hovering out in the street past the motorbikes with indefatigable arms that hold up their wares. Their sad, sad eyes stare out at us, trying to bridge the worlds of abject poverty and Western wealth, their only option to continue the dance of trinkets and smiles . . .

A man with a wooden tray secured around his neck like cigarette girls in nightclubs of old hustles his goods: lollipops, cigarettes, chocolate bars, chewing gum, pens, calculators, jaguar fangs. But as a bent, five-foot-tall Peruvian grandmother in her sixties comes up to the table and begs for a sole, she finds these hardened, battle-scarred travelers have already learned to say no.

Suddenly a black SUV with *RADIO PATRULLA* written on the side cruises past and lets off a burst of sound from their sirens as they flash their lights—it's a cop car. The *motorcarro* taxis double-parked in the street outside the Yellow Rose all rev their engines and quickly disperse and in seconds all the hawkers, merchants, and beggars have likewise melted into the day. The cops double park and Mariana goes out to take their order.

"Bad boys, bad boys, what cha gonna do, what cha gonna do when they come for you? Bad boys, bad boys . . ." Bob sings cheekily.

"*Caliente?*" Shane says eventually, trying to ask for the bill.

"That means hot," Margaret corrects him.

"*La cuenta?*" Mariana says with a smile, like she's seen a thousand crazy gringos and this is just the latest batch to wash up here at the end of the world. We are all of us crazy from their point of view, and the ayahuasca tourists are the craziest of them all, to come so far to drink a foul jungle brew in the hope that it will heal them, connect them to their god, or open doorways that no one else even knows are there.

And as I sit here in the morning light, taking this all in, I wonder whether the mystery isn't more of a puzzle, or a joke, and the joke is on us all . . .

2

Wheel of Fortune

Parthenon Hotel, Iquitos

FRIDAY JUNE 30, 2006

Early Friday morning I catch a *motorcarro* taxi a few kilometers out from the center of town to the Hotel Parthenon—the biggest convention space in Iquitos—and step through the giant faux Roman pillars framing the main entrance. Standing in front of the registration booth is yet another Aussie—Theo Valis, the psychedelic alchemist who initiated me into ayahuasca three years ago in the Australian bush. He's tall and lanky with a curly, receding hairline and a teenage mad scientist vibe, like he's just stepped out of his lab and forgotten his white coat. He's here to give a presentation as a speaker at the conference, and sample the local wares.

He's a bit of a wildcard our Theo, and he likes to do things his way. But, God love him, he is also one of the best bush-shamans Australia has produced. His expertise with the acacia plant and his own self-doses of discovery were the stuff of underground legend.

"Here's Rak now," Theo says to a tall, older man with mousy blond hair next to him, weighed down with two big packs of photographic equipment.

"I was just asking Theo if he'd seen you. I'm Vance Gellert—your photographer," he says with a friendly smile, holding out a hand.

Vance is a distinguished photographer, a babyboomer who studied pharmacology at university in the Sixties and was inspired by the jungle adventures of botanical explorer Richard Schultes seventy years ago. He lives in Minnesota where he runs his own gallery space and has been coming to the Amazon off and on for three years, photographing *curanderos* and the native culture for a book and exhibition he's working on. I'd been given his details through friends of friends in the ayahuasca network, and arranged for him to take shots to accompany the feature for *Australian Penthouse.*

We exchange some small talk and have a wander around the hotel, which hosts a cavernous open-air conference room surrounded by palm trees, a small round changing room hut with no walls called a *maloca* and a large swimming pool. It's all very *Melrose Place* but there's a tinge of *Fawlty Towers*—the hotel is still unfinished and little things like the wiring, room fans, and amenities are still being installed. Theo tells me it was the same last year, which suggests that it's been largely idle all this time, waiting for the business the conference brings to afford to finish construction.

New Age earth mothers, bearded academics, hippies, students, and global gypsy travelers mill around, mingling with everyday folks in t-shirts, shorts, and sandals, waiting for the lectures by and about shamans to start. It all has the feel of a Florida "Amway" meeting gone awry.

The crowd appears to be from all over the world with a heavy proportion of Americans and an equal number of men and women. I meet New Age sound workers from London, psychic healers from Brighton, hedonists from New Zealand and Australia, website coders from L.A., and crew from Switzerland, Spain, Lapland, Israel, California, Oregon, and Vancouver. Many of the participants are from a global electronic community centered around the forums on *ayahuasca.com,* and are getting to know each other for the first time face-to-face in this hot, humid cultural melting pot.

It could be clichéd, but a lot of the women are in their late thirties or early forties and appear to be going through a spiritual sea change, embracing energy work and holistic practices. Most of the guys are the same, but they also have that macho-warrior ego of the man on the path, oblivious to the fact that the Goddess is the destination.

I spot Frank, the long-haired professor surrounded by a gaggle of other doctors and academic types in open neck shirts and shorts, trading notes. And sitting at one of the long tables with yellow covers is the Steven King look-alike, still beaming with an inner glow. Overall though, the thing I really notice about the crowd is the concentration of young backpacker types, the adventure-traveler market turned on to the spiritual high of ayahuasca.

As I walk around this mimetic melting pot, past locals selling art and crafts at stalls lining the sides of the main conference area, my brain abuzz with the packaging of indigenous spirituality, a rough, raspy voice to my left says, "The Indians have been trying to get out of the jungle for 3,000 years and now we're trying to get back in!"

Jack's a short, wiry, mustachioed dude in his early sixties who looks like somebody's archetypal uncle, but says he is in fact, the father of Michael Stipe from REM. I'd met Jack at Alan's place yesterday when registering; a chiropractor by trade, he tells me he's also running an ayahuasca session on Sunday if I'm interested. And he's not the only one.

It turns out there's over two dozen speakers at the conference, including indigenous *curanderos,* Western shamans, academics and scientists, journalists, photographers, and media makers. A good half of them are running ayahuasca sessions, or "circles" as they are known, where participants drink around the inside rim of round, thatched jungle *malocas.* As over a hundred conference attendees pour in from all corners of the globe, ayahuasca is not only the "mother of all medicines," it's the best game in town.

One of the first things I've learned here in Peru is to let go of my expectations and that goes doubly so when it comes to shamanism. Ayahuasca's practitioners aren't even shamans in the sense that the West has constructed them to be. The word *shaman* comes from Siberia as a cultural import via anthropologists studying indigenous medicine men. Some commentators believe it reflects the root of the word "sham," reflecting the non-hallucinogenic alternatives shamans utilized due to the lack of psychoactive plants for much of the frozen Siberian winter.

But throughout the Amazonian medicine tradition—one of the longest unbroken threads of connection with the earth—the locals refer to these plant doctors as *curanderos,* from the Spanish, "to cure."

And surrounded by the mighty Amazon, where over eighty percent of the planet's biodiversity lives, these healers draw upon that diversity to work their magic.

Thousands of indigenous healers populate every village, town, and city throughout South and Central America, with many sub-specialties to the craft for those populations big enough to support it. There are *vegetalistas*—those who diet and work with many medicinal plants, who believe that each and every plant and tree has a spirit in it, and that the spirits can be contacted to give advice on their properties, what they cure, and how they can be used. Then there are tobacco healers—the *tabaqueros*, who use the jungle tobacco *Nicotiana rustica* exclusively to cleanse and cure; *perfumeros*, those who work with flower essences; *encantos*, who work exclusively with the strong, deep power of magical stones; and a raft of others.

The first speaker of the day is a familiar face from the Yellow Rose—Ron Wheelock, dressed in a simple white t-shirt and cut-off denim shorts. The set and setting of the conference and the urban trappings somehow make it hard to imagine Ron, or any of the other Westerners who claim to be shamans, are the real deal. For all his down-south simplicity, this *hillbilly ayahuasquero* doesn't seem to fit the archetype I have in mind when I think of a medicine man. His three-and-a-half-year-old son, Queto sits next to him on stage, and at turns climbs into his lap while he's speaking:

"For me, ayahuasca has literally changed my life . . . It's made me more aware of the world around me," Ron says in an endearing Southern drawl. "It hasn't been an easy path to follow . . . I never charge for any of my work, because God put everything on this world for everyone on it. The ayahuasca told me this the first time I used it." His raw beauty shines on through as he talks, and you realize that despite the color of his skin, the country of his birth, or his background, Ron's straight down the line following the call of spirit.

"Deep inside I knew what I had to do. Ayahuasca showed me my death and [how] if I lived a normal life enjoying the pleasures of the world my death would be very painful. But with ayahuasca my death would be glorious," he says, like an old-style preacher with the congregation eating out of the palm of his hand.

Ron's always been interested in shamanism, but one day back in '96 he decided to come to Peru and find himself a teacher. The first *curandero* he drank with was don Jose Corale Mori, a renowned local healer and a *banco*, a "master of sky, water, land, and the spirits." He took him under his wing and taught him the ways of the jungle medicine, making him diet with medicinal plants and cleansing his energy field to be more receptive.

"One really suffers in the *dieta*," Ron says to the crowd, "but nothing comes easy in life." Don Jose is ninety-nine-years old now and in a nursing home, and Ron looks after his *maestro* as best he can, while also bringing up his son. Queto tugs at his legs playfully as Ron smiles and continues his tale. Someone from the audience asks him about how he manages his role as a father with that of a shaman.

"We did nineteen or twenty ceremonies together, and he was by my side for every one," Ron answers. "Four times in North Carolina he drank half a teaspoon or a spoonful, but now if I ask him if he wants to drink, he says, no Papa, but he still licks [the ayahuasca] off the stick."

Queto—*Quetzalcoatl* (the Meso-American sun god or "feathered serpent") Louise Anguila Wheelock—is having an interesting childhood, that's for sure, hanging out with his dad at ayahuasca ceremonies, sipping the brew and now attending conferences, learning the ways of the jungle science and the business that supports it in the modern world. Shamanism is often a hereditary path, and those singled out are trained from a young age, so there's nothing new here, just a shift in cultural perspective.

"Once in California I smoked 5-MeO-DMT [scraped] from a frog and I seen [sic] spirits in the desert . . ." Ron says, leading into a talk about his shamanistic work with smokable DMT, found in its native form in various plants and added to the ayahuasca vine when it's brewed up, causing the startling visions that ayahuasca trances are famous for.

DMT is not only in thousands of plants across the world, but in animals, insects, and us humans. Dr. Rick Strassman, author of the book *DMT: The Spirit Molecule,* believes DMT may be secreted by the pineal gland and used as a neurochemical regulator that may explain our connection to higher-dimensional realms.

"It's called the spiritual world because it's populated by spirit beings," Ron reminds us, and as I look around at the crowd fanning themselves in the early morning humidity I'm struck by the sea of expectant faces just hoping for a glimpse of that world that the West has lost connection with.

"If we're multidimensional beings, isn't it time as a species we became aware of it?" the next speaker, Kevin Furnas, asks in wry tone. "We're on a world level now; the old patterns don't work anymore. We're transiting from an individual level to a species level, and if the reason we're here is to learn from the 'University of Life' then we have to work together with the plants…"

Kevin's a long-haired gringo from San Francisco in his late thirties with angelic good looks and hazel eyes. He's been wandering the world and learning about traditional belief systems and indigenous medicines for over a decade, and he trained for two years doing an intensive *dieta* with medicinal plants at the famed Sachamama Ethnobotanical Gardens outside Iquitos.

"The diet is an energetic relationship," he explains. "You have to leave space for the medicine. No salt, sex, sugar, meat, or alcohol. This facilitates the merging of our spirit with the spirit of the plant, by reducing ego identification and lessening resistance, which helps our minds become more flexible."

Kevin's a bit like Ron—gentle, intelligent, and he speaks from the heart. He also knows how to woo the audience, especially the women. He could be the Fabio pin-up boy for this emerging subculture, but he's also too nice a guy to run with that, or let other people's projections control him. And as he says, "Ayahuasca is the movie star of the [Amazonian] system"—not him. It's the plants that are the real teachers, the ones his training has allowed him to access.

This is a common thread running through many of the talks and speeches—like all priests who have put themselves between God and his people, the shamans are just the middlemen. The energy and consciousness they channel and connect to is that of the plants, the spirit allies, and the Divine. The *plants* are the real teachers and if you diet and are sensitive enough to register it, they'll tell you that themselves—apparently.

"Plants are sentient. You can talk to plants, and they can talk to you . . ." Kevin explains. "The body cries out for help and the plant spirits help. Each tree, each plant is a specialist. The spirit of ayahuasca goes inside you, it looks for blockages and it triggers you to vomit them up. It does intensive healing by working on your higher energetic self. Plants have a vested interest in helping us to heal as individuals and as a species. In fact, an ayahuasca ceremony is like an inter-species pow-wow—life forms come together to communicate, to build a bridge. That's how we are taught by the spirit of the plant.

"And what is a *spirit?* What is *ayahuasca,* or a *tree?* In the Amazonian system the plants and trees have a higher energetic self that develops a relationship with your higher energetic self, like student and teacher. The plants take you out of your cultural syntax, leaving you in the rainforest with just you and the universe."

Wow. Mega-download from the Gaian networks there. Around the cavernous open-air conference room the ayahuasca tourists are drinking in all the knowledge, some taking written notes or with their laptops out, others recording the talks, or just listening, serious students all. But my Hollywood conditioning stills hungers for an *authentic* native shaman, which is where the next speaker comes in.

Percy Garcia is the first indigenous *curandero* to speak. He's in his early thirties but he looks younger, with shining skin, short black hair, and the stocky build of native Peruvians. He's been trained since he was a boy in the world of the spirits, and of the great plant medicine ayahuasca.

"Ayahuasca is *Quechua* (the Incan language) for *'vine of the dead (souls),'* but at the same time, as a healer, we don't call them dead spirits—we call them allies," he explains through an interpreter. "Ayahuasca is medicine. It is strength, intelligence, wisdom, and healing. In this way everything is in accord with tradition. While nature represents what life is, ayahuasca is the mother of us all," he says, radiating a boyish enthusiasm as he talks.

"I feel myself I am a healer, not a master. All my life I will be an apprentice," Percy says humbly. "The spiritual masters, they fill me up with their gifts, but I'm just an intermediary."

He's a simple man who radiates a good nature. Like young Queto, he was trained from an early age to be a *curandero,* in this case by his grandfather, Enrique Garcia Mozombite, to use his skills for the benefit of his community. "I am the only grandson that follows the tradition. I started at ten years old with all kinds of traditional plants. He prepared me to have the strength to complement ayahuasca, and I have used the vine since I was fourteen years old," he says to the applause of an eager audience.

After dinner the talks start for the second session with Norma Panduro, the *shamana,* on first. The set and setting are jarring, Western, and like the male speakers she is surrounded by lights and audio equipment, cameras, and a wall of front-row media all conspiring to give the participants a caged animal feel as they prowl up and down, baring themselves to the audience.

"I'm very pleased to be a mother, a grandmother, and a great-grandmother," Norma announces as she comes on stage, dressed in slacks and a flannel shirt, with a Rasta-colored headband framing an archetypal grandmotherly face, full of love and compassion. She adjusts her glasses and walks slowly but confidently to the center of the stage.

Out of almost two dozen indigenous healers, Western scientists, and academics, she and her apprentice and business partner Paula Harbrink Numan (aka *Tarzana*) are the only women speakers present. A handful of other Western women are in the audience with "Estrella Ayahuasca Center" t-shirts on—black and pink tank tops with the Estrella star logo on them, advertising Norma and Paula's ayahuasca retreat.

Norma introduces herself via a woman translator and tells the story of how she became a *curandera,* a female shaman. Like many initiates her path with the medicine came through crisis, when she was diagnosed with tuberculosis in her teens. Her illness led her to a shaman to be cured, and to the jungle medicine ayahuasca and the world of spirits.

"One day my *maestro,* who was Shipibo, turned to me and said, 'Norma do you want to learn the ways of the jungle?' And I said yes. '*Then drink ayahuasca.*' So I did, from seventeen, with much respect to this master plant. And through this process I learned what it is to be a good shaman. Someone balanced, healthy, and in integrity in terms of his or her soul. [You] can feel suffering and suffer along with the sufferer."

Ayahuasca also set Norma on a path as a female magic worker in a male-dominated culture, where she was repeatedly challenged and oppressed by men who thought a woman shouldn't be dabbling in such things.

"Those of us women who study the plants are known as healers, doctors, and also shamanas," Norma says. "We spend years studying the properties of just one plant and the gifts of healing they provide. The deeper you go in the study of a chosen plant, the more prestige you can carry in your field. And by communing with the master plants we recognize and diagnose thousands of types of illness.

"Traditional medicine is very important, especially for those who Western pharmacology fails, [then] they turn to the plants as a last resort . . . But because of [the] use of traditional plants [shamans] have been persecuted by authorities, like the church. Even I have been persecuted by the police and [told the] ayahuasca ceremonies I'm con-ducting are Satanic practices. They've extorted money from me under threat of incarceration. Here is my vision of hell."

As the only female practitioner many of the women, and indeed some of the men have a lot to ask Norma, especially when it comes down to brass tacks and talking about sex. "Sex is welcomed by the body, ayahuasca recognizes that. Sex is a good thing," Norma says with a down-to-earth grandmotherly voice, as if she's giving advice to her daughter. All the male shamans visibly bristle at her words.

"It's like the abortion debate and the right of a woman to choose," Norma explains. "If a girl gets pregnant early, anywhere from twelve to fourteen, sometimes through rape, why not use medicinal plants to prevent unhappiness for these people?" Fair point. And from the pharmacological abundance of the jungle, hundreds, if not thousands of medical concoctions are made, supplying indigenous cultures which still respect the plants and their curative powers, and who also can't afford the Western drug alternatives.

There's just one little problem though, when it comes to sex and ayahuasca: there is a sex taboo in Amazonian shamanism for three days either side of an ayahuasca ritual. The process of the medicine entering, cleansing, purifying, and connecting a patient to the spiritual dimensions can be an exhausting and demanding experience. Many shamans like to close off the energy body opened up by ayahuasca with flower baths, smoke smudging, or other forms of energy work, as well as advising ayahuasca drinkers of dietary restrictions on sugar, salt, alcohol, etc. for at least a day after a ceremony. Too much too soon can throw the newly sensitized body out of whack, and the sex taboo is top of the list for whack.

Most *curanderos* say the energy field of another person we open ourselves to with intercourse is too strong when you are still ayahuasca-sensitive, and ignoring this rule can result in energy imbalances and sickness. Of course, "too strong" is just the type of hyper-accelerated libido most Westerners are actively pursuing in this day of legal lifestyle drugs like Viagra, and the increased circulatory and energy flow post and during ayahuasca is reportedly a mighty aphrodisiac in itself, if you stay on the base chakra level.

I am told that the real work with the medicine of ayahuasca, however, is to move up the chakras and connect with the spirit, which is perhaps why shamans frown on sex until the body has come down again. Norma, however, is not one of the naysayers. In fact, of all the male *curanderos* at the conference and indeed later throughout the Amazon, she is the only one I come across that is hep to getting *jiggy* in the presence of ayahuasca.

There's also the issue that many of the male shamans, as women in the audience have pointed out, have reputations that precede them. One male *curandero* later tells me that most male shamans have two major problems in their lives: *women and money.* The charged energy generated in working with ayahuasca is often an energy that gets spent and grounded in their sexual encounters. If ayahuasca is the "movie star" of the Amazon, as Kevin Furnas joked, then ayahuasca circles can potentially turn into casting couches if the wrong energy and intent is projected.

"There was once a woman at her wit's end, desperate, who went to see a shaman," Norma recounts. "She said to him, '*maestro,* my true love has left me. I ask you to do something for me, as I really love him.' He said to her, 'okay you must do as I say' and she agreed. 'Take off all of your clothing. Lie down and I will blow tobacco smoke over you; later I will put magic powder over my penis and introduce it to you. Does this feel good?' And this she did without any shame. But I feel the shame of this; it is a real shame, which brings me a feeling of dishonor... A good shaman never attempts to seduce his patients or give the 'evil eye' to anybody."

Part of me feels I've stepped into a talk show confessional, like I'm in the audience of an episode of *Oprah.* Yet Norma's also forthright, not afraid to call a spade a spade or a man a bastard, as if her own suffering has merely strengthened her inner convictions.

"Why isn't a woman recognized?" Norma asks. "[She is] the foremost member in the family: cooking and cleaning—holding the space." The Women's Liberation Movement has come to the jungles of Peru a few decades late, it seems, but it's full of a righteous fire that threatens to burn through this outpost of machismo.

"Women's rights and sexuality need to be encouraged," Norma says. "We should be teaching little boys to caress the body, how to kiss, how to please a woman; this is all natural. We should be teaching girls how to assert themselves in intimate situations. A woman should never be ashamed of her sexuality and afraid to express where she wants to be kissed and touched," Norma concludes to a round of applause from the audience.

Taking ayahuasca means making yourself vulnerable, and taking ayahuasca in a remote jungle setting with a shaman of dubious moral character is a vulnerability many of the women here seem rightly cautious about. Norma's also encouraging women to be themselves, and for many at this conference it's exactly what they need to hear.

"I don't feel like a goddess—I am a woman. I have my habits. I make my mistakes. But day-by-day I try to improve myself. I feel infinite gratitude to God, who has brought me into this world, and I am proud to be an *ayahuasquera.* Many blessings to President Bush, and I hope one day he will come and drink ayahuasca!" Norma finishes, and this time the audience is standing up and the applause is thunderous.

It's definitely high-rollers night, and the last speaker is another successful shaman—Guillermo Arévalo, who seems to have mastered the knack of walking between the old world and the new.

Guillermo is one of the most famous Peruvian *curanderos,* having starred in French filmmaker Jan Kounen's feature length psychedelic spaghetti western *Renegade* (released as *Blueberry* outside the USA), which reportedly conveys the visual hallucinations and experiences the spirit of the vine can bring.

When he comes on stage, however, there's a stark simplicity about him—at 5' 2" and stripped of any robes or ceremonial trappings, he's a simple man in Western pants and a t-shirt, his cropped gray hair speckled with white and a tight-lipped smile across his broad Peruvian face. It's a bit like seeing Tom Cruise in the flesh for the first time and realizing he's shorter than he seems on screen.

"I give thanks to the universe for the powers I have," Guillermo says to us, his dark eyes squinting like an eagle in flight. "I'm self-taught, and by not choosing any path I've acquired the skills I have. My Shipibo [his native tribe] name is *Kestenbetsa,* which means 'universal echo,'" he explains patiently through the translator, as a wave of lights firecracker across the conference room from all the cameras.

Guillermo is descended from a long line of healers and was initiated into the shamanic world in his twenties in his hometown of Pucallpa. He's used his business know-how and media presence, alongside his healing skills, to build a formidable botanical sanctuary, Espiritu de Anaconda. There he can host upwards of thirty seekers a night into the mystery of ayahuasca at between U.S. $50–$75 a pop, making him more money than most Peruvians can dream of. But why not?

Capitalism has long since invaded the jungle, ever since the Rubber Boom here back in the late nineteenth century. Guillermo invests portions of the proceeds back into his community, and connects with the West, touring Europe and North America and leading ayahuasca retreats to spread the word of the vine. He is reputed to be a *maestro*—a master with the brew, leading seekers into the deep, unchartered waters of the spirit world.

And as the number of ayahuasca tourists increases, the number of seekers that burn through the tourism layer to genuinely engage with the work of *curanderismo,* or healing, is also on the rise. Western apprenticeships are common with many *curanderos,* especially those like Guillermo who have the ayahuasca retreats and the space to facilitate study over long periods of time.

"From my Shipibo practice I see the youth gravitating towards the religious experience ayahuasca embodies," Guillermo says. "But the *dieta* is often too hard for them, so *ayahuasquero* numbers reduce. I see fewer and fewer traditional shamans in the future . . . So if Western people are interested in preserving traditional knowledge I support that. It's a shame my Shipibo people aren't so interested . . ."

Guillermo's got his support team with him up there on stage—his wife Sonia, who is also a practicing shamana and helps him out in large ceremonies; another Peruvian woman; and a Westerner called Francois, who has been training with Guillermo for two years, after being treated with ayahuasca for addiction at the famous Takiwasi rehabilitation clinic in the nearby city of Tarapoto, run by the French doctor Jacques Mabit.

The first stage of Guillermo's apprenticeship is an introduction to the plants, their properties and consciousness, learning the ways of the *vegetalista* or herbalist. The second stage further develops the individual's consciousness and awareness of the spirit world, allowing them to contact it for clearer visions and to see, divine, and travel the spirit realms. The third stage is traveling to other dimensions, connecting to the astral, which takes great discipline and fasting to master, Guillermo says. He doesn't have the robe, or the lightsaber, but he does have the gravity of a Jedi to the eyes of this Western audience, and the archetypes it understands.

"Being a *curandero* is a long journey. It is difficult. It begins deciding *this is it,* what you want to do," Guillermo explains. "So I respect the theories and practices of every *curandero*. There are those who deal with light work—and the darkness... For me the Devil doesn't exist. In nature we see the light and the dark, so we can extrapolate from that.

"There are many different dimensions and astral energies, and the sun, moon, and planets connect energy to the spirits. It's through the plants we connect to the astral. The most important thing is having practical knowledge, and the master plants assist in this. Apart from the plants, we can't say there is any traditional knowledge left in the Amazon. People hold to traditional knowledge... but there is a mixture of beliefs and properties."

Ayahuasca healing is a central focus of the vine's use, and even without the added combination of DMT-containing plant admixtures to the brew, the vine on its own is still considered the "medicine." "When I heal an illness and look for a cure, there are spirits which travel the world, UFO type spirits," Guillermo tells us. "I connect with an energetic being who shares the knowledge of how to cure this disease... It's like channeling the DNA of a plant into a cancer patient [for instance], to improve their quality of life."

But healing only pertains to a specific illness. And in the magic-realist worldview of the *curanderos,* spirit healing is just one facet of the role of the shaman. Another is to traverse the worlds.

"*We live to die,*" Guillermo says, black eyes glinting like a condor as he pauses for his words to be translated into English and settle in our brain. "There will come a point in time when it's your time to die. Accept this—it's natural." The words hit us like the shock wave of a sonic boom, as the glamor of Hollywood shamanism starts to hit home on an emotional level. *Life and death, good and evil, spirits and other dimensions...*

We're knee-deep in the cosmic juju now, and it's starting to get heavy—and pretty late. We're all tired, but Guillermo is the last speaker. It's hot in the city tonight as I catch a *motorcarro* back to the Plaza de Armas with Theo Valis and share a guilty yoghurt milkshake and some fries at Ali's Burgers on Calle Prospero.

The plaza is packed full of locals trying to keep cool in the park, and sex oozes from every pore in this heat, like the whole city's horny. The Peruvian attitude to sex is a lot more laid back than in the West, despite the Spanish-Catholic imprint, and the locals seem to revel in their natural urges. In a country where everything closes down for a few hours during the day and few people have TVs, it's no wonder where all those kids are coming from.

"*Companiano?*" one of the streetwalker women asks me as I pass back down Calle Prospero on the way to the hostel. There's a flock of prostitutes on the main corner nestled in among cigarette sellers and taxi drivers waiting for a ride, all of them waiting for one customer or another. It makes me think of Norma's presentation tonight, and of the whole open attitude to sex that this country has.

Dozens of undernourished stray dogs also prowl the night, not dangerous enough to bite anyone, but wounded enough to make you feel for them. That is, until you see the humans.

I spot two young boys who were hassling me this morning to buy their trinkets, or just give them money, now curled up asleep in the doorway of a bank, covered by torn cardboard boxes. Next door to them a military policeman stands guard in another doorway, oblivious to their plight. The poor are so common they're invisible, just part of the ambience of this place. I tuck a few soles under them as they sleep and walk off, feeling like a guilty tourist here for thrillseeking in a culture that's trying desperately to survive.

Can shamanism help them? I wonder, as I make my way back to the hostel by moonlight.

Beggars and merchants clog the streets the next morning around the main plaza, hawking their wares. There is poverty aplenty, that is true, but the people of Iquitos also have a freedom the West has lost, a laissez-faire philosophy they exude from their roadside stalls selling candies, sweets, fruit juices, cigarettes, telephone calling cards, and tourist bric-a-brac. What you see is what you get in this hot, humid jungle outpost. The people have a down-to-earth gravity that can't help but rub off on you. *This is life,* they seem to say.

There's no ambition—or rather, as the locals struggle to make a living, there's less of the Western pressure to "get ahead." Most people I see look too busy just trying to survive—cooking food on their front porches or hanging onto their children with their many mouths to feed. *Hustling, selling, buying, crying, eating, and fucking* behind doorless and windowless walls.

There are, of course, many locals who hang out in the city cafés and watch TV and absorb the media dreamings. Downtown Iquitos is also filled with Western-style shops selling clothes, electronic goods, and hand-me-down First-World lifestyles. But you get the feeling that for the vast majority of the poor here these are unattainable fantasies. For all the locals who fill the streets, or live out their lives in their front doorways waiting, just waiting, not for anything they can put their finger on, just waiting the day away till *mañana*—they have already arrived.

In the early afternoon I share a *motorcarro* back to the conference with John Bowman, a straight-talking, bearded dude from Vancouver who's wise beyond his twenty-three years and who turned up in the dorms at the Hobo Hideout this morning, armed to the teeth with broadcast-quality audio recording gear ready to tape the shamans.

I haven't yet figured out how to work the new MiniDisc I bought the day before I left Australia, and considering I'd pitched an audio documentary to the national youth radio station, Triple J, this seemed like divine providence. I ask the questions, John records the audio, then we put together a package with all the interviews. Flanked by Vance as our photographer, we three *media ayahuasqueros* were now covered on all bases—see no evil, hear no evil, speak no evil.

Being a journalist and reporting on a new culture is somewhat akin to being a locust in the wild—you swoop down and devour all the information you can to build up an accurate impression of the place, but hopefully without stripping it bare. I was interested in the concept of ayahuasca as a spiritual tool, but I was also not going to whitewash the business culture that was booming around it. I wanted to tell it like it was and the more data I had to capture the essence of it, the better.

A group of gringos sit in deck chairs by the hotel pool, basking in the sun. One of them is reading Carlos Castaneda—*The Ring of Fire*. Half a dozen small Peruvian kids run around the pool chasing each other, full of life, and suddenly there's a loud splash as little Queto falls in the water. Ron's right at his side, pulling him out again and making sure he's okay. As I head to the refreshment table I spot Carlos Tanner, a gringo apprentice to don Juan, a local *curandero*, surrounded by a clutch of conference attendees like autograph hounds, to whom he's explaining about the sessions Juan runs.

"Healers are like the white blood cells of the planet, and they're much needed now," he says, with a knack for spin. Carlos is tall and skinny as a beanpole, with crew-cut hair, glasses, and a red Che Guevara baseball cap. He looks like a university anthropology major gone native.

I've been emailing him and plan to spend some time with Juan and his "school for shamans" they're setting up after the conference.

Sitting against the wall to the left of the stage is a Peruvian man with short black hair and glasses, dressed in a blue-striped shirt and tan pants and another baseball cap. He has the air of a Western family doctor and he sort of looks like the photo on the conference website of don Juan, maybe after a talk-show makeover. There's a surly frown on his face as he waits for his slot at the crowd, like he's uncomfortable with the whole showbiz angle of it all. But when Alan introduces him after Julia Ona-Hay's finished her talk about her work with MAPS (the Multidisciplinary Association of Psychedelic Studies), an American drug-reform non-profit, he springs into action like Jackie Chan, marshaling some inner force and focusing it to life.

"People expect me to perform miracles but I am no saint. A *curandero* is a person of learning and wisdom. I perform a diagnosis—I look into them and tell them what's wrong, but then they must work on it. They must develop the mental awareness that they can do as they will with their minds," Juan says with the fiery charisma of an evangelist TV preacher. It's hard to believe he's fifty-six years old, but perhaps it's the last forty-three years of dieting with ayahuasca and other medicinal plants that keeps him young.

"The science of *curanderismo* is a science of God... God is a fountain source of knowledge and understanding, but we don't necessarily have the capacity to bring it out in ourselves, mainly because of our own bad habits that we steep ourselves in; our own humanity is what holds us back."

The first step, Juan says, is to open your mind to receive the intelligence of the plant life. This is the science of *vegetalismo*. It's a discipline, not unlike Occidental medicine. Where Western doctors have specialists like obstetricians and psychologists, so too, do *curanderos*.

"There are *mayras* and *bancos,* all fields of specialty. In order to become a *curandero* you must purify yourself on every level," Juan says passionately, and I get a little tingle up my spine. "Then you can have insight into seeing right into a person's ills and read their thoughts and emotions. Ayahuasca also increases your sensitivity to light. And when your eyes are sensitive to UV light you can see the spirits that are already there.

"Its greatest strength lies in the power of the mind. [Ayahuasca] investigates and cures illnesses. The cure is through the discovery of unknown things, through the use of plants to access other worlds and dimensions. It's not for everyone—it's not easy to attain. But if you want to become a good *curandero* you must learn the *icaros,* and deliver them through a cleansed body that has dieted," Juan stresses, booming into the microphone.

"I'm not Michael Jackson. This is not rock'n'roll. It's communication from various sources: spirits, plants, animals, the astral, the great beyond, whatever you call to assist healing the patient. It's like a telephone call to whatever entity is out there that has insight to your problem." You could call it *Google for the vegetal internet,* I guess.

I find that Juan's got a sense of humor, but as he talks I can sense something sad about him, as if he too, has been touched by *brujeria,* the dark side of shamanism. "Ayahuasca has its dark side, all the plants do," Juan says as he winds up. "It's thirty percent bad, or drug, and seventy percent good, or medicine, and some people are using the drug side, looking for hallucinations and power within themselves."

The rumor around town is that there are more witch doctors than *curanderos* in the Amazon—and one reason for this is that it's the best paid job. Men flock to the *brujos* to get back their girlfriends, women go to make men fall in love with them, and some people use them to revenge themselves on their enemies. So the *brujos* work their black arts, projecting their will via *virote,* magic darts that hit their opponents and lodge in their spirit bodies, causing physical pain, and oftentimes, death.

One must always be careful, for the art of shamanism is fueled by the power of the will, interacting with the power of the plants. And it seems all too easy for some shamans to warp that power to dark ends, to the "shamachismo" that can drive them to serve selfish ego desires.

Power corrupts, and the spirit world can corrupt absolutely if it's not approached from a perspective of openness and servitude.

"So am I a magician, sorcerer, or *curandero*?" Juan asks cheekily, staring into the cameras and flashing a trickster smile. "It doesn't matter," he says sternly. "You must submit to a teacher's expertise and be guided and corrected, like a martial arts discipline."

I look over to see Carlos looking up at Juan respectfully from the front row. The force of his will makes me revise my first impression—this *curandero* is more akin to a neurosurgeon than a run of the mill family doctor. For a second I see through the role he plays of the good doctor of ayahuasca and another archetype flashes through: the Sorcerer Supreme, Dr. Strange from the Marvel comics. You can take the boy out of the popular culture, but all those comic books, sci-fi shows, and otherworldly media are imprinted deep within me, and as I grope through this foreign culture and its world of magic and spirits, they're all being triggered.

Sayre Tupac Wiracocha is meant to be on next, but he's hurt his back surfing in South Africa or something, and after a brief introduction he postpones his talk for a later session.

Tupac claims to be a descendant from one of the last pre-Incan families of Peru. He wears a tight-fitting brand label tank top, designer pants, gold bling-bling, and has buzz-cut short hair and the clean-shaven, poster-boy looks of Antonio Banderas crossed with the relentless salesmanship of motivational speakers like Anthony Robbins. He is the *Armani shaman,* and I later hear his workshops are filled with the beautiful and the cool in their matching sunglasses and latest season fashion, those who can afford U.S. $100 a session for his hallucinogenic cactus-inspired wisdom.

After another talk by Frank from the Institute of Integral Studies, the Ecuadorian *curandero* I saw having breakfast at the Yellow Rose the first day I arrived gets up to speak. Elias Mamallacta, the shaman son of a famous Ecuadorian family of *curanderos,* said at last year's conference that "ayahuasca is the sacred mother of humanity and that is why we must take care of her. She can't be sold. Many use her as a business. These are not pure, true people."

I'm glad someone's saying that, because it's all too easy to lose track of the spiritual foundation that all this ayahuasca use is meant to be embedded in when you're surrounded by white plastic lawn chairs, palm trees, and the sound of splashing from the pool.

"Amazonian plants are the lungs of the world," Elias says now as he takes to the stage, striding commandingly about, "and we are the guardians . . . of these plants. But our traditional knowledge is in danger of being lost." In provinces like the Nueva Loja frontier, where Ecuador meets Colombia and Peru, indigenous tribes like the Siona, Secoya, and Cofán are not just losing their traditional knowledge; they're also suffering at the hands of Western oil companies that are exploiting the jungles in their search for black gold. Lake San Pablo has been totally contaminated with oil, causing water pollution and sickness and the people there are suing Occidental Petroleum. As the roads and trucks go in and the oil comes out, the jungle and the plants like ayahuasca it supports are endangered.

"My family, the Mamallactas, is trying to create a university specializing in passing on plant knowledge," Elias explains. "In Ecuador the role of shaman is passed along hereditary lines to the first born son, or the first born girl if there is no boy. I had my first ayahuasca session at eight years old, [administered] by my father, who has been a shaman since he was born." The idea of lineage, of continuity to the past and to the future is one of the bedrock foundations of indigenous life that Elias embodies. And with these solid credentials a lot of the conference participants are hurriedly signing up to drink with him as attendants walk around with clipboards and lists for the rapidly filling up ayahuasca circles tomorrow.

I'm starting to feel really pressured by the dilemma of having to choose a shaman to drink with. It strikes me that this is just like a Western doctors' conference, full of sick people that don't even know they're sick, all listening to the experts explaining their medicine and different points of view—and you have to choose which one you want to be healed by.

Which shaman would you like tonight? What's your poison? Choosing your shaman is a bit like that game show, *Wheel of Fortune.* Spin that wheel full of *curanderos,* witch doctors, entrepreneurial gringos who know a good wicket, and wonder. There's various options, all with scaling payoffs, but only one top dollar—and of course the bankrupt trick prize. In a town where every man and his dog claim to be a shaman, the trick prizes are out there.

"It's a man's world!!! Really... it's a man's world! Not that I mind, because I love men. But still... it's a man's world," Paula Harbrink-Numan says as she comes to the microphone. *Tarzana,* as her beloved mentor Norma has called her, is every inch the jungle heroine—but don't mistake her for Jane. She's a commanding figure that inverts gender roles—tough, with a muscled physique like Linda Hamilton in *Terminator 2,* long chestnut curls falling past her shoulders. When she smiles she reveals metal braces that look like they could rip through your throat in a second and spit out your corpse before moving on to her next feed. She has a kick-ass attitude and the balls to put most men to shame—there's no mistaking who wears the pants in this family.

"Last year at the first conference I'd expected to find many wise and enlightened shamans, but did I ever find myself in a *machista* world," she says with a firm tone. "And to my total horror and disgust I learned that it was no exception that some shamans here and there displayed a womanizing behavior that went from innocently grabbing titties to pure rape! Disillusioned, I found a powerful but humble, compassionate shaman, with no macho behavior. Why? She was a woman—Norma Panduro."

Women shamanas are still few and far between in these parts—apart from Tarzana and Norma at the conference only Guillermo's female apprentice and his wife have been trained in the science of *curanderismo,* but a few more *curanderas* reportedly operate in Iquitos—when their husbands let them.

"By the time a girl is bleeding and able to access her shamanic power, she's often pregnant or tied to the family, and the target window of opportunity is gone," Tarzana says sadly. "But when you do see [female *curanderas*] they are often very powerful." Looking at her up on stage, I believe it. Tarzana later tells me she believes she was a powerful shaman in a previous life, and that energy is apparent here and now, watching her in her power.

There has been so much knowledge to process in the last two days—historical, cultural, academic, and experiential—that I'm all conferenced out. As the night's presentations draw to a close I still don't know which shaman to choose, and I can feel that spinning wheel of fortune coming to a slow, *top dollar, top dollar, top dollar*...

Finally I sign up with Percy, mainly because Bowman wants to, and a good journalist taking extreme hallucinogenic plant medicines needs an audio recording if he's to remember anything at all of the experience, I figure. So Percy it is.

The wheel has been spun.

My fate awaits me.

3

Jungle Fever

Hotel Parthenon, Iquitos

Sunday July 2, 2006

There's an electric air of expectation out front of the hotel Parthenon this morning as over a hundred ayahuasca seekers push through the wall of Shipiba fabric hustlers and other amassed locals that have surrounded the gate to wait for their buses to nirvana. It looks like a scaled-down Peruvian version of the crowds that used to besiege the Beatles when they first toured America in the Sixties. Three-wheeled *motorcarros* are pulling up in clutches and depositing fresh-faced tourists already starting to sweat in the humidity, and among all the usual suspects I spot Vance with his two bags of photography equipment and go over to chat.

Vance, Bowman, and I are locked in to "Percy's Posse," along with Hal, the Steven King lookalike; Muriel, a gray-haired, spiritual woman from the Blue Mountains in Australia, who's just finished an intensive twelve-session san pedro cactus retreat; Lincoln, a quiet, tall, bearded guy from the States in a sun hat that makes him look straight out of *Gilligan's Island;* John and Sarah, a sweet young couple from the Midwest who have drunk ayahuasca before, but seem just so awfully nice that I can't imagine them vomiting their guts up on a hallucinogenic jungle vine; Sandria, a chirpy department manager of a large corporation in Chicago; Jay, a successful independent businessman in his fifties from North Carolina; and Eliza, a shy, bespectacled, curly-haired girl with the air of a kooky librarian.

Shane, Margaret, Marty, Rachel, and Bob are all in Norma's group with a host of other gringos, affectionately dubbed the "Stormin' Normas" by Tarzana. The pairing off into groups makes it feel just like *Survivor*, like competing tribes on a reality TV show.

Marty offers to share a joint with me to blunt the underlying nervousness I'm feeling about the prospect of finally going native, getting out of this sweaty, congested city and immersing myself in the unknown jungle and the magic of the vine. After days of talking about ayahuasca and shamanism we were finally doing it, and now the enormity of the situation was starting to bleed through.

The prospect of losing my mind on an alien hallucinogen was starting to come into focus. I had this underlying fear of losing control, of not being able to concentrate on the job at hand, *the reporting,* and that threatened to cascade into a bigger reservoir of doubt about this whole gonzo expedition.

Stoned by the gates of the Parthenon, I realize that this gaggle of everyday ayahuasca tourists in their t-shirts and shorts, baseball caps and sunglasses could be going anywhere. It feels like a tour group going off to Disneyland, to see the magic kingdom, but instead of Mickey Mouse ears and other branded merchandise, everyone's adorned with jungle beads and hand-carved knick-knacks.

A local Peruvian hustler in traditional costume with a feather headdress on is beaming a smile at every gringo as he tries to sell us bead necklaces with jaguar fangs, and he's doing a roaring trade. It starts to rain lightly and as the constant patter drenches this Contiki-tour of consciousness, the group energy buzzes like a livewire in the rain, building towards a charge.

A tall, white-haired American with glasses and a cigarette in his mouth ducks for cover and presses against the wall next to me. I recognize him as Chuck, Percy's gringo … accomplice, I guess. It's hard to get a handle on what's what in this shifting cultural melting pot, but Chuck seems to be less a translator or apprentice than the young *curandero's* manager. He laughs when I tell him that, translating it into Spanish for his Peruvian girlfriend under the umbrella next to him, who giggles at the thought of it.

"I wouldn't say manager, more of a facilitator," he explains. "I try to be somewhat of an intermediary between the people coming down here and Percy. I understand our culture much better than he does, and I try to put gringos in the right frame of mind, although most of 'em don't listen." He stubs out his cigarette and immediately pulls another out of the packet and lights up.

"Percy's good energy," Chuck continues, doing the soft sell. "He's only been dealing with gringos for a year, before that he worked in his local village. He's sincere—gosh, he didn't even know about business cards!" he laughs, dragging on his cigarette.

He hands me a business card for Percy's services: *Percy Garcia Lozano: Curandero, Vegetalista, Ayahuasquero,* it reads, with a picture of Percy in a white t-shirt holding out some medicinal plants. Wow, my first business card from a shaman. A blond woman in her forties dashes out of the rain and comes up to us, eyeing the card.

"Y'know I'm also available to do the cover art for Percy's CD when he gets it together," she says to Chuck, and I realize she's the one who designed the card. It turns out she did Norma's CD art, too, recordings of her singing her *icaros* that are for sale in the market area on the outer rim of the conference auditorium. Apparently the next big thing is for all shamans interested in marketing their business services to Western seekers to record a CD with their *icaros,* their healing songs.

As the indigenous *curanderos* chase the gringo dollar the slippery slope of twenty-first-century marketing demands they keep up with the usual brand-bombing strategies and utilize business cards, websites, CDs, t-shirts, etc., like any other business. But perhaps the strategy of disseminating indigenous medicine through modern technologies and paradigms is right on the mark. The first entrepreneurial *curandero* who signs a deal with iTunes might sweep the world, but the interesting thing will be to see the effect that magical healing songs have on a mass Western audience.

Percy doesn't speak any English so it remains to be seen what he thinks of his gringo-run marketing campaign, but I'm sure he's catching on quick. He's standing in the light rain with a khaki waterproof poncho on, chatting with another group of *touristos* via his amigo Carlos, who's translating. Carlos has the same short crew cut and stocky Peruvian build as Percy—they look like brothers or cousins, and they have a gentle humor that passes back and forth between them.

Suddenly an aqua blue Mercedes Benz tour bus pulls up and one by one we all file on, giggling like school kids on an excursion. The destination sign at the front reads Kilometer 74, but I have a feeling we're going a whole lot further than that. We ply onto the bus, racing for the best seats, and are enveloped in the constant chatter of conversation in Spanish-American accents.

Bowman sits behind me and shows me his recording gear, which captures 16-bit stereo WAV files for broadcast quality audio. It turns out he's an electronic goods salesman back in Vancouver and he really knows his tech. He was in town last year doing recordings of ceremonies and sharing them as bootlegs with friends, seeding the ayahuasca vibe—and he's not the only one.

All of these ayahuasca gringos are frontrunners, in a way, exploring fresh territory in the jungles and in the *terra incognita* of the mind and bringing back reports of their experiences to the folks back home. It seems that ayahuasca knows what Madison Avenue has only recently twigged to—that viral marketing is the most effective way to increase brand presence.

Vance sits opposite me, clutching all his photo gear like he's been to South America before and knows how bad the roads can get. It's already put his back out lugging it this far, and we haven't even made the jungle yet. Bob's behind Vance, sitting next to a shy little seven-year-old boy with a matching crew cut and glasses, like a miniature version of him, but I don't know where his father is. In front of me is Phoenix, a clinical psychiatrist from California with long sandy blond curls and a Janis Joplin-like energy.

"I feel like I'm back at the high school cafeteria," says Eric, a permanently cheerful, rotund lad with a blond crew cut and a wisp of chin hair, like he's been growing it but he still doesn't have to shave much. Eric's an ayahuasca virgin, he explains with a beaming smile that just doesn't seem to dim. He makes me feel like I'm on ecstasy.

Eric's taken LSD a few times he quickly confides to me, and got into psychedelic headspaces after only his third marijuana cigarette. He's a poster boy for the War on Drugs, for sure. It turns out he's also on anti-depressants, so he's not going to be taking any ayahuasca because SSRIs interfere with serotonin uptake, which can react badly with the DMT in the brew. It's ironic, because ayahuasca is reportedly one of the best natural anti-depressants around, but oh well, Eric seems happy enough just to sit through a ceremony and watch what happens to everybody else.

Tarzana's standing up front looking resplendent in a fluro-orange t-shirt and bright blue gumboots. She does a little salsa dance, the anaconda dance she calls it, and all the Estrella women laugh and cheer. Phoenix stands up and shakes her hips, rattling her bead girdle, belly-dancing any bad spirits away. The Stormin' Normas are, it seems, the cheerleaders of the spiritual revolution.

Tarzana reads out a roll call so the gringos can confirm which *curandero* they're drinking with and at what kilometer to get off for their specific lodge. The Iquitos-Nauta highway is the only road in and out of Iquitos, a hundred-odd kilometers of bitumen that connects the small village settlements along the way with Nauta at the end of the line.

Guillermo's Espirit de Anaconda retreat is at Km 14; Brazilian *curandero* Roberto Merhino's borrowed *maloca* is at Km 20; the Stormin' Normas are headed to Norma's Estrella retreat at Km 45, with Percy's Posse not far past that out at Km 45 and a half. Those are just the main stops; dozens of other *curanderos* ply their trade from simple *maloca* huts through to ethnobotanical gardens and retreats all the way along this jungle highway.

The local trinket hustler has been doing a roaring trade in spirit girdles and hand painted skirts with shell tassels for fifty soles, and is packing up his bags. He's giving Eric a run for his money in the smile department as he sells his last bead necklace to Malonie, a skinny blond woman from Canada in a black Estrella t-shirt who's sitting next to Tarzana and taking group photos of us all. Someone tells me her nickname is Butterfly Girl, because she apparently becomes a butterfly thirty minutes into each ayahuasca session, making flying motions and talking like a faerie till comedown. Seeing me looking, she shakes her wings suggestively.

The last *touristos* finally arrive with Alan and Percy, who takes off his rain poncho to reveal a short-sleeved red tank top with "Faculty de Education" on it, like he's the physical education teacher all the girls fall in love with at school. His skin is still shining.

Everybody claps as the bus pulls off and the trinket man waves goodbye very, very happily. *Ayahuasca Disneyland here we come!*

As we drive out of Iquitos the rain stops and the roads look fresh and wet as the suburbs give way to deforested strips of green that border the highway, dotted with villages. Dirt poor huts and palm trees frame images of Peruvian school kids playing soccer in the streets. As three-wheeled *motorcarros* glisten in the sun, villagers potter about their front porches. Even the dogs by the side of the road look clean. Outside the bus windows the vibrant skin of mother earth is singing in a dozen shades of green. In front of me, Phoenix is singing her own private *icaros,* cleansing the air. All the gringos have their cameras out, recording the moment unfolding all about.

Sitting next to me is a friendly brunette in her mid-to-late twenties with a Midwestern girl-next-door kind of smile. Her name is Melissa, and she's here in Iquitos on a mission.

"My son died last year and I'm here to contact him on the other side, just to make sure he's okay, and to come to peace with it myself," she says, her big brown eyes holding back an enormous hurt. "I wasn't even sure that it was possible to do this, but then I read that article in *National Geographic* about shamanism, and I knew I had to come here, to try it myself..."

The March 2006 edition of *National Geographic Adventure* magazine, a companion to the regular title focused on adventure and first person accounts of traveling experiences, had recently published "To Hell and Back" by journalist Kira Salak, chronicling her stay with American shaman Hamilton Souther out at his Blue Morpho ayahuasca lodge not far from here by Km 56. It was reportedly one of the best-selling issues for *National Geographic Adventure,* spurred on by the growing interest in shamanism by mainstream readers. Almost all the gringos I spoke to at the conference had read it or heard about it, and some, like Melissa, had been inspired to come to Iquitos to find their own shamanistic healing by it.

While the West is still grappling with integrating a spiritual dimension into its own cosmology, indigenous peoples already have a magical framework hardwired into their reality tunnel, and the *curanderos* deal with the spirit world all the time. Melissa has organized to drink exclusively with don Juan Tangoa de Paime over her three sessions: "I don't know if that'll be long enough to make contact," she says, and pauses, holding back tears, "but I hope so."

I'm willing to believe in the possibility of her making contact with her dead son, but I'm also wary that many people could take advantage of someone like her in a precarious emotional state. As she gets off on the outskirts of town at the turnoff to the airport with a sad and hopeful look in her eyes, biting down on her upper lip to keep herself together, I sure hope she gets what she's looking for.

At Km 14 a hunched, nervous-looking, middle-aged white male with glasses gets on with two more tourists, and Guillermo's group piles out to continue their adventure. Our new passenger's quiet demeanor is topped off with an unnerving wry smile, like a little boy who's just skinned his first rabbit. I'm sure "The Smiler" is a lovely man, but he has the archetypal appearance of a serial-murderer. I wonder absent-mindedly if he's left a few bodies behind him.

He gets off not long after at Roberto Merhino's stop, along with Eric, a few of the European ayahuasca tourists and some locals. Alan

Shoemaker also takes the opportunity to head back to town now we're all strapped in, with no turning back. A few kilometers later we pass two military police who have roadblocked the highway, their SUV's lights flashing, but when they see we are good tourists they pass us on.

We wave goodbye to the Stormin' Normas at their stop and before long we've arrived at the remote outpost of Km 48, where we're greeted by a road sign and a small thatched roof *maloca* at the top of a hill. There's a village a few hundred meters in, and men are carrying sacks of coal almost as big as they are on their backs and down to the highway for transport into town.

We watch the bus disappear down the road, leaving blue skies in its wake. No other traffic is about—we're alone. The sun beats down and a sea of green surrounds us. One by one we gather up our backpacks and gear and head down the path past the village, into the jungle.

The trail is alive with the sound of birds, frogs, insects, and the screech of monkeys deep inside this fecund landscape. About ten minutes in we cross over rickety log bridges strapped together over a little creek. A light rain falls that evaporates on our skin as soon as it hits.

"I guess this is why they call it the rainforest," I joke to Vance as I help him lug his photo bags through the lungs of the earth. *The Amazon. I am in the jungle at last.*

Up ahead of us on the gringo trail is Chuck, chain-smoking his tailor-mades as always, a shiny new machete in his hand. "You can get these for two dollars in Belén market," he says, swinging wildly at a passing frond, really enjoying hacking his way through the undergrowth.

Soon we arrive at the ceremonial *maloca*, a kilometer or so past the last village. It's a simple wall-less hut about twenty feet long with a thatched roof and wooden floorboards, surrounded by a forest of eight-foot tall plants. A hundred meters distant giant palm trees tower about, closing off the outside world. It looks like an alien vista, but tonight it will be our home and sanctuary.

Percy lights *mapacho* cigarettes to chase away bad spirits—they're filled with raw jungle tobacco, *Nicotiana rustica,* with eighteen percent nicotine. The smell of the tobacco wafts through the *maloca* as we drop our bags and Chuck unrolls the mattresses. "They're a luxury out here," he says.

It's getting towards early evening and after we get settled Percy takes us down to the river a hundred meters away to bathe us in flower essences. We swim in the cool water and let it rush over and refresh us as Percy prepares bowls of flower petals dipped in *agua de florida,* calendula, and rose that reminds me of the smell of holy water in Christian churches. He's creating an "essence" from the flowers so that the individual vibrational imprints are becoming infused into the water. It's the same in the West, where flower essences are usually taken with brandy and water under the tongue.

One by one we are called up and leave the river, baptized into the ways of the jungle by the fading dusk light. Percy bathes our heads with flower essences and blows smoke down the back of our necks and over our crown chakras. It feels like the hot breath of nightclub smoke machines but it's a very intimate situation, and as I look up at Percy's always beaming face with his shiny skin and dark black eyes, he still looks like he's just stepped out of the World Cup *futbol* tour.

But he is also a *curandero,* a healer, and I start to realize the responsibility he has, that tonight he will lead us through the subtle zones of the spirit.

Up by the bushes where we've left our towels a million giant red ants are swarming over the ground and back towards their nest. One bites me, the sharp sting seeping into me, through me, in a burning wave of pain. The pain triggers a memory of a lucid dream I had just before leaving home, of giant ants cresting a horizon like in a 1950s atomic mutant movie . . .

When I saw the ants I realized the essence of them was the sting, and the pain that they brought. But I also realized it must be accepted, absorbed, and integrated. *Accept it all, the dream seemed to say, let go and become it all.* And here now, with the ant's sting in me, it all comes flooding back to my conscious mind. As I pull the ant off my foot its jaws are still lodged in my skin. The power and life force of this creature has transferred from it to me in the Gaian shuffle, as I start to tune in to the interdependent ecosystem I'm embedded in . . .

As we wander back to the *maloca* in the crisp night air its thatched frame is lit by dozens of candles that Chuck and some of the others who have stayed behind have lit. It looks like a faerie house in the jungle. As we take our spots on the hard wood floorboards and shake out our sleeping bags, Carlos explains to us that Percy comes from a long line of *curanderos,* in a tradition where you are born into the role. You don't choose to become a *curandero,* and the few that do will enter the science because they are called by spirit, he says.

Percy was prepared by his grandfather, a *banco* shaman who started grooming him in the plant medicines at the age of ten. Percy started drinking ayahuasca at fourteen and learning from other teachers after his grandfather died, rising up to become the village healer. He's now the patriarch of his family, the main breadwinner looking after his wife, their three children, his mother, father and grandparents, all through the work he does with the plants.

The night is alive with the sounds of insects and animals, like a constant hum of electricity. Percy changes into his ceremonial garb—a curious mish-mash of Western clothes and indigenous bling-bling that visually sums up the changing nature of shamanism: a tiger t-shirt, silk spotted pants and sneakers, a feathered parrot hat with blue, red, and yellow feathers, offset by Christian rosary beads and a *shacapa* leaf fan in one hand.

He sits behind a makeshift altar, a wooden box covered with an intricate, geometrically patterned cloth like those the Shipiba women were selling, the visual trip reports of the ayahuasca headspace. The altar is covered with ceremonial objects: little rainbow bead dolls, wooden cups, and about a hundred giant *mapacho* cigarettes. And last but not least, in plastic two-liter San Luis water bottles, a thick, dark-brown liquid—*ayahuasca, the "vine of souls."*

"Being here in the jungle, you may consider me a teacher, but I am just another student of Mother Nature," Percy announces. "I am only a leaf in all this Mother Nature. The *doctores* are the teachers, those who guide me to perform my healing," he says earnestly, puffing away on his pre-ayahuasca *mapacho.*

"When you have the cup in your hand, ask the spirit of ayahuasca to guide and show you your personal visions. You may see forms in the darkness—these are the '*night doctors,*' the plant teachers. I am the intermediary for them through my *icaros.*" His shaman songs are infectious melodies that roll over and over in your head, giving you paths to follow in the hallucinogenic shaman-space ayahuasca takes you to.

Percy doles out the ayahuasca by torchlight and we drink one by one, going up to the altar and taking the medicine in little wooden bowls. The brew is dark and phlegm-like, and like all medicines it tastes foul, an earthy flavor that hits the quick of you and threatens to come up again. People burp and rinse their mouths around me as I clench down the bitter flavor and breathe through it, feeling its warmth sink down into my belly.

. . . The blood of the vine, plant medicine to make you strong. Keep it down, let it pour into you, fill you, this plant-human interface . . .

Outside the sounds of the jungle deepen, monkeys screech, parrots call to each other, and the ubiquitous sound of insects, as always, are switched on. Now, so are we.

As the minutes go by we collapse into our mattresses, and the sound of vomiting fills the air. *La purga* the natives call it—the purge. Wracking heaves of spew usher forth from gringos all around me, as the ayahuasca reads their energetic bodies, finds the sickness within and brings it up and out, sometimes from both ends.

I'm actually feeling okay, slightly spacey, but the steady warmth of the ayahuasca in my stomach is nothing compared to the gag reflex from all the vomiting gringos. I'm by the bottom right hand corner of the *maloca,* so close to the edge I should be able to lean over and vomit when it comes time to purge myself, and part of me wishes it would happen sooner rather than later, just to get it over with . . .

When you're surrounded by a group of fellow ayahuasca drinkers in ceremony their energies overlap your own. And as the ayahuasca heightens your senses the sound of gringos drinking ayahuasca and vomiting and rolling around can be overwhelming. Every noise, every word, every look and breath sinks into you, until you can't look at them; you need to reel in your own psychic energy and contain it within yourself, not contaminate it with others' energies, no matter how good-natured. You have to pull in your aura and weave a cocoon, a sacred space that you can fully let go in and be yourself in to concentrate on you and the ayahuasca there on the psychic floor, naked in your raw emotion.

I can feel myself gently slipping away into a light trance by the quarter moon light as the candles are blown out, and my last thought is that we have gone back to the jungle, back to the great green womb—we have returned full circle from whence we came...

The ayahuasca starts to come on slow, snaking in and out like a lover, tantalizing me. The spirit in the plant is playing hard to get—or, more likely, she's finding me hard to get. She's interfacing, overlapping energy fields as her jungle medicine comes on strong. There's a flash of vibrant green as something starts to happen, as I fall into this target window of curious circuitry-like patterns, lines of energy that are called "ayahuasca rivers." Locks deep inside me that I never knew were there are tumbling open and I am spilling into the spaces they reveal.

Wrapped inside the Mother, she who nurtures and destroys in her endless embrace, all those I love flash before my mind's eye in a slow-motion emotional retrospective. I feel like I'm being unwound and examined but I'm not sure if this is for me or for the spirit of ayahuasca to get a quick vibrational diagnostic on the patient. I am an open book to her gaze as I circumnavigate these heart spaces and heal the way I feel to each of my loved ones. Then *madre* ayahuasca shows me bits of myself that lay forgotten or unused, like rooms to a house I've lived in all my life but never entered.

Suddenly Percy cuts through the night with his haunting voice, singing beautiful rhythmic chants that carry healing energy on the currents of their tone. *Da da da da dada da da de da da da* he sings, sweet and gentle as mother's milk, like a nursery song sung to babies while suckling at their mother's breast. The base riff is also hauntingly familiar—it's the tune of a thousand spaghetti westerns, Clint Eastwood in *A Fistful of Dollars,* a sweltering horizon at noon as the man with the black hat rides into town.

Percy comes around dutifully, blowing *mapacho* smoke over us, smudging us, shaking loose any negativity into the ether. The circuitry patterns come and go as I struggle with the vine in me now, still holding on and breathing through the cramps in my stomach and the pressure building up in my bowels. I feel like the ayahuasca's getting to know me from the inside out, but I'm trying to control her; I'm static and blocking her ability to come through. It's only when all the others seem to have fallen asleep in the wee hours of the night can I bring myself to get up and creep out deep into the jungle to purge.

As I look up from my vomit I can see water particles hanging in the air like a swarm of liquid bees; tiny glowing beads of moisture, jungle dew. Glistening among the beads are glowing mitochondria-like amoebas illuminated by the light from my headlamp. I can't for the life of me figure out what they are: they hang there preternaturally in the light, and as I reach out my hand and wave it in the air the beads curl and swirl in an equal and opposite reaction to my motion. Then it hits me: *this is the breath of the Mother, visible and exhaling all around.*

God, the ayahuasca's hitting me now, changing my perceptions, deepening my emotional connection to the web of life... It's like there's an invisible thread and if you pull on it the whole picture will unravel, revealing the true pattern underneath. I feel I am intimately connected to everything around me by my vibrational wavefront, to that great atomic sea where we are all one. Safe in the great green womb, I am remembering what this connection means, who—and what—we really are.

Later, I make it back safely to the *maloca* and sit there in the moonlight, the hard wooden boards under me, my head still fugued by the vegetative consciousness of ayahuasca. Most of the gringos are awake again, so we ask Percy questions about our experience, translated by his buddy Carlos.

It feels like some type of initiation that we've all gone through together, some psychic trial by fire. An essential part of us has awakened and blossomed to the touch of the vine and the planetary consciousness it's connected to. It's like we've all just discovered sex and now we're in the post-coital cosmic afterglow, coming down and trying to integrate what we did, what we had in ourselves the whole time but never knew. *Ayahuasca virgins, deflowered by the vine.*

The sound of the jungle is rich and deep, cicadas and insects singing their praises to this wet, amphibian Eden all around. I'm trying my best not to lie back (the spirits like it when you sit up, apparently) and to face Percy, but the inside of my head is exploding with images and emotions, all my stored memories and hurts rising up from within and flooding my mind. I'm drowning in my past.

I manage to get a few hours' sleep, and at dawn all the gringos rise from their caterpillar-like sleeping bags and shake loose their new wings.

"Where are you from?" Jay asks Sandria as she offers some Tibetan goji berries to us all for breakfast. In his white baseball cap, t-shirt, and pants, Jay looks like a middle-aged, but slimmer, Marlon Brando.

"Chicago. And you?"

"Raleigh, North Carolina."

"My name's Hal and I'm from Heaven," the Steven King look-a-like says to them both, chuckling and beaming now, just like the "Smiler"—we all are.

"I know what you mean, pal, my whole body was light, it was incredible to feel that, like a spacesuit," Jay responds, as we all fall into discussing our experiences last night.

Hal goes on to tell Percy, translated through Carlos, that he received a message from the spirits for him. It involves Jesus, John the Baptist, Miriam, Jesus's mother and her father, the rabbi, and some past-life connection. He's gone all post–*Da Vinci Code* on us, and proselytizing to the natives is so old world. Percy nods all simpatico-like at the crazy gringo Jesus freak who may or may not be onto something—but after what we've been through I'd be willing to believe almost anything...

Sarah is down on the floor of the *maloca,* curled up in her sleeping bag, her fiancé James kneeling with a supportive hand on her back as she sobs in a creaking voice, "What do we do now? I mean, how do we help take this to the world, to heal?"

A little seed in me says we don't have to do anything. As the vine spreads its tendrils round the globe, people have to stop thinking they're in control and sit back and have faith...

Or maybe I've got the jungle fever.

4

Space Cadets

The Yellow Rose of Texas, Iquitos

MONDAY JULY 3, 2006

"Are you seeing Jesus yet?" Eric the ayahuasca virgin asks me this morning over a late brunch at the Yellow Rose. The place is packed out with chattering, bubbling ayahuasca seekers still shining from their transdimensional experiences last night, filling the tables out front and spilling over into the Gringo Bar next door.

We're trading visions like trading card stats, comparing our different *curanderos* and gossiping like schoolgirls while the street vendors and fabric hustlers stand around by the dozen. Six local boys have climbed all over a three-wheeled taxi *motorcarro* parked out the front waiting for a gringo, everyone waiting, catching the tourists' eyes and forcing them to look away.

"Am I becoming Jesus would probably be a better way to explain it," I respond, and it's true. I feel like I'm walking on water. The aftermath of the ayahuasca experience is glorious: I feel lighter, cleaner, like a hard drive that's been defragged and all my pathways are re-linked up to each other, whole, and able to express joy once again. *This is what it feels like to be healed, my whole body radiates from the inside-out.* Any pretense of journalistic objectivity, which of course has never been my aim, is totally obliterated in the face of the ayahuasca experience.

"It was amazing, Eric, amazing. I could feel the interconnected web of life and my place in it, like there was no break in the circuit of energy that animates everything," I say excitedly, but words just don't do it justice.

"Well don Roberto's brew was weak, the others said, no real visions, but it sure was interesting to watch. It was bad form though—as soon as the ceremony was done around 10:30 p.m. he brought everyone back from the *maloca,* when some people were still under the influence. It felt like he was trying to get rid of us as quickly as possible."

God, I can't imagine trying to catch a bus while coming down from ayahuasca—that sounds beyond the pale. Despite the holiness of the sacrament and the worlds it can open up, Eric reminds me that the whole experience is still wrapped up in a spiritual tourism paradigm that is inevitably going to have some teething problems.

"Well at least you got back—our bus never arrived," says Bowman opposite me, clutching his papaya juice. "We all had to hitch back to town in vans this morning . . . it was kinda cool, actually."

The post-ayahuasca comedown leaves us feeling not just cleansed and elevated, but very picky over the greasy food menu this morning. "Myself personally, I have no taste for alcohol whatsoever," Bowman announces sagely, like he's been on a Betty Ford intensive. "I've drastically cut down cigarettes, and the idea of fried foods or meat isn't sitting well . . . That's one of the most interesting things about the [ayahuasca experience], the profound healing that occurs."

"Ayahuasca is an awakening to a state of mind. Its best gift is giving the eyes to see it after, when you come down," says a voice from the table next to us, and it has the ring of truth about it. A tall, thin man with dark hair and a black beard lit with white streaks smiles at us. He looks like Michael J Fox's dad in *Family Ties,* but introduces himself as John Bernstein, a fellow ayahuasca seeker who has drunk over two hundred times in the last two years across South and North America.

I spot Alan Shoemaker digging into a late breakfast special on the other side of the tables and wander over to say hi. "That was pretty amazing last night," I tell him, asking if he drank himself. He's been too busy organizing the conference to sit and take the medicine, he explains, and in fact it's rare he gets a chance to drink anymore at all, what with all his business interests.

"It's been over two years," he confesses, wiping the last of the runny yolk off his plate with the crust of his bread and asking for the bill.

Back at our table Vance has succumbed to the relentless gaze of the Shipiba fabric hustlers and is actively browsing by the curb, surrounded by half a dozen women all trying to show him their wares at the same time, like a synchronized dance of the seven veils. He returns from the scrum with a collection of astounding hand-woven fabrics that depict grid patterns, energetic mosaics that are commonly seen in ayahuasca visions. With their blocky pixelated style and street-like dotwork, some of them look like indigenous visions of the early Atari game *Pac-Man*.

The Shipiba women don't usually take ayahuasca themselves, instead they are taught the shape of the visions by their mothers and grandmothers, who were originally instructed in the work by male shamans, some of whom still update the designs today. These women travel hundreds of kilometers by boat from their communities on the Ucayali River around Pucallpa to Iquitos and back, following the tourist trail and the money it provides. What many people don't realize, though, is that it also keeps their indigenous art and culture alive, where other tribes are absorbed into the homogenization of the encroaching global village.

Gobi, one of the little boys who has been bugging me for days, swoops down with his *companianos,* and I let him finish my papaya juice and have some loose change. But as his friends start arguing over the coins I realize I've created a source of imbalance between them, that in a way, that's what we do as tourists.

"The poverty down here is so grinding, huh? And the expectations are rising," a familiar voice says, and I look up to see Chuck, all fresh-faced with a cigarette dangling from his lower lip like a midday cowboy. "People don't realize," he says, taking a seat on the other side of our table. "I'll argue over 50 *centimos* and some people will say, well that's only 15 cents, and I'll say it's not the point. It's that [the locals] are getting that greedy vibe and they see us as targets for enriching themselves. Our presence is a real corrupting force."

Chuck orders a coffee as he unloads his gripes about the ayahuasca trade and the attitude of some "spiritual tourists." "I think a lot of people come down here and take ayahuasca … and I heard one fellow say he wanted to maintain self-control!" Chuck exclaims. "Ayahuasca is about no self-control, it's about losing the sense of self…There's an erasure of one's personal identity and most people cannot stand that.

"I was in this ceremony last week…You had people laughing and joking and talking about their jobs and parties they went to and this and that—and it absolutely goes over their heads. They have no idea what it's about and I'm not one to tell them what it's about. If they're not ready for the message they're not going to receive it," Chuck sighs.

It all comes down to intent, he argues, that many ayahuasca tourists see the experience as another thrill in an over-stimulated world and are taking it as a drug, rather than as a sacrament.

"And what do you think ayahuasca's message IS?" I ask him point blank, trying to avoid the eyes of the Shipiba women over his shoulder flashing me their wares. "What's going on in that spirit space?"

"I always considered ayahuasca more like a vaccination," Chuck answers with a glint in his eye, enjoying this chance to vent. "I think you're vaccinated by ayahuasca. I actually believe it to be an external entity, to use a kind of a hacker word. I consider it to be a force, a power. And when I go out to the jungle there's a unification as far as spirit's concerned. I think it's a very powerful one and that with the help of ayahuasca you can contact that spirit or force …"

It's amazing how much people will just open up when it comes to talking about ayahuasca, like the vine has ripped the lid off their emotional armor and they're compelled to communicate their experiences. I feel the pull of that, too, even after my first ceremony.

Chuck's a grizzled veteran of the ayahuasca scene in Peru, and has been coming down here for almost thirty years and drinking with the *curanderos.* And while he has a very valid point about the intent of the tourists drinking ayahuasca, and of the industry that has developed to cater to it, I can't help but see the looks of wonderment and vibrancy on the faces of all the ayahuasca seekers here.

They have experienced a buoyant sense of transcendence, however fleeting, and for many of them this is their first time through to the "other side." They really are like kids courting the mystery of ayahuasca, full of youthful exuberance, and the ones who remain on the path will soon learn the duties and responsibilities that the science of *curanderismo* demands, and find their healing.

On my freelance writer's budget I'm hoping to find a hostel even cheaper than the Hideout, and after brunch Bowman and I check out the two-story "Mad Micks Jungle Emporium and Bunkhouse" opposite the Yellow Rose, which at ten soles a night must be the cheapest place in town.

Mick's Peruvian office ladies potter around the small cluttered store and information exchange like bored housewives, surrounded by gumboots, mosquito nets, and maps. Suddenly a pained voice screams out, "Elizabeth …!" from past the bunkroom, and I feel like the prodigal son returning home to mom and dad while they have a domestic.

Elizabeth waves us through to check out the digs, a simple but clean room with four bunk beds, tourist posters, and a small bookshelf—but all the bunks have lockers at the bottom, and there's a fan, thank God.

Beyond the bunkroom is a rotund, friendly Englishman in his fifties who's lying in a hammock in the kitchen. "Mad Mick" as he's affectionately known, beckons us in and rolls over to show us his bum—which has been bitten by a bott fly, an ugly parasite that burrows under the skin and lays eggs that hatch and eventually crawl out after feasting on you for days.

It reminds me of tourists and the sometimes parasitical relationship we have to the countries we visit. We get under the skin of a culture, root around and make it part of us, taking in the sights and experiences, but what do we offer in return?

Mick's been here eight years now, and he runs the local tourist newspaper, a black and white bi-monthly broadsheet called the *Iquitos*

Times, which often has articles on shamanism and ayahuasca. He estimates that there's about two thousand *touristos* here every month in Iquitos—which is only about a tenth of what they get in Cuzco—but this frontier town attracts the more adventurous spirits, he says.

Of that two thousand, Mick reckons about ten percent again try ayahuasca for the experience—another kick in a jungle wonderland. But four or five percent of those who try ayahuasca are drawn to it, he explains, they can feel the call of the spirit in the vine.

Mad Mick's only taken ayahuasca once—as part of a BBC documentary from a few years ago. The English media makers gathered eight people together on an all-expenses paid BBC jungle tour. One person chickened out of the final ayahuasca ceremony and two people were rejected by the shaman as too weak, so the final footage wasn't all that exciting.

"It's not for you," Mick recollects the shaman's advice. Four people had a slight effect from the brew, but Mick says he was left unchanged. "It didn't even touch my sides," he laughs with an old-time English comedian's accent, swinging back and forth in his hammock.

"Oh, you little bastard!" he screams finally at the bug in his behind, grimacing tightly and getting out of the hammock. "When he comes out I'm going to stab him!" he growls, his face flushed red.

All in all, the Bunkhouse seems the perfect nerve center for our media crew, and Bowman and I get our luggage and relocate, Vance agreeing to join us when his room back at the Parthenon is up tomorrow. The show must go on. There's been so much conferencing, ayahuasca, and culture to experience that there's been no time for integration—and now we've got a 1:00 p.m. appointment with Dennis McKenna on the other side of the plaza and we're running late.

Bowman and I get to the rented apartment on Calle Yavari, however, to find Dennis is running even later than we are, finishing off another interview with a Spanish documentary crew. He comes walking up the boulevard, a man in his fifties but with the mischievous smile of a little boy on his face, an echo of his late brother, Terence, in it.

Dennis is one of the leading figures in the global psychedelic and scientific communities, investigating entheogens (substances which "evoke the Divine within") and indigenous plant medicines. He was involved with the "Hoasca Project" in the early 1990s, studying ayahuasca usage by members of União do Vegetal (UDV) and he recently issued the 2005 manifesto "Ayahuasca and Human Destiny."

Along with his late brother Terence he cowrote the book *The Invisible Landscape,* which revealed their psychedelically influenced insights into the nature of reality and space-time they received during "The Experiment at La Cholerra" in South America in 1971 (later recounted in Terence's book *True Hallucinations*).

It was on that infamous trip that Dennis and Terence tried to "end history" because they "thought it needed to end" by vibrationally cross-bonding with a mushroom and exteriorizing the soul, creating translinguistic matter. Or something like that. Terence went on to become a global underground celebrity and advocate for plant entheogens before his untimely death in 2000, and Dennis has since continued the scientific research and discussion about entheogenic issues.

Two days ago Bowman convinced me to spend half a day's budget on an early morning nature walk through some botanical gardens outside Iquitos, hosted by Dr. McKenna. Dennis's original trip in the jungle in 1971 still echoes down the years and influences "psychonauts" (as a whole generation of innerspace explorers term themselves) today, as they search for their own pathways back to the Divine.

Culture, like nature, goes in waves, and as the tide of history builds and spends, we modern day *ayahuasqueros* are just the latest wave to brave the shores of consciousness. So as an elder figure for Western seekers, Dennis has much knowledge to share, and if it was to begin with some basic botany then I figured that was just part of the story.

The bus ground to a stop somewhere near Km 40 as Dennis McKenna stepped out to lead the group like a boy scout leader, sunhat covering his balding-scientist head, ever present pipe in hand. The dozen or so gringos formed a single file, cameras loaded and ready to shoot as we picked into the jungle with a native guide leading the way.

We passed through the green labyrinth and stopped to inspect *datura,* ayahuasca, and the dozens of mushroom species growing everywhere, sprouting on tree trunks in a delicate lacework and from beneath giant palm fronds. It seemed like cosmic synchronicity to watch Dennis among the mushrooms and it triggered the memory of what happened to the McKenna brothers that has since become part of psychedelic folklore...

Dennis and his brother Terence were drawn to South America in 1971 by a curiosity with DMT and plant entheogens that connected to other dimensional realms, but they soon found themselves taking advantage of the abundant hallucinogenic mushrooms that were to spark Dennis's own shamanic initiation and color all his later scientific work with plants.

Magic mushrooms, containing the active chemical *psilocybin,* were still an exotic unknown in the States at that time. Albert Hofmann, the Swiss chemist who had infamously isolated *D-lysergic acid diethylamide* (LSD-25) back in 1943, had only isolated psilocybin some sixteen years earlier in 1955, and it was a legendary substance that rarely showed up on the streets. Dennis says he remembers things sold as psilocybin that were really LSD—frozen store mushrooms that had been sprayed with LSD—but the real vegetal sacrament was unknown in the concrete utopia of the Haight-Ashbury in its hippie prime.

"So we started taking psilocybin mushrooms and at first kind of recreationally, and then... we started incorporating them into our diet because there wasn't a whole lot to eat. We had canned food, we had rice, we had bananas—whatever you could buy in the village—so we started ingesting these things, a lot. We were in such a state we were kind of half-loaded all the time," Dennis says to me now in his downtown Iquitos apartment. He's definitely got the gift of the gab like Terence had and he likes to wax loquacious about his experiences. And like a good ayahuasca boy scout I'm taking it all in.

"It produced such a flow of ideas and such interesting conversations and such apparent insights into the way that the jungle was working and how plants and insects and everything were generating these web of messages, and so on. It generated a lot of talk, a lot of chat about all kinds of stuff, and you have to remember who we were. We were pretty verbal people anyway, intellectual and curious and steeped in Jungian psychology and alchemy and all this crazy, esoteric stuff."

The two McKenna brothers were like mutants from a future age born into the repressive intellectual cultural milieu of 1950s America, but as the psychedelic sixties blossomed their thirst for experiential knowledge seemed to mirror that of the counterculture at large. As Dennis is the first to admit, however, at the time he and Terence were young and "had what we thought was knowledge. We had enough knowledge to be dangerous to ourselves," he laughs, puffing away on his pipe.

Their esoteric expertise ranged from alchemy, genetics, chemistry, and philosophy, all the way through to science-fiction and hippie cosmology, but it gave them an *ideogrammatic blueprint,* a word-map to try and grasp the unfathomable reaches they were to experience. They had the hubris to spit in the cosmic ocean, and find that the cosmic ocean spat back.

"One of the aspects of taking mushrooms was this sound that we could hear at high doses. You could hear a sound at the edge of detection that seemed to be a kind of high-pitched, electronic buzzing and popping sound. It's the sound you can hear very strongly when you smoke DMT. The sound of ripping cellophane . . . or things like that. On mushrooms you could hear it," Dennis says animatedly.

Psilocybin, they quickly discovered, was a perfect orally active form of DMT that is absorbed and metabolized slowly and converted into *psilocin* in the body. Psilocin is very close to DMT but it takes longer to be eliminated. At high doses of psilocybin you can get to a dimension that's very much like a DMT trip, the active hallucinogen contained in the ayahuasca brew.

"And so we developed this idea that if you could listen to this sound, and not only listen but imitate the sound, you could sing it . . . you reached a point where it sort of locked on to this internal resonance . . . And your mouth would open wider than a mouth has any right to open and your tongue would stick out and this stuff would just literally rip out of you, you couldn't stop it. It would just pour out of you; it was like a harmonic lock . . . And there's a whole visual thing going on . . . in the hallucinogenic state it seemed to have a very strong visual component. To a certain extent you could even make the air shimmer—or so we thought. But y'know, we [were] totally ripped on psilocybin."

The McKennas believed they could generate an opalescent "psycho-fluid" from their bodies, a magic mirror substance with the properties of a scrying stone, to see into the past, present, or future and to work their magic with. They also believed they could lock on the sound they would make and "fix" it onto the body of a mushroom—*fixing the mercury* it was called by the medieval alchemists.

The two brothers had gotten the idea from anthropologist Michael Harner, whose 1969 article "The Sound of Rushing Water" in the *Natural History Magazine* quoted the Jivaro Indians in Ecuador performing these feats in ayahuasca ceremonies, and they filtered it through their rich cross-cultural imaginations into a grand unified possibility of neo-science.

"We were trying to recreate the Philosopher's Stone," Dennis says without a trace of embarrassment, "which is in some ways the ultimate artifact. That thing that exists and is both mind and matter and responds to thought . . . and can do anything you can imagine.

"And so we performed the experiment and what we postulated was going to happen didn't happen, obviously. How could it happen? It didn't happen that the mushroom would explode on a cloud of super-condensed glowing crystals and leave a violet disk in front of us, no. That's not what happened, y'know. That was the hoped for result, that we'd be able to get in the saucer and fly away, and end history in the process.

"What did happen after I got through making the sound and proclaimed in this state I was in that the experiment had been complete . . . As [Terence] described in the book . . . we were looking at this mushroom, it was dark, and it was a fully opened mushroom. My shadow fell across [it] in such a way that it was perfectly bisected, half of it in dark, half of it in light, and I looked at it and said,

"'Look at this. We're looking down at the earth from 23,000 miles out. You can see the continents, the cities, all this.' Because we were loaded you could see all that, right?

"And so then Terence awoke and said, 'Is that IT? Is that all?'

"And I said, 'No, listen.'

"And he said, 'Listen for what?'

"And I was quiet, I said, 'Just be quiet for a minute.'

"I was hearing what he was thinking and I was answering the questions, and I was in a telepathic state, or so I thought. I said, 'I'm . . . I've tapped into the universal database. Got a question for me? So ask me a question.' And he started this process and I started giving answers. What is the name of this plant? What's going to happen six months from now? I had ready answers—I don't know if any of the answers were true or not, but that was convincing to him.

"What was happening to me on the subjective level at the time . . . what I was experiencing, was that essentially I had traveled back to a point about six months previously when I was living in Boulder and I had smoked DMT. And I have this experience about being so completely blown away by the DMT that I was spread—literally to the edges of the cosmos. My psyche and my mind, what was left of it, was co-incident with the boundaries of space-time.

"And I had this feeling that I had been literally smeared over creation by this experiment that we'd done. I don't know what the connection was to the previous smoking of DMT, except I had a real strong advocation that this had taken place then—the present moment at La Cholerra and this previous moment were like the same moment. And so I was spread all over creation. *I was literally a space cadet* . . . And then

70

I just started raving and speaking in tongues ... and [Terence] was on the outside looking at me behaving like a complete, raving madman."

It took Dennis two weeks to come down from this cosmic high, during which some of his companions thought he had gone mad, in an isolated jungle village hundreds of miles from help. Terence looked after him as he experienced a slow collapse over each twenty-four hour period, from the edges of the universe to a concentration. Dennis remembers: "For the first twenty-four hours I was the whole cosmos, and then in the next period I was like the galactic cluster, then the solar system, then the earth and so on, it was mapped that way."

Modern neuroscience would say that he experienced a prolonged MAO-inhibition that screwed up his brain chemistry, but from the vantage point of decades later, Dennis thinks that's a very reductionist way to look at it.

"I've thought about [what happened] a lot since then, and really the only model that fits is not a biochemical model or a pharmacological model. The only model that fits is a *shamanistic initiation,*" he says, straight down the line. "I didn't ask for it, I wasn't prepared for it—but that's what happened. Because in shamanic traditions in all cultures over the world, there is this notion of being literally torn apart and put back together—in a better way than you were before.

"I feel—and I'm not a shaman, I'm not claiming to be a shaman, I didn't ask to be a shaman—but I got the initiation and I do feel that ultimately it was a very integrative thing. It was a healing thing that happened to me ... and it totally influenced my future career."

Dennis returned to the States and threw himself into scientific study, changing his academic direction from anthropology, philosophy, and comparative religions and receiving his Master's degree in botany from the University of Hawaii in 1979. He went on to earn his Doctorate in Botanical Studies from the University of British Colombia in 1984 for a thesis on "Monoamine oxidase inhibitors in Amazonian hallucinogenic plants: ethnobotanical, phytochemical, and pharmacological investigations." The fieldwork for this paper was conducted in the Amazon Basin ten years after he'd had his shamanic initiation into the vegetal world.

"In a way that was done as my own personal effort to redeem myself, to say yes . . . I can go to the Amazon without going crazy. I can do science, I can do this work, this very reductionist, ethnobotanical, ethnopharmacological type work—and I'm a competent scientist."

As the thesis title suggests, McKenna went back to the jungles and explored the pharmacology, botany, and chemistry of ayahuasca and that other DMT-rich hallucinogen, *oo-koo-hé*. In 1990 he joined startup Shaman Pharmaceuticals as their Director of Ethnopharmacology, and he later worked for more mainstream companies like the Aveda Corporation, where he was Senior Research Pharmacologist developing natural products. In the corporate world McKenna found the usual paradigm of bottom-lines, end-results, and return for investment that all corporate botanical research demanded for useful and patentable products.

"There has always been some interest from 'Big Pharma' to look into Amazon plants for potential sources of new medicines," he explains. And sometimes, when profits go before ethics, it leads to cases of "biopiracy" where indigenous cultures' knowledge of plant medicines is exploited and stolen.

In 1986 Loren Miller, the director of a Californian company, the International Plant Medicine Corporation, applied for and was granted a U.S. patent on an Ecuadorian strain of ayahuasca, saying he had been given permission by indigenous people for his research. The claims that it was a distinct strain with different colored flowers from other plants of the species were repudiated by botanical experts, and the patent was overturned in 1999, only to be reinstated on appeal.

Miller however, was not able to modify the ayahuasca or derive any medicinal product from his research, and the seventeen year patent on ayahuasca expired in 2003. But the precedent remains, as does the larger problem of an economic–intellectual rights system clashing with an indigenous knowledge system and sacred plants.

"The indigenous peoples of the Amazon basin believe that commercializing an ingredient of our religious and healing ceremonies is a profound affront to the more than four hundred cultures that populate the Amazon basin," said Antonio Jacanamijoy, the general coordinator of the Coordinating Body of Indigenous Organisations of the Amazon Basin (COICA) in a 1999 statement.

"I'm all for finding new drugs in the Amazon," Dennis explains, "because I think it really helps—if you do it in an ethical way . . . it helps to preserve the Amazon and the medicines that come out of it. But you have to be ethical about it, you have to acknowledge the debt to the indigenous people and you have to do everything in your power to make sure they get something out of it."

There's a smile on his face like he's wrestling with something, like the scientist and the space cadet are both appraising their perspectives on indigenous plants. "I'm still curious about ayahuasca and I still think science can tell us a lot about [it]," Dennis says finally. "But I have given up my pharmaceutical ambitions to turn it into a drug, or a drug that can be used clinically. I've gotten a strong message that . . . ayahuasca is a sacred thing and I don't want the pharmacological industry to corrupt it. The less it's regulated and the less they try to make a drug out of it the better we all are," he says emphatically. It's a curious path for a scientist who has strayed from academia to the corporate sector, but perhaps the only ethical alternative for a man of his experience.

It's been a long interview, and Dennis takes off his glasses as he collects his thoughts, polishes them, and puts them back on, a sincere look in his eye.

"I think the world is in serious need of healing and in some serious need of waking up," he says finally. "The destruction of the environment, the changes we're making to the global climate, the unwillingness of the powers that be to even acknowledge that this is going on, let alone do something about it . . .

"The interest in ayahuasca is encouraging in that people are waking up to the fact that you have to rediscover not just these substances, but the context for their use [and the] archaic traditions where people have developed over millennia ways to relate to these plants and their traditions...

"[Ultimately] I think that those who need to find ayahuasca will find it," he concludes. "I think that ayahuasca will find those it needs to find."

While what his brother, Terence, called "dominator culture" tries to wrest control of the plants and natural resources to prop up a sinking materialist economic system, the spirit of nature is seeding its own agenda, trying to regulate the human monkey out of control. And a Western cultural integration of the hyperdimensionality these plant interfaces bring could yet "end history," or at least expand Cartesian reality in ways indigenous peoples have already been navigating for millennia.

As Dennis leans back in his chair and refills his pipe, puffing away meditatively, it strikes me that like the mushroom before it, ayahuasca has found the right person to be its spokesperson in this shaman–scientist.

And that maybe he wasn't such a space cadet after all, but a herald of things to come...

5

Cosmovision

Iquitos
WEDNESDAY JULY 5, 2006

In the early hours of July 4, just after midnight, a mob of locals stormed the Yellow Rose, chanting anti-imperialist slogans and attacking *touristos* in their assault on gringo central. The restaurant has been an ongoing target of Peruvian discontent with Americanos, their Free Trade Agreement, and the encroaching globalization threatening their culture and living. Texas was under attack once more, but unlike the battle of the Alamo, Gerald wasn't going down to the Indians, hell no.

Armed with a baseball bat Gerald fought off the marauding hordes as the *touristos* grabbed their cameras and barricaded themselves behind tables and chairs, standing their ground—and with nowhere to run. For a good hour this bastion of Western imperialism was on its knees, but by the time I arrived for breakfast this morning it was all back to normal, a political aberration on my spiritual itinerary but a forceful reminder that as Chuck said, our presence here is changing things.

Iquitos is electric with noonday humidity as Vance, John, and I wade through the horde of locals hustling trinkets outside the Parthenon gates and join the other ayahuasca gringos amassing by the pool. It's Bowman's birthday—he's twenty-four today—and drinking with Guillermo is going to be his present.

We're waiting for Alexis, a blond, twentyish dude from Washington D.C. who's going to help translate the interview with Guillermo I've lined up. Alexis is a Princeton dropout who's backpacking around on a spiritual path, drinking ayahuasca with shamans and asking critical

75

questions to deepen his own understanding. He's drunk with Guillermo four times now and calls him "a fucking Jedi." When he turns up an hour late, wearing a *Corey Feldman School of the Arts* t-shirt, I know he'll fit right in with our media crew.

Vance wants to get out to the Espiritu de Anaconda, Guillermo's aya-huasca retreat to take some shots before we lose the afternoon light, so we pile into two *motorcarros* and speed away from the front of the Hotel Parthenon before the *touristos* bus has even arrived. Before long our *motor-carros* get bogged on the dirt road turnoff from Km 14, a long undulating strip of mud from recent rains, and we have to get out to walk. The local villagers are busy building a concrete footpath to run from the highway past their village and towards the ayahuasca retreat a few miles in, and part of me wonders if this will facilitate t-shirt and refreshment stalls springing up wherever the gringos go, like mushrooms after a fresh rain.

Before I'd left Australia I'd watched a pirated DVD of the hard-to-find psychedelic western *Renegade,* which shot Guillermo to fame, and a little of the Hollywood spin had rubbed off. In the Hollywood feature, cowritten and directed by French filmmaker Jan Kounen, an ayahuasca drinker himself, Guillermo plays a master shaman who initiates the lead character, Mike Blueberry, a Civil War cowboy, into the world of ayahuasca and the spirits.

It cost U.S. $34 million to make and flopped at the box office, mainly because of bad marketing. The special effects were as accurate a copy of Kounen's own ayahuasca journeys as the digital rendering could repli-cate, triggering flashbacks among many of the ayahuasca seekers who watched it and unsettling revulsion in others.

When I'd interviewed Kounen last night, after the screening of his documentary *Other Worlds,* which tells the story of his own apprentice-ship to Guillermo in over one hundred ayahuasca drinking sessions, he said that it was vital for him to make films about spiritual reality, and ayahuasca.

"There is . . . a tremendous knowledge that we cannot imagine in our culture, you have to make a bridge to that to make people consider, just consider. The culture protects itself from these concepts. It's like a philosophical issue but it's also like a keeper that doesn't want you to go outside of your own culture."

Kounen has bright shining blue eyes and the calm and grounded nature of a man in his forties who has found inner peace. This French music video and feature film director has carved out a career specializing in bringing aspects of the spiritual world to the screen. As well as *Renegade* and *Other Worlds*, he has also filmed a series of one-hour documentaries for TV called *Another Reality*, and his latest docu-pic was on Amma, a modern day Hindu saint, who purportedly performs miracles.

"Cinema is a great tool to deal with modified states of consciousness and different perceptions, [just as] shamanism, or meditation, or other ways, help us to understand how the creatures that we are, work," Kounen said. "If you start to think of [perception] as separate channels, then you start to know how to work the channels, all relative to the information." And if you shatter the channels, which is what he believes ayahuasca does, it can "reveal information . . . going to the deep meaning of what it is to be human."

In essence, media itself is an altered state of mind, Kounen said, where the director can closeup on an eye or change the sound, and thereby change the perception. This might explain his transition from Hollywood director to ayahuasca drinker, and also the synchronistic fit with the casting of Guillermo as a master shaman playing the master shaman, art mirroring life.

Bowman, Vance, and I feel like *media ayahuasqueros* ourselves as we walk under the blue sky and marvel at the giant cumulonimbus clouds billowing overhead, and take some panoramic shots with our cameras, capturing everything but the spirit of this place. We're in a funny position here as Western media reporting on these spiritual realms—no matter how many mediums we record in, the essence of the ayahuasca experience can't be replicated, only approximated. And even then just crudely.

It's *translinguistic,* as Dennis McKenna would call it. The shamans say that nature speaks in signs, in the overlapping coincidences and resonances of the natural world and the beings in it. Walking down the dirt road through the cleared jungles, awash in a sea of grassland, it's speaking to me now.

After a few kilometers we reach a sign, which reads "Espiritu de Anaconda." Walking over wooden bridges we pass the lush cultured rainforest and enter into a sprawling multi-unit complex designed to cater to Western standards. The central *maloca* is about 30 feet in diameter with a conical roof that reaches almost as high again and houses over two dozen people.

It's booked full tonight with conference attendees wanting to drink ayahuasca in this Amazonian cathedral, fully mosquito-proofed, leave your shoes at the door, please. Add a dozen smaller *malocas,* guesthouses, the dining room, and toilets with porcelain bowls and doors and this starts to feel like the Club Med of ayahuasca. I half expect Elle MacPherson to come out of the jungle clad in a leaf bikini, offering a selection of fruits and nuts.

Guillermo moved here from his native Pucallpa and built the center only two years ago, after money from *Renegade* gave him the capital to expand. "It's safer here, you know," says Carlos, a native Iquitian who works here and meets and greets us ayahuasca gringos. "We have the army here, and the police—and there is nowhere to run. Pucallpa has the bus to Lima and many exits—someone can kill you and never be caught, they could get out of town in any of a dozen ways."

It's an oft-repeated wisdom and there may be some truth it, but I imagine Guillermo might have been a target himself down in Pucallpa. Despite being a respected healer his expertise has also brought him fame and fortune that most locals can only dream of, and other *curanderos* have been targeted and blackmailed before.

We've arrived early but there's no sign of Guillermo himself as we have a look around and Vance sets up his photography equipment. Rama, a tall, beautiful black woman with a large afro introduces herself as an anthropology student from France, who has been studying with Guillermo as part of her work documenting indigenous cultures for her fellowship in neo-shamanism.

She films one of Guillermo's helpers who's boiling up crushed ayahuasca vine and other plants in a giant soot-blackened cauldron in a wall-less hut behind the main *maloca*. As the flames lick up and spray into the air it resembles a witch's pot, with the attendant in his shorts, t-shirt, and baseball cap looking like a *mestizo* Beverly Hills pool boy.

A plume of thick gray smoke billows out, stinging my eyes, and when they clear I can see the jungle medicine, ayahuasca, brewing, bubbling, writhing with life in the boiling phlegm-like green brew. A giant witches cauldron full of snot, and around the thick, brown vine bark are green admixture leaves that contain the active DMT.

I get a whiff of the brew and it makes me want to vomit. A surge memory of ayahuasca washes up—the taste of my last experience catching in my throat. I struggle to force it down. They say it takes a few years for the ayahuasca drinker's body to get used to the brew and properly acclimatize. But the soul? That takes longer—sometimes forever...

Ayahuasca is not a drug—not in the Western sense. It cannot be abused like recreational chemicals because the taste and experience are so demanding and the hallucinogenic effect is never the same twice. Rather, it develops a relationship with the drinker, sometimes healing the body, other times illuminating the mind, or deeper still, taking the soul on journeys beyond.

But it will do none of this without the participant putting effort in—it's not just "pop the red pill and escape the *Matrix*." Serious students have to give up their Western ways and embrace a rigorous diet low in foods containing tyramine, a chemical which can react badly with the MAO-inhibiting properties of the vine. No red meat, pork, salt, sugar, fat, caffeine, acidic foods, alcohol, or sex, all of which affect the body's sensitivity to ayahuasca. But tell that to a bunch of Western thrillseekers looking for some jungle kicks.

The dark clouds gathering on the horizon all afternoon finally break and a late downpour cleans the air as the other conference gringos start to rush in. They take off their coats and shoes and leave them by the door and pass into the main *maloca*. We all form a concentric circle hugging the wall while far above a spider-web criss-cross brace of poles supports the high cone roof.

We're an eclectic bunch—I spot Jay, whom I drank with at Percy's, dressed in a one-piece vomit-proof ayahuasca jumpsuit, Frank the professor, and other familiar faces. Dennis McKenna's here holding court, his bald head gleaming in the late afternoon light as he sits on his mattress and puffs away on his pipe, chatting about altered states. "A lot of psychologists are into science fiction," he says. "It's the closest we can legally get in the West to other worlds..."

Next to him is his seventeen-year-old daughter Caitlin, who's going to college in the fall and is taking ayahuasca tonight for the first time. She's reading a fantasy novel in the dim light like she's in an airport departure lounge waiting for take-off. With her hair back in a bow, glasses, and soft, mellow energy, she looks like she'd be more into ponies and horses, maybe some Christian rock.

"I haven't done any psychedelics before, I haven't felt it was time," she tells me with the honed nonchalance of someone whose father is one of the planet's most pre-eminent legal psychedelic researchers. "This is my first ayahuasca experience. I have no expectations, y'know. I'm keeping it open."

Everyone waits patiently and swaps ayahuasca stories and travelers' tales, letting our collective energies mingle in the flesh before they meet in the spirit. After my previous problems letting go around the energy of a group, I wonder if this many people all in one *maloca* on ayahuasca will turn me into a psychic pressure cooker ready to explode.

"The word on the *ayahuasca forums* is that Guillermo's brew is one of the strongest in town," Bowman tells me with a wry smile as he sets up his recording gear down by the edge of his mattress. "The crew who drank with him on Saturday night say he's definitely loaded the brew to kick gringos' butt!"

"I haven't really seen any *spirits* or anything of that sort," Alexis chips in excitedly beside us. "But it's really . . . I've felt it, like, going through every crevasse, on a subatomic level of my body and my spirit . . . And anything it finds that's dead . . . or not life and movement . . . it gets rid of, or fixes or makes me vomit. I remember the first time I drank I vomited, and each time I vomited it would show me a picture of all my bad habits and my life that I was vomiting up and getting rid of."

Great. Everyone seems to vomit up easily but me; it's going to be another interesting night. As the rain keeps falling down and the sounds of the jungle come alive, I start to feel the fear. *Fear of the real, of the deep ayahuasca experience and the madness it can bring.*

When Jan Kounen apprenticed with Guillermo to make his documentary, *Other Worlds,* on Shipibo shamanism, he went mad for a time, temporarily schizophrenic when he failed to respect the diet and ayahuasca. He says the difference between a madman and an *ayahuasquero* is that the madman can't communicate what he's seen. Trapped in a recursive psychic groove, the hapless psychonaut doesn't have the guidance, or the ability to escape, and sometimes when he does, not all of him returns.

The trained *ayahuasquero,* on the other hand, can navigate the abyss and integrate it, even bring a bit of it back and ground it in this realm. This, Kounen told the conference audience before the screening of his documentary, is the role of the artist and the magician. I guess that tonight will be the test of my magic.

There's still a while before the ceremony, so I meander out to the main dining room with the thatched roof and meet Kathleen, a fiftyish American woman from Denver with a blond bob, blue eyes, and the warm, nurturing appearance of Carol Brady from *The Brady Bunch.*

She looks like somebody's mom doing ayahuasca—and in fact, she is—but she's also a clinical psychologist who's here for her own healing. Kat's drunk the brew once before, ten years ago, and the thought of going back into that raging dimensional flux has gotten her all nervy. She gets out her rosary beads and says prayers over the dining table as I fix us a cup of herbal tea.

There's a half dozen other ayahuasca seekers milling about as Guillermo himself walks in casually, followed by Sonia, his wife, and Rama, who at six foot two towers over the others.

Guillermo's got a very down-to-earth air about him, and as heads turn and everyone looks he doesn't react, just sits down at the table. With his broad face, graying hair, and mellow vibe, he looks like a Peruvian version of Lorne Green on the Ponderosa, tucking into his dinner of chicken, rice, and vegetables. Apparently he's not worried about a strict diet before drinking ayahuasca, but I guess he writes the rules. Only the Timex watch hints at his affluence, and there's still no hint of the mystic who will lead the ceremony tonight.

One of the gringos asks about the mix of the ayahuasca brew, and Rama translates Guillermo's explanation that the DMT-containing *chacruna (Psychotria viridis)* that he usually uses still hasn't reached maturity in the new gardens. Instead he's using another plant analogue—*chagraponga,* which is native to the Iquitos area, but is just as powerful, he promises. This worries Kat, who doesn't want an overwhelming experience.

"Will you help us, Guillermo, if it's too strong for us? Will you look after us?" she pleads with her big blue eyes. "Francisco said he would at Sachamama, but when I cried out for him he was overwhelmed helping others, and he wasn't there for me."

Guillermo assures her he will look after everyone and because of the big size of the group tonight his wife Sonia, who has also been trained as a shamana, as well as another apprentice shaman, will be brought in to help facilitate the circle. In today's tourist market with different sizes and physiologies, the *curanderos* control undue effects by measuring the dose of the brew they give their customers, and they also claim to be able to psychically tune in and help control the journey while it's happening. *Nobody wants to see Carol Brady freaking out on ayahuasca, nobody.*

"I drank three times, then no more," Rama says as she tells me more about her own ayahuasca experiences. "The brain has the memory of the plants so I am still connected to the visions. After [ayahuasca] I had flashbacks in my dreams and when awake."

She's known Guillermo since she worked as a translator on Kounen's *Renegade* film, and tonight she will also help facilitate the ceremony. She's not the only French speaker here at the center—probably because of the fame of Kounen's movie and documentary in his native France, there is a disproportionate number of French seekers here, and French-Canadians. Perhaps to stave off the rapidly spreading interest by French front-runners, in 2005 France became one of the first countries in the world to ban ayahuasca usage outright, regardless of religious considerations.

Back in the ceremonial *maloca,* Tobin from Denmark is tending the altar with a small Swiss-Peruvian boy with a bowl haircut who is in his pajamas, while his mother rests close by on a mattress near the door. The boy has a sweet, confident spirit as he melts the bottom of one candle and joins it on top of another, like he's at an adults' pajama party and he knows the drill.

"Will you be drinking tonight?" I ask him, and he shakes his head calmly from side to side.

"No. Tonight I just watch," he says, and I wonder how old he is—seven? Nine? It seems natural that he is here with his mother and family, participating in an ayahuasca ceremony, witnessing the healing that the medicine brings. It makes it feel more real, like the way native South Americans have been taking ayahuasca for millennia as part of their village life, no War on Drugs or war on consciousness, just plant medicines connecting to a greater spiritual whole. *How can you hide this from your children, this secret from the jungle that unlocks the universe?*

At sunset, we drink. I learn that when you spend the night in pitch darkness with a large group of people and take ayahuasca, purging, sweating, dying, and rebirthing together, you get to know each other pretty well. You might not remember their names, but afterwards you remember their faces and the sound of their suffering, and they yours, and there is a special bond between you.

To my left, Bowman darts forward and crouches by the round plastic bowl placed at the end of his mattress. Gripping it with both hands he makes a swift, sharp gurgling sound and vomits quickly. I can see his shape and the outline of his back in the diffuse moonlight as it shines through the thick mosquito nets that surround the *maloca,* heaving over and over.

Around the circumference of the room another drinker scrabbles for their bucket, as if set off by Bowman's vomiting. Dry wracking heaves and the choking of dry bile reverberate through the dark as the drinker gets caught with nothing to bring up. The vomiting goes on in successive waves across the room and through the night, for three, four, six hours or more, and just when you think you've kept it down, or purged as much as you could, the spirit of ayahuasca finds another dark crevasse and helps bring it to the light.

I find I'm a bit lighter than the first time, but I still have blockages. I'm sitting cross-legged on my jaguar-spotted blanket with the heels of my feet tucked under me, spine straight, chakras aligned and my crown pointing up to the stars.

Ayahuasca is a fickle mistress—she likes it when you put out for her, make a show of it, and put some effort in. But ayahuasca is also a plant medicine, and as such she reads you and what you need, and that changes every time, both as you progress on the path and as new issues come to light. Like a high maintenance girlfriend, the relationship with "aya" can be hard work, but the rewards far outweigh the sacrifices.

I'm starting to come on slow, a warm billowing headspace enlarging to take in the whole *maloca* and the spirit zone phasing in. My head is awash with the psychic detritus of my own mind: past loves, mistakes, issues from my life all flash before my eyes, but I'm not sure if my brain's just hyperactive or if there's something deeper going on . . .

Like last time, there appears to be some subtle inter-species relationship in this fugue where ayahuasca is reading me as I reexperience my issues and my head pours out my subconscious into my conscious mind. The vision dreams don't stop, they plague me all night long in wave after wave of emotional torment, little things blown out of all proportion. Maybe this is part of the healing, that as I remember I also let go, for *la purga,* she is coming, I can feel her building . . .

In the Amazonian *cosmovision* everything on the earth has a spirit animating it and the bridge between the earth and the spirit world is us, the living things. Guillermo says that there is a unity between everyone and everything, an "ecological bridge between the living systems." And this extends beyond the material plane to a multidimensional universe, he believes, where the shaman has to work on a superior level to accomplish his will.

Working with the plants is the first level, he says, and the second is to "control the occult elements of the spiritual world." The third is a purely spiritual level that affects the physical—for example, the knowledge of how to become invisible, or how to travel in the innerworlds, the sub-aquatic world, or the cosmic world. The other dimensions you go to depend on the person drinking ayahuasca and how they want to work, he says. Spoken like a true Jedi.

The candle goes out and it's pitch black. A heavy stillness hangs in the air like a burlap curtain—maybe it's the spirits. Everyone is quiet, moving around slightly, the silence of the moment punctuated by the inevitable Promethean heave of another drinker vomiting. As they vomit up come all their hurts, their pains, their suppressions and ills.

There's no point of focus in this darkness, no sense of time progressing. To the unprepared this could be hell. Possessed by a strange spirit, your body wracked by wave after wave of nausea, vomiting up green bile in crushing waves.

In the darkness my mind is up to its old tricks, trying to imprint form on the primal chaos. I want to see snakes, alligators, jaguar totem spirits, and I want it so much my mind is doing its best, grabbing at the shadows and seeing eyes, slithering obsidian dream snakes. It's as if the world of spirits is playing itself out as shadows on a black canvas, tantalizingly beyond reach. It must be the *chagraponga* Guillermo's using in this brew; it's less full-on visual than the *chacruna* after all.

The flash of mental thoughts continues and at times it's impossible to tell which bits are me thinking, which bits the ayahuasca speaking, and which bits the ayahuasca making me think I'm speaking. The voice of aya is soft, subtle, and yet again it has the emotional nuances of a relationship. She speaks in concept-images, in that post-McLuhan symbology where you become what you see, and in the overlapping you know it, message-medium as one.

On the dark of my vision I see a flash of a seed snaking through the void of space, coming from beyond. The funny thing is, as I see it, another bit of me is sifting through the mental dialogue and saying, "That's not one of your thoughts."

"*Whoo hoo hoo…*" Guillermo's staccato breath punctuates the dark— short, pitched sounds that strike like compressed air darts and cut through the heavy atmosphere around us. It is one of the most eclectic sounds I have ever heard. Distinctly sentient, with an intelligence behind it, but at the same time insect-like, alien and just beyond the reach of the conscious mind. The sound is his *icaro,* the first wave of his bag of tricks to pierce the veils that separate the worlds.

"*Whoo hoo hoo ooo…*" His *icaros* cut through the dark, tuning in my consciousness as something cracks along the back of my skull, some slight tweak as the muscles tighten and now I'm feeling lighter, different, but it's hard to place. Guillermo's tuning us in, sinking us into a shared phase space and voila: the curtain is pulled back and we're smeared across the invisible canvas. *We've arrived.*

Outside the *maloca* a wave of insect consciousness is resonating back a whoo hoo hoo pitch that matches Guillermo's *icaros* and as the two meet and cancel each other out I feel as if I'm breathing in a dreaming universe …

By the moonlight I can see the wooden beams of the roof shimmering like a vast spider web, the central pole flashing with mythic resonance like the World Tree of Norse myth, connecting the *axis mundi* with the worlds above.

And suddenly around the circumference of the roof a billion, billion eyes come into view like a shimmering peacock tail, all veiled behind a dark lens. They drink me in, blink and stare again with a reptilian coolness, images warping one into another rapidly. I feel like I'm looking into some sort of hyperdimensional mirror and that the thing on the other side is experiencing what it is to be human through my eyes, all our eyes...

Sometime in the dream Guillermo comes round and blows smoke down our necks and backs. He beckons me to lower my head, not out of respect, but to cleanse my crown chakra, and his touch has a gentleness and a collected strength. Then quite suddenly the darkness erupts with a thundering growl, bigger than us all, big enough to hold the world in its jaws. Snakes, crocodiles, writhing anaconda spirits, and jaguar eyes imprint from my subconscious onto the canvas of the night, all my fears spewing forth with them.

The ayahuasca makes urgent rumbles in my belly and as a wave of nausea washes over me I muster the fortitude to stand and grope my way through the dark to the door. Mercifully it opens as I push it and stumble out into the night, punch-drunk with the spirit of the vine in me and threatening to come up quick.

The silhouetted jungle is bathed in a silver spectral light as Peruvian helpers stationed outside the door point me towards the toilets, a shimmering ball of light only twenty meters away that seems to skip in my field of vision. My whole body feels like it's underwater, that the consciousness trying to drive it is doing so from very far away and under challenging circumstances.

After an eternity on the path, lost in the trees, I finally find my way to the toilets and an empty cubicle. The porcelain bowl and seat is a miracle, as is the fresh toilet paper, and as I am bathed in the bright artificial light the ayahuasca in me judges all is ready. With some secret psychic trigger I'm not in control of a violent rush of vomit erupts from me and into the basin next to the toilet, then another and another, my whole body gripped with peristalsis and squeezing out sickness.

The lightness of my body post-vomit feels wonderful. As I cough and splutter over the sink and try to hang on to the shifting space-time coordinates around me, a trick of light draws my attention to the warm sick backed up in the sink.

It's still bubbling like a fizzy drink, like ayahuasca-cola, but it has a curious opalescent film to it, like oil rainbows on water, or the eyes from the other side of the mirror. A magic mirror, perhaps, created from my ayahuasca vomit. As I look into the magic mirror the eyes become spots, and the spots move with the shape of a large cat, a jaguar stalking the jungle.

He stops in front of a grandfather tree with thick snakes of flowering ayahuasca vine twining around its frame and looks back, as if he can see me. Suddenly he pounces, muscles rippling and claws extended, and shreds the thick vine into shards and starts nibbling on the leaves. *Then he starts tripping out, rolling around with glazed eyes, and then he's vomiting too, and I realize it's me, me in the jaguar skin, and it's me who's vomiting once again into the sink.*

I meet my fears and they devour me, and with another roar of the jaguar-god melts the realization—it's the thunder of a jumbo jet overhead—the 10:00 p.m. flight back to Lima, back to civilization. As the hallucinogenic jungle envelops me I start to wonder if I can ever come back from this, ever return to civilization as I left it, or if something inside me has now changed forever, and the jaguar is the one who stalks the world in my skin . . .

But there's no turning back now, no off switch, just me alone with the universe and the jaguar in the forest, two crazy cross-species trippers sharing a cosmovision that says we are both one.

6

Hamburger Universe

Hotel Parthenon, Iquitos

Thursday July 6, 2006

"Dude, I've got to tell you something about my ayahuasca session last night," James says, coming up to me in the lobby of the Parthenon Hotel.

Deep into the sacred space of ayahuasca James had a vision of me, drinking ayahuasca, too. But it wasn't just a seeing, it was more a becoming, as our two souls overlapped and became one in that spirit zone. James's spirit merged with mine, he became me, he says, taking on my mannerisms and personality.

"I felt like I was interfacing with this 'Rak' persona. And then I hurled...!" Psychic fallout from my own journey, I wonder, out in the jungles of the collective unconscious?

It's been a long week—an amazing week—and as the conference nears its end things aren't slowing down any. We're learning that the world is a whole lot bigger than we were ever told, and once you've expanded out to merge with the universal intelligence, it gets harder and harder to squeeze back into the same old box of rational Cartesian materialism.

Last night was the tip of the cosmic iceberg. I've seen enough now to have an inkling of just how big and different it really is out there, and like all early explorers charting new lands, I've found the sights can be intoxicating. The funny thing is that it all seems so natural, that not only is our spirit-journeying an innately human thing that the West has forgotten, but that the time seems right for it to resurface on a larger scale.

Many, many ayahuasca seekers I spoke to at the conference and later all pointed towards a loss of faith in Western religious systems and a deep need to reconnect to the spirit. Len, a tall, long-haired twenty-four-year-old from Chicago who looks like a drummer in a heavy metal band, said, "[There is] a spiritual sickness that's permeated our society and culture, and not just in Western nations but the developed world over. I feel the sickness as a lack, an emptiness in people."

Len was drawn to shamanism versus other mystical states that have already penetrated the West like meditation and yoga, because, he says, "It's pure spirituality. If you can get in touch with that, there's an enormous wealth of power, and knowledge, and freedom to be had. If you connect with that with a pure heart, you're not going to grab or attach or try to control, you're just going to give."

This lack of a Western spiritual connection is not just at the root of the spiritual tourism boom—it also permeates our culture and its institutions, and may explain the return of the sacred to the intellectual agenda. Science, which has inherited the priesthood's responsibility for defining the universe and our relationship in it, has been drifting for over a hundred years into a reciprocal, dynamic cosmology not unlike indigenous beliefs across the globe.

As a modern quantum physicist like Michio Kaku, author of *Hyperspace,* posits, "I often think that we are like the carp swimming contentedly in [a] pond. We live out our lives in our own 'pond,' confident that our universe consists of only the familiar and the visible. We smugly refuse to admit that parallel universes or dimensions can exist next to ours, just beyond our grasp. If our scientists invent concepts like forces, it is only because they cannot visualize the invisible vibrations that fill the empty space around us. Some scientists sneer at the mention of higher dimensions because they cannot be conveniently measured in the laboratory."

According to Kaku, who is, by the way, a Harvard *summa cum laude* graduate who has been professor of theoretical physics at the City University of New York for twenty-five years, and an international best-selling science author, the energetic nature of reality is much like the shamans say it is. Other dimensions exist—Kaku says that "hyperspace" (or high dimensional space) contains at least ten dimensions, and that each dimension is embedded within and is oblivious to the dimensions above it, unfolding like Japanese origami through infinity.

Kaku is also the co-author of the "superstring theory," which says that the basic forces of the universe are nanoscale string energies vibrating in a higher dimensional space, the understanding of which may one day lead to a "Unified Theory of Everything." Or so Kaku would like us to believe—the Western shaman-scientists are still battling it out to interpret the story we live in.

Stripping away the scientific language, what you find is that our most eminent minds agree that on the subatomic and quantum scales the universe is full of invisible energies that not only affect our reality, but on a fundamental scale create and support it.

One of the latest scientific conceptualizations is that of "dark matter," an astrophysics term that describes matter that doesn't emit light or electromagnetic radiation, which we can't see, but which nonetheless has gravitational effects that we can measure. Up to ninety-six percent of the universe's mass is thought to be attributed to dark matter and dark energy, which affects the rotational speed of galaxies and played a large role in the "Big Bang"—yet science can't see it.

The indigenous science of *curanderismo* deals with just such unseen energies, but with their vegetal technology they claim to be able to alter their perception in a way that allows them to see these forces, and then go on to interact with them. A few days ago at the conference don Juan's gringo apprentice, Carlos Tanner, said, "There is so much more to what we think is real ... In fact, on the scale of all reality, the human being can only sense less than one percent of what's there. A perfect example of this is the light spectrum. The spectrum of light is immense, but the visible spectrum is tiny. It's this tiny, tiny bit of the light spectrum. Beyond red is infra-red, which we cannot see. Beyond violet is ultra-violet, which we also cannot see. If something reflects ultra-violet light it's invisible to us, even if it's right there we cannot see it.

"We use our other senses for the same reason. It's like frequencies that go up too high, you can't hear; you go too low you cannot hear them. We can basically only exist in one tiny little fraction of what reality really is. And what we call reality is really just one tiny piece, one dimension if you will.

"What ayahuasca does, what makes it possible for us to find out information in these other worlds and dimensions is that it increases our sensitivity. So much so that the sensitivity to light in our eyes expands, to the point where we include ultra-violet, infra-red light. Now we can see the entities which reflect ultra-violet light. They are always there. Spirits are always there, and when your eyes are sensitive enough to light you can see them. That is the beauty of ayahuasca.

"I feel scientists will soon recognize the presence of this power, which is at this time not understood and inactive. And it's inactive only because it is not recognized. Spirit is the primary, vibrating, originating power. You may enter into spirit and use its power by the simple acceptance or knowing that it does exist. This is the root of *curandero* philosophy. *Nothing is impossible if you believe.*"

It's one thing to read a book or accept a scientific equation saying multidimensional reality exists, but it's another thing entirely to step into it and interweave with forces you can barely contextualize. Ayahuasca tourism is no simple thrill-seeking tour activity to tick off your checklist with bungee jumping and the ruins of Machu Picchu. It has the potential to literally blow the roof off your reality grid and send you smearing through hyperspace where, like all travelers, you will be accosted by natives wanting your attention and a bit of baksheesh.

It's no walk in the park, but where Western quantum physicists have laid the intellectual groundwork, the indigenous *curanderos* are now helping seekers put that knowledge into practice and come back alive—and sane. Outerspace meets innerspace, East meets West in "Ayahuasca 101," and today the classes continue back in the baseline reality.

Each day here at the conference gets a little more surreal than the one before and as I stare into the muddy, unblinking eyes of a *Phyllomedusa*

bicolor frog and jostle for elbow room as it's surrounded by a mass of gringos photographing it, nothing seems out of the ordinary.

The frog has brilliant wet, green skin with a tan underbelly that shines in the light of the *touristos* camera flashes, but according to the Matses and Mayoruna tribes of the Upper Amazon, where Peru meets Brazil, when stressed its skin also secretes *sapo* [Spanish for "toad"]—a powerful chemical that is 2,000 times more potent than morphine. A crew from Colombia have brought half a dozen frogs here to the conference to string them up, stretch them out, and torture them slowly with sticks to secure the sapo and then administer it to the gringos by burning them with the venom for U.S. $50 a pop.

The frog, known as *dow-kietl* by the Matses, is said to be "ordeal medicine," and the "power comes from surviving it," says amateur enthobotanist Piers Gibbons. The indigenous use of sapo is reserved for sharpening the senses while hunting, or strengthening the body, but here at the conference it's being presented, whether intentionally or not, as the ultimate test of your manhood.

A group of men all sign up for the experience, including Bob, who's keen to try out the frog poison. "I'm here for the healing, so whatever it takes," he says, as the participants arrange a time for the ritual back at a hotel. I can only imagine them there in an air-conditioned suite, intimately prodding the frogs to secrete their magic toxins, their macho men screams attracting the management, who walk in on these drug-fiend gringos, caught in the act . . .

"They burned me, those sapo frogs," Bob tells me the next day, and lifts up his shirt to show me the burn marks on his back. Then he points to the large tattoo on his left forearm, a lurid green, yellow, and red amphibian that jumps out at you with its vibrancy.

"The chicks love it, dude, more here than in the U.S.," he says, a frog convert from way back, and I know he'll use the burn marks as a pick-up gimmick for as long as they last. Amazonian pharmacology may provide a window into an amazing medicinal cornucopia, but Western culture will always find its own use for these things.

Sapo was first written about by American journalist Peter Gorman, (who's speaking later at the conference) in his 1993 *Omni* magazine article, "Making Magic." As he describes,

"My body began to heat up. In seconds I was burning from the inside... I began to sweat. My blood began to race. My heart pounded. I became acutely aware of every vein and artery in my body and could feel them opening to allow for the fantastic pulse of my blood. My stomach cramped and I vomited violently. I lost control of my bodily functions and began to urinate and defecate. I fell to the ground.

"Then, unexpectedly, I found myself growling and moving about on all fours. I felt as though animals were passing through me, trying to express themselves through my body. It was a fantastic feeling but it passed quickly, and I could think of nothing but the rushing of my blood, a sensation so intense that I thought my heart would burst. The rushing got faster and faster. I was in agony. I gasped for breath. Slowly, the pounding became steady and rhythmic, and when it finally subsided altogether I was overcome with exhaustion."

There is an up side to the intense physical sensations—Gorman claims when he awoke his senses were not just cleansed, but amplified. His vision, sense of smell, "everything felt larger than life, and my body felt immensely strong," he wrote in his *Omni* article.

Gorman's discovery of the sapo lead to more scientific research on the use of amphibian peptides as potential medicines, and, like most people in these parts, he's also tried ayahuasca, and written extensively on it and other healing plants. "Once you open the door it doesn't close, once you've tasted the medicine the spirit of ayahuasca will never go away. You might ignore the message—but she won't go away," he says later, during his presentation.

The crew from Colombia who've brought the frogs includes Jimmy Weiskopf, an intense sixty-three-year-old author and translator whose wide open blue eyes convey a permanent look of shock that matches his explosive personality. Jimmy's spent the last twelve years as an apprentice to a shaman in Colombia, drinking ayahuasca, or *yajé* as they call it there, and writing about it in books like *Yajé: The New Purgatory.*

"I'm not a shaman, I'm not a healer—it's too much responsibility, it's a big job. I'm a writer, I drink with my friends," Jimmy says honestly up on the stage to the amassed gringos, his thin legs crossed and his wiry frame radiating an intensity beyond his years. He's here with his nine-year-old son, whom I'd spotted days before on the bus out to Percy's, on the way to the first ayahuasca ceremony.

"What's the wisdom of this plant?" Jimmy booms frenetically down the microphone. "Why drink it? . . . Ayahuasca is like the Amazon River—it's an umbilical cord. And the Amazon is like the puberty of the world, the juices and hormones of plant chemicals and essential essences. It's the sex of the world and it's being milked to connect with the cosmic orgasm of the spirit world."

Jimmy's like an elderly boxer who's been hit in the ring too many times over the years—he's taken a few knocks and given a few, too. His mad, blue eyes burn down at us as if straining to communicate the far-flung dimensions they've seen beyond the veil and the wisdom he's experienced. But his words stay with me as I flash back to the journey at Guillermo's last night, and the reality of this multidimensional world that has cracked open to reveal itself to me.

"Don't be one of the unplugged in the *hamburger universe,*" yells Sayre Tupac, the *Armani shaman* as he comes on the stage after dinner, wearing a tank top that shows off his pumped biceps, hair groomed short, and tribal paint on his strong, Inca face. It looks like he's just come from a *GQ* photo shoot and as he sways onto the stage and into action with the Latin American sex appeal of Ricky Martin crossed with Carlos Castaneda, I can tell we're in for a show.

"Just become yourselves, not a shaman," he says, a fierce magnetism radiating from him. "You were sent here. Why are you here? No one knows why you are here. I will tell you why you are here.

What is the time? What is the question? What is the *Matrix* is the question!" *Ay carumba!*

He's a hustler, a shark among the fish, but he's so damn funny in his relentless salesmanship, contradicting himself at every turn, and his tone and pitch sound just like the local advertisers spruiking their wares on the radio, that I can't help but love him.

"I don't see plants as plants, I see them as information," Tupac says, working the audience from up there on stage. "Stop thinking of things as things. They just found out about the string theory that unifies the quantum field. Big deal! We *ayahuasqueros* have known about the energy fields forever! Don't limit nothing [sic], everything's limitless . . . I work with limitless possibilities, but you are part of it . . . you can't be something you are not . . . This is like a commercial by the way, yeah . . ."

It resembles, in fact, a self-help talk crossed with an Anthony Robbins motivational forum. But his salesman sound bites do resonate with the crowd and perhaps in a post-modern clash of cultures way it works, after all.

"He's good for people who aren't already awake," Margaret says beside me, perfectly summing it up.

Tupac has a spiritual retreat in Urambumba, a small town in the Sacred Valley outside Cuzco, but he also spends a lot of time in Lima, illuminating the entheogenic cognoscenti there with his homegrown san pedro wisdom. He claims lineage to the Q'eros people who have lived in the highlands of Peru and were never conquered, not by the Spanish, the Incas, or the pre-Incas. He also says the Q'eros live in balance with nature, maintaining an eons old lineage and keeping the traditions, which go beyond the plants or even the stones, all the way back to the energy itself, which they can perceive without any hallucinogenic interface. Their high priests call themselves *alto misayoc* or *pampa misayoc,* the ones who have a special connection to the natural world.

"Our work is to download information." Tupac says. "Why are you full of visions that hang round life to life? You don't know why you're here . . . We clean the hard disk with the means of the software devices—the information contained in the plants...We download it, and for that we use songs, compressed intention, and motivation to benefit countless sentient beings..."

As he talks his entourage sets up a slideshow to give us an intensive understanding of his shamanic practices. Speakers blare with a splash of fast, hard techno music as one-by-one the slides show Tupac surfing in Africa; Tupac in Lima hanging out at the bars, being the MTV shaman; Tupac at sunset; Tupac hiking; Tupac hanging out with beautiful women...

Finally the slideshow finishes and as Tupac sings some *icaros* a wave of base chakra energy radiates out from him. Women get up and dance, beta males following suit as the crowd falls under his sway like a snake charmer at work. As if testing our complicity, Tupac gets us all up to do some exercises, some dancing to get our chi working to all that hard-assed techno backbeat. It's full on spiritual aerobics for the next ten minutes while he does his Anthony Robbins spiel to the crowd, exercising their bodies while he exorcises their souls.

He's been arrested three times for his shamanic practices, and it's cost him a lot of money to get out of jail, you know. "You don't have to make a church, don't believe what they tell you man, proof [sic] it yourself... you don't have to do anything. Super police they told me, I know what you know, they said...

"We had all these reports from the United Nations about ayahuasca, the police told me. I sorted it three times with attorneys, and I didn't say I'm part of a church and get out of it that way...You get a few Jewish attorneys and you sue the police and get your medicine back, yeah!" he shouts, stabbing the air with a fist.

"This is so ironic," Margaret says beside me, opened-jawed. "When Shane and I did the pedro session with him the other day it was definitely another reality. His entourage was full of hip 'it' girls in matching sarongs and big, chunky, latest fashion sunglasses, the men with aftershave on and perfectly groomed hair—y'know, the *fashionistas*," she whispers while half the auditorium is up and swaying to the spiritual aerobics.

"He dosed everyone up really strong, yeah—Shane got really sick from it because he put an extra dose of cactus powder under his tongue, he overdosed him trying to be macho. Then, when the cactus starts to come on—and we're all in his hotel room, yeah—at one point he turns on the TV and makes everyone watch key scenes from the *Matrix* whilst tripping off their dials. It would have been hilarious if it wasn't so enduring."

His motivational speaker act is getting grating and Tupac starts turning on the crowd, blasting them with his machismo while he pummels their egos down like a drill sergeant in the army. People start booing him, but he takes it in his stride.

"I'm from *hyperspace,* you know, so you can boo me but it's no problem..." It's unfortunate, but his massive ego is getting in the way of all the traditional knowledge he's learned and being able to share that with the crowd. "Don't forget guys, assume your responsibility, throw away the hamburger universe! *Free yourself!!!*" he cries, and slinks off stage with his entourage.

Tupac isn't the only person to deride our "normal" world of sensory input as something materialistic and disposable—ever since the split between religion and science during the Reformation the material world has been analyzed, quantified, and deconstructed to see what makes it tick, and the idea of an animating spirit or energy has fallen from favor.

Discoveries and advances by scientists like Galileo, Francis Bacon, Isaac Newton, and others promoted a mechanistic paradigm of a "clockwork universe," but that paradigm has itself now been superseded by modern quantum physics. Indeed, Tupac's "hamburger universe" sound bite is actually a quote from the successful indie documentary *What the Bleep?* which was all about quantum physics and redefining the way we see the world.

American physicist David Bohm was one of the key minds who created insights into what the nature of quantum reality really meant in a way that would be intimately familiar to *ayahuasqueros.* Bohm upset the scientific applecart by suggesting that the everyday world of our senses is in fact a projection broadcast from a deeper level of reality in a similar way to how a piece of holographic film is used to create a hologram. Bohm named this underlying foundational dimension the "implicate or enfolded order," and our dimension the "explicate, or unfolded, order." According to Bohm the manifestation of all matter in the universe is the direct result of the continual enfoldings and unfoldings between these two dimensional states.

Einstein's general theory of relativity suggested that space and time are not separate, but are in fact parts of a larger time continuum. Bohm went further than Einstein, saying that everything in the universe is part of this continuum and that on the implicate level *everything is seamlessly connected.*

Bohm further argued that consciousness itself is a subtle form of matter and on the implicate level it is inherently embedded in everything, everywhere. Think about that one for a while, and how a conscious universe changes your view of reality. There is no longer a need for any distinction between living and non-living things as everything is alive and has consciousness, including energy itself and everything made from it. *There is no separation, says one of the greatest quantum physicists of all time.*

Trickle-down quantum teachings have definitely hit the mainstream, but as we attempt to navigate the unknown on our shamanic explorations they also give a vocabulary to help understand the dimensions we're experiencing. The fact that I'm now seriously open to the possibility of spirits, and trying to ground it in a layman's scientific understanding, however, is something new. Something has shifted in me that a lifetime of Western-reality tunneling has never breached.

Am I on the slippery slope to becoming an ayahuasca true believer? You betcha. What's the alternative? That I'm going mad in the jungles of Peru, entertaining facets of my subconscious and maybe the collective unconscious of my fellow trippers? That the set and setting of the shaman's ritual is triggering pre-set archetypes and it's all just a construct of our own minds?

Sure, that'd be the objective, scientific response. But it wouldn't be the emotional truth. Benny Shannon, a professor of psychology at the

Hebrew University of Jerusalem who is also here speaking at the conference, says in his book *Antipodes of the Mind,* that "while the generation of hallucinations is a major effect of ayahuasca (and other agents), surely it is not the only one. Indeed, one principal message conveyed by the ... ayahuasca experience is by far too rich and complex for the brew to be characterized merely as a generator of non-ordinary perceptual effects ...''

Benny has participated in over a hundred ayahuasca circles, but says, "I do not believe that there are physical places other than those in the ordinary natural world. I do not believe that there are beings and creatures just like us who reside elsewhere in other realms, I do not believe in reincarnation and paranormal travel ... I recognize that experientially, under the intoxication people do, indeed, feel that what is seen in the visions are wondrous realms that have actual, independent existence. I have experienced this firsthand."

Ayahuasca may however, allow the mind to contact something akin to the Platonic world of ideas and archetypes, he counters, trying to ground the realms the vine opens up in some comprehensible paradigm for the Western mind.

"However, I am a Western university professor, a psychologist, and a philosopher, not an Amerindian shaman ..." he continues. "Thus, acknowledging the enchanted nature of the ayahuasca experience, I am trying to account for it while at the same time respecting frames of thought and canons of judgment that define my own cultural and professional heritage."

So I figure I'm not mad as long as I'm aware that I could be mad. That's my story and I haven't got anything better, so I'm sticking to it. But I also have a deep-seated need for some grounding in just what the hell is really going on in the universe at large, some bridge between science and spirit that I can trust. Someone who's bridged the cultures and their ways of seeing.

Because I understand now, that the Peruvian *cosmovision* is different from ours. We see the surfaces of things, the exteriors, and we quantify them and think we comprehend the workings of the universe. The

Peruvians feel it; they see the connection under the skin of things and the way it threads together. And that changes the way they think and speak, and their relationship to the cosmos. And from what I'm learning about ayahuasca and the spirit world, once you change the way you see, what you see starts reacting differently to you.

Thus it is that two days later I meet Kevin Furnas, the eloquent gringo shaman from San Francisco to talk about indigenous cosmology and how it relates to the Western understanding of the universe. Bowman, Vance, and I interview Kevin by the foreshore in Iquitos, on the *tourista* boulevard, jumping the balcony to find a quiet spot past the roar of *motorcarros* and city life, the screech of traffic, and the constant hustle of the Shipiba *manta* sellers.

Foraging through the scrub past the foreshore we find a patch of dry swampland and are drawn to a magnificent grandfather tree with bright orange flowers blooming from its crown, rectangular chunks of skin flayed away from the bark where locals have scalped it for its medicinal properties. We sit in the shade and talk about spirit, the spirit in us and the spirit in the plants and trees, how we connect to them, and the cosmic ecology that feeds us all.

"In the Amazonian system they believe that each plant has a mother, if you will, a spirit," Kevin says, laying his hand on the tree and connecting with the energy in it. "What is a spirit then, from a Western point of view? Well to understand the spirit of a tree it helps to first understand who we are as human beings. We have a physical body which modern science is quite aware of...

"What modern science is not so aware of is our energetic matrix, how we're made up, how the human body is set up on an energetic level. In our body we have rivers of light flowing through us and where these rivers intersect twenty one times is a major chakra. And chakra is an Asiatic term—here [in Peru] they're called 'eyes of light.' So a major chakra is an energetic vortex. It's a receptor point of energy.

"Each chakra is processing different vibrational frequencies, different colors of light. Energy from outside enters into our chakras as perception and is changed into memories. Who we are then is a conglomeration of memories. What is often not understood is that each chakra has an associated energetic body. So what I'm saying is that as human beings we're actually inter-dimensional. We have different sets of energetic bodies that overlap each other. They're super-imposed over each other and they all have different qualities and work with different things. The higher ones exist in different vibrational realms completely, like the heart—the associated energetic body is the astral body.

"So to get back to the question what is a spirit? Well a tree, for instance, has chakras as well," he says, placing one hand on the rough bark of the tree we're shading under. As he closes his eyes and concentrates on the energy before him, he looks every inch the plant Jedi, long dark hair braided with beads and his black shirt unbuttoned almost to the bottom, billowing in the light breeze.

"It's set up a little differently than humans. Different spirits can live in one tree, for instance, whereas with a human, just one spirit can live in our physical bodies. The chakras on a tree are movable; basically the higher chakras on a tree and their associated energetic bodies are existing in a vibrational frequency much closer to the celestial realm."

He opens his eyes and smiles. "It's a higher energetic frequency. So the higher energetic self of a tree, for instance, is actually quite advanced and quite intelligent. While the physical tree might be quite simple on a physical level its higher, almost physical self, is quite advanced, quite intelligent, and quite wise."

Kevin speaks about lessons learned in other lifetimes, karmic connections and energy work with the spirits of the plants, but he does so in a way that lacks any dippiness, in a calm and sincere voice as he looks you right into your eyes and reads you.

As we all sit here under the tree it suddenly strikes me that we are like all the bodhisattvas and saints from times past who have achieved illumination with plants: Buddha had his Bodhi tree, Christ his wooden cross, Odin the World Tree, and so on and on; plant-human symbiosis encoded in all the world mythologies. The plants and trees have always been opening us up to the greater reality—but we've been too blinkered by our egocentricity to see it.

"So basically the Godhead, the Dharma, whatever you want to call it, is a sea of energy, intelligent energy," Kevin says calmly. "You break off as a bubble, and you have part of the sea inside but you have water outside, and you get placed in a nursery. This is the birth of a soul, of YOU. They put you in the sky in a nursery, and after a while you go into your soul group of two to fifteen souls—bubbles—this illusion of separateness from the Godhead, from everything. You are pure energy and light, a little bubble of energy or light that comes from a place of unconditional love...Then you start coming down and doing your first lifetimes in this school...

"The earth school is pretty hard. You go through something called the 'seven gates,' which are the seven chakras...During those lifetimes ...they blank out your memories so you don't remember who you are ...and you enter a physical body. You have the desire for sex, protection, food, comfort. As you learn through these lifetimes, becoming accustomed to the physical body, the color of your aura changes and you start moving [from baseline red] towards orange as you work with feelings and how you use your emotions...

"Then you start moving up to the solar plexus and the associated body, which is yellow, and you start working with the intellect. In these lifetimes you're that kind of nerdy scientist up there doing mathematics and all that [laughs]...Then you start moving up to the astral and its associated body, which is green in color, to the green chakra and its associated body. Then you start doing ayahuasca and these type of things, yoga and working with energy. This is the bridge between the lower three chakras and the top ones. Then you start working with spirit stuff, the third eye, y'know. And there's different levels...Each of these bodies associated with each of the higher charkas exists in a different vibrational dimension. So there's a lot to learn in the spirit world.

"Then when you're done with the earth school . . . you work on your specialty trade. At some part you leave your soul group and go into your specialty group. So then maybe you'll be trained as a celestial guide . . . For me, I work as an explorer scout, so I go and travel and take students on field trips to planets that are suitable for becoming schools. And when you finish the earth school you go on to your trade school and the levels above it . . .

"Ultimately what you are then," Kevin says, pausing as a plane goes overhead with a mechanical roar and the cloudless blue sky reaches over our heads, "is this little bubble [of the Godhead] that goes through this progression, and being incarnated is the hardest part of the whole progression. Then you go to the schools in the sky and you continue learning, and eventually this little bubble merges with the whole sea, the sea of energy, [until] there's no difference between you and the entire universe."

He smiles then, as if he's just said something so simple, something basic that isn't stretching my reality paradigm onto a whole other plane, frying up my hamburger universe with onion and pickles and serving it up to me on a plate.

I look out past the marshy foreshore at the Amazon River and the boats on it, plastered over a clear blue sky as the nuclear fusion reactor in the sky beats down upon us, the secret all around. Energy. We're all energy vibrating at different wavelengths, interpenetrating and discovering one another in our hyperspatial chrysalises.

Like a caterpillar emerging from its cocoon, Kevin's cosmic lowdown has transformed me. Reality hasn't been the same since my visionary ayahuasca experiences began, but by embracing the indigenous cosmovision and grafting it with my own grassroots scientific understanding, at least things have some sense of structure. It's possible, if a whole lot different than I ever thought probable.

And like the proverbial butterfly, I'm now staring out at a whole new world, blinking back the light of day and flexing my wings, ready to fly . . .

7

Surfing

La Rosacita, Iquitos

FRIDAY JULY 7, 2006

Ron Wheelock stares at me with cloudy gray-blue eyes ringed with hardship. He's practically bald on top with a shiny forehead, just a light scalping of thinning hair and long side hair that falls down past his ears. He's in his early fifties, with a worn-down, weather-beaten look, faded denim pants, and a Western style t-shirt with a picture of a Navaho Indian on it. It's like he's just stepped out of a John Steinbeck novel, the haves and the have-nots, the raw, all-American salt of the earth trying to make good and struggling against the system.

It's not just the system, though, it's the responsibilities he carries being a single dad and with his mother back in the States and all his furniture, or the roof that leaks in his house that he never gets to fix because it's Iquitos, y'know, and here in the jungles of Peru it's like, raining all the time, or threatening to, and even the chicken coop got fixed the other week but he's still suffering in that ramshackle house of his out by Kilometer Nine. It's a simple two-story log cabin not far past the Quistococha Zoo and lakefront. He brought the property off his *maestro,* don Jose Corale Mori, and there's an abundant supply of thick, mature ayahuasca vine sprouting round the back that Ron uses in his shamanistic ceremonies with gringos.

Then there's his ex-wife, whom he met at an Americana burger joint in the plaza one night and has been sapping him of all of his money, all his mojo, and she knows it and he knows it and everybody knows it, but he's a nice guy, you know, and he tried to make it work for as long as he could. Her parents pushed her to marry him and she's been draining him ever since. She killed his fighting chickens, she almost killed his *maestro,* and she neglected their son, he tells me.

When Ron was called back to the States unexpectedly he left her with the responsibility of their son, Quetzalcoatl and don Jose Coral Mori, his teacher, who's now ninety-nine and in an old age home here in Iquitos. Ron pays his bills and looks after him as best he can, but when he came back to find his wife hadn't been looking after him properly and Mori was almost dying from malnutrition, that was the last straw. He checked Jose into the hospital and has tried to look after him as best he could ever since.

So many responsibilities, and he's doing the best he can. His first priority is to his boy, his beautiful lil' Queto. "He's not even my blood, y'know—I had a vasectomy in my twenties, but he's my boy," he says with a fierce pride, the unshakeable bond of a father and his son.

The two are inseparable, and for the entire last week of the Shaman Conference I would see them walking around, Queto playing with the smattering of other kids near the pool. The two are like a lone wolf and cub, taking on the world together. But who knows, Ron's mother reckons he looks like him, and that connection they have . . . well, they're like two peas in a pod.

But it's not even all these things, which might be burden enough for a man to shoulder in this world. It's that other world, the world of spirits, of *brujeria* and witchcraft, of "shamachismo," competing energy and egos and the black magic that every seeker on the path comes across eventually, that finally got to him.

"Why, last week I did a circle for these folks that came out to my place, and I've done like hundreds of circles before," Ron explains in that Southern accent, like he's about to ask you ever so politely to pass the apple pie and cream sauce, m'am, and tip his hat and smile an old-fashioned smile and burp at the pleasure of a well cooked meal and your company. "But shit, I don't know, something happened this time, and I went to take a shit in the outhouse and I swear I couldn't get back up the stairs to my own home. I was crawling on my hand and knees and I could feel some real *brujo* hanging on me.

"Around Y2K I started doubting what I was doing, you know. I had nine people that were meant to come out and drink with me and one by one they all made excuses and canceled. I was like, what am I doing, man, this shit is crazy. I'm going to throw it all in and get like an 8 to 5, clock on, clock off—a normal life, yeah? So I started internet dating and I just wanted to settle down, to give up this crazy path and have a normal life. But I couldn't give it up."

It's still strange to think this *hillbilly ayahuasquero* is a shaman, that it's possible to just pack up your bags and train with indigenous *curanderos* in the jungle and do an intensive *dieta,* and learn with the spirits of the plants. But that's just what Ronald Joe Wheelock did when he first came to Iquitos ten years back. It wasn't until around the time of 9/11 that the spirit in the ayahuasca told him to stop doing circles in America.

"I had a calling, you see … [Ayahuasca] told me to come back here to Iquitos, and it told me not to charge for what I do." He shrugs good-naturedly, his big round eyes bulging out like a fish. "Well, what can I do? The spirit, it calls me and she hasn't let me down yet. I've gotta trust her," he says.

Early Friday morning Ron drives me out to his house in his three-wheeled *motorcarro,* along with his friend Juan Acosta, a bearded, hawk-faced scientist and ayahuasca drinker originally from Mexico, now at the University of Washington in Seattle. His specialty is doing mobile QEEG (quantitative electroencephalography) scans on people on his laptop, a classic mad scientist on the frontiers of consciousness who's traded his castle for a thatched hut and his lab coat for Bermuda shorts and beads.

Juan reads the brainwaves, and shaman Ron supplies the smokable 5-MeO-DMT that catapults seekers into the deep reaches of innerspace, like a tag-team that unites the modern with the archaic, science and shamanism. Juan's been getting readings off dozens of gringo tourists coming through Ron's place and collecting the data for his own private research into consciousness. I'm here to interview Ron and experience firsthand the raging torrents of DMT space, where Dennis McKenna has already worded us up on the joys of being smeared across creation.

Queto rides in the back with Juan and I, the wind in his face, loving every minute of it, and as Ron turns back, aviator-style goggles on his face and smiles it all feels so *Easy Rider*, cruising down the Iquitos-Nauta highway in search of the ultimate mystery.

As we get out at Ron's place I notice a carved sign above the gates adorned with wooden flowers that says "*La Rosacita*" (the Rosy Cross), with a little red love-heart dotting the "i" in "Rosacita." Maybe it's having young Queto here, or the good vibe I get off Ron and his down-to earth manner, but this place immediately feels like home—where the heart is. By the time Bowman, Vance, and Oran, a shaven-headed Israeli friend of Shane and Margaret's all arrive in the second *motorcarro*, driven by Ron's Peruvian friend who's also called Juan, I'm already settling in on the porch, admiring the flowering psychoactive datura lilies in the front yard.

The smell of ayahuasca wafts through the house as we all drop our bags inside and take stock of our surroundings. There're two jaguar skins across one wall and another on the ground, army camouflage curtains and chains for the dog, a small black creature curled up in the kennel outside but making itself known by its barks. The walls are long, thick planks of untreated wood that give the place a rustic, down-south Civil War reenactment feel, decorated with hand-carved wooden idols and knick-knacks.

Past the living room with its skins and trappings is a thick wooden picnic table in the dining room which doubles as an altar space when Ron conducts ayahuasca ceremonies, and beyond that is the kitchen with its Western refrigerator and appliances. The ayahuasca is boiling in a big shiny chef's pot on the stove, its dark surface bubbling a green froth. Ron grabs a wooden spoon from the sink and begins stirring as Queto runs around his legs.

Seeing Ron and his son here in the kitchen with the ayahuasca reminds me that this is not just a business for this gringo shaman, it's also his home. Queto usually sleeps beside him or goes off to bed by the time a ceremony begins. He's dipped his fingers in before but he's been taken aback by the laxative effect of the brew and doesn't like to do it no more. As he darts around the kitchen I remember he's a bit niggly this morning because he saw his mom last night and he misses her, and he's got a cold, but he's still full of beans and excited by all the visitors.

"Let's go upstairs," Ron says, leading us up to the second floor. "There's mattresses up here if you need them and room for the computer and all your equipment." It reminds me of suburban crash pads across the free world, except it's a log cabin in the jungle. Light streams in through mosquito-netted windows as Queto jumps on a mattress and digs out some paper and crayons to draw with, tracing my hand and his on the page.

Bowman sets up his video camera and plays with Queto and me as Vance positions his own photography gear in the light. Juan sets up his laptop loaded with five grand of proprietary software that analyzes EEG readings. To capture the data he's going to strap on a skullcap laced with nineteen electrodes that are wet with gel to conduct the brain's own electrical activity and pipe the data through a rainbow BUS cord that will connect me to the computer. *Full on.*

"This is my first time—I hope I don't electrocute you," Juan says in a deadpan tone, getting me to sit in a seat and fitting a blue plastic skullcap over me before discarding it for a red one that's tighter. Before I know it he's sticking in a long, prodding instrument and squeezing in the conductive gel. Juan claims to be a professor from Washington University currently doing neuropharmacology research, and to be honest, as he wires me up it never occurs to me to question otherwise.

He's been working on consciousness issues throughout his career, he says, and was previously involved in harvesting frog eggs and injecting them with purified RNA from rats' brains, and then measuring receptor site activity. The leap to measuring humans while on entheogens seems the next logical step, so sure, wire me up and fire me into the mind of God; it's all in the name of science, after all . . .

"It's like a multi-track recorder of the brain," Bowman quips from across the room, shooting me a look of concern. Queto waits till his dad's not looking and puts a *mapacho* smoke in his mouth and puffs away before Bowman grabs it off the cheeky little monkey.

"The gel's cold, huh?" I wonder out loud, trying to remember everything, the adrenalin in my body feeding the mind, the ego as it prepares to be obliterated.

"It's last night's semen . . ." Ron jokes, a broad grin across his face, his front gold tooth shining. I can tell he's trying to keep everything calm and light-hearted as I'm wired up to all this technology and the expectation of the unknown builds. I've smoked DMT before (but not 5-MeO-DMT) and the results have been as alien and profound as most other psychonauts report. But here in the Amazon jungle, in the very, very odd circumstances of our current "experiment at La Rosacita," everything seems exaggerated.

"That smell in the house—you think it's ayahuasca, but it's not—it's fried brains!" Ron says with a guffaw, as he starts cleaning a glass pipe and packing it with an orange crystalline powder—the 5-MeO-DMT. There's something curious about this psychedelic neurotransmitter, which is found throughout many of nature's creatures in a swathe of plant and toad species.

Renowned psychedelic chemist Alexander Shulgin claims in his book *TIHKAL: Tryptamines I Have Known And Loved,* that "DMT is . . . in this flower here, in that tree over there, and in yonder animal. [It] is, most simply, almost everywhere you choose to look."

As he mentioned at the conference, as well as ayahuasca ceremonies, Ron also works with smokable 5-MeO-DMT. Despite its powerful psychedelic effects, 5-MeO-DMT's chemical properties, which are present in plants and animals alike and are central to indigenous plant-based shamanism, are not illegal at this time in Peru. 5-MeO-DMT is also much more fast-acting and intense than the orally-active DMT present in ayahuasca brews, but also quickly recognized as native to the brain and rapidly metabolized.

The mechanism of DMT is believed to be intimately connected to consciousness itself, where its similarity to the neurotransmitter serotonin allows it to bond to serotonin receptors in the brain and trigger hallucinogenic activity. Some medical researchers, like J.C. Callaway, of the Department of Pharmaceutical Chemistry at the University of Kuopio in Finland, believe it may be involved in producing the visual hallucinations we experience in dreaming.

Dr. Rick Strassman, who wrote the book *DMT: The Spirit Molecule* about his legal research with volunteers taking DMT at the University of New Mexico in the 1990s, also hypothesizes that a surge of DMT is released from the pineal gland at peak experiences like birth, the point of death, or a near death experience, which may also explain spontaneous "contact" experiences throughout the West, whether that be with angels or aliens.

Drug information portal Erowid states the effects of smokable DMT include "a powerful rushing sensation; a change in the perception of time; an experience of the 'void'; profound life-changing spiritual experiences; internal visions; muscle jerking, twitching, abnormal vocalizations; sensual enhancement and occasional euphoria; fear, terror, and panic; disassociation and even unconsciousness."

Entheogenic advocate Terence McKenna said that DMT is utterly idiosyncratic in that the experience is so bizarrely alien it is almost beyond our comprehension, yet it is beyond our comprehension precisely because we don't have the words for it. In many of his taped talks about the DMT experience that helped fuel a generation of psychonauts, he said that the more attempts we make at languagizing it the more possible it becomes to share some of the content of the experience, and then we can culturally integrate it into our species skill base, as we did with other shifts of consciousness like art, or language itself.

"And then, if you've taken enough DMT (and it has to do entirely with physical capacity: did you cross the threshold?) something happens ... for which there are no words," McKenna says. "A membrane is rent, and you are propelled into this 'place.' And language cannot describe it—accurately. Therefore I will inaccurately describe it. The rest is now lies."

So just for the record—everything I say here is a lie, too, an approximation, a paltry word-shadow patina of concepts, a multi-level linguistic smattering of emotional responses to something so alien and profound that we don't have words for it. That's the thing that both Terence and his brother Dennis tried to convey about the DMT space, too, the sense that it was beyond language, or *translinguistic*. It makes me think of Ron's bible downstairs on the dining room table, which I'd flicked open earlier at a random page—John 1:1 "*In the beginning was the Word . . .*"

Juan's finished fitting the skullcap and I'm all wired up. "The cap has nineteen placements and they cover the frontal, temporal, central, and occidental regions of the brain . . ." he explains. "It's a bit noisier than the rest caused by muscle tension . . . we're filtering at sixty hertz to get rid of any noise . . ."

"You have a rainbow coming out of your brain," Oran jokes as he points at the BUS cord connecting me with the computer in interspecies symbiosis. Juan puts little foam circles over my eyes and lowers the blindfold, reducing eye movement and "artifacts," the noise that each tiny muscle of the skull and jaw creates in the EEG readings. In the pitch black the screen of my mind calms down and the EEG readings even out.

"A perfect reading," Juan says, calm and collected. "There's a lot of alpha." He's watching the streaming waves of peaks and troughs on his laptop screen and recording at fifty microvolts . . .

"How you feeling there, Rak?" Vance asks, and it's good to hear his voice here too, shuffling around with his camera gear, and lil' Queto crying out for his Papa from the mattress as Ron shushes him. There's a group intimacy that is the complete opposite of the previous ayahuasca circles I've done, a trust I have for my groundcrew around me that lets me open up on those emotional levels I've held back from before. That, and being around Queto has activated my heart chakra and awakened the unconditional love I have for Afra, my own daughter back in Australia.

"I feel like that first monkey they fired off into outer space back in the 1950s!" I say, trying to hold still and not create any "artifacts" on the readouts.

"He was from my hometown, Independence, Kansas," Ron says, which seems an appropriate resonance.

It strikes me again then how odd this all is, to be in the jungles of Peru about to smoke a plant extract responsible for deep spirit journeys, administered by a Western shaman, wired to a computer reading my brainwaves and the whole thing filmed for posterity like the launch of a manned mission to the moon. Our DIY jungle psychonautics into the innerspaceways have the low-budget, cutting edge feel of the Apollo missions, of the days when astronauts were exploring new frontiers and changing the world with their discoveries. *And I'm the lucky chimp.*

Queto is running about, offering me water and helping me drink it, the water boy to the space monkey. Ron's saying, "Queto don't be doing that," chastising him. "We need silence now..." In the dark of my mind's eye I can hear the sound of chickens in the yard outside, and I know it's time. We're ready to launch.

"Ron and Oran and I are going to be here watching you and holding you if we have to, just making sure that you'll be fine," Juan says paternally. Ron passes the glass pipe to my lips and I grip the smooth weight of it. He lights it and I toke slow and strong, letting the DMT smoke enter me. A soft numbness comes into my mouth like the taste of burning plastic as my reality grid starts to melt into another space. I can hear the call of parrots and the squawk of chickens and the shuffling of little Queto around the room...

"Get it all in?" Ron asks as I fall backwards into the pillows and the smoke curls down my throat and the rabbit hole falls away under me. I can feel the hot jungle air all around as a wash of DMT rushes to the synaptic pathways of my brain and from here on in it's all words, yeah...

As I go under kaleidoscopic images fill the screen of my vision and as each geometric shape overlaps into the next I'm grokking the vibe; it's reading me and I'm reading it, both of us melting into each other in that sacred space where the heart of all consciousness resides . . .

This space fills me and it feels like I'm drowning, but it's not water it's . . . something else entirely . . . energy . . . a consciousness independent and larger than me . . . And that consciousness is drinking me in and getting inside me at the same time, or filling the negative spaces with its essence, or stripping away layers of illusion to reveal itself always within me. Part of my mind is still on automatic pilot, experiencing all this and deconstructing and processing it as best I can while the other part just hangs on for dear life at the rushing cannonball surge into this thing. It is as sixties hippie scientist, philosopher, and author Alan Watts described, "Load universe into cannon. Aim at brain. Fire."

Last night during the last conference presentation Dennis McKenna said that if the brain is a receiver of consciousness, then perhaps consciousness itself is a singularity point much like black holes, where energy is compacted so densely in on itself that it collapses. That collapse in the brain may be what causes consciousness. So adding an injection of DMT to the endogenous levels of DMT already in the brain may act like the collapse of a star into a black hole, as the brain receiver tunes into an ultra-dense state, reading deeper than ever before. It's the raw heart of creation here and it recognizes and absorbs your consciousness back to the Source.

The Hindus believe that in the beginning was sound, a pure vibrational ohm, and as I surf these wave emanations I feel like I've locked onto the fundamental frequency. Seconds go by on the outside but inside it's eternity, outside time and space and back where it all began . . .

00:20

Twenty seconds in the first stirring of interspecies communion register . . . It's like a lover . . . A smile breaks across my face as I recognize where I am again, holy mother of God, I'm melting into it, tilting my head back, falling, I can't go deep enough it just goes on forever and ever, amen . . . I'm groaning now, the energy is melting me like liquid on liquid mixing with the other, our waveforms overlapping . . . And there is no fear, no holding back, just pure consciousness merging with where it came from, the Godhead, the Overmind, mother-matrix union . . .

I'm in the rocking chair all wired up and I'm leaning forward, into the God-space, pushing through the dimensional envelopes . . . And as I break through the space like the skin of membrane a little "ugggh" escapes me and a feeling like a popped blockage releases . . . and I'm in . . .

Somewhere within I can feel the broadcast of a pattern signal, a cosmic heartbeat like the pulse of life from a baby within the mother. The feeling keeps flowing as I break through layers and pop dimensional membranes. Wave after wave of energy and I'm breaking through an infinite kaleidoscopic matrix of pure unadulterated consciousness . . . The current of life is streaming through me and it's like a brainwave of God and I'm surfing it . . . surfing God's wave . . .

As I go with that energy I melt further into it and the signal gets stronger, it becomes me, and I make the sound back at it, a broadcaster myself as well as a receiver. I'm groaning like I'm coming, but on the inside where it's outside and where it's all IT, IT's IT . . .

. . . And as I break through each layer of illusion the lesser bardos peel away and I'm just melting into the heart of the GOD-consciousness . . . And each groan is a sacred sound vibration recognition and it's whispering in telepathic union to me yes, yes sound that's it, make sound. I'm sound, it's all sound you're swimming through sound and the groan starts to become a reverberating waveform, an insect-like repeating staccato carrier wave that connects me to the Overmind and expresses it on the outside . . .

UUhhhhooohooouhhhooohhoooohhuuuooohhooohoohohohoyuoooo

Long syllabic strings until I'm singing-coming, channeling the vibrational wave of God . . . and the sound is coming out of me in pure liquid translinguistic magic mirror form, but I'm inside it now, I'm IT and IT's me . . .

01:54

Juan comes and puts a reassuring hand on my shoulder . . . I'm starting to shake as the vibrational energy builds and courses through my flesh body, my mind far above outside space-time, my spirit totally abandoned in the heavens . . .

02:00

Two minutes in Godhead and I'm still surfing the vibrational waves of bliss . . . I'm shaking, trembling, my legs vibrating like those of cicadas as they make their high-pitched waveforms in the night and Ron and Oran both hold me down as my flesh body rolls about . . . It's insectoid consciousness . . . The same vibrational patterns that are shaking my body connect the insects to the Source and the sound you hear from them every night as they sing their song of creation is the sound of God coming through them . . . The insects know, they hear, they receive the signal and transmit it on . . .

03:46

Over three minutes in . . .

And my head kicks back and I let out a long central breath as I rise inside and it's like cosmic orgasm, a total interface with the Godhead, merging overlapping becoming IT, IT becoming me, full telepathic union—no separation, no fear, all the levels of maya and illusion and noise stripped away and this is IT and IT is all there is and all is love . . . My throat elongates, stretches and a deep guttural sound emanates from somewhere deep within me . . . The shaman's song being born, throat chakra activation . . .

AHHHHHHHHHHHOOOOOOOOOOOOOOOOOOOOO OOOO . . . AHHHHHHHHHHHOOOOOOOOOOOOOOOoooOooooooo OOOOOooooO

Primal glossolalia pouring out of me like water, riding the vibrational waves of sound, channeling it . . . I'm spewing out sound . . .

04:10

They're still holding me down as the energy courses through me like electricity, a cosmic orgasm into the Overmind ... And the Overmind likes the sound, it's agreeing with it, echoing it back, yes, yes it says, and this makes me laugh a jagged glossolalia laugh, ha ha ha ohh ohh oh ...

Still riding the primal OHM wave, and I'm smiling I GET IT now, I've locked it in, I know what to DO in this space—you make SOUND, that's how you navigate in here ... Ahha ha ha ha hah ha I'm beaming, held down my Ron and Oran ... Ohh ha ha ha HA HA HA ha the voice rises up and down, recognizing sub-modalities traveling on the carrier wave, getting the grip of the steering wheel ...

Four minutes in I start circling my index finger around, making a circle, a loop, I can FEEL the current, the wave, how to ride it in here, deep in the Godhead, how to use SOUND to bodysurf the emanations from the Source, the vibratory waves that make up this heart of creation ...

Once I've GOT it it's got me and we harmonically lock onto each other ... Aha ha ha ha he hee hee hee I'm still circling a finger round and round riding it, riding the wave ... And then I start to experiment, I'm tapping my finger up and down and on the inside, still endlessly surfing the vibratory waves, the brainwaves of God ...

04:34

A chicken crows and I'm pinching the air, making the OK symbol ... ha ha ha ha hee hee hee hokey dokey dokay riding sound as we ride each other, voodoo dreaming in the drowning universe ... Si si si I'm saying to IT, to the me that is IT and us all, si, I understand you my creator, my God I understand what we are in this space, si and the flash of it sets me OFF, and I'm rolling my fingers round and round and like a bandmaster calling for a windup, and then I pitch forward and WHOOOP the air, piercing the moment, crying out in primal recognition of the code that is life, screaming it to the raw face of the day ...

04:49

Bilililililililililiboo boo boo blulililililililil bili bili bili bilib boo boo BOO BOO! I'm pitching the sound now, using rolling sonic mantras to express the energy and let it come out through me ... Bub bup bup bup bup bup billlli bOOO! I'm crowing like a rooster, purging/expressing raw naked sound, my DMT icaro ... Later, as I watch the video Bowman took of the event, I can see that I look like a mental patient being held down, about to foam at the mouth and expressing pure ur-language ... AAEEEEEEIIIIIIIHHHHHHHHHHH I cry, letting it out of me, heaven on earth pouring through me like molten sound ...

OOOHH I'm jostling around now squawking like a chicken, pitching short snippets of sonic sound like a monkey screaming in the jungle ... Ron's exerting firm pressure to hold me back as I flail around possessed by the sound-God, screeching liquid language, monkey man peaking on the Godwave ... OOOHHHHHH my body goes erect, straight as an arrow as I let off sonic steam and ride the wave. I'm surfing. My fingers are waving like I'm playing the sound ...

05:16

Ohhh AHHH aayyyiieee ahhha hah OH thank you mama mama and I'm clutching my hands over my heart, the sacred and the Divine ... kissing my fingers that have been at play with the Lord ...

05:40

REENTRY

I'm coming down, spluttering language, the wave is coming to shore and I'm grounding it, spitting it out in sonic mantras and somewhere a dog is barking and I can hear the parrots and the people and I'm riffing off their energy and vibrations with my melting raw *glossolalia* ... I feel like I've barreled through a hundred-foot wave and skimmed back to shore to do a few loops. I'm in total control, harmonic lock of this experience. I lean forward and something in me pops, I'm pure liquid mental quicksilver, liquid intelligence overlapping and interfacing with the GOD consciousness as it absorbs me back into the womb matrix ...

The Buddhists and other holy men state that the whole purpose of being alive is to cultivate consciousness and lock in the ability to remain lucid in the after death states, to transcend the body and retain awareness in the lower bardo frequencies where the larger cosmic playground begins ...

The more I be, the more I sit back and melt into the Godhead the more it melts into me, like cosmic interspecies sex of pure unadulterated consciousness, and the more I know a brief glimpse of what they mean ...

It builds, it melts, it becomes *deeper, deeper, deeper like a wave ...* The Sufis say there are fifty thousand veils of illusion or maya between you and God (but none between God and you) and right now I know with a certainty that all of those layers are alive, and they're not veils but filters that sift the soul, stripping it of heavy vibrational frequencies and purifying it enough to be able to interface with the core, *the Source.*

05:50

And I'm shouting, I'm thanking *la madre,* the saints and the mother, the mother mind of us all and whoop whooping liquid quicksilver glossolalia words all melting out of me. My head is ballooned out, I can hear and understand everything in the cosmos at all times, the language of nature, the trees, the animals, the mad trippers holding me down in the room as my legs shake with the energy and I'm grounding GOD into the matter world with my language ... Thanking him/IT...

"It's IT!" I say and there are no other words to suffice. We are all IT, IT is IT, the dense heart of a star in our heads and it knows me and I know IT. I have to shout to the heavens above to honor the connection

I still feel, fading fast within me now as I return, Tarzan cries and insect *icaros,* I'm living language, *the WORD made flesh . . .*

Ron and Juan and Olan are around me and maybe they're talking, I don't know . . . But I can *feel* the spirits, I can SEE them . . . I still have the blindfold on but I can see spirits for the first time in my life, white silhouette outlines of people, brother shaman spirits that are there whispering to me, guiding me back into the body, pressing down on me here, letting me rise up there, and their voices are like whispers, like the caress of the *icaros,* helping sounds . . . They are layering me back into the world in a hundred Photoshop layers all spliced together to make four-dimensional space, and I'm tuning into all the separate levels as my shaman guides protect me and guide me back home to my body for reentry.

"*Whhsss sss hsss mmmaa*" they whisper, and over to the left I can feel the spirits watching me . . .

"*Whhss mmaa ma sssee*"

"*Mmee hasss nooo . . .*"

They caress me with their voices, wrap me in their sonic protection and bring me back to the world safe and sound. There's no fear, they bathe me in their soft supportive light and love, they lay their spirit hands on me and readjust my energy; they help me back into the flesh . . .

05:55

I'm back down enough for words.

"OKAY . . ." And I'm putting on the brakes, fluid translinguistic creature that I have become. "John, I hope you're getting this . . ." I say to Bowman, hovering out there with his camera, but of course he can only film the outside experience and the inside is where the miracle is as fresh as a new day, all the things on the inside that can't be put into words because they *are word,* the WORD, vibrational essences . . .

"I got it," he laughs. "Holy shit . . ."

"Okay. I'm ON. Thank you, oh, I don't know the words," I cry. I feel like I've just been hit by lightning, *liquid language lightning, the WORD of GOD*... I can't stop tapping my leg up and down, moving my fingers in fluid mantras, vibrating, singing, *translinguisticizing* like a baked potato hot out of the microwave, still radiating the frequency of Heaven.

07:05

"OH MY GOD." I'm back... laughing, ohmygoding, bathing in the afterglow of cosmic union... *Jesus Christ almighty*... The groundcrew are all laughing, too, the nervous bubble of tension broken.

07:43

"It's IT," I say definitively, trying to ground it in words, to bring something of it back for the tribe, then realizing the impossibility to capture it in lower sound-language.

08:00

"It's fluid it's IT it's IT it's IT there's nothing BUT IT... It's self-reflexive code—but how does it get to be self-reflexive code? And GOD—YEAH!!!" I'm gesticulating wildly, still connected to the BUS cord and the electrode helmet, and at one stage I nearly pull the whole laptop down with me, crazy monkey.

"I LOVE IT. IT LOVES me. We're IT... I'm coming down... it's all just words now... It was fluid... IT's the mainline... It's scary going in losing all your cultural imprints and layers, all your YOU melts away till there's nothing left but IT and you ARE IT and IT is IT and on and on in perfect radiating superunion... But the weird thing is *how is it IT without NOT being IT?*"

08:56

The blindfold comes off and my eyes blink back the light with the wide-open innocence of a babe. "What's the context? I LOVE IT . . . It's IT, it's IT—there's nothing but IT . . . that's the weirdest thing of IT . . ." I say, shaking my head back and forth, wires and cables spilling about.

"Thank you for being there with me . . ." I say with raw emotion to my friends around me. "But you know what? We're ALL IT . . ." and I laugh.

"Everything is ONE," Ron says, a gentle smile on his face, the room still full of a diffuse light like my eyes are reading more of the UV spectrum.

"But there's no context to it, how does IT GET to be IT?" I can't get my head around IT; I'm covering my eyes, clearing my vision and head, trying to make sense of that which is beyond the monkey brain . . .

It's scary and alien but I've gotta go back there . . . And once you're there, there's nothing to do but BE . . . It's like floating in an amniotic ocean of the cosmic womb, you just be and the more you just be and tune into the BE-ing, the more the waves of energy come and come and come and the more IT you become, and it just goes on forever, deeper, deeper into IT, into just BE-ing . . .

"Surrender, nothing to do but just be, yeah," Juan agrees, reading my mind. "In that place of everything . . . Full oceanic bliss, right . . . There's no room for anything else . . ." He knows.

I realize that while he's done readings on dozens of gringo seekers here in the jungles of Iquitos, he's also done it himself, and he knows what we're going through as the remembrance takes hold, as the hyperspatial memory of self surfaces from the noise of "normal" consciousness. Which makes him either more of a mad scientist than I first thought or the world madder for this great cosmic game we're playing with each other.

"I don't know if you got anything I can work with," Juan says finally, pouring over the spikes and troughs of the EEG readings on his screen.

"You went in too deep, too high and strong a frequency. All that convulsing won't be good for a clear reading, which is a shame, because if you don't get a good data set it's not worth doing."

I'm still seeing holographic imprints on my field of vision and radiating the vibrational wavelengths imprinted on me by the Godhead, so an accurate data set is about the last thing on my mind. *Fuck me, what WAS that I just went through? Amazing.*

As Juan points to an unusual spike on the EEG readings I can feel the bit where the new signal is coming from, directly above the right eye and in, the frontal post-orbital section of the brain. The vibrational wavelengths are still strong; I can tweak them all around. It feels like the wings of a hummingbird fluttering over me, my eyelids trembling and eyes rolling back as my perineum muscle tightens and I try to squeeze that bit of the brain that connects me to the Source. A signal flares up on Juan's screen, splashes of delta among the alpha.

"You keep on saying 'IT,' can you explain?" Bowman asks, his concerned brown eyes peering into me. I'm so raw.

"There's nothing in English but it... IT's IT... It's GOD... You're surfing God, it's the groove... It's the wave, a tsunami, but you're not surfing it you ARE it, you are the wave... the ALL..."

"Hence the liquid... 'cause your movements were very liquefied..." Bowman says, stroking his beard as he tries to grok the translinguistic Other in words.

"I couldn't hold back once I got IT, I had to ride IT, BE IT..." I laugh, eyes downcast, still reeling from the infinite splendor all around...

"But what the FUCK is IT?"

8

Ayahuasca Disco
Pilpintuwasi Butterfly Farm
SATURDAY JULY 8, 2006

The shimmering, iridescent blue morpho butterfly flutters its wings and takes to the air surrounded by its cousin the *buho* or owl butterfly, with large spots that resemble owl's eyes on broad, tattered wings. The enclosure is awash with a cloud of multi-colored butterflies of various sizes and as they swarm around me like moving shards of light, I feel like I'm back in the kaleidoscopic DMT realms, in my own alchemical transformation.

The morpho's brilliant blue wings aren't caused by pigmentation, as with other creatures. Instead this clever insect reflects layers of light to create an interference pattern that changes according to the angle of the observer and the wavelength of light reflected. Reality, like this butterfly's wings, is in the eye of the beholder.

It's the day after the "experiment at La Rosacita," and Vance and I have caught a boat to the Pilpintuwasi Butterfly Farm outside Iquitos on the river Nanay, near the village of Cocha Padre. Pilpintuwasi, which means "butterfly home" in the native Quechua, is run by Gudrun Sperre, an Austrian woman who has been living here in Iquitos since 1982, breeding exotic butterflies and teaching tourists and local school children the wonderful ways of this most symbolic creature. With her Peruvian partner Robier Morano she has set up a number of enclosures connected by twisting stone paths through the exotic gardens, and outside the mesh-covered main house I find myself in are a number of parrots that screech through the late afternoon air.

The conference is finally over, although a final ayahuasca circle remains tonight. It seemed to end with a whimper, not a bang, but that's probably because of my own weariness from all my entheogenic adventuring.

After all the hands-on ayahuasca circles of the last few days and the intensive information downloads from the speakers' presentations, most of the other gringos were tired too, but ripe to spread their knowledge and do something with it practically. The atmosphere in the conference auditorium felt like a charged seed that was ready to germinate. Or as "Lil' Merlin," one of the *ayahuasca.com* forum moderators, said that final night, "Maybe there will be trouble, like in the Middle Ages with the witch hunts, but I have to live with the consequences of my choices [taking ayahuasca]. You cannot stop the movement of ayahuasca once it had started. Thousands of people have seen it on the internet and they are interested, you cannot block that knowledge now..."

And as the conference showed, the business of shamanism is booming. All the shamans smiled and made out that they could stand each other for the cameras, because a unified front is good for business, but the truth is a little different.

"Not everyone wants to participate in the 'We Are All One' ceremony," Kevin Furnas explained to me, his piercing hazel eyes looking right into me. "It's all political, y'know. Some *curanderos* are jealous of each other—it's a business to them and they're all chasing the gringo dollar, or they just don't get along, whatever. There's not much cooperation—it's all competition."

As the blue morpho settles back on Gudran's outstretched finger I wonder about the dichotomy of our systems models, of the seeming supremacy of the Darwinian view of nature and the actual cooperative, Gaian model of interdependent networks that appear once you step back and see the synergistic context.

I know that while some *curanderos* might have their personal differences, and on a surface level competition for business is rife, there's also a deeper dynamic occurring where humans as a whole are interfacing with a vegetal intelligence that seeks to *unite,* not divide. And that the gringo seekers of the mystery, myself included, have been changed for the better by our ayahuasca experiences.

There are forty-two distinct species of butterfly bred here that feed on one or two kinds of plants, flowers and fruits, as well as Pedro Bello, an adult jaguar that was left at Pilpintuwasi by a man who had bought him off some natives and tried unsuccessfully to sell him around Iquitos; two black Huacary monkeys with white faces and long, bushy tails; Chavo, a red-faced Huacary which is part of an endangered species native to the region; Rosa, an anteater; and a tapir called Lolita.

After the intense DMT session yesterday and the wind-up of the conference, it kind of feels nice to be taking it easy this afternoon and doing the usual tourist route for a change. There's a large American family here and as we all listen to Gudrun explain about caterpillars and their life-cycles and the afternoon sun beats down, I lose track of time.

It's getting late as Vance finishes reacquainting himself with Pedro the jaguar, his totem-spirit that he took photos of last year and that he shares a special spiritual connection with. "He's the missing link," he laughs, as I tell him about my own jaguar experiences at Guillermo's, entranced by the animal's graceful movements on the other side of his cage.

By the time we get back to the Yellow Rose and grab a bite to eat, and, cheekily, a few *cervezas* that break diet rules, all the other ayahuasca seekers have left for their last ceremonies tonight. Bowman's already headed out to Norma Panduro's Estrella Center out by Km 45, and as the sun starts to set Vance and I take a *motorcarro* down past the markets of Belén and hire an honest-to-goodness car to speed us to the Center. If the DMT trip at Ron's house yesterday was an entheogenic *acid-test,* then tonight is due to be the graduation ball, and I'm determined not to miss out.

We speed through the choked streets of Iquitos and onto the Nauta highway, breathing in the exhaust fumes that spew out of dodgy bus and *motorcarro* mufflers. The vehicles communicate by beeping their horns for every action, a symphony of bleeps and whirrs that sound unerringly like R2D2 and the other "droids" in *Star Wars*. As we turn a bend in the road an oncoming bus thunders towards us in our lane, on the wrong side of the road. It's de rigueur in Iquitos—motorbikes, three wheeled *motorcarros,* buses, pedestrians—everyone uses both lanes and overlap continuously, hogging the road till the last possible second.

There's no speed cameras, no traffic police, no worries as we hurtle along at 140km/hr, cruising to Spanglish techno music inside the car and breathing a sigh of relief as the bus glides back to the other lane and passes us. Outside the sun is heavy and melting into an orange dusk as it sinks over the treetops, mirrored on the left by an almost full moon. In little villages along the highway kids are playing volleyball in their front yards, joy on their faces.

The Estrella Center is a healing retreat for ayahuasca ceremonies a half hour into the jungle by Kilometer 45.5, on the Iquitos-Nauta road. It's just down from where Percy hold his ceremonies, set among beautiful tropical rainforest surrounded by fruit trees, with small paths frilled with flowers joining the guest's cabanas to the main grounds. Behind the ceremonial *maloca* a meandering stream slowly snakes through the earth.

It was opened by Norma six years ago as a non-profit organization called Clinica Naturista Jose Torres Vasquez, after the patron who helped her set it up. When Tarzana met her a year ago and became her apprentice—and business partner—they renamed it the Estrella Ayahuasca Center, "for the research of ayahuasca and other medicinal plants." Norma is officially President, and Tarzana is the Vice President.

It's since undergone a flurry of transformation, expanding from one to seven cabanas for the rising influx of ayahuasca tourists pouring in, building a new kitchen and adding a large new common area. Business is booming, and the main reason seems to be Tarzana, whose business skills and years managing a condominium business in Mexico have shaped the raw essence of Norma into a slick, competitive package.

The professional marketing touch can be seen everywhere in the revamp, from the Estrella logo—a yellow and green ayahuasca vine in cross-section overlaying a shining pink star—to the website and business cards, to the black and pink branded tanktops that the goddess entourage were wearing at the conference.

The Estrella Center never advertises itself as a women-only establishment, but it touts its femininity in bright shades of pink at every opportunity, offering a package that focuses on healing with ayahuasca in a nurturing, feminine environment.

"Being a woman facilitates the participation of our female visitors to the healing qualities of ayahuasca ceremonies because they are in the safe care and protective guidance of a kind-hearted and knowledgeable shamana," the Estrella website reads. The business angle is paying off, attracting a large number of Western women, and a fair number of men all seeking nurturing and enlightenment. *The Goddess is on the rise again in the jungles of Iquitos.*

Tarzana gave a PowerPoint presentation at the conference on the role of women healers throughout history, or "His-Story" as she called it. She quoted a wealth of evidence, much of it gathered by archeologist Marija Gimbutas, that points to the fact that not only were there women shamanas in ancient communities, women were in fact, in the majority when it came to healing.

In the 1950s archaeologists in the Czech Republic found the skeletal remains of a shaman from the Upper Paleolithic era, over 60,000 years ago during the last Ice Age. The skeleton had the body of a fox in one hand, a shamanic spirit totem for many cultures from Europe, Asia, and even the Americas. The skeleton was later identified as the body of a woman.

From the west coast of Europe to the east coast of Siberia, little clay figurines of women with large breasts, bowed heads, and no faces have been found made of limestone, mammoth tusk, and ceramics. These "Venus figurines," named after the Roman goddess of love, have been defined by male archeologists as signs of a "fertility cult." But recent explanations by feminist academics have turned this idea on its head by suggesting the Venus figurines were made by women shamanas—for women users—in earth rituals that formed the foundation of a larger religion honoring the Goddess.

Tarzana claims that much of the evidence of women shamanas has been overlooked or marginalized by academics, anthropologists, and archaeologists trained in the patriarchal paradigm of the nineteenth and twentieth centuries. Cave paintings at Pech-Merle in France depict, among male hunters with erect penises, pregnant women dancing, but these were for a long time interpreted as "bison." Historical records of female shamanas throughout the Mayan culture in Mexico and Central America, Siberia, Mongolia, and China were all downplayed or ignored to fit existing currents of the male hunter-shaman archetype. Add that to the wholesale slaughter of over seven-and-a-half million women branded witches in the sixteenth century, and you start to see why the archetype of the female shamana has all but been erased from history.

Vance and I finally arrive by the full moon light and head straight to the central *maloca* where the ceremony is about to begin. Inside, the space is lit by a candle and a lamp at the central altar in the middle of the floor, which is also adorned with flowers, crystals, shells, tarot cards, perfume, and jungle rattles—creating a lush, warm atmosphere. Norma's in her seat in front of the altar to the left of the toilets, positioned in front of a giant tan-colored Shipibo wall hanging with concentric circles and ayahuasca river patterns that match her ceremonial gown. People are laying out their sleeping bags, water bottles, and paraphernalia on the mattresses provided.

I see Jay and John Bernstein from the Yellow Rose. Next to him is Alex, a young guy from Alaska that looks like a raver, and of course Bob, who's here for his third session drinking with Norma to get that female healing he's so desperately seeking. Finally I spot Bowman on the right curve of the wall, setting up his audio gear.

"Just in time," he says with a grin as I plop down beside him. Vance is sitting on the only other spare mattress on the opposite side of the room to us. "I thought you guys weren't going to make it."

"And break up the team? No way. We were just running really late and had to catch a taxi out here. It was the first real car I've been in whilst in Iquitos—the driver had a seatbelt and everything. What's the drill?"

"Norma's setting up. The goddess crew are cleansing the space and it's due to start any minute."

The "goddess crew" are the three or four American women who have been drinking ayahuasca here at Estrella for a while, and are now helping run the ceremonies. A strong Californian New Age vibe has settled as they surround themselves with crystals and incense, faerie pictures and power items. I recognize Phoenix in a squatting position around the altar, staring into the candle flame and singing *icaros* to herself. Back on the bus she told me that she's a clinical psychologist in California, but here at Estrella she's a handmaiden to the goddess, bringing out her inner divinity.

And there's Butterfly Girl, sitting in a lotus position with hand-painted faerie pictures behind her. A number of other women, including Ashera, the sound healer from England, are clustered together over one side of the circle, giggling and hugging, offering mutual support, all of them in their power.

Stretched out on the mattress to my right is a tall Peruvian boy who I'd seen at the conference handing microphones to the speakers. He speaks better English than I speak Spanish, and it turns out he's only fifteen and he's never even had an alcoholic drink before. He's heard of ayahuasca, of course, and his peers and family have taken it, and from what he's learned at the conference this seems like the right time for him to take the first step with it, he tells me. I wish him luck, and tell him I'll be here for him if he needs me.

The ceremony room is layered with intimate feminine touches that create a soft, nurturing atmosphere. It has the lush vibe of a spa as the aya goddesses come round the circle administering drops of eucalyptus into the vomit buckets and putting flower essences on our wrists.

Norma begins pouring out the ayahuasca by torchlight, a really strong brew that's been fermenting for a while. Like most *curanderos* throughout Peru she keeps the sacred medicine in clear plastic bottles recycled from the Cola companies, recycling materialism for a spiritual pursuit. Tarzana comes through the shadows with a small wooden cup containing the dark brown liquid, *the goddess bearing the holy, holy grail.* She is a priestess of the night, of all the deep, primal, feminine archetypes triggered by this ritual.

The grandmothers of the Amazon Basin still believe that the first shaman was a woman who painted her face red every month to mark her menstrual cycle. The shamanic powers of a woman *curandera* are believed to be stronger both before and after a menstrual cycle because of higher estrogen levels and a rise in the amount of neurotransmitters, allowing them a heightened sensitivity to the spirit world. Tonight under the light of the full moon, the goddess is loose and on the prowl...

"*Salud!*" I say, holding the cup up to my third eye and sending out my intent for connection with the feminine, nurturing aspect of ayahuasca, the spirit-mother in the plant. The taste is unbelievably bitter, potent, and earthy, and as soon as it goes down it comes up again. My throat opens and elongates, jaws stretching like the mouth of an anaconda as I vomit prodigiously into the basin at my feet. *La purga* flows out and out and out of me like a waterfall, no holding back, no resistance. It feels sublime.

When I'm finished vomiting Tarzana appears before me with the grace of a goddess, another cup of ayahuasca in her outstretched hand. "Are you ready for your medicine now?" she asks.

"Si," I moan, and swallow, clenching down hard. The snake medicine is in me, hurtling through my blood. Within minutes I can see it moving, undulating and shifting in whip-like arcs, giant snakes that overlap, merging with the spirit of the plant. Once again I'm swimming through an endless canvas of spirit energy, interfacing with my genetic memory and being healed on a cellular level. *The snake is in me, in my DNA, shedding its skin to be born.*

The connection between the snakes and serpents one sees on ayahuasca, the role of the serpent in almost every world mythology, and the double-helix of DNA itself has been drawn by Canadian-born, Swiss-based anthropologist Jeremy Narby, author of *The Cosmic Serpent*. In the book Narby says that shamans are accessing the genetic level of information with their consciousness, and that this DNA-knowledge is what they call "spirits."

Narby meticulously details the almost ubiquitous presence of serpents in shamanic cultures across the globe and draws parallels to the double helixes of DNA and the vine, rope, and ladder motifs in these cultures. It is within the shamanic trance, or a "defocalized" and "non-rational" state of consciousness that the shamans dip into the DNA memory for their amazingly accurate botanical and medicinal knowledge.

Narby also says that "research indicates that shamans access an intelligence which they say is nature's, and which gives them information that has stunning correspondences with molecular biology." His theory goes on to posit that there is an active intelligence contained within the DNA of all living things, which is a new tweak on James Lovelock's "Gaia" or whole system theory hypothesis, now cautiously embraced by science.

Narby's book, which is hugely popular on the ayahuasca circuit, also offers a scientific explanation for how *ayahuasqueros* see these visions, explaining that scientists proved that the cells of all living beings emit photons at 100 units per second, per square centimeter of surface area. Finely tuned measuring devices perfected in the early 1980s showed that DNA itself was the source of the photon emissions, and, furthermore, that the wavelength at which DNA emits these photons corresponds exactly to the narrow band of visible light: "Its spectral distribution ranges at least from infrared (at about 900 nanometers) to ultraviolet (up to about 200 nanometers) . . . DNA emits photons with such regularity that researchers compare the phenomenon to an 'ultra-weak laser'. . . Inside the nucleus, DNA coils and uncoils, writhes and wriggles. Scientists often compare the form and movements of this long molecule to those of a snake."

Right now as the snakes envelop me in my hallucinogenic womb all of nature seems to unfold and embrace me. I realize then that you don't do the jungle, it does you. It's bigger, older, the green mother that nurtures and destroys.

You can feel the spirit of the jungle working on you in the heat of the day, in the humidity in the air, the buzz of insects and the cry of the birds—all living creatures riffing off this vibrant ecosystem. All living things give thanks to the jungle, letting it pour through them, and that's why they make the sounds they do, it's the pulse of life flowing through them from the Source, *gracias to the mother in every cry*, every movement reverberating and feedbacking the energy being received. And like the jungle I can feel the ayahuasca working on me now, coming on strong.

I am enveloped in a greater world, this spirit jungle; I can feel the energy of ayahuasca feeding and bathing me, getting inside me and awakening the bit of me that is really her. The snake spirits, jaguar eyes, and monkey chatterings all merge with the "Dolby Surround-Sound" of the spirits on their multiple levels, and each sound is a sonic caress that works on my body and soul, like aural Reiki straight from the heart of the world.

The visions continue to unfold like jungle VR: subtle animal totems, hallucinogenic space, and geometric sigils of hypercondensed information abound. I am floating on a sea of sentient dreams, and these information-spirits are layering me, helping me release and let go, to fully surrender to the current and draw me out from the shore to a deep, deep ocean world where the heart of aya lives.

A small Indian boy-spirit appears before me and offers me his hand. *Come play with me,* he communicates wordlessly, smiling, inviting my inner child out of the man-shell and into the cosmic playground. The spirits are all around now, flitting like insects, taunting, caressing, coming in waves, and everything is alive and beautiful, beckoning me to join it.

Suddenly I can feel more spirits tugging at me, the ancestor spirits with old, weathered brown skin and smiles. Their spirit hands caress me with a weight that says they're really there, holding my head as I lean back into the mattress and melt into a stream of higher consciousness. The spirits are bathing me, holding me, baptizing me in the eternal flow of life and as it carries me away my sense of self melts into the river. *My mind bleeds out of my head and becomes one with the universe . . .*

Do you see now why ayahuasca is not a drug, but a plant sacrament, something that connects to the sacred? You don't take ayahuasca and get the same reproducible effect every time. You have to work at it, develop the relationship with the spirit in the vine and let go of the ego. Then she may, if she chooses, melt into you till you and she are one.

Minutes or hours go by. Norma, Tarzana, Phoenix, Butterfly Girl, and Ashera are singing sweet, sweet *icaros* now to melt the soul. "*Gracias, muchas gracias del amoooore . . .*" Norma croons. She is daughter, mother, and grandmother all wrapped up in one, giving and receiving.

There is a pure spiritual energy pouring through her song and activating my heart chakra. It is a blessing, a love song of praise and a call of thanks to the mother spirit of ayahuasca. To the tweaked ears and cleansed spirit the medicine has brought, it is the *Amazing Grace* of *icaros,* and it brings me back down and makes me whole.

I remember what Tarzana had said about Norma's *icaros,* and how in a trance ayahuasca reveals to her "luminous geometrical patterns of energy." These filaments drift towards the shamana where light is metamorphosed into sound, the chant or *icaro,* which "is a conduit for the patterns of Creation." Norma is then able to "reestablish the balance of [a] patient's body by chanting *icaros,* the geometrical patterns made manifest in sound, where the visual codes are transformed into acoustic codes."

Norma, however, also likes Western songs without any spirit blueprints in them, and pretty soon the *maloca* is awash with a karaoke hit parade. Norma is accompanied by Tarzana and the other women, their voices playful and mellifluous, blending together into sacred harmonies. But it's slightly jarring when they start singing, "Turn, Turn, Turn" by the Birds and the "Sounds of Silence" by Simon and Garfunkel. When "Hello darkness, my old friend, I've come to talk with you again . . ." echoes through the room, I'm starting to feel trapped in an ayahuasca disco.

"I feel like when people say they are drunk?" the boy beside me says, his own ayahuasca trip coming on now.

The psychic tide is turning and it's starting to feel like a sing-along, not a sacred ceremony where you focus on your own inner journey and relationship with the plant. In the raw altered state of ayahuasca inebriation the lyrics pour over me and trigger Western thoughts and memories, and seem to distract from the sacred state of mind we're trying to engender.

"C'mon guys, we want to hear you sing," Tarzana says to whispers and giggles from the other women. To my surprise the boy next to me launches into a high-pitched and pretty good rendition of "Unchained Melody" from the movie *Ghost,* which seems appropriate considering the circumstances. John Bernstein blows out pure primal sonic vibrations on his didgeridoo, the waves of sound traveling through and cleansing us.

The didgeridoo sound triggers a DMT flashback as my eyelids flicker and the spirit of the *mariposa,* the butterfly energy, like a hummingbird's wings flutter over my eyes. I'm inducing deep theta waves and the more I induce them the easier it gets, the mind-space deepens and the energy rushes in. I'm in dreamspace, and on that psychic canvas more visions come. A rush of images of times and places I've never seen: *jungle visions, villagers, Indians, the river, the mighty Amazon carrying me away as it snakes through an iridescent sea of green.*

John Bernstein's still pumping out sonic didge mantras as he launches into his own *icaro,* which he later tells me he learnt from Darpan, the Australian shamanic practitioner whom I first drank with earlier in the year:

Be in the now you will find
And be in the heart you will see
Be in the now you will find
And be in the heart you will see
This love that flows so deep inside
Within there lies a seed
This love that flows so deep inside
Within there lies a seed

> A seed has been planted inside your heart
> And love is the water that feeds
> A seed has been planted inside your heart
> And love is the water that feeds
> With love eternally it will grow
> My mother / father / the force / ayahuasca makes it so
> With love eternally it will grow
> My mother / father / the force / ayahuasca makes
> it so . . .

"This is the strangest circle," Bowman says from the mattress to my left, shaking his head in amazement as some people get up and sway to the music.

"It's not a circle it's a square," I whisper. "It feels like a slumber party, an ayahuasca disco!"

The ayahuasca disco is in full swing and the room has taken on the charged atmosphere of a harem as invisible energies ripple through our blue-light party. Underneath the need to connect with the higher realms on an intellectual masculine way, the goddesses have connected with the spirit, and are pouring out love and open energy that is received by the guys and channeled into a sexual tension that hangs in the psychic atmosphere. Or maybe it's the other way round; it's really hard to tell with the goddesses frolicking around, teasing us to join their play.

"The sky is singing the color of the clouds, singing to us . . ." Butterfly Girl is saying in lilting faerie tones as she comes round to massage us all individually. Before I know it she's sitting on top of Bowman's back, straddling him like a Reiki cowgirl and cleansing his blockages. I'm next, as she drops down beside me in my blanketed cocoon and holds my wrist. The touch of skin on skin is electric as she begins to massage me, turning me over and working on my chakras.

"The spirit of the anaconda is here, it's in you," she whispers. I'm sure. The *Karma Sutra* positions and increased energetic and psychic flow are all screaming sex, but my higher mind will have nothing to do with it, or her, and there's no physical reaction. It's too contrived, like a black widow entrapping her male.

Butterfly Girl is pretty high on ayahuasca herself, flapping her woven fans which make a sound like giant butterfly wings enveloping me. Norma says that Malonie is a new soul that hasn't lived a human life before. She's been an animal twice, and in her last incarnation she was a butterfly, hence her strong totem identification with them in this life.

"You've got a lot of blockage in your crown chakra," Butterfly Girl says chastisingly, reading my energetic wall. "Leave your mobile phone at home!" she commands in that Tinkerbelle fairy voice she hides behind.

"Let go, imagine a silver thread connecting the back of your head to the cosmos. Draw down the cosmic energy through you and into the earth." And with that she disengages and goes on to the next man in the circle . . .

"Is it getting a bit soft porn in here or what?" I ask Bowman beside me, drawing him out of his own ayahuasca trip.

"Definitely," he agrees. "When she was on me, it was very sexual. I felt aroused but I didn't want to."

Somewhere in the back of my mind I remember Norma's attitude to sex, and I'm sure everyone's thinking the same. The air is charged with that electric expectation that precedes a group orgy, as someone tells the story of the couple who made love in their sleeping bag at the previous ceremony, breaking the prime taboo.

Ayahuasca ceremonies are usually very structured rituals where the shaman or shamana holds the space and guides the drinkers on their journeys of discovery. The shaman is not just administering the hallucinogenic brew; he or she is also calling in their allies, banishing evil spirits, and safeguarding the immediate physical environment—playing the role of psychic bouncer. And while personalities vary, the role of the shaman in anchoring the physical and spiritual worlds is inviolate, and should be treated with respect.

Many *curanderos* have rules about what can and can't go on in the sacred space of an ayahuasca ceremony, which may include no frivolous talking, respecting others, no shining torches or lights, and focusing on the spirits they are calling in. The baseline energies of sex are definitely a spiritual no-no. This ayahuasca ceremony, however, has exploded all these rules in a laissez-faire atmosphere of anything goes. Most of all it resembles an entheogenic slumber party, with the girls on one side of the *maloca,* the boys the other, and an infinite multidimensional universe between us.

And while there's definitely some merit in the idea of a freeform ritual, of exploring the group dynamics in an open, supportive environment where you can express yourself, some participants weren't comfortable with it. As Jay, and other men were later to report, the resulting group freedom was "distracting, disrespectful, and chaotic."

As if feeling the psychic backlash from some members of the group, Tarzana breaks the mood with her own sweet *icaro,* then makes a speech. "There's strong healing going on here," she says. "Just because we're playful don't think there's not a lot of work going on. If the women wake up first then the men have a harder time connecting."

Well that must be what it is then—I'm just having a hard time connecting. As the full moon beams down on our ayahuasca disco, illuminating us with its full and ripe energy, Alex, the young raver guy from Alaska, says out loud, "It's like a hologram. Depending on how much you take in you can alter your level of engagement with it. You can go really deep and look at the grid structure underlying everything, or stay in the wading pool and frolic with everybody."

And he's right, but every culture has a different name for it: *Indra's Net; Godhead; Mitaqueasen; Logos.* The way the parts contain the blueprint of the whole and connect us all together.

And tonight, here at the ayahuasca disco, we are all embracing the hologram, men and women moving to the universal strobe light...

9

Logos

Rio Itaya, Iquitos
Sunday July 9, 2006

I'm wading through a mountain of sawdust that goes up past my ankles and covers my shins, slogging my way through the ancient bodies of grandfather trees in a sawmill graveyard down by the Itaya river. Bowman is with me, trailed by a dozen local kids from the nearby shanty town that have walked over giant sawn logs and past an ancient nineteenth-century cutting wheel as big as an elephant to follow us loco gringos.

It's a pleasant Sunday afternoon and we're on our way to the Soga Del Alma ayahuasca church a few miles downriver, chasing, as always, the mystery...

As we near the riverbank and a flotilla of boats we find John Bernstein, didgeridoo under his arm, his glistening brown eyes hinting at the friendship we've formed last night at Norma's. He's come along to try smokable DMT for the first time tonight, administered by Theo Valis.

As the late afternoon sun plays on the water's edge, Theo pops out of a boat and greets us with a youthful enthusiasm, throwing his tall and lanky frame into action for our imminent entheogenic adventure.

Theo's been busy sitting ayahuasca circles with Percy, offering his services as a facilitator. He's run his own ceremonies—sometimes with up to thirty people, back in Australia. Percy was reportedly bemused at the thought of such large groups, but wasn't threatened at all by what Theo describes as "pseudo-shamanic dick sizing."

After some light haggling we hire a boat and float down the Rio Itaya in the late afternoon light, people bathing and frolicking like naked apes, water glistening off their bodies and good energy all around. On the right hand riverbank are the most amazing hulks of ships, old two-story paddleboats and steamers left over from a previous era, like beached whales of the Rubber Boom years in the early twentieth century. Their rusting bodies are still inhabited by local Peruvians who smile and wave at us as we gently float downstream, becoming one with the water and the energy of the day.

As we turn a riverbank a shimmering band of rainbow juts out from thick cloudbank ahead and juts back in again as soon as you please. The day is just perfect, sublime, the birds singing and insects buzzing. Nature is in harmony all around us; our cleansed, post-ayahuasca bodies are receiving the Gaian signal clear and strong.

We arrive at the other shore and walk through the jungle path to Soga Del Alma, Alan Shoemaker's ayahuasca chapel, a beautiful big *maloca* with two ensuites, one bathroom, and one kitchen, mosquito netting all around and polished floorboards inside.

It's the perfect sacred space for our journey back into the vibratory seas of the Godhead, and as I laze in a hammock above the ground, Theo explains that the DMT extract was harvested from the bodies of Australian acacia trees felled in storms, their essences carried away by nature and prepared for ingestion into us.

I've done a few circles with Theo before and while he's well versed in chemical extractions and has had DMT over a hundred times, and ayahuasca as many again, I've always been a little cautious of his laissez-faire attitude towards psychonautics. Theo's a maverick—always doing things his own way and braving new frontiers, without necessarily providing the anchor or safety net for others that *curanderos* do in ceremonies here in Peru.

"DMT is the ultimate gnosis," he explains, sitting cross-legged down on the wooden floorboards as he unpacks his alchemist's bag of tricks. In the flickering candlelight the shadows dart across his face. "It's about consciousness and the Godhead, not necessarily aliens. I'm not a shaman—I simply provide the materials for people and a safe environment.

I give people the space to explore and awaken their own consciousness," Theo says, then quotes J. Krishnamurti: "Truth is a pathless land."

I remember. How could I forget? DMT is called the "spirit molecule" because it is in countless living creatures on the earth—it links the plants, the mammals, and the insects like a neurochemical key, a receiver-transmitter of the Divine that some say connects us to the Dreaming and the after-death realms.

It's only been two days since the "experiment at La Rosacita" at Ron Wheelock's house, where I experienced a spectacular immersion into the holographic matrix, surfing the brainwaves of God and becoming living language. I'm a bit afraid of making a spectacle again, but even more afraid of not being true in the spirit world. *When you meet your maker it has to be with an open heart, fully embracing the Divine and letting it flood into you.*

This morning at the internet café on Calle Arica I'd googled Terence McKenna to refresh myself on his take on all this hyperspatial action. He calls the numinous presence of the "Other" the "Logos." In one of his many raps on the psychedelic experience, the 1984 lecture "New Maps of Hyperspace," McKenna says,

"What psychedelics encourage, and where I hope attention will focus once hallucinogens are culturally integrated to the point where large groups of people can plan research programs without fear of persecution, is the modeling of the after-death state. Psychedelics may do more than model this state; they may reveal the nature of it. Psychedelics will show us that the modalities of appearance and understanding can be shifted so that we can know mind within the context of the One Mind. The One Mind contains all experiences of the Other. There is no dichotomy between the Newtonian universe, deployed through light years of three-dimensional universe, and the interior mental universe. They are adumbrations of the same thing.

"We perceive them as unresolvable dualisms because of the low quality of the code we customarily use. The language we use to discuss this problem has built-in dualisms. This is a problem of language. All codes have relative code qualities, except the Logos. The Logos is perfect and, therefore, partakes of no quality other than itself. I am here using the word Logos in the sense in which Philo Judaeus uses it—that of the Divine Reason that embraces the archetypal complex of Platonic ideas that serve as the models of creation. As long as one maps with something other than the Logos, there will be problems of code quality. The dualism built into our language makes the death of the species and the death of the individual appear to be opposed things."

From my last trip I now believe that a big dose of DMT causes a collapse of the normal substrate of consciousness and a mini-black-hole phenomenon, a *singularity* where we fall back into the mind of God, the primal matrix where all life comes from and goes back to—a total death experience. But I'm also drawn back to it like the proverbial moth to the flame and filled with an irresistible urge to fully understand it, to become IT. Whatever IT is, it deserves to be engaged, and like all good explorers I have a thirst to penetrate its depths and drink of the mystery contained there.

The problem is how to *communicate* what I find. As McKenna warned, the experiences of one state of consciousness are often not just unintelligible, but untranslatable to another state. And the more distant the state the more difficult the translation can be. Philosopher Charles Tart called this a problem of "state-specific knowledge." Early reports on the mystical revelations of nitrous oxide by nineteenth-century consciousness explorer William James brought back linguistic solipsisms like "There are no differences but differences of degree between different degrees of difference and no difference."

All I could say after my last incursion was "it's IT," over and over again, while knowing full well IT couldn't be reduced to words. DMT-exposure, whether by natural plant material like ayahuasca, mushrooms, or brain-induced altered states, often overwhelms the brain in pure linguistic phenomena. So unlike the normal descriptive function of language, trying to describe the DMT-phenomenon with English often involves describing energetic states of being and the emotional responses they engender, but it cannot, of course, communicate the *feeling* of those energies themselves. Something is invariably lost in the translation—yet I have to try.

More travelers arrive and as the sun sets the background hum of crickets rings out of the jungle, enveloping us in a blanket of subtle vibrations. Nicole, a perky brunette from California who has been doing ayahuasca circles at the conference but has never tried DMT before and Shylo, a dreaded, Eskimo-dude in his twenties from Nelson, Canada, who's been staying here at the *maloca* all week, both join the circle.

Last but not least, my jaguar-brother Vance turns up just after the sun has gone down, drawn by the strange attractor of the most singular thing we are invoking, *the Logos on high.* Seven loco gringos and Nicole's Peruvian boat driver sitting quietly in the corner watching us all, taking it all in as if it's something to warn his grandchildren about.

By candlelight Theo makes a homemade bong from a water bottle, some hose pipe, and a metal cone, sealing tape around the hole. Everyone watches, unsure of what they are about to experience, our fear mingling with the expectations of this drug. John Bernstein tries a blue lily smoke, an herbal mix of various plants to test the vehicle and together he and Theo scale it down to a smaller water bottle and are ready to begin. A little nervousness hangs in the air, mixing with the sweat and sounds of the jungle. Incongruously, the neighbor's Western salsa music drifts in from a few hundred meters away.

Theo packs the bong with the acacia mix, sprinkling it with fine crystals of N,N-DMT, some ayahuasca vine, and other trace elements of plant material. "You can have any intensity from four to eleven point five," he jokes, flashing one of his trademark wry smiles as he lets people feel assured in how much they're taking of this most potent psychoactive material.

Bowman goes first, eager to reconnect after his last aborted flight at Ron Wheelock's house after my own journey, where he'd had a sub-threshold dose and not broken through.

Once again I am reminded of the romantic notion that we are like astronauts of the innerworlds, going on our neurochemical journeys and exploring this new, yet archaic frontier inside us, those places that few Westerners now dare to tread, walking with the angels and spirits. We're putting a man on the moon but the stars are inside, alive and waiting for our return.

"Innerspace is the most outerspace you can get," Bowman says, lowering a black eye mask that John Bernstein has produced and psyching himself up for his manned mission into the Godhead. I remember a cultural resonance—the name of the astronaut hurtled through a cosmic stargate and evolved into the next form of life in the movie *2001: A Space Odyssey* was also called Bowman.

As he smokes the DMT bong and falls back into his hammock, I imagine his mind racing backwards and going IN—into the writhing sentient matrix that I remember so well. I know right now he's seeing a sea of swirling colors and shapes, like being inside a cosmic kaleidoscope as it shifts and turns round and round endlessly, but it's melting into him and him into it and it's all happening at light speed.

Of course, on the outside all you see is the caterpillar body in the cocoon-hammock, murmuring slightly, sometimes saying words, sometimes gesticulating, the meat body-shell left behind while the soul rejoins the Source and the drop returns to the ocean and remembers that all is One, *telepathic Overmind consciousness ingressing in through the lens of you* . . .

Minutes go by and as I sit behind Bowman on a thin yoga mat on the floor I can feel the DMT rush myself; my own brain's still sensitive to the frequency from the experiment at La Rosacita. When I close my eyes and focus on him, his journey, trying to create a safe space and be a guide and sentinel for him, my eyes start blinking rapidly again like I'm entering rapid REM, and that familiar heavy, vibrating butterfly/

insect wing consciousness descends on me. I can feel the frequency, the DMT signal from his brain to mine, so close it's rubbing off on me . . .

"Godddd . . . that was . . . oh man . . . oh man," he says on reentry, trying to grasp the experience, trying to assimilate it into monkey-words.

One by one the others take their excursion into the God-matrix, and I sit with them and guide them on their journey, softly blowing air and making click-whirring noises to help the souls navigate, to give them some hooks and lifelines in there, in that infinite mix, because sounds intensify and potentiate in the DMT zone.

All that kaleidoscopic color is, according to the Shipibo-Conibos tribe of the Ucayali River, resonating vibrational frequency, that is, it's actually *sound* we're seeing and immersed into, it's *sound* that is washing over us and into us and as it does so it's interacting with our own vibrational wave form and cleansing the lens of our consciousness. Later I'm reminded that Carl Jung, one of the premier Western scholars, also believed in a universe of harmonic vibrations that the Collective Unconscious he proposed was always in tune with.

Nicole takes a level seven dose, what she hopes is safe, but it's her first time and she struggles against the alien sensation, crying "Help, help me, I need help, it's too much!" She's writhing in the hammock and Theo, Bowman, and I are there, comforting and holding her, creating a sacred space and waiting for her reentry.

Bernstein is next and as he settles back into the hammock and lowers his eye mask he radiates the aura of an experienced "head," like a gentle, oriental mystic going in, and under. He's chosen a big dose—level nine—but he seems ready to grok the experience and makes a few guttural ur-sounds as he navigates the unknowable.

He comes down gently, quietly, the memory of it all tantalizingly beyond the reach of his conscious brain. When he can talk he says it all happened so fast that he wasn't able to process the information overload, and like a dream the meaning slipped off because it never stuck in the conscious brain.

Halfway through his own trip, Shylo takes off the eye mask and gets lost in the fractaling geodesic patterns that overlay on the air around him, tracing the light trails with his hands like he's sculpting light and spirit. Then he goes outside to hug the earth and ground himself in the mother.

Vance falls back into the Logos and thrashes slightly in the hammock like a big cat for a few minutes, making a few sub-vocal growling noises as he groks the Divine and lets it wash over, through, and into him.

And finally, it's my turn.

If last time I felt like the first chimp about to be shot into space, this time I feel like Chuck Yeager, totally next level up. This time I go in forewarned and armed, knowing something of what to expect, what to look for, and how to glean the raw spirit essence and truths and ground them down into words, into language.

This time I'm going in to bring IT back. Thank you, *Australian Penthouse*, for assigning this humble gonzo-embedded journalist to the Ultimate Story. But there's no way in heaven that your readers are ever going to understand anything I report.

I'm the last to cross over and as I take Bernstein's mask and close off the light to my eyes and suck down the DMT bong, an eleven hit on the scale, Theo warns me there may be some memory loss, it may be, as the Spanish say, *bastante*—enough, too much . . .

. . . Rushing tunnel of light like hyperspace in Star Wars, and each bead is a frozen liquid angel, a condensed vibrational being, another drop in the cosmic ocean all around. And the angels are alive, they pulse with welcoming light-love, they caress and become me as I enter the DMT space and everything becomes infused with holiness, with a sacredness beyond words, felt in every fiber of my being. This is what the saints say, what the enlightened ones experience, the lower bardos and the shores of the heavenly realms . . .

All I have to communicate it to you, dear reader, is these poor words, these little niños. They are but shadows of the thing for the experience is translinguistic—beyond words. Underneath the semantic skin of words are vibrational wavelengths that attach to the essence of the thing that is named.

The vehicle of the Word is like a freshly minted wave packet to contain energies that are burst open here as I swim through—in—become one with the core, the Source of all things, the Logos that creates and is pure Creation itself . . .

I cross over to the other side—where the angels live, where all spirit and energy is manifesting on different levels, the fifty thousand veils of maya and the Sufi myth, the infinite masks of God. As I let the Logos in, I embrace the onrushing Divinity and it fills me, becomes me, until I'm swimming like a dolphin cutting through the water, yet the water is me and there's no separation from IT, it's all IT, and it's all sound that manifests as light and it wraps around me as the caterpillar leaves the hammock-cocoon and becomes the cosmic butterfly . . .

Here and now, writing these words, I know how all this sounds. But listen, over there, a dimensional frequency away, a raging torrent is flowing that is the Source of all things. The spirits I describe are so much more than that word, so real. They are the feeling of your lover, the first time you kissed, the birthday cake when you were ten, your first sunset, the love from your mother, a dog's tongue on your skin, sleeping in last Saturday, learning colors in preschool, the smile of a stranger, the secret name you've never told the world, the flight of an eagle as the wind lifts its feathers and a lifetime of things besides . . .

A billion feelings are all stored within the holographic matrix of my DNA and as I join the vibrational matrix of the Source it not just polishes the hologrammatic lens, it unlocks the chakras to unleash all my memories and emotions. I'm being read like a book and the reader is God, the Logos, the thing with as many names as there are namers. It reads my stored memories and they cascade around me like a flower in bloom.

The spirits caress me and laugh with me, and as I get it, as I get that flash of recognition that I've felt these feelings before, the spirits say si, amigo, yesss, and they laugh and lift me higher. They sing me their secret songs and I smile and remember and become and feel all of this in the touch of this one word: spirit. All of this hypercondensed into each single crystalline moment reflecting the glory of God in the molecular rainfall of my journey.

It's like "Dolby Surround-Sound" hologrammatic code. Hologrammatic, grammatic, grammar, the Word, the word of God . . . we're in the WORD you see, and the WORD is a sound, a vibration. And the more I don't fight IT the more I let go and embrace IT, the more perfect a vessel I become for the Logos, a living Logos that incarnates within. All at godspeed, smearing like a camel through the eye of a needle ...

A timeless state ensues, and I'm wrapped in this being and I AM this being, I always have been. In this state all is one is one is one forever and ever without end, and the visual hieroglyphics and the colors and kaleidoscopic patterns wrap themselves around me. Each one is another layer of the being, multiple strands of consciousness. The Logos is a modulating waveform made up of layers of vibrational sentience all overlapping with me, creating a ripple-like interference pattern as on the surface of a pond.

I can feel every molecule in my being vibrating at the same time, singing a song of joy, the same song the birds sing in the morning to the dawn and the animals sing when they run across the ground in the hunt or a lover whispers to their mate in the heat of passion. Molecular rainfall all around, sentient superstrings showering space-love, unity, unity, unity. I am IT and IT is you. We are all One. And this goes on forever, and the whole time I'm melting and hurtling and blossoming and becoming and caressed by spirits and angels and cumming holographic chakra blossoms, totally transdimensional, till I lose myself, and there is no me left to remember separation. I'm drowning in it, back in the dreaming universe ...

My heart chakra opens like an eye to the sun and drinks in its energy essence. This timeless world of spirits wraps itself around me like a cloak of eternity that goes on forever in all directions, beyond words now, IN the WORD now ... And I can feel the spirits, they caress me, hold me, they teach me how to swim and breathe and they whisper their own icaros to help me navigate, those vibrational patterns that create cosmic ballast. I am at play in the fields of the Divine, swimming with the spirits ...

After some time a memory of being Other returns, and like a deep-sea scuba diver I struggle to return to the surface. Even though "I" can't remember who "I" am or what it is I'm trying to do, a feeling remains that I've done something, this is it, I've done something I can't come back from.

This is what it must be like to be dead, lost in the current of the Source and merging back to the zero point, unanchored from the body. But I'm just visiting, I'm bungee jumping the lower bardos and just as I can't remember I'm an "I," I feel the pressure of being a million miles from home, and the call of the Other that is "I" begins . . .

I fall out of pure unity and start descending back the cosmic ladder to the matter world below. Reentry begins. The spirits rejoice; they caress and sing to me on the way back down; they play with me and guide me back to my body. The *icaros* they sing are hologrammatic tools that carve me back to the right shape to fit my flesh. They pat me back down into myself, back into the "I." It feels like being born.

I'm back on the wooden floor of the *maloca* but the Logos is still in me, seeing through my eyes and the spirits are all around and there's a diffuse light like I'm seeing everyone's auras lighting up the room. I can still feel the Source connecting me to all living things around in perfect hologrammatic unity . . .

Here I am sitting spilled and spent, spat out of the Godhead spewing forth translinguistic currents of energy: "Tuesday crimson Jerilderie sweetheart, wappa loopa baby what I say . . ." I've trapped a bit of myself in each word I've ever mastered and now when I say them that energy is released again, like splitting an atom.

I can feel an immense grace like the shadow of God is in the room with us, the energy thread of the hologram, the Great Spirit that connects us all. And this grace rubs off, it's shining through every living thing, every person, every sound, it's all in on the game we're playing down here, and I know this in a truth beyond words, as real as my breath, no illusions—the veil has been lifted.

It's like *The Truman Show*, that comedy where Jim Carey is being watched his whole life, but it's the whole universe watching us. The liquid angel spirits are all here, maybe they're creating the light all around, and we're ALL the reality TV show . . . it's an organic collective consciousness, it's grace, and I'm crying with the knowledge and the fullness inside me, thanking the blessed Mother and all the angels . . .

And I'll say, "Waa wa billl boo hoo coo CHOO," and behind me the birds in the night will echo the sound exactly, they pattern match—

complete it with a cry, they hear the signal I'm giving off, the pattern recognition of the living Logos. And I'll "ooh ooh ooh wah nee nah boogna yip yahh" in reply and the insects by my feet will sing a vibrational concerta of joy as Vance murmurs a supportive phrase and my heart reels it in and riffs off it, because the thing I'm connected to has no beginning and no end and the brain state I'm in now perceives it, *shaman–wordsmith–fallen angel.*

There is a translinguistic thread that connects all life in the language of the gods, and when the birds sing they hear it, the spirits whisper it, the thunder echoes it back, they're all talking, all connected, and I can hear them in my head and make sense of it and there's no end to it. Send out a signal, and the jungle responds with its cry. This is the hologrammatic universe science dreams of made flesh, visible, manifest. Booming right back at'cha.

The night is alive and love connects us all, and all my media imprints are firing. I feel like Steve Austin, the "Six Million Dollar Man" gone up to the heavens and melted like Icarus into the sun. Now I'm crashing down and they've rebuilt me, bigger, better, stronger than before. It's the ayahuasca, I know that, and the *dieta,* the purification of the plant spirits. I am so raw, so purified by the *purga* and the diet that it allows a better pattern recognition to the DMT signal, the receiver of pure God-consciousness and the caress of the spirits. Norma's *icaros,* her ode to love, "Muchas Gracias del Amore" washes over me in memory, the "Amazing Grace" of Spanish songs, and a heaven-sent feeling radiates out.

Everyone is talking but I can hear-feel the words and the energy like a billion levels of Photoshop wrapped around me, but God is the picture yeah, and all these layers of reality are threads I can pull and make words to now, and it's all sentient and it's all holy; *holy holy holy God,* most sacred of spaces, the raw holiness of Creation is still right here now.

So we play with each other. My heart chakra is open and all my loved ones are around me, their spirit forms are here waiting and hovering. When I invoke them they flood into and connect with me, and I can channel their essences.

I am, however, still rolling round on the floor of the *maloca* while the others look on, still possessed by the Logos, loving the Logos, spitting out ur-sounds and pure glossolalia, surfing the vibrational waves still coursing through me and letting them ooze out my fingers in little hand mudras that complement the words. I'm living language and it radiates from me. I twist and turn and writhe like a snake and it feels so fluid I could burp up Shakespearian metaphors and primal *ursprache* assembly language.

Nature calls and wraps me in her, the animals sing back because they can hear the signal I'm giving off, the floorboards creak in expectation, the night whispers its secrets and I *know*, I know it and am it, everything is language, it's all alive and now I know its grammar, the secret language of nature . . .

God speaks through me and the Word is made flesh.

I'm so happy that I've come back because I'd forgotten I could come back, that I was separate from the All, and knowing that I can come back means that I can also return. It really feels like the early Apollo missions, the first manned missions to the moon. Not only do these other spaces exist, but we can travel to them and return safely. We can survive the experience. We can make sense of it, the hypercondensed black hole of space-time-love that is the Logos, it can be integrated. It can be downloaded. *The idea of IT can be brought back.*

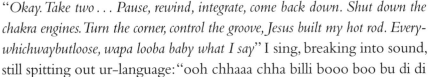

"*Okay. Take two . . . Pause, rewind, integrate, come back down. Shut down the chakra engines. Turn the corner, control the groove, Jesus built my hot rod. Everywhichwaybutloose, wapa looba baby what I say*" I sing, breaking into sound, still spitting out ur-language: "ooh chhaaa chha billi booo boo bu di di di diiiii . . . !" If this is the afterglow of cosmic orgasm then I'm rolling in the translinguistic wetspot of our union.

I can still hear all levels of sound as a multi-track recording of reality, as layers of the night: the jungle, the birds, the insects, the neighbor's music, the sway of the hammocks, Bowman's voice, the shake of a rattle,

Vance's paternal utterings; all of us are riffing off each other like a giant cosmic pinball, but it's not random, it's connected, and in my holy state I can feel and see the connection.

I know everyone here sees and feels it too; we're all in on it—even if our matter bodies aren't quite aware, our higher selves are. It's the singularity that the DMT dimension reveals—it also draws everything else into its web, warps all other living things into the gravity pit, so everything is consensually drawn into the experience on a spirit level where we are One.

When the insects sing their vibrational song it is the Source that triggers them and comes through, and so too with us humans. We may blink, or burp or fart, or suddenly have a thought or say a sound or call out a name; but when in the heavy tow of the DMT singularity all of those actions are understood as reverberations of the spirit world where everything originates. We are all connected, and everything is feeding the whole.

I'm still on the floor, surrounded by my ground crew, and I get control of it, start to navigate it for the sake of reentry . . . "*Wheee hoo ha hoo nahhhhh*" and I'm spewing forth the translinguistic Logos again, staring at the people staring back at the DMT mess I have become on the floor, writhing around in his own psychic juices.

Oh my ground crew, my brave psychonauts, *muchas gracias,* thank you for being you, for being there for me, for all of us together, for the things which bind and the things which sustain us.

I have had my *cosmic consciousness* connection, as Richard Maurice Bucke would call it, that experience of Jesus and Mohammad and Buddha and all saints and mystics throughout time, the inherent possibility that we all have to connect fully with the Divine. And I know it is within each one of us to become this thing, and that the time is coming when a greater relationship with that spirit world will be needed, when this "spirit gene," this consciousness will activate in greater numbers in us all.

And I'm still molten language, *ursprache* assembly language, but I know the controls now, the on and off switches, the volume control, fast forward, play, pause, and rewind. I feel the shamanaut, the master of the experience, not the lost soul. I can navigate the Logos, I can speak its WORD and do its will, I am master and child to its love and it is ALL . . .

"Fuck me . . . gorgeous, intense, beautiful . . ." I have to get some air.

I step out of the *maloca,* some ten minutes after reentry and I'm still buzzing, still connected, still sacred. I look up at the stars and marvel at their beauty and, of course, the stars wink at me—one by one left to right—letting me know they're in on it too, we're all still connected. And oh, the beauty of *la luna,* the moon, she shines down her deep love to me, and the night is alive and I'm totally telepathic, still immersed in the hologram, kissing the dirt and feeling the mud on my fingers and streaking it across my face, Mother Earth, so sweet, Mother Earth, and still the connection is there.

Days later, in the streets of the slums of Belén, I see a picture of Jesus and he's opening his cloak to reveal his sacred heart, and it's glowing with an aura and I know just what it means, coded in its religious iconography.

The *curanderos* say that the heart chakra connects to the spirit world, it sends you off on astral journeys, and part of the upward thrust of your spirit travel is the energetics of the person you are, the vessel you can be for the Logos in you. The less fear you have and the more you accept and embrace the onrushing becoming of you in IT, the more it gives and the more you receive till you have the Holy Spirit in you, your heart chakra is pulsing open and accepting in the light and it's you and you're it and the seed in your heart has germinated.

Every word, every action, every deed, everything I learned about people and energy and the flow of life and the secret things beneath the surface, all of that came together in this journey, in my ability to recognize IT, what it is and what was going on, and to ride it and become it and bring a tiny piece of it back with me, however small.

And for that I feel the most special blessing, the most sacred gift of all. The gift of IT is alive in me and I am crying on the inside, transmitting the love of the Lord, giving thanks for this gift and the remembrance ...

I have been to the stars and they tell me to share their message, their essence. Blessed be, Great Spirit, the all-in-one.

All is one.

All is one.

ALL IS ONE.

10
Night of the Black Puma

Pasaje Colon, Iquitos

TUESDAY JULY 11, 2006

Don Juan Tangoa Paima's house is in the suburbs of Iquitos, a stone's throw from the airport, down a quiet little cul-de-sac called *Pasaje Colon,* which seems appropriate for the good doctor. We arrive to find him busy working around the house with his seven children and three grandchildren all in attendance, running around playing while his wife Leonore does the washing out the back in colored plastic buckets and sets it out to dry in the morning sun. There's a healthy looking golden labrador lazing in the shade of the house—and a healthy looking dog in Iquitos is rare, and a good sign that the master looks after all the inhabitants of his home.

Juan's very unassuming and down-to-earth, dressed in a green t-shirt with the slogan "St. Patrick Old Rock Church, since 1843" emblazoned across it, tan shorts, and blue flip-flops. But there's something about him, a pain on his face, in the slight down curl of his lips as he carries himself, not from his own woes, but as if he's taking on too much, the pain of the world.

Carlos Tanner is looking serious by his side in a t-shirt and shorts and his ubiquitous red Che Guevara baseball cap. He's been studying with Juan for over three years now and they're pretty much inseparable, this indigenous *curandero* and his gringo apprentice. It's like a Peruvian inversion of the superhero / kid sidekick archetype—if Juan is Dr. Strange from the Marvel comics, as I'd posited earlier, then Carlos is his Wong.

They've got reason to be concerned though—there's been a break-in at the house but it doesn't appear that anything's been stolen. Still, Juan is worried. He says it may be *brujeria*, and that he's often under attack from other sorcerers who are jealous of his power and position. You see, while he may be a healer for the local community, the equivalent to say, of a local family doctor, he's also much more than that. He's a *maestro* shaman who's been studying the science of *curanderismo* for over forty years, and he seems to have made a few enemies along the way.

The energy of kids running around mixes perfectly with the ayahuasca on the boil in the big pot in the back yard, in the shadow of the giant grandfather trees. There are half a dozen mature ayahuasca vines here in this suburban shaman's home. Giant thirty-foot palm trees are entwined with ayahuasca vines a shadow of their size, but the upstarts have taken control. The roots of one magnificent ayahuasca specimen twist around a palm tree creating a sigil shape like a musical note, or a dollar bill sign. High up above in the canopy the vine flowers into a brilliant deep green cluster of ayahuasca leaves, drinking in the light.

There's a swagger of gringos here to do the six-week ayahuasca initiation course Carlos is running in conjunction with Juan, the first step in their ambitious "shaman school" project to launch a stream of global shamanism. "We're pioneering a new form of shamanism with roots here in the Amazon rainforest but with branches that reach out to other parts of the world," Carlos explains to me later. Four Americans are here for the full six weeks, and Ariel and Meera, a couple from Israel in their late twenties have been here for a while already, learning the ways of the medicine.

Today they're sitting in the warm morning sun and hammering the ayahuasca vine, mashing it down to rich brown splinters that flash through with a tan colored cream center, the blood of the wood. Ariel's bare-chested with long curly dark hair, a beard, and piercing almond eyes; Meera has long black hair and a sweet Hebrew face, both of them in light and simple clothes like they've just stepped out of the Old Testament. As they hammer away they sing *icaros* to the vine that Juan has taught them, interspersed with some Santo Daime songs Meera knows, and the air is filled with a spiritual energy.

"Ayahuasca is what we use in order to investigate the problems of the people that come with sicknesses," Juan says to Carlos, who translates for us as Bowman and I record the interview here in the backyard and Vance sets up his photography gear. "But it's an investigation that takes place in another dimension, the spiritual dimension, so with ayahuasca you can then enter into a world where information is readily available, where you can ask the spirits or look at a spirit of a person and find out the roots of those afflictions and what can then be done to alleviate [them].

"And this is done in the spiritual dimension in the same way that a doctor would use in this dimension information about your history, your lifestyle in the past and find out a formula or a way of healing it using their books. But because they don't understand the spiritual dimension and because many of them don't believe in a spiritual dimension they have no access to [it], which is where all the work that I do takes place. I keep stressing—in the spiritual dimension *nothing is impossible*. All of the work is used because of ayahuasca, which allows you to work in that spiritual dimension."

There's a kind of comic book context to what Juan's saying, that he performs a kind of "psychic surgery" with his astral body on his patient's astral body. It's just like in a hospital, he says, that "there are spirits that come and assist me in the same way that nurses are assisting the doctors. I have done operations myself where I have removed the heart of a person, like a heart transplant and replaced organs." It's almost identical to physical surgery, Juan claims, except that it's taking place in the spiritual dimension. "So in essence your material liver is not being removed, but the spirit within that liver is being replaced by the spirit of a new liver."

It's not only spiritual healing that many people come to Juan for. Some come with a mystery pain that has no physical cause. Others are sure their wife is cheating on them and need to know who it is she's seeing. Others want to know things beyond their senses, or contact spirits of the departed.

"I work for the community and for everyone that is sick," Juan says earnestly, his dark eyes shining. "I know many, many people that don't have any money and can't afford to go to the hospital to see a doctor because they have to pay for that. I work for free, for the good of God, and so anyone who comes to me, regardless if they have money or not, I will heal them. I want to heal everyone from anywhere around the world, but we also heal all the people from this community."

Some women come looking for love, for a spell to enchant that boy they really, really like, but won't take an interest in them. Juan doesn't humor them, however—he entertains their desire and lets them see what their emotions won't.

The lovesick girl, for example, gave the full name of the boy she liked, and his spirit was summoned to the ceremony, conversed with, and asked if he had any interest in the girl. The spirit, like the boy, replied he wasn't interested. He wasn't ready to settle down and he was happy chasing girls and he didn't like her like she liked him. If you told that to her face her heart would still pine. But when the spirit doctor says it in the context of the ayahuasca ritual, her heart was open, she listened, respected what he had to say, and she moved on.

I ask Carlos about Melissa, the young American woman whom I'd met on the bus during the conference who was coming to them for help in contacting her dead son. Over the course of a few ayahuasca ceremonies Juan and Carlos established contact with the spirit of her son, and managed to assuage her worries. "He came here to do important work, and now that mission has been completed he has returned to the spirit world to continue that work," Carlos told her.

"My son led me to ayahuasca, and now ayahuasca has led me back to my son," Melissa said to me later about her experiences. "I feel like I can move on now."

This isn't some new age charlatanism. Until you've felt the world of spirits it's all words, all something you've seen on TV in shows like *Charmed*. But the world of spirits is a raging quantum hyperdimension right next door. We can't see electrons, or neutrons, or the spin and charm of atoms as they move in their subatomic dances, yet we believe in them, our entire Western culture's high technology is built on this faith. In the jungle there's no room for faith. If the shaman can't heal his patient, they die.

And more than that, if the patient stays sick for a long time it's the *curandero* who is paying for the herbs and the plants, the medicine that treats them. The crucial difference with the Amazonian worldview is that it's the plants and trees they call *the doctores*. They are the ones that heal; the *curanderos* are just the facilitators. The world of spirit is an energy rich ecology which those with the right training can enter and manipulate—for good or ill.

"This is my work, money's not important. It's best to have good people here," Juan says, pointing to his new students in the house. He says he found the Shaman Conference draining, mainly because so many people were all after a little bit of him, and some people had the wrong attitude to the medicine. Westerners may have an interest, a mental calling, but in the world of spirit everything is energy, so how you approach ayahuasca affects how it approaches you. This energy work is draining and some people suck his energy, he says, they take and take and someone has to give back.

Now I know why he has that pained look on his face and where those mixed messages in his body language come from. I feel like I know him better, the good doctor and his gringo apprentice, Carlos. They're good people, working with the spirit in servitude, trying to further the science of *curanderismo* from humble beginnings here in this suburban home. Not to say that *curanderos* opening up healing retreats and charging tourist prices aren't also doing good work, but the simplicity and earnestness with which Juan approaches the science is inspiring.

After all the *brujeria* worries Juan wasn't sure he was going to do a ceremony tonight. But after our arrival and talk with him, and shared energy, well, it shifted things.

After our interview we head back to town and get ready for the ceremony. At approximately 5:30 p.m. that afternoon I have a flash of

DMT hangover, like someone's opened up my head to the astral plane again to have a look in. *Brujeria?* Or Juan doing a quick diagnostic spiritual once-over? I feel like the ayahuasca's kicking in already and I'm slightly nauseous, like I shouldn't have had those salty chips with Theo Valis at the Yellow Rose an hour ago.

I mention this *brujeria* feeling to Bowman, who's feeling wary about tonight. For some reason he's got it in his head about black magic, too, and he seems to think the break-in that happened at Juan's and the claims of *brujeria* have put some psychic dampener on things, that we're warping the probability fields with these type of thoughts and attracting the very energy we're scared of.

So when the taxi we're in with Vance goes one block around the Plaza de Armas before the tire punctures, Bowman and I look at each other with concerned looks: "*Brujeria*" we say in unison. The black magic cloud is hanging over us like a self-fulfilling prophecy. Our second taxi drops us at Juan's and I see the Sanctum Sanctorium all lit up in full splendor from within like a mansion. Cautiously, we enter.

A few more gringos are here from the conference—Johan, a long, dark-haired website coder with olive skin and sad, haunted eyes like a bloodhound; Alan, a young English teen who looks like he should be gearing up for a night out; and some middle-aged women from the States. As Bowman, Vance, and I take a seat on the cold marble floor in the good doctor's ayahuasca waiting room—the family lounge room—I look down and realize that I, too, am wearing black, a black t-shirt overlaid with a long black sleeveless kaftan, which seems to match our *brujeria* vibe.

Just then I look up at the wall opposite to see a painting of a black puma, one green eye all glassed over, a subtle smile hanging on its face like it's seen its prey and is about to start the dance. Like many *curanderos* throughout South America, Juan has adopted the black puma as his spirit-totem.

It's a powerful ally to have, and is said to help connect to the heavenly realms, as well as being a ferocious fighter and a cunning opponent. Juan calls him up when he has to go into battle on the spirit-plane, along with his other ally, the green dragon, to fight the *brujeria* that haunts him. He's sitting opposite the puma's steely gaze now, drinking in its power.

The flash of recognition I see in the puma's eyes jolts a hidden memory embedded in that dream I had before I left Australia. It started with the giant ants, and the lesson of acceptance their sting brought. After the acceptance I had a lucid vision of a black puma walking into my bedroom as cool as you please, escorted by Amos, my black cat. The two felines padded onto the carpet right through to where I was sleeping and I awoke in full consciousness within the dream, watching them without fear. The mighty black beast's muscles rippled under smooth skin as it walked low to the ground with the dignity of a king and approached my bed.

Part of me completely freaked out at the reality of a black puma there in front of me, living, breathing, stalking its dream-prey. But the rest of me knew it was not just my friend but my ally, my power-totem for my South American journey, and as it accepted me I accepted it. Now here I was, under its gaze...

The sounds of Hollywood spirits roll out from the TV in the room opposite our waiting area, where Juan's wife and children sleep. The door opens and one of his young daughters walks through brazenly and goes into the kitchen for her dinner.

This is the family home, and all the domestic rhythms of life must coincide with the spirit world. There's no altar, bones, skulls, or clichéd magical paraphernalia here—they don't serve any purpose in healing, Juan says; to him they're simply things for show to please the tourists. There's no Shipibo cloths here, no beads; Juan follows the simple procedure of having us sit in the dark and drink ayahuasca and receive healing. "*It has nothing to do with the feathers in your hair and everything to do with the feeling in your heart,*" he says.

Juan has his feet up on the table, hands behind his head, relaxed, the master. The ayahuasca is in a four-liter plastic water bottle on the waiting room table. There's an air of surety about him as he tips the ayahuasca bottle up and down and gives it a good stir. There's ten gringos here tonight, including Juan's apprentice Carlos, and one local Peruvian man—Cesar, a cousin or something of Juan's who studies the art with him, helping out in ceremonies with *icaros* and energy work.

I'm sitting with my back to the kitchen wall. The Israeli couple is opposite me against the far wall, under the window. Ariel looks like an ayahuasca Jesus in his long white robe and beard, his partner Meera all calm and centered.

This is the first chance I've had to meet the American students that are here for the initiation course and they're an interesting bunch of twenty-something seekers themselves. They're not your usual clichéd hippies, or new agers, but everyday Americans from all walks of life that have felt the call of spirit, and traveled all the way down here to Peru to follow it.

Len is six-foot tall and stocky, with long dark hair and a cheeky smile. He looks like he should be a WWF wrestler, but he also has the quiet and gentle demeanor of a seeker. He chain-smokes incessantly and has an opinion about everything. He's sitting on a chair closest to me, and it turns out this is his first ayahuasca session tonight, and he's a bit nervous.

Next to him is Jolane, a mid-thirties American woman who's been living in England for a number of years. She's a big girl and is acclimatizing to the diet and the rigors of the medicine, but she's also well versed in psychonautics and countercultural thought from her formative years in Bristol with the *Dreamhaven* crew. She's ridden out the rave nineties and now finds herself smack dab in the middle of the Peruvian jungle, learning to let ayahuasca into her life.

Next along the wall is Julia, a tall, slim woman with a nest of blond dreadlocks framing a long face, tied up like an Egyptian headrest that accentuates her height. She carries herself with a quiet dignity, a well-balanced poise that echoes a Nubian priestess gracing the streets of some lost Ur city from prehistory. She's been a regular participant at Santo Daime masses in California, and her respect for the spirit of the vine shines through. She's also the Director of Educational Outreach for MAPS (the Multi-Disciplinary Association of Psychedelic Studies), a well-known American drug reform non-profit, and was one of the speakers at the conference.

Her friend, Carina, is a little harder to figure. She's quiet and pretty, with shoulder length dark hair, and has just finished an apprenticeship with herbal medicine in New York State. It looks like she should be curling up in front of a good DVD, not drinking ayahuasca, but appearances can be deceiving.

Juan watches the locals arrive for their healing, greeting them warmly one by one. I realize that this is the first ayahuasca ceremony I've had in Peru that isn't just gringos, that has indigenous people coming for healing, not visions or other Western desires, and it humbles me. But there's not enough room for this many people in the one room, so the paying guests come first and the local overflow relocates to the kitchen. It makes me feel a bit weird being one of the "first class" ayahuasca drinkers, but no one seems to mind.

Carlos goes round smudging us with *Nicotiana rustica* smoke in a beautiful Tibetan metal urn, swinging it to cleanse the air and lowering it over our backs and crown charkas, cleansing us. "During the ceremony Juan will do a personal healing on you," he explains, instructing us how to go up when our names are called, edging our way in the dark, and sit on the small table in front of the maestro.

Finally he fixes the curtains to block out the moonlight and noise, and we're ready to begin. I can feel the kundalini rainfall down my spine, tingling beads of energy building at my base chakra, and I grip them and bring the energy up a few notches to help fuel the imminent lift off. I look over at Bowman and we catch eyes and smile. Here we go.

"There's a chance you might encounter bad spirits outside, away from the protection Juan's cast around the house," Carlos warns, taking a seat next to his teacher. They both think there's *brujeria* about from the break-in this morning, and I dart a glance at Bowman and see him nervously twiddling his thumbs at all the black magic talk. Sitting here under the gaze of the black puma, its one clear eye staring down, a mainline to the spirit world, I don't know what all the fuss is about.

"Bad spirits don't like tobacco," Carlos continues. "It's a form of protection and it also maintains visions and potentiates the ayahuasca. Keep your eyes open and look into the total darkness to find your vision spot. Don't fall asleep. Stand up if you have to, be vigilant. Work at it."

Over in his chair, Juan begins pouring the ayahuasca. The waiting room has become the journey room. One by one don Juan calls us up to take our medicine, going counter-clockwise around the room, with Julia first. Early today I was talking to Theo Valis, telling him about my ayahuasca experiences throughout the conference, and he urged me to up my dosages to push beyond the threshold I had been encountering. Two cups, up front, he said, see how you go. So I ask Carlos to ask Juan if that's okay, and Juan doesn't mind.

"*Salud!*" I say, scoffing down two little wooden cups in a row of the dark brown liquid. It's surprisingly smooth—the cleanest brew I've had yet. Juan doesn't need to drink, he says, he can ride on our wings when we're flying, but he takes a small dose to be part of the group, nonetheless. My base chakra energy is buzzing and my crown chakra feels open, my heart light. I am ready to journey.

"Keep in control, like a cat," Carlos offers. "Don't cry out, don't lose control, focus on the spirits—they're here to heal you."

As the lights go off the ayahuasca comes on strong. Within seconds a ballooning consciousness expands in my head as the ayahuasca rivers spill into the center of my vision like water going down a plughole, a swirling, concentric whirlpool formed on the canvas of my mind. It grows and envelops my own vibrational wavefront till I am stripped raw and rising and becoming this thing; it has swallowed me whole and then it spits me out the other side as Juan begins singing his *icaros*.

I'm plunged back into darkness, but this time I'm not alone. Each *icaro* brings forth visions, fleeting hyperspatial entities that streak past and sometimes stop and chat. Hundreds of spirits come and go over the course of the ceremony like dream people, moving too fast to stick in my conscious mind.

At one point an insect spirit appears, a small, bright buzzing mantis, red, green, and orange fluttering like the hummingbird, a red hot chili pepper that bares its private parts to me as if offering itself up to be known. I stare at it for a few seconds, long enough to ensure it's really there and it's really trying to communicate with me, but when I'm unable to engage it in conversation everything melts and the scene shifts to other transdimensional offerings.

The feeling of merging with a greater force is omnipresent, and it's only through a huge force of will that I'm able to hold my vibrational pattern together and not merge with this cosmic ALL. I feel like the drop struggling against joining the ocean. The magnetizing pull of this force is so overwhelming, so strong, like the event horizon of a black hole that I have to ride away and down from it, performing hitherto unknown locks and holds on my energetic body to bring myself down.

I'm talking to myself in my head, by the way, but not in words. It's like speaking in *spirit,* in proto-emotional bursts that supersede words. I'm also speaking to spirits that are telling me things, secret things about myself and the cosmos and how to navigate it all. I smile and chuckle and realize there's so much to do here, so much to learn, it's like I've finally been born into the cosmic brotherhood and all my friends are here to help me on my journey—but there's so many opportunities and options cascading by they're overwhelming.

I smile and ask the spirits if I can do this, but after, and use the hand signal mudras I've picked up on DMT to navigate our communication, quick finger rolls to signal speeding up and the thumb and forefinger together to make the OK symbol to agree with the thought energy bursts they're sending. I want to go back to this later, I beam to them, to not forget the beauty of this hyperdimensional communication, and I use the finger mudras to place the information they have given me over my heart, to lock it in there for when I will need it. Later, of course, as in a dream, the information is gone from my mind, but I know it is still within me like a seed, waiting for the right time to bloom.

After the interspecies chatter it's back to the event horizon. The overwhelming energy returns, the ecstatic merging into the Godhead, but unlike the DMT flash, this time it's all in slow-motion. I feel like Jesus on the cross, I know what he felt then, the unbridled merging with the vibrational energy of the Creator, the raw and overwhelming energy of soul disintegration. It's too much for any human to bear, that's why he had to be nailed down, to be forced into a position where there was no return, no off switch. Because even though he was the Son of God, he too was flesh, and the flesh is weak and has inbuilt mechanisms to defend itself. I have to pull away...

My spiritual navigation kicks in to protect me and I pull back from the core to a safer distance, still observing its Promethean energies. "Jesus Christ," I say without irony, exhaling into the shimmering dark. *Bastante.* It is very strong, this spirit medicine, these two cups are stronger than any brew I have had before. I feel like I'm reading the book of ME and the instruction manual was inside all along, hidden away in the back of my head where I never thought to look for it.

Outside the house the roar of motorbikes peaks and then suddenly slows, right outside the Sanctum Sanctorium. The purring idle of their engines rolls out into the night like beasts on the prowl, a pack of black pumas marking their territory and hunting for a pure heart to feast upon. I worry that they can smell my open heart as I invoke the spirit of the black puma guardian and thank fuck that I'm his spirit brother and he is my ally. I can't see him but I know he's there, staring down at me in the dark, watching and devouring me, and I honor him for it.

Along the wall to my right I can hear Vance groaning a soft spirit cat-throat sound in hologrammatic resonance, and everyone in the room shifts posture in response to the moment, letting the energy settle. I have the intuition that when I feel something, everyone else in the room is feeling it too, as we tune into the group mind.

It's that "surround-sound" feeling again; I can feel an empathic carrier wave of consciousness all around and focus in on individuals or become one with the group. The ayahuasca headspace is like a web browser—where do you want to go today? Who do you want to be? What are you giving back? The Tao is in flux, the feedback loops ache for the return of what they give, and once you've fed you must feed in return. The student feels, knows, becomes, and then reciprocates.

Back in the physical zone Juan's still singing his *icaros* as people shuffle about in the dark, getting up and vomiting outside on the front lawn. Don Juan calls up the ayahuasca drinkers to sit in front of him on the table and receive our personal healing. It feels like we're being called to meet our maker, to open ourselves to him and let his vibrational wisdom flow into us. I can feel Juan's own energetic being, his vibrational wavefront before me and it's heavy and dense and radiating power, like a gravity wave that threatens to crush me in its wake. Jesus, it's all so strong, so much, I haven't even purged yet. I can't handle that one-on-one.

I'm feeling a bit sick; the medicine went down so smooth and stayed down for so long, working its juju deep into me, and for a long while I thought I wouldn't purge. But now it has come upon me with a sharp weight in the gut. I take a deep breath and stand up to get some fresh air, fumbling in the dark and pulling back the curtain that leads to the kitchen and the doorless entrance to the backyard, passing a huddle of local Peruvians scrambled on the floor to the left on a blanket, tripping hard on ayahuasca themselves.

As I walk outside past the dogs I do a little jig, the ayahuasca energy coursing through me and connecting me to everything and everyone, every moment fresh like a newborn babe. The golden labrador is awake and staring up at me, sparkling, and we overlap our wavefronts and play before I head step-by-step down the path to the toilet, concentrating firmly on my motions, my body drunk and that feeling like I'm walking underwater upon me.

The sky is alive tonight with la luna peeking through fractal cloud webs, full and ripe and shining down in the backyard, lighting the trees and the ground with its spectral grace. I stop and do a complete rhythmic series of mudra hand signals and aerobic exercises with the fluid muscles of my flesh, feeling my hands and arms and spiraling round and round and round in the moonlight. Heading to the toilet I stop to purge spectacularly in front of a small tree, gripping it for balance as my mouth opens impossibly wide, and a wall of green vomit spews forth, covering the tree and me in ayahuasca retch.

Then I'm heaving and heaving and heaving over and over again, more times than I've got fluid in me to bring up and the world's spinning and the spirits are chattering away and I'm translinguistic again, erupting into glossolalia sound commands, speaking with the spirits and the night to regain my center. "*Whoo bil bill boo be bup radaaa da doo da deech cho chala la lun lu looga,*" the words just spill out of me, secret words, power words, word-vibrational essences whose very sounds are ways to sculpt the world: the Word.

I'm vomiting hard: five, six waves of peristalsis that leave me wracked. Suddenly there are chunks of purge stuck in my throat and I can't breathe, and the anaconda is coming through me again ... The snake splashes against the tree full force, taking the brunt of all my fears and sick, the tree takes it all in and lets it come out of me. And when I've hucked and spluttered and managed to breathe air again, I rub my hand up and down her central trunk, I caress my tree lover, thanking and honoring her, before moving onto the toilet, finally, for the second type of purge.

In the fluorescent light of the toilet cubicle my jungle superpowers come on strong as the ayahuasca vision kicks in. My eye is perceiving more than the usual twenty-four frames per second. The shutter of the eye is opening to drink in the streaming multidimensional movement of flesh against the invisible canvas. It looks like I have six hands, like an insect, that I'm smearing across time, streaking, hyperdimensional. This is amazing. How does the posthuman deal with the baseline needs of the larval reality? How much higher dimensional reality would you be willing to permanently integrate, I ask myself in telepathic dialogue, becoming superhuman, posthuman, up the vibratory scale?

Not quite THIS much, I realize as I reach for the toilet paper and light trails smear in the wake of my hand as if under a strobe light. I feel like my skin is an eggshell permanently cracking to reveal the yolk within in some sort of alchemical transformation. The thought of navigating a world permanently strobing like *Koyaanisqatsi* on fast-forward frightens me back to the baseline. I'm speeding-hallucinating-melting with an expanded awareness, hot flush and anal cramps, needing to shit and receive God in the same eternal now. Elvis died on the porcelain throne, I remember, as my second purge bleeds out my behind, cleansing, emptying, and letting go of all my stress and negativity.

It feels like my spirit ballast has reset itself, that with my physical lightening I'm now able to let go on a vibrational level as well, and I might be able to face the waves of force back in the ceremony room. After a few infinite lifetimes I drag myself back into the dark, warm room and the sound of Juan's *icaros* envelops me. And then it's my turn to make my way up to the *maestro*.

"Rak...Rak Rollerskate Razam—is that really your name?" Carlos asks in the dark.

As I stand up the ayahuasca kicks back in strong and clear, like it's locked onto the carrier wave. I can feel Juan there two meters in front of me, magnetizing and pulling me in with his spiritual tractor beam. I'm tuning into him in a harmonic lock and he's buzzing, I can read his energy, and he is the father, the doctor, the *maestro*. His wavefront hits me with such force that I feel flattened. I am raw and open to the waves of energy pouring into me with such spiritual impact that I barely manage to sit down on the table in front of him before I faint.

"*Wee wooo boo ba da na ba geeeee whooooooo,*" I groove and everyone breaks into laughter. I can feel a concentric circle pattern in the spirit space before me, hanging there like a forcefield and it's so strong I have to lock myself down. I pass my right hand over my heart and wave it across like a touch-sensitive light, and lock down my spirit energy a few notches to be able to cope with just being in Juan's presence, the *maestro* of the black puma and green dragon.

Juan laughs at my glossolalia noises and he checks me out, reads my energy body there in the dark and starts singing an *icaro* he thinks is appropriate for what healing I need. He's holding a ritual *shacapa* leaf fan and as he hits me on the stomach with it a ball of golden energy ripples back in reaction. The *shacapa* shaking starts climbing up the stomach to the chest, over the heart, over the throat and onto the face, right over my third eye.

It settles into the same pattern as the hummingbird's wings, like the DMT vibration that invokes theta wave state, beating down again and again and again and again till something shifts and opens and gushes out, like spiritual-pineal-juice. And that DMT feeling, that theta wave eyeball rolling in the back of my head feeling descends on me, and the ayahuasca hummingbird has arrived. It's on my third eye now and it's merging with me as Juan moves up to the crown chakra and cleanses it and the waves of energy are coming and coming and coming out of me, like my head's broken open and spilt my essence into the stars.

My body is still sitting there in front of the good doctor as he blows smoke over me, cleansing and purifying, but I'm loaded, barreling through the cosmic energy all around me, trying to stay sane. The *shacapa* beats against my chest now, harder and harder, and as I tune into its *chuk chuk chuk* rhythm it tunes me further into the tryptamine groove, threatening to spiral out of control. I'm holding onto the edge of my soul lest I slip over into the abyss of infinite vibration . . .

On some fluid, astral level I instantly go into action, assuming protective mudras with my fingers and adjusting my psychic ballast. I open secret doors within myself and lock down my energy, closing off the upper harmonic receptors in case I faint and die. It feels like what the flower does at the end of the day, when it curls up its buds against the night. *I lock my heart down.*

Like he has throughout the night, Juan sings again, magic *icaros* specially chosen to match our vibrational wavefronts and smooth and heal whatever anomalies he finds there. The doctor is in the house. And then just like that, he stops singing and it's over. Sweet Jesus, I break into a glossolalia thank you, a "*whip bib aabbaoo abooo,*" and everyone laughs again.

Dazed and spent I stumble back in the dark to my place by the wall, under the hidden gaze of the black puma, and slowly the ceremony winds up and the lights go back on. Bowman looks over at me similarly dazed and spent, and we both know we've gone through something immense.

It feels like the aftermath of a thunderstorm, after the spaceship has landed. I'm feeling drunk, ayahuasca drunk, definitely an altered headspace hanging over me, echoes of ayahuasca vision as I look across at my fellow ayahuasca drinkers strobing like cartoon cells. We all blink and look at each other with the stunned-mullet smiles of post-coital bliss and awe, breaking into giggles and sighs.

Bowman's sitting next to me whistling gentle *icaros* into his camera recorder. Our media chakras are engaged and as I break out my laptop and try to form thoughts and type them out with numb fingers. I'm coming down but the brain is still receiving the signal, the field pattern recognition, so Bowman and I go outside to get it all down, data-dump the experience into his recording gear by moonlight in the front yard.

The funny thing about all this is the remarkable similarity of all our experiences. We're both intelligent white-boys with a smattering of quantum know-how and anthropological awareness; we can both pour forth language to navigate the transcendental experience. Yet when it's put into words it's immediately diluted:

"Aya opens you up on a molecular level, and you can feel the molecules of your body vibrating with other vibrational beings. This is the book of You, the next step beyond the objectivity of science and the living science of the universe. This is the global child becoming the global adult, taking on the power—and the responsibility—of this awareness," I pontificate in the night, my heart chakra open and pulsing.

We're not alone, far from it. We're surrounded in an infinite sea of cosmic awareness, of being, and waveforms of sentient energy layering all the way to the core, the Source that births and contains all in the delicate cosmic ecology that must be maintained. I've come back from my ayahuasca journey with a deep sense of compassion, responsibility, and servitude to the Great Spirit in all things.

I can feel the connection we have with it, how we take from it, every breath, every thought and deed, and how it feeds us. It is the mother, the father, the Source of all things. And it must be fed in return—reciprocal maintenance, as the Armenian philosopher Gurdjieff called it. Our energy feeds the moon and the moon feeds the sun, the sun feeds the galactic sun, and so on through the synaptic web of the universe. And when the web of life isn't fed it takes what it needs to maintain the cosmic balance: earthquakes, floods, tsunamis. Gaia is alive and like a good mother, must be treated with respect.

This knowledge and sense of purpose fills me and I can't contain my joy—I'm up on the grass and spinning like a whirling dervish, round and round, cutting through the air, feeling the weight of my body as I try to ground myself back down, into the flesh. It feels as if the more I spin the denser the movements become, that I can crack the vibrational barrier entirely.

But somewhere in my mind I know I'm peaking too early, that this whole cosmic dance I'm on must slow down to be integrated, and that throws me off-kilter, down into the grass, twisting my left ankle.

I am, to paraphrase Oscar Wild, in the gutter and looking at the stars. Or as the Sufi poet Rumi so eloquently said, "There are hundreds of ways to kneel and kiss the ground."

Later, still high in vibrational attunement with the Source, I fall asleep on the front lawn, staring at the moon, feeding her waves of my own energy and bathing in her love and light. Juan's *icaros* are still coursing through me, sonic mantras imprinted on my waveform, sunk deep into me. My fingers are tapping the beats of his song onto my chest, over my heart, affirming and sealing them deep within me—for next time.

Sealed within is the key to the kingdom and the secret to the mystery, the mystery of the ONE, the ALL. I have hidden it away in my heart, this infinite wonder, this thing that is too big and shocking for the monkey mind to hold.

I have put it deep within me where it will be safe, for when I am ready to accept it.

11

Downtime

The Yellow Rose of Texas, Iquitos
WEDNESDAY JULY 12–THURSDAY JULY 13, 2006

What do you do the day after storming Heaven? The day after all your preconceived notions of reality are exploded and you're left coming down off God?

Bowman, Vance, and I are lounging across two tables at the Yellow Rose of Texas, our Western comfort zone, basking in the afterglow of our cosmic communion. It sort of feels like the "Last Supper" but it's the "First Breakfast," with ayahuasca Jesus and the disciples of the vine. Even the ayahuasca comedown is cosmic bliss. I can feel the God-essence shining through and animating us all, just a heartbeat away. Enjoy every moment, the world around me sings, be present, drink in the light and the now.

The holographic resonances are shining through the day, wave packets of information from beyond the curtain, the Logos peeking out in the smile of a small child, the path of a bird as it sails against the wind, in the way it's 11:11 when we look at a digital clock, and a million other things besides. It's reassuring to be around Gerald and the cowgirls, and *la bonita senoritas* from El Gringo bar next door as they bat their eyelids and flirt with us. Now in our still-heightened perception I can feel the energy they radiate, as if I'm tuning into a favorite radio channel and there's a warm pool of familiarity.

It feels funny to be here with the other ayahuasca seekers and run of the mill jungle tourists and missionaries. I see that family that was at the Butterfly Farm with Vance and me the other day at one of the

Gringo Bar tables and wave. I wonder what other tourist attractions they've seen, and if they've figured out yet that the celestial realm is alive and well and they, too, can backpack its light-filled vistas, basking in the inner sanctums of Creation.

There's a number of familiar faces converging on the Yellow Rose for breakfast this morning—Marty and Rachel, Johan, James and Sarah, Bernstein, Theo Valis, Kevin Furnas, Jack, Phoenix, and others, and everyone has their own stories, their own experiences of the central mystery we've all experienced on ayahuasca. We kind of sound like rejects from a science-fiction convention babbling on about experiential quantum theory and psychic healing, hanging out at the university of life café. Ayahuasca is our school, our teacher, and our passion.

Yet in the back of my head the journalist in me is aware that we're commodifying the ayahuasca experience, condensing it into something comprehensible that will trickle down and be shared with other Westerners, who will themselves be drawn into its web. Iquitos has the feeling of Goa in the early days of the trance music scene. It could easily become the next global party town for seekers and thrillseekers unless they're helped to see the medicine the vine embodies—and I'm sure the vine will be the first one to teach them that.

It strikes me now how far we've all come from those first virginal days at the start of the conference, listening to the *curanderos* and scientists talk about ayahuasca. Just how quickly the brain adapts is evinced by how normal it seems today to be describing the spirit worlds and the central mystery. We're knee-deep in our apprenticeships now, giddy like schoolchildren recounting our jungle experiences, a firm bond of camaraderie between us. And to be fair, we're not just consuming the ayahuasca experience like another commodity, it's also changing us, consuming us, and there's no guarantee who or what we'll become at the end of all this.

"Vibrational sound energy... It's what happens when you tap into the *cosmic consciousness*," Bowman theorizes. "You really learn that it's all about sound. Even physical matter is just different vibrations of sound energy. In theoretical physics they call it 'string theory,' which I think is absolutely correct. Superstrings resonate at different frequencies; vibration and sound is the key. It is the all."

"Yeah, well," Vance says in dulcet radio announcer tones and with a gentle shake of his white-blond head. "I always ask ayahuasca for the same thing and I never get it. And that's for courage." As I look into his blue eyes framed by crow's feet, I think Vance's age is catching up with him. He looks younger than his sixty-one years, but hiking through the jungle and drinking hallucinogenic brews is a young man's game, and he's feeling it. Yet no matter what the rigors of ayahuasca and the jungle throw at him, he keeps going back for more.

"Vance I would say you have courage, because you show up," Bernstein offers from two tables down.

"I'm realizing courage is like in *The Wizard of Oz*—it's always in the person you just have to wake it up inside them," Vance agrees with a tired smile.

"You're not the Cowardly Lion, Vance, you're the jaguar," I say, remembering the animal essence he gives off in ayahuasca sessions, the purring of his spirit, my cat-brother.

One of the best things about full ayahuasca immersion into the holographic wavefront of the Implicate is that you can come back from it. I feel that we ayahuasca drinkers are like prehistoric fish testing the air outside the seas, mutating and freaking out at the enormity of it all before crawling back into the water on our long journey of evolution. You do come back, but never the same. The ability to disengage from the wave, to integrate the experience and take stock, this too, is one of the gifts.

But as we sit here sipping on papaya juice and watching the other tourists overlap in their particle realities, I can't help but be aware that underneath our play of forms, the game of us all, is a hyperdimensional matrix that animates and sustains, that we are just a three-dimensional shadow of.

As I'm trying to sneak a look at the Shipiba women's fabrics without them seeing I'm looking, and taking that as initiating the dance of the *manta*-sellers, Bob pulls up in a *motorcarro* taxi with a good-looking model couple from L.A., just back from an ayahuasca circle with Percy last night.

"I had lots of visual effects for the first time," L.A. guy says, smiling and gesticulating as a Frank Sinatra song blares out some crazy-cat vibes, and we're tweaked onto it, reading the energy embedded in the song as the roar of motorbikes and three-wheeled *motorcarros* stream by, and snippets of conversation weave in and out across the tables.

Bob's looking pretty darn despondent this morning and Phoenix puts a big, motherly arm around him and says she'll take him out on a boat trip down the Amazon this afternoon to cheer him up. After all those ceremonies drinking with Norma he still feels he has issues to work on—ayahuasca sure hasn't been a quick-fix for him.

"It's not like that; this isn't a Western drug that you turn off and on like a tap. The visitation and enlightenment of the spirits can happen at any time," Bob says with a forlorn look. But a shaman isn't going to cure him, the brew isn't going to fix his problems with women, not alone—he has to be able to open up and unlock the safeguards we all place on ourselves, and he knows it.

Bob's an augur of things to come, and my own problems with women are about to begin. The rest of the day is spent indulging in some serious downtime, recharging the batteries and falling back into the Western comfort zones. That night the spirits come to me in my dreams and give me a good wake up call.

I'm still body-high and flushed clean from my ayahuasca session, charged with kundalini sex-magic, a ball of energy coiled but not spent at my base chakra. I'm horny as a teenager. In a psychic flash I know the spirits are here too, drawn to my energy like an open book, or maybe an *Australian Penthouse* magazine. I still have to write that bloody article before God knows what new overwhelming hallucinogenic encounter overtakes me. I just don't have any idea how to tone down the enormity of what I've been through for a newsstand men's magazine. Or for any mainstream audience, for that matter.

As I toss and turn in the hot and humid bunkhouse that night, my energy wavefront casting out into the shadows, I can literally *feel* energy-signatures dancing around me.

Just before midnight a sudden jolt of energy hits me and wakes me from a light sleep. A stab of energy hits my groin, and there's a feeling like a hand reaching for my erection as it rages into life. I'm in the dark on a top bunk. The spirit women are all around and I can feel their invisible touch, like cobwebs brushing on skin and a slight breeze . . .

There're no visuals but I swear to God I can feel this spirit woman caressing me, a ghost face teasing me as I react under her touch. Before I can stop myself I'm tonguing this invisible goddess, licking the rim of her lips, kissing her passionately and my senses have no trouble affirming that she is there and I'm not doing this alone. There's a slight DMT buzz in that familiar front part of the right brain, and as I kiss her liquid language *la la la la li* slips off my tongue as our mouths meet.

I'm drawn into her, our essences meeting, but then I'm fighting it, loving it. I'm scared and still reading the spirit-DMT energy and feeling the spirits here, multiple spirit-women. I'm a beacon to them and I don't even know how to protect myself, or if I even should. Succubuses, or should that be succubi? What the fuck am I doing? There goes the ayahuasca ban on sex; here I am making out with a harem of ghost women the first chance I get out in the astral.

I block the succubi with my psychic intent, disengaging from their omnivorous embrace and force myself back to sleep. But that doesn't stop them. I know the feeling of this frequency, it's the DMT wavelength. I'm awake, lucid dreaming, ayahuasca dreaming. Whatever they are they return in my dream and as I struggle they morph into withered crones, descending on me like a flock of divorcees.

They have incredibly wrinkled faces, like the way your fingers and toes go when they've been in the bath too long, and their faces are revealed to have one giant Cyclopean eye. I get the same vibe off them as from the Shipiba *manta*-fabric sellers, like they're native to this place, with that same patient energy, waiting, just waiting to engage a gringo.

The dreamscape shifts and I'm thankful that I'm not having sex with them, now their real faces are visible, but there I go, look out, do I ever learn?

Suddenly I lie down with a younger, more beautiful Cyclopean sister, and we sleep side by side in their realm . . .

"You have beautiful eyes," says Diane, one of the Gringo Bar girls the next morning. "Are you married?"

I'm hot and sweaty and horny as all hell. Iquitos is full of it this morning. So much sex in the air the clouds finally burst and rain down their cool seed on us. The ayahuasca healing has made me fit and healthy and I can feel that kundalini build-up pinging up my back from the base chakra, playing the superstrings. And, strangely enough, from breakfast on, all the women of Iquitos are flirting with me. They're feeling it, too, reading my energy and giving me back fluttering eyelids and deep stares.

There is life beyond the air-conditioned comfort of the Yellow Rose, but as the ayahuasca seekers return from their day as normal tourists soaking in the sights, we all find ourselves back in its Texan-down-home ambience yet again for breakfast. The sex energy is strong today and as like energy attracts like, Tarzana pulls up in a *motorcarro* with "Jungle," the Lapland boy-shaman under her arm. With his long straight hair he looks like a knight right out of *Lord of the Rings*.

They look like they've been fucking all night, their hair freshly washed, skin radiant with afterglow. The news firestorms around the tables that she's actually married him, and as I go up and congratulate them I imagine they're both big cats, shape-changing shamans that love to fuck.

That's when I realize that if drinking of ayahuasca is like a relationship, then there comes a time when she wants to have sex with you. Back at our table Richard Grossman, the sound therapist from L.A. who plays a mean didgeridoo, tells his own story about home base with ayahuasca:

"We're going to fuck," the ayahuasca spirit told him on his strongest ever brew. A beautiful blue-skinned woman materialized and proceeded to devour him. The ayahuasca was so strong his eighty-six-year-old *maestro* couldn't stay in his place; he lost control and fell to the floor. And on the occasional ayahuasca journey Richard still sees that blue-skinned goddess; they now have a long-term on and off again relationship. Me? I just lie down with Cyclops women.

The smoke that cleanses and protects, the *mapacho* smoke is what I need to master, that's one of the wisdoms aya told me in her visions the other night. The women here have a term—*amontes*—which they reserve to describe the raw sexual need men have. It translates to something like "a thorn in his side," that feeling of sexual energy they use to explain why men stray from monogamous relationships and have multiple partners.

Some women here not only put up with their men straying, they become actively involved in making sure their man goes with a woman they know and trust, a girlfriend or a relative, to keep it all in the family, so to speak. As I feel the spirits circling, good and bad, I know I have to get back in control lest I spend my sex and lose my power in the spirit world. Ayahuasca, fickle mistress that she is, might not forgive me.

So in what I am starting to understand is no coincidence, Vance announces over fruit salad at breakfast that he has lined up a photo shoot with a *tabaquera*—an indigenous woman who performs her psychic work through "smoking" patients, reading their energy and calling on the spirit in the tobacco to help her heal. It's funny, after all my sex dreams, to be going off today to interview a *tabaquera*. It's as if my Jungian unconscious is picking up on the Freudian pun of all those cigarettes being smoked. Sounds like just what I need, but there's just one problem—and her name is Mariella.

Mariella Noriega de Shoemaker, wife of Alan, the conference organizer, and mother of two. Vance has also organized with Alan, who's away in Cuzco with a post-conference tour group, to have Mariella act as our guide and translator with the *tabaquera,* and as we swing by the offices of her *Chinchilla* (Dragonfly) tour agency on Calle Monero, the magnetism of this woman hits me. She is so beautiful, like a flower in spring, and my energy field is buzzing and overlapping as I read her womanhood. I'm drinking it in and so help me, I want her.

The three of us take a *motorcarro* to out near the airport, deep into the shanty town suburbs of Iquitos, and I have to be careful not to stare at Mariella's chiseled, gentle beauty opposite me.

The *tabaquera,* Sara Alicia Ferreira Yaimes, turns out to be a middle-aged housewife who has a nice, modest brick home by Peruvian standards. There's a dog calendar on the wall and a TV in the lounge room—an old black and white model screening American sitcoms with Spanish subtitles. *I Dream of Jeannie* is on, an appropriate choice for the house of a female shamana.

Sara is very neat and proper in a light pink dress, her raven hair tied back in a hair ring and a blush of lipstick on her lips. Her eyes sparkle with an indefinable spirit and joy, brimming with motherly love, like an Italian mother who always says "you're too skinny" as she pinches your cheeks and fattens you up with a big plate of spaghetti, but this time she's feeding the soul. Not the witch woman I was expecting at all. She also has a passing resemblance to Oprah Winfrey crossed with Condoleezza Rice. That same strong smile, that same inner strength and confidence, a fierce but friendly energy and passion that exudes out of her.

Sara works with *Nicotiana rustica,* the Amazonian jungle tobacco also known as *mapacho,* which has up to eighteen percent more nicotine as the common variety, *Nicotiana tabacum.* It's frequently used in conjunction with the ayahuasca brew to heighten the hallucinatory effects and to cleanse a space and a person during an ayahuasca ceremony. The relationship is so synergistic that the myths also intertwine—where ayahuasca is said to be the daughter of the earth, the tobacco plant is said to be the daughter of ayahuasca.

Tobacco has been used as a shamanic inebriate for millennia throughout the world. In the South American tradition tobacco is used for purification, connecting with spirits and healing. Unlike social smoking in the West, tobacco is considered a sacred plant here in South America, food for the soul. It also nourishes and feeds the spirits themselves, strengthening them. It can be used for protection, cleansing spaces of negative energies, and amplifying whatever intention you create for prayer and manifestation.

At the ayahuasca circle with Juan the other night he was praising tobacco, saying that with the protection of a single *mapacho* cigarette he can walk through the jungles of Peru or the urban canyons of New York City unharmed.

When healing, the tobacco cigarette itself is used to create a focus point or "eye" to examine the patient and see the spiritual cause of their illness, Sara says. The way the smoke from the cigarette travels as it rises also divines meaning for the *tabaquera,* as it represents the connection between heaven and earth. Tobacco thus provides a direct connection for the soul of the shaman to the realm of the ancestors—the spirit world.

Sara's altar-workspace is in her bedroom, away from the worldly distractions of the house. The altar consists of a white cloth over a small round table, with a plastic two-liter bottle-vase containing brilliant pink, red, and white roses. To the left of the flowers are half a dozen small bottles of perfume essence, incense sticks, and matches. At the front of the altar are a range of colored candles arranged in a row like a rainbow, scaling down from black, green, red, and yellow to a white candle. Sara works with the healing spirits through the candles, as well as the tobacco, cleansing and purifying any bad energy. In front of the row of candles are five neatly sorted piles of *mapacho* cigarettes, thickly rolled and ready for the ceremony.

She begins by lighting the candles, going down in color from black to white. Nimble fingers carefully choose a cigarette from the pile on the altar. She draws it up under her mouth with the reverence of rosary beads and softly whispers prayers on it. It's a process called *soplaring* (blowing), invoking the spirits of the tobacco to cleanse and purify the space of all negativity. When that's done she lights the cigarette and draws in deeply, letting the smoke enter her.

Sara puffs away furiously, holding the *mapacho* to her lips with the index finger of both hands and letting the ash burn down. A billowing cloud of gray smoke engulfs her as she closes her eyes and draws in the other world. When the cigarette has burned down at least half way she opens her eyes and reads the way the ash has curled and fallen. This, as well as the shapes in the billowing smoke, tell her the answer to her question, or instruct on how the patient is doing.

When the patient has a bad illness Sara moves into high gear, summoning the spirit of the tobacco plant itself, a powerful spirit "ally." "The spirit that comes to me is a *blanco* and she appears as a white woman dressed in a black dress and a black hat, every time," she explains to Mariella, who translates for us, looking deep into me with big, doe eyes. "I never see her face—it's always downcast. But she is the spirit in the tobacco, the mother of the tobacco who comes here and helps me to heal patients."

Mariella agrees to be the "patient" so Vance can get some shots of Sara in action, "smoking" her client. To test her connection with the spirits Mariella asks Sara to ask them about some money that went missing at the conference. She feels she knows who took it, but needs a confirmation. She sits opposite Sara by the altar and looks like a goddess, silhouetted in the light from the bedroom window, a halo of light around her head. As she rubs her ankles I can feel the touch of her skin on skin, her long hands cupping her shins.

Sara lights a *mapacho* to divine her question. She sucks on the cigarette in tuk-tuk-tuk short drags, the red-hot tip glowing lightly in time to the pull of her breath. Then she exhales, closing her eyes and going into a trance. A large ball of smoke envelops her head in a gray mist. As her connection with the spirit world deepens, the two women hold up two arms and clasp together their palms in unison.

Sara blows smoke into Mariella's cupped hands and it curls around her in the light like dancing spirits. She holds out the cigarette, now a long, curled pillar of ash, and her lips raise up into a knowing smile as she whispers to her, "I'm feeling it was someone close to you that took the money." Mariella nods, taking it all in. She asks some more questions about her husband's health, and Sara listens to the spirits and relays their answers.

Then she strategically cleanses the top of Mariella's head, her back, and feet with the sacred smoke before bringing out the flower essences and lightly bathing her with them. "I feel like I'm getting married," Mariella jokes as a shower of white and pink petals fall across her face and down to the ground. The smell of roses fills the air.

The flower bath is a ritual purification ceremony that cleanses the spirit. Sara says it refreshes and revitalizes the body and soul and makes your spirit happy, so "all your sins go away." Standing here watching Mariella under the microscope of my lust, I need a flower cold shower. This is wrong; she's a happily married woman, a mother, a sovereign being. But the sex-energy in me is strong; I am reeling in her essence-energy and it's addictive.

I'm watching the marriage of flesh and flower as the petals make the shape of a star around Mariella, gathering at her feet. "A powerful sign for a good life," Sara says, then spits tobacco juice into a small wooden bowl on the ground that's full of a sandy paste and spent *mapachos*. Suddenly there's the cry of a small child from outside the bedroom, the sounds of cooking and the *I Dream of Jeannie* theme shimmying in from the lounge, as the mundane world seeps in.

Sara's been practicing shamanic healing since she was twenty-two. She comes from a Brazilian family of plant workers and has a sensitivity or "gift" with the spirits that has been nurtured by her mother and grandmother before her. It's an important skill passed down the generations through the bloodline, but out of the six girls in her family she was the only one with the power.

"I worked with my mother healing with tobacco for many years," she tells me. "After she died and I started dieting with the plants more, it was like the angels started talking to me." It's not easy work, healing. Sometimes she cries when she feels information coming through from the spirits on the other side. Sometimes she reads from the Bible, letting the spirit answer her questions with random passages. And sometimes she uses ayahuasca to heal her patients when the problem is too strong for the tobacco itself.

"When I drink ayahuasca a lot of spirits come. They show me the patient's spirit body and show me where the problem is. They also tell me what plants will fix the problem. Then I go to Belén [market] to buy the plants that are needed, or I go to the jungle to find them. After the spirits have diagnosed the problem I have another consultation with the patient and I blow them with tobacco, with the *mapacho*. I might then prescribe a certain diet they are to follow to help cleanse their body, or a flower bath or perfume to take."

Perhaps because she's a woman she also seems to get more female patients asking for help with their personal lives. They want to find true love and to get married, or to have more money, and Sara helps guide them to the answers they seek—and sometimes the ones they don't. She also treats children and babies that are sick with minor ailments like gastroenteritis, and uses the smoke to call in a spirit that helps heal the child, following a long practice of using tobacco to cure *mal de aiyre* or bad air by Amazonian shamans and shamanas.

As one of the few women shamanas in Iquitos, Sara has also faced hostility and jealousy—both from outsiders and fellow healers. In traditional Amazonian culture women are not allowed to smoke, so a female shaman—and one that works specifically with tobacco—can be frowned upon. And quite often it's by the other women who are jealous of her position.

Sara bathes and smokes Vance and then me, also, in turn. The smoke curls around me and gets in my hidden places and sweeps them clean. As Sara pours the scented rose water over me and its cool essence calms me, I let go of the spirit-women, the beautiful and the demonic energies that have possessed me all day. I try to bring up my base chakra energies into my heart, to set good intentions once again.

After the bathing my energies do seem balanced. Mariella is careful not to catch my eye as we all head back to town in a cramped *motorcarro,* and Vance and I rejoin our fellow ayahuasca classmates at the cafeteria.

"Iquitos was buzzing today," Bowman says, digging into his tuna melt. "It feels like aya's been tuning in our vibrational bodies—all the gringo freaks have been bouncing about, freaking out the town."

He's really keen to see the new *Superman* movie tonight at the theatre around the corner on Calle Arica, and as the ayahuasca crew all gather back at the Yellow Rose in time for the 8:00 p.m. session I realize we've all been picking up on each others' energies. The aya magic is in us now, in our downtime and the way we interact and the things we manifest. What we need now is a unifying archetype—or at least some eye candy and a night on the town.

"This whole trip has been getting more and more mythical the longer it goes on," I tell Bowman and Vance as we wait for the others to arrive. The reason multi-generations of Western seekers are cruising round the jungles of South America like vegetal Jedis is the same reason *Star Wars, Lord of the Rings, Superman,* and the heroic archetypes sell so well in Hollywood: they fill an ancient need. All our Western dreamings are a longing for the hero, the mythic one who goes beyond the boundaries of the known world and returns with knowledge to heal the tribe.

Unfortunately the archetype's been degenerated to action heroes and car chases, endless explosions and the fuck-heat-death of global terror flashed on the screens of the world every night at 6:00 p.m. Despite the ongoing buildup of heroic memes, there's no cultural release—unless you join the army or play football—and no process of initiation for our Western youth.

Earlier, when I interviewed Jan Kounen, the director of the ayahuasca initiation movie *Renegade,* he touched on the power of the hero myth in Western culture:

"We are lost," he said, because "in our culture only the women are initiated, because they give birth. And maybe this is something we have to reinvent because it doesn't exist in our culture: to transcend. To become adults." Some tribes in South America still put their kids in a deep pit they dig for initiation ceremonies. They teach them to conquer their fear by spending a whole night in the pit with a cobra. "Sometimes the kid is bitten and they die," Kounen said. "But very, very, very rarely. Less often than with a motorbike accident in our culture, because you want to transcend, so you go alone at two-hundred kilometers an hour . . ."

Indigenous cultures respect the role of initiation and the need for a real connection to the forces of nature to invoke this. As Kounen said, "When you go out of this place [the cobra pit] you are an adult. You have transcended. So I think it's more important to find a more secure way of initiation. Like the Vipassana meditation, ten days in silence— it's a start. So is ayahuasca, or something else. We need that initiation because our culture is lost. Without it we just become greedy kids and forget about what life really is, and live in an ego trip."

I guess I'm playing the hero role myself tonight. I'm adorned with a sarong with stars and suns on it, a cosmic cape tied round my neck, over the top of my black rave top with the atomic symbol on it. I've really kitted myself out, yeah, and it feels good to be playing, all us gringos together in our downtime from ayahuasca. I can still feel the quantum threads all about, the hologrammatic resonance that binds us all, the invisible dominos of cause and effect, and I feel like my every action and thought is riding those waves into the future.

Bowman and I head to the cinema where we meet up with Vance, Marty and Rachel, Sarah and James, Johan with his strange, haunted eyes, Juan the mad scientist who wired me up to his computer the other day to monitor my DMT session, and Gorbi, the little nine-year-old street hustler who has adopted us during the day, eating our leftover french fries and bugging us for loose change.

I've treated him to come to *Superman* with us, even though it's screening late and I don't know where his parents are—I'm sure he'd literally be sleeping in a doorway if he wasn't here with us, and it feels right to bring him along, his little face beaming at the prospect. But when we get to the ticket booth they've sold out for the 8:00 p.m.

session and we're forced to see the 9:15. Worse still, we're crushed when the ticket booth attendant tells us that there are no subtitles— it's only in Spanish.

A stocky, well-built English guy with bright blue eyes and a handsome face sits with us while we wait. He's come to see *Superman,* too, but won't go in as he wants to see it in English. His name is Jem, and he reminds me of George Reeves, the 1950s black and white TV *Superman,* that same confidence and brawny strength to him; it can't be a coincidence he's here and entered our event horizon. Like energy attracting like, again and again all through the day if you have the eyes to see it, synchronous resonances of the hologram, facet-moments rubbing up against each other in hyperdimensionality.

Jem's good-natured and a likeable guy, it's just that he's full on alpha, and a lot of the other ayahuasca seekers are a tad intimidated with his larger-than-life energy, especially his sexual licentiousness and braggadocio. Then it hits me: he's my shadow. Not necessarily a villain, but he who is the opposite of the hero, a mirror image inversion of the qualities the hero must balance out within himself.

The idea of something evil seems reductionist to me after multiple immersions into the web of life, especially since the last ceremony at don Juan's. Any fear has replaced by a feeling of servitude to the Great Spirit and acceptance of all beings. I've learned that when approaching a strong energy front that it's the intensity that often feels uncomfortable, not the person themselves.

Similarly, it doesn't hurt to shop around for the right *curandero* to not only fit your ideological needs, but your energetic needs as well. It's just like getting a second opinion from a doctor. A few people mentioned a discomfort around don Juan and get mixed signals from him, a strange vibe that puts them off.

Bowman himself was worried about Juan's energy, paranoid that he might be a black magician, a *brujo,* but after meeting him and sitting with him in circle and soaring the heavens, Bowman and I both agree that Juan is simply a *maestro* with a strong energy that can react to other sensitives. Juan is a servant of the light, of that I am sure, but his energy is so bright it may appear surrounded by the dark—if only in comparison. So too, with Jem. As he heads out to a bar to check out the booty, I have a feeling I'll meet my shadow again.

Johan shares a pipe or two of homegrown maryjane outside on the footpath around the corner from the theatre, to get us in the mood, and I explain the archetype of Superman to all the stoned gringos:

"It's funny, yeah, 'cause a culture can only receive information when its ready for it, and Hollywood is one of the gatekeepers of the planetary consciousness. The subliminal messages, the archetypes it pumps out are crucial to the global mind understanding the evolving message of life and acting on those symbols. We can only evolve as fast as our ability to drink in the cosmic message and then repeat it, to learn the language of the gods . . ."

It's like this, I tell my gaggle of stoned ayahuasca friends—in magical theory as well as in Platonian archetype, all the gods are alive and real, independent but synergistically entwined with us. It is our faith that brings them alive, our steady channeling of mental energy that sustains and makes them strong, and when a religion and a culture is in decline, the gods die with the culture.

So have passed the Babylonians, the Chaldeans, and a host of forgotten races before the tide of history, reduced to words and archetypes that carry on as new gods. The Egyptians, the Norse, the Greeks, the Romans: their light has dimmed, but the names and power still remain. And the twentieth century, the age of science and reason—it had no place for gods, and so the archetypes survived—transmuted into tales of heroes and superheroes to fill young minds with wonder.

Which brings us back to Superman. He was "invented" in the late 1930s by Jerry Siegel and Joe Shuster, two Jewish kids from the Bronx, and he epitomized the underdog, a force of good let loose in a bad world. But what most people don't know is that coded in his archetype was a resonance and connection to all the mythologies that had gone before, especially the Hebrew heritage of his creators.

Like baby Moses being put in a boat and carried to safety down-stream, baby Kal-El came to earth in his rocket ship, and was raised as an earthman.

"El," his family name, is the abbreviated name of the gods in the Jewish faith, the "*Elohim.*" And woven through his life, everyone that is important to him is also graced with the sound "El" through the initials of their name: Lois Lane; Lex Luthor; Lana Lang. The vibrational sound of God, El El, echoing through the twentieth-century mythology of the god made flesh.

"The New York publishing scene was filled with talented Jewish writers, artists, and editors, and their stories became Superman's stories. So the history of Krypton is awash with parallels to the Old Testament, and by extension, Superman is the story of Jesus, and his adventure on earth is the New Testament, yeah. He is, of course, the savior, the one who redeems us from the evils of the world. All this encoded in the four-color comics that litter our youth, the secrets handed down amongst the trash..."

"Whoah. You're fucking full on, Rak," Marty says, stoned, shaking his long blond dreads back and forth. "Let's just go see the movie, I'm ripped."

So we pile in with the natives into a small cinema, seating less than a hundred, and Bowman's right, everyone's buzzing—especially us grin-gos. As the curtain pulls back it segues right to the start of the movie, no previews, and this is it, the new planetary message from the hologram-matic intelligence pulsing through.

It's B-grade, definitely, but even without the English translation I can see the archetypes, and in my post-DMT ayahuasca hologrammatic receptivity, I can read what it's saying to us all, to the planetary culture...

Superman returns from a full seven-year cycle in outer space, con-necting with his Kryptonian heritage in the heavens. And Lex Luthor, playing the devil role again, steals into his Fortress of Solitude and takes a knowledge crystal, a piece of heaven, and warps it with kryptonite and lets it loose on the earth. Heaven comes to earth, but the lens is dark, clouded, twisted by our fears and egos.

Superman is, of course, a plant. He gets his power from the sun; he photosynthesizes the energy of the stars and drinks it in to make him strong. And like a plant, he seeds. The twist of the movie is that in the seven years he's been gone Lois has married a mortal man and had a son to him. But when the chips are down and the Superman-savior needs help, Lois and her family rush to Superman's aid. In the process it's revealed the son has super-powers, too, that he is the son of a god, the son of Superman.

And the archetypal message seeps through. The cross-pollination of the gods with the humans has begun, but it's no longer about Superman saving the world, it's about the humans saving it, becoming gods ourselves. We must become the heroes, tune into the spirit of ayahuasca and the plants, the spirits which animate them and the light which feeds us all. It's OUR time now, not some other, someone from somewhere else to save us. What ayahuasca teaches you is that there IS no other—WE ARE ALL ONE.

A flash seed-memory wells up inside me from the ayahuasca ceremony at Juan's house the other night, the realization where all this ayahuasca tourism is headed. Just as a yellow sun powers the photosynthesizing Superman, yellow is also the color of the solar plexus chakra and a whole generation of internet nerds totally consumed by the mind and the mental zones. But that means a whole global generation of kids are primed and ready for the next stage, which is the heart chakra, the green astral level where the web of life becomes apparent and we all make reverberations through it. Green like kryptonite, like the plants that are teaching us their gnosis.

When that generation now coming online and researching ayahuasca reaches critical mass, and cosmic consciousness, a *planetary icaro* will clear from our throats and be sung, connecting us to the plants and the planet, and on into the stars . . .

In the seat next to me is Gorbi, mesmerized by the action unfolding on the screen. I nudge his elbow and he smiles, totally rapped, whispering, "*Gracias, senor,*" and I feel the hologram tugging and overlapping and the strange coincidence that tonight of all nights, and this movie of all movies would be the one I brought him to, with its message that the child shall lead us.

Germination time is drawing near, six years to the end of the world age, the end of the Mayan calendar in 2012. The ayahuasca spirit is spreading her vibratory tendrils throughout all who drink of its knowledge, and the garden is being tended. Now it's time for the seeds to sprout, all of us who have felt the touch of spirit.

After, in the streets of Iquitos, Gorbi and I fly down the sidewalks, my sarong cape fluttering stars and suns behind me, the smile of my native son beaming back at me.

"Superman," he cries, "Superman..."

12

Seeds

La Rosacita, Iquitos
FRIDAY JULY 14, 2006

Monika has her legs straight up in the air and they're shaking like she's been hit by lightning but its smokable 5-MeO-DMT she's taken in. She's howling like a jaguar dying and rebirthing upside down in the bushes, like she's trying to push herself back into the earth as she shakes uncontrollably, waves of energy streaming through her. She's having the most extreme reaction and Gavin's beside her on his own journey, the other DMT tourists in varying degrees of cosmic comedown back in the house. *Jesus fucking Christ this is like home footage of some species mutation caught on handycam in the jungle.*

But wait; let's step back a bit, this is too full-on, too much to explain now. We are, of course, at it again.

Bowman, Vance, and I have come out to Ron Wheelock's place outside Iquitos to finally nail down that interview we never got around to after sampling his smokable 5-MeO-DMT ourselves last week. He's mashing up some ayahuasca vine with a hammer in his backyard this sunny Friday morning as we arrive, getting a brew ready for a circle tomorrow night. Ron slips in his good teeth, the false set with the gold front tooth for the close up photos. We media curate him into a perfect Harley Davidson bandana with the American flag on the side and a bald headed eagle on the front, over his forehead.

Ron tells us his story as he beats the wood, his journey from the Kansas heartland of God's country to the jungles of Iquitos and he sings some *icaros* to assuage the spirit of the vine along the way. He's got this slow drawl that can't hide his down to earth simplicity. It becomes mesmerizing and after a while you feel his openness and are drawn into it. It's something about that hillbilly accent imprinted on my Western subconscious from TV, which combined with the indigenous knowledge he's learned from the shamans he's studied with makes it the perfect mix to slide in real good like under the skeptical defenses.

Ron's sure ain't no cowboy, though, no siree. More like the latest karmic incarnation of a southern Civil War soldier gone AWOL in the jungles of Peru, sitting here in the sun as easy as you please, mashing the vine of the dead and talking about plant medicines and hyperdimensionality. Somehow, it all fits, like he's done this before.

Quetzalcoatl is with him, watching, playing, absorbing everything he's doing as only a three-year-old can do. Today he's out in the sun with his own junior hammer and bowl, mashing up ayahuasca vine like his father. The day is overcast and cool, a temporary relief from the omnipresent heat and humidity of the Amazon basin.

Even here, in this suburban patch of jungle, the sounds of animals and birds are plentiful, and a constant bubble of sqwarks from the chicken coop with its newly fixed roof out the front backtracks our conversation.

Ron breeds roosters for fighting cocks and has a few champions there in the shed—as incongruous as it might seem, cock fighting is still practiced in Peru, and while a common pastime from the villages to the cities, it can also be a handsome little moneyspinner if you win. When in Rome, I ponder, as the chicken sounds fade and I tune back into the slow, steady thump of Ron hammering the vine.

Ron's main source of income is the growing stream of tourists coming to Iquitos in search of the healing and knowledge ayahuasca offers. Yet like many of the good *curanderos* I have met on my journey, there is an air of acceptance and duty about Ron, of listening to the spirit and being guided by it, and so if the spirit says you can't charge money, he obeys.

"I just ask God to provide me with a living, no more, no less. So I don't have to go hungry and I have a roof over my head. All the rest is extra. And it's far exceeded that ... I mean, I get some local people to drink with me, five soles they give me; other people come, maybe ten, fifty soles. But I came back in January and I've had a pretty solid flow of foreigners come in and work with me so I can sustain my life here."

The number of ayahuasca tourists has definitely been growing, and since that *National Geographic* article came out earlier this year it's threatening to become a torrent. The times are definitely changing, the wave is building, and good people like Ron that have answered the call of spirit are in the right place at the right time to help facilitate them.

"I mean it's planting seeds in people's minds to wake people up," Ron says of his work. "Even though I probably won't do much work in the States anymore, it's not the whole world. [Ayahuasca] is global. I see ayahuasca as all vines. The vine it starts growing on something and it just starts trying to take over everything. And ayahuasca is also a vine. And through us, every *ayahuasquero*, we're like another limb on the vine. And she's trying to embrace the world."

It's funny but having been on the inside of that cross-species communication, I find I have to agree. It might sound like a science-fiction concept ripped from *Invasion of the Body-Snatchers*, the book and films that proposed an alien invasion by a plant-consciousness that killed the human hosts and replaced them with emotionless "pod people" doppelgangers.

But while the movie was also an allegory commenting on paranoia and social mistrust, and colored by Hollywood Manichaeism, it also introduced the concept of a plant-human symbiosis to the mainstream consciousness. Now in this age of biotech wonders, where the gene of one creature can be inserted into another to hotwire the genome, is it that hard to think that nature herself has been doing her own experiments on and through her creatures all this time?

"They say that ayahuasca [is] changing our DNA," Ron says, looking up intently from his work. "I believe that's true. So these plants are changing us and preparing us for the changes. So we will be ready. I think it's all part of the scheme of things. Evolution is always at work."

It's an interesting thought—that there is, as my ayahuasca and DMT experiences have led me to believe, an active intelligence behind or in nature itself, that it's working as part of the cosmic ecology to nurture us monkeys, not possess and replace us, but to improve and better us to play our role in the web of life. Nature is full of reciprocal relationships, and the spirit level is no different, according to *curanderos* like Ron. Ayahuasca is certainly helping us, but it's in its—and all life forms'—best interest to get us humans back into a sustainable groove.

"In my opinion we're caretakers of the earth," Ron says. "They need us. This I've even seen in my ayahuasca visions, y'know. Many of us are very concerned about the earth changes . . . the Mayan calendar ending [in 2012]. I think even the government's very concerned about that . . . I think it's going to be a very interesting time. I think something will happen then. I mean we've had many wakeup calls here recently. The tsunami in Asia—250,000 people—whooossssshh! Gone with one sweep of a hand. The war can't even do that . . .

"What I have seen with ayahuasca—we're all doing exactly what we need to do, subconsciously. We're not aware that we're doing these things, [like] sucking all the petroleum out of the earth. The earth needs us to do that to bring forward all the earth changes. She can't do these things on her own. To bring this toxic thing over here and mix it over there—she can't do that. She needs us.

"Anybody that's done much work with ayahuasca will tell you—we don't choose to work with ayahuasca. She chooses us, and I find that very true. There are hallucinogenic plants all over the face of the earth. Peyote, san pedro, Syrian rue, opium . . . all of these plants. And I see these plants selecting the caretakers. The teachers. That when the earth change comes, many, many people are going to die. Many people. But the human race will not vanish . . ."

This is a huge concept to get across and also a huge responsibility. That's why reporting on ayahuasca is so important, why Bowman and I joke about our "media chakras" being opened by the vine. Kenneth Tupper, a Ph.D. candidate in the Department of Educational Studies at the University of British Columbia, said during his presentation at the Shaman Conference, "The movement of people and the medicine to the Amazon is very fast now. In the early twenty-first century we're seeing ayahuasca come into the mainstream consciousness.

"Ayahuasca defies linguistic expression—but to pass along the knowledge we need to find ways to explain it in words. So there's an opportunity for change here, and the media can play a role. More and more *ayahuasqueros* are sprouting who share their knowledge. And the internet means people can find information about the use of ayahuasca. It's not all valid or true—but you can look for yourself and it's harder for the government to control. There seems to be an increase in . . . the ability of seekers from the West to handle these experiences."

Perhaps that's the key—the tourists are coming because they are answering a call they hear deep within themselves for reconnection. Whether that awareness comes from the state of DMT-gnosis that can occur with natural plant material, as in the ayahuasca brew, or synthesized DMT made in a lab, often doesn't matter. And the synergy between the two extremes—science and nature—is coming to a head with this new wave of consciousness explorers trekking through the jungles of Peru in search of a God-fix.

Erik Davis, author of the book *The Visionary State: A Journey through California's Spiritual Landscape,* has said, "DMT was around in the sixties but it never became a cultural force—you'd have to be a real Head to have taken it. But there's something about the televisual, hyper-dimensional, data-dense grandiosity of the DMT-flash that seems to resonate with today's globalized, hyperreal culture."

The players are gathering round, spreading the knowledge and the connection so that when the time comes to sing the *planetary icaro,* a critical mass will be attuned to the right vibrational wavelength. Every group mind, every ayahuasca circle on the path of that journey of becoming is a lesson, not just for us as individuals, but for the group. Every action, every thought, every deed is reflected and stored in our emotional bodies and we carry this energetic baggage with us to the final target window. "All of history a dress-rehearsal for the species evolution," as Terence McKenna once rhapsodized.

Which is when the psychonauts arrive at the front gate of La Rosacita, ready to smoke DMT and storm the spirit realms. They're accompanied by everybody's favorite mad scientist, Juan Acosta, who's rounded them up and eager to get some more brain scans for his collection. So yeah, we're at it yet again, but this time I'm on the other side of the fence. I know the drill; now this is my chance to watch these DMT tourists plunge the depths of perception and see what they make of this most extreme adventure.

There are five of them—Susan, Eliza, Monika, Gavin, and Kat—that all cram into the top floor of Ron's little two-story wooden *tambo*. Three of them—Monika, Gavin, and Kat—are Aussies in their twenties; Susan's an Englishwoman in her early thirties; and Eliza's an American in her mid-twenties. It's too crowded up here so they arrange among themselves a pecking order, and while Susan starts the laborious process of being wired up via the skullcap to Juan's QEEG equipment, Ron prepares the first pipe for Eliza while the others wait downstairs. Bowman, Vance, and I fuss about quietly like nurses, making sure everyone's comfortable and lil' Queto is there offering people water from a plastic bottle, loving the excitement.

Eliza drank with us at Percy's, and her friendly girl-next-door demeanor almost masks her nervousness as she sits on the bare mattress down on the floor, rubbing her arms and waiting for the ritual to begin. She looks into Ron's eyes as he brings the pipe to her lips and goes in strong, catapulted into the dark spaces before the light. She stays under for a few minutes, murmuring to herself and writhing about, fretful, tormented. Five minutes in she sits bolt upright and stares off into space. Ron's there for her, smiling. She looks into his eyes again and sees her reflection looking back, and for a second there's a flash of recognition.

"Oh my God," she says.

"He is—all of us," Ron says.

"I am so grateful," Eliza cries, then her face contorts. "I hurt, Ron. I'm so scared."

"Don't be afraid," Ron answers, holding her arm.

"Will you hold me?" she asks in a little girl tone, and he cradles her in his arms and their hearts beat together before Eliza falls back, exhausted and spent.

Queto looks at her gingerly, like he's seen it before and wants to help.

"Thank you baby. Come over here," she beckons, and Queto goes to her like he would a wounded animal, offering emotional succor. They lie there on the mattress on the floor; reentry time.

And she's back now, back in the body, fallen from grace and crying, purging, becoming, crawling out of her psychic cocoon. Crying tears of pain and joy, sacred mother, joy and blood. Now she too, has broken through the monkey shell and into the game of it ALL. A rooster crows. Eliza cries and cries as Ron whistles gentle *icaros* to soothe her.

"These experiences can be very life-changing," Ron says, testing the waters to see if she's ready to talk yet.

"Oh Ron," she sighs, and he holds her in his arms for the longest time. "Oh, Ron." She's shaking, the tears are falling and the game of her is broken. Ron and Eliza rock back and forth as the pain subsides. The pain of her body, the pain of separateness from the ALL. But I can see it in her face, a bittersweet smile, a hint of recognition that I can recognize because I've been there, too. Then she smiles. Her eyes flutter and her smile grows and grows and grows. "I'm so beautiful!" she cries.

"Welcome back, butterfly," I say.

Just what is this strange drug doing to us in the jungles of Peru? A hologrammatic consciousness is a bit like Google—you can see the threads that connect together among a sea of floating data, because the whole truly is contained within each part. And while ayahuasca tourists are drawn here to answer the call of their own nascent spirituality, I suspect we may also be fulfilling a larger need.

As I have often heard here in Peru, the Inca prophecies say that this is the time when the eagle of North America and the condor of South America fly together, which symbolizes the earth awakening. One side cannot be complete without the other. The steady stream of Western *ayahuasqueros* learning the ways of the vine also fills the gap left by the indigenous youth who have been seduced away by materialism, as the two cultures merge.

"*Muju*" means seed in the Incan Quechua language. This can refer to a literal seed that is planted in the ground or in a metaphoric sense as a spiritual seed within a person. The Q'ero realize that this spiritual seed can be awakened within us all. In their Andean cosmology they have a phrase to describe this process of awakening—the *Hatun Karpay,* or the Great Initiation and Transmission. Only an initiated one can provide the living energy necessary to germinate the seed, but perhaps a "living one" includes the plants and the spirits contained therein. As I look at Eliza now I realize that there is definitely a seed in her that has been awakened.

It's funny how things evolve, how the *Superman* movie triggered thoughts of humanity as seeds ready to blossom, and now today I'm witnessing it here in the *tambo.* Post-humanity, emerging from the spiritual backpacker circuit, the seeds within them activating via a DMT-induced germination of the species.

Our second passenger, Susan, is now all wired up and ready to roll. She's a curly, dark-haired English woman with an air of confidence and a wry sense of humor. She's done DMT before and is a bit of an experienced Head. "I can't use that pillow, my mother was a nurse, I won't be comfortable unless the pillow's clean," she says seriously as Juan potters around her, connecting her skullcap to the BUS cord and the EEG monitoring equipment on his computer, oblivious to the rustic setting.

"Let's get a backup reading here," Juan says as Ron gets a clean towel to drape over the pillow.

Everyone makes peace with their God in a different way. While Eliza is still crying on the mattress, sobbing softly and integrating the realization of what she really is, the hyperdimensional creatures that we are, Susan goes deep within, meditating silently. Her face has the look of concentration of someone scanning the fine print of a contract to see where they're being ripped off as her alpha waves stabilize and Juan gets a good take on her EEG readings.

"All the back channels look beautiful," Juan says, the mad scientist at work. "The top channels are real noisy, though," and he points to the screen at a thick band of black seismic brainwaves. They're the same to him as the ayahuasca vibratory patterns the Shipibos weave into their colorful *mantas*, I realize, watching his hawk-like face in the blue glow of the screen.

"It's Bastille Day—shall we storm heaven?" Susan jokes.

"How are you feeling?" Juan asks.

"Oh great, I love skullcaps, I hear they're all the rage in Europe right now." She's ready for launch, all right.

"Now there's some muscle tension, not much electrical noise. Susan, I need you to focus on making a soft face, we just need five minutes of good, clean data before we start." Juan's got his top off and is mad scientist-ing around with a hairy chest and his Bermuda shirts, loving his job. "All those big waves on the screen are shifts in the DC potential across the scalp associated with emotional states," he explains to us. "All recognizable rhythms. Okay, we're ready for liftoff."

Ron fills the glass pipe three quarters full of 5-MeO-DMT and Susan tokes it down and into the rabbit hole. She's smiling and smiling and smiling, totally beatific as she tumbles back into pattern recognition with the world soul.

"Tense muscle signals," Juan says worriedly, she's hitting a high frequency. Susan starts to groan slightly, breathing heavily. A rooster crows. "Her alpha's coming back but the tension component is still strong..."

"I don't see anything, Juan," Susan says suddenly, with clarity. "No, you're perfect . . . Okay, well, that was fun . . ." She's back, a smooth reentry. "You can't put the ineffable into words without losing some of it, but I believe it was a God experience," she says in a running monologue. "It was a healing context—I was healing a cyst within myself, in my ovary..." Susan's a pro, a psychedelic nurse, allowing the procedure to happen to her, ideologically ready to go with it.

"I still have the motion to tune back in, I can feel it still," she says, smiling.

"No, now we need five minutes silence to get a good EEG reading," Juan orders, stroking his beard, and the hawk-like gaze of his eyes on the computer screen reminds me of some Egyptian high-priest offering up his hidden knowledge to Horus.

Two down, another to go. The next entheonaut is Kat, a beautiful, blond-haired woman from Melbourne, Australia. She has a bright, breezy attitude to all this, like it's just another experience among many, but she reminds me of a psychedelic Paris Hilton about to smoke 5-MeO-DMT and forever have her psychic virginity shattered.

Kat puts the pipe to her lips and takes it in and falls back gently, like she's daydreaming. She's smiling like she's suppressing a laugh, the remembrance of it all. Lying back, arms on her chest, she is a serene goddess at play in the fields of the Lord. Bliss is coursing through her and onto her face—she's in the hyperspatial wading pool. There's a rustle of chickens outside and an explosion of squawks and Kat starts going off, grokking it all.

She's breathing steadily as an inner sun rises and shines on her and she's breaking into an even wider smile as it overlaps and becomes her. Kat turns her head and opens her eyes to orientate herself before closing them again and going back under for another dip. She's beautiful, radiating bliss like a cosmic Buddha, laughing at the rooster sounds we make back to the squawking chickens, a slumbering babe adrift on an amniotic ocean.

At four minutes in she laughs suddenly and opens her eyes, her hands running up and down her face, massaging it to feel the solidity of the body. She's giggling, riding the energy wave, grounding herself on the mattress and patting herself down, into her body. "It was blissful," she says, beaming a smile as big as Texas, still rubbing her hands down her legs.

It's then that I hear this unbelievable sound, a cry piercing the noon air, barking like a beast in the heat-death-birth of a star. Bowman and I race out of the house and into the backyard towards the sound of the storm, the thunder coming from a figure down on the ground. It's Monika—there she is split like the moon from the sky. Good God in heaven—that a human can make these sounds, that they can be birthed through us, in us . . .

Monika's a six-foot artist from Sydney here on an Australia Council grant to study indigenous Peruvian culture and integrate it into a performance art piece. She's covered in tribal tattoos and has a punk energy that she seems barely able to restrain. During the conference she drank with Juan and each experience was more powerful and dangerous than the last. She's a sensitive, with a fierce warrior strength that guards some deep emotional blocks ayahuasca hasn't been able to break, but the 5-MeO-DMT has.

Ron's standing over her holding her carefully, trying to sing *icaros* but it's like trying to woo a wildcat. She's wailing a death cry and flailing about like living lightning, and next to her Gavin's curled into his own innerspace ball and trying to ride out the storm. Ron's *icaros* eventually guide her into a sacred space and she calms like a babe; she's broken through. And lil' Queto is right there with his dad, helping this wounded beast, a hand on her leg.

Then she's back, in the meat, the body. Monika's eyes open wide and she's laughing manically and crying, and shaman Ron's there, the healer, at the ready. He's riding her soul in from the heavens, from where it's been storming the astral jungles. Her DMT-connection is still strong and as she puts two hands up to cup her face there are no words to describe what she's feeling, so she holds out her arm with a red love heart tattoo on the underside and a cursive script atop it that reads, "Love," and points at it and cries.

Monika's broken now, but stronger in the broken places. All of us now are stronger in the broken places.

There's one psychonaut left, though, and reentry hasn't been so kind to him. Gavin's a tall, good-looking Aussie with short dark hair. He looks like he should be the captain of a football team. He's guarded, cautious of us media *ayahuasqueros* with our cameras and audio gear, and he's not okay with us watching and filming the sanctity of what's going on. Fair enough. Eliza asks us to put our cameras down and of course we agree; it was more of an instinctual thing to click and point as the drama unfolded, engrained into us.

But Gavin's struggling on his journey, holding onto the negative spaces and still enmeshed in Monika's energetic web. He's the moon to her sun as they circle each other in neurochemical orbit. He's holding himself back because of her and us, and the negative emotional thrust is building. We're stopping him from letting go, fully rejoining the Source and thus it's no surprise that we become the canvas for his pain.

We've overstepped our bounds. Media vultures so intent on chasing the shot, the image, the angle, the full content package, that we forgot about the sacred space these people were going through, the thing which cannot be bought. After Gavin recovers he's off; he walks away leaving us all without a word, just a note to remember him by:

If any image I am in is seen beyond here
I will find you.
I did not invite you in.
You invaded my space of healing and turned
It into something else.
Fuck you.
G.

When the particles rejoin the wave we're all there, and all our actions affect one another in that raw, sacred space. Gavin's pain is our pain. His bad trip is reflected in the bad vibes he projects upon us; as above so below, and now we all carry that weight. Gavin, seed brother: *In'Lakesh.* Our media chakras are black, we filmed your sacred space, your healing space, and we pained you. You've allowed us to see the shadows, the *brujeria* building these last few days, the black magic that is ego-based desires that was in us, all along.

When Eliza questions me and asks to see the photos of her, to see if they were appropriate, it's only when I look I realize I have no shots of her because that first seed I was busy nurturing, sitting, and giving her some psychic protection, making gentle breathing sounds and whistling some soft translinguistic *icaros,* navigational commands I picked up in my own time in the DMT zone.

The best thing you can do for a psychonaut about to journey inside the vibrational Overmind is to be present. Sit with them and let your energy field overlap theirs; let your thoughts and heart and intentions create a space for them in their raw psychic becoming. And that is what I failed to do for Gavin.

Now that all the seeds have sprouted and burst upon heaven's shores, their souls ebb back into the vehicles of their bodies as they gather here in the backyard to integrate. Ron's drumming and singing raw *icaros* that burst into life, the primal sounds of the beat, the heartbeat of creation. He's a wild man going for it in his jungle backyard on a Friday afternoon on the day of germination. And then he blows *mapacho* smoke over all of the seeds from a hand-carved pipe shaped into the bust of a native Indian, cleansing their auras.

"Ah," he says, picking a little bambino spirit from Kat's aura and flicking it quickly out of her. Healing her and the others before they go back into the world.

What a day. The light and the dark all birthed and brought to the surface.

The psychonauts gather their things and head back to the baseline reality. Ron's Peruvian friend Juan, the *motorcarro* driver, takes us back to town, pointing to the dark horizon ahead.

"Look senor, the storm is coming," he says, eyes off the road as he hurtles along, weaving in and out of the crazy Iquitos traffic, buses and other three-wheeled taxis, pedal bicycles and pedestrians all timesharing the same thin strip of bitumen they dare call a highway.

The clouds roll in, dark and gray and heavy with the psychic sweat of the day, mirroring all we have gone through. The *brujeria* has been hanging in the air for days now, building up its dark charge. The lesson, I see now, was all about how to integrate it, to embrace the shadow and give it its time in the light.

Finally the sky splits open, and it rains, and rains, and rains.

Let it fall.

13

Beasts

Quistococha Resort and Zoo, outside Iquitos
SATURDAY JULY 15, 2006

Everything has a fresh, clean glow this morning as Bowman and I slum it with the other tourists at the zoo. Located over ten kilometers from downtown Iquitos, La Laguna de Quistococha Natural Park is a mecca for tourists to gaggle at caged and free-roaming animals and for the locals to beach themselves on by the white sand lakeside. The complex sprawls over 360 hectares and includes a small museum of natural history, an aquarium, the zoo, a café and bar, and a sumptuous piranha-free lagoon.

We're both feeling the psychic hangover from yesterday's DMT session with the germinating seeds and Gavin's reaction to our "ayahuasca paparazzi" routine. Humans have burnt us out, so we're here at the zoo to mingle with the animals and get a little breathing time before our next ayahuasca ceremony tonight. Once again I'm reminded how important it is to integrate each ayahuasca/DMT experience, to cling to the normality of the baseline world while the inner processing goes on.

As usual of late I can feel the ayahuasca signal hovering on the fringes of my consciousness. It's been three days since my last sojourn, but the hologram still flashes through the noise with archetypal signals and the language of forms that the world-spirit speaks.

Bowman and I gaze at the spider monkeys in their enclosure and some lizards and turtles, and the warm safe energy of the beasts registers on me. We take some happy snaps with a baby six-foot anaconda around our necks for a sole, and the feel of the snake, this giant muscle in my hands is like an undulating phallus moving about me. I must still be riding the base chakra sex-wave from the other day, I think, but it's funny how the hologram layers the journey, how the beasts and animal spirits now leads back to the sex thread, meshing the old with the new.

In one of the cages up ahead we stop to watch a dozen brown capuchin monkeys—instantly recognizable as the poor sods attached to organ grinders and busking on the streets of the twentieth century—shriek and bound about a large cage. These little fellows look so much like miniature version of us humans that you feel like you're watching rambunctious hairy children swinging about, demanding your attention. The genes are almost the same, essentially—there's just that spark of consciousness that separates us and them.

They're so playful, swinging with the precision of acrobats across the four walls of the cage and darting their paws out past the criss-cross wire to grab at whatever they can get—including a totem I carry with me for good luck, a child's plastic yellow monkey from the game *Barrel of Monkeys*. As I hold it up for them to grok on the image of the man-made monkey with the real deal, a cheeky capuchin swipes it, moving faster than my eye can see, and instantly bites off a yellow plastic hand.

Quite a few of these capuchins also have erect penises, their animal urges up front and made plain to see. They're holding nothing back as they express what we've learned to suppress. The male monkeys usually get hard-ons when excited, I'm told, and can often bare their members when greeting as a way of showing respect. Their sex organs are about three or four inches long, ending in a mushroom head, but the monkeys themselves are only one or two feet high—so let's just say they're well hung.

As our energies overlap I can hear aya sharing her secret language with me, and in a flash a voice says, *Beasts. Totems. Animal-spirits. Your journey tonight will be all about beasts.* It will also be the first ayahuasca journey without Bowman at my side; post-conference he's striking out on his own and plans to drink again with Guillermo, just up the road from here.

It's no small thing to say how important Bowman and Vance have been to me on this odyssey of self-discovery, how much I've come to value their friendship, formed in the fires of innerspace and tempered on the road and over interviews. But all good things have a time, and my initiatory days with the training wheels of the conference and my fellow media *ayahuasqueros* is coming to an end, making way for deeper territory.

New challenges await, and the first is in the form of the King of the Beasts himself—Jem, the British traveler we met back at our night at the movies seeing *Superman.* His stocky, alpha-male form is ensconced in one of the bamboo seats out front of the Yellow Rose as Bowman and I reconvene with Vance for lunch. Jem's wearing a U.K. football jersey and at first glance looks like a potential soccer hooligan, but those cool blue eyes and Hollywood good looks also hint at some archetypal hero.

He's been traveling for a while and has just returned from Brazil, where he regales in telling us of his sexual exploits with smooth-skinned Brazilian women and the nurse that he made a home-made porno with. "She sucked me off, rode me like a bull and then slipped my tool deep in her ass to come. I taped the whole thing on my new Sony hand-held, do you want to see it? I showed it to all these Peruvian guys on the slow boat down here from Leticia. They were mad for it."

Jem's a walking fuck-machine, King Cock—just like those capuchin monkeys at the zoo, offering up their erect penises as a show of greeting. But still, you can't help but like the guy. As the waitresses from El Gringo Bar flirt with us as they always do, Jem sizes them up and says in an aside to me, "We could do a tag-team with those two, they're keen for it," and flashes me a smile. I'm tempted. Just being around his machismo is a challenge for my own cerebral nature, the ayahuasca monk I've become, here to write about the whole thing for *Australian Penthouse.* The irony is delicious. But I remember that the shamanistic ideal is not to suppress the base chakra sex energy, but build it, bringing it up the chakras for heightened illumination.

I wonder if that's my role in this little drama—to bring this king of the fucking jungle into awareness of the levels of psychic energy, to introduce him to the royal road of higher consciousness for his personal evolution? That may sound egotistic, but my newfound feeling of servitude to the spirit of aya is matched by my awareness that same spirit works in mysterious ways, bringing people together here, introducing concepts there, sculpting the culture to some grand plan beyond our ken.

Jem's been hanging out at the Rose with us over the last few days and hearing about our ayahuasca journeys and now he's keen to try it himself. I mentioned this to the crew last night, but Bowman flatly refused to even countenance the idea, saying there's no way to predict what someone like Jem might do on ayahuasca. If he went wild, Vance agreed, it'd be my responsibility—and the guy's built like a brick shithouse. The idea of holding back a raging madman while on ayahuasca sure put a dampener on things, but now here he is, putting me on the spot.

In a mind-flash I know that I will invite Jem to drink with me tonight at Ron Wheelock's house, that the symmetry is perfect with Bowman going to Guillermos and Jem filling the space, and that he is also a beast himself, a primal Kong among primates. And so it is that in the early evening I find myself in the back carriage of a taxi *motorcarro* with Jem—and his Sony handycam—speeding past the sprawling fringes of suburban Iquitos and out onto the highway to Nauta and Ron's place.

"I'm writing a book myself," Jem says, dragging on a cigarette as he films the countryside flashing by. "I'm right into Charles Darwin, yeah—evolution and the theory of natural selection and all that? I'm heading down South America, towards the Galapagos Islands off Ecuador to meet the people and animals there, where Darwin first bridged the gap of evolution." What he really wants to find, he tells me, is evidence of the missing link, the proto-ape-man that joins us to the other primates.

I tell him about Terence McKenna's theory that it wasn't an ape at all, but a mushroom that came into early hominid's diet and catalyzed higher states of self-awareness, bootstrapping us into art and language and other forms of human expression. Jem takes all this in his stride, nodding and staring at me with those blue, blue eyes of his.

What makes us speak? What spark animates the tongue, the fire, the soul? My own ayahuasca/DMT experiences say it's spirit. I believe that each sound is a vibrational wavelength, a compression of energy in sound that emanates itself from a higher source. Monkeys make sound to express their animal urges, but only humans use it for multi-track communication of the complexity that sifts meaning from noise and drives some to love, to war, and even back to God.

Language may be the true missing link, and we monkeys are but hosts to its magic. The idea of apes and mushrooms—us and plant interfaces—is really the same thing reemerging on the planet now. As we left behind the early primates to inhabit ever-richer plateaus of consciousness, so too, this new wave of entheogenic explorers is re-colonizing higher-dimensional space.

As we pass a number of roadside stalls back in the baseline grid I impetuously ask the taxi driver to stop. I run over and buy two big bags of bananas to invoke the sacred monkey tonight during ceremony, as an offering to Hanuman, the monkey god and all the beasts.

When we arrive at Ron's he's stoking the pot of ayahuasca out the back and he tells me the bananas are no good to eat and will have to be slow-roasted in the embers of the fire under the ayahuasca pot. The bananas look like erect white penises when peeled, sacrificial phalluses whose power enters me when I eat one, shunting to my base chakra. Later, two dogs are humping on the road out front, hammer and tongs, getting a good groove and licking and sexing each other as Queto and I look on.

"Fire," Queto says, pointing to the two dogs and giggling.

When Juan Acosta (who's just winding up some more DMT experiments upstairs) comes down and announces that he's bought a bag of magic mushrooms with him—*Psilocybin cubensis*—to add to the brew for tonight's ceremony, the ritual seems complete.

The current synchronicity of events and ideas is no longer strange; the event horizon of the spiritual realm seems to warp and distort the canvas of the world and the people in it to create its own picture. I look at a few delicate little shrooms in Juan's outstretched hand and recognize them as "gold tops," as we call them in Australia, mixed in with some "liberty caps," their long, thin stalks ending in a phallic helmet. *Penises and mushrooms, monkeys and bananas, missing links, language and the Logos.*

The DMT tourists wander down from the launching pad on the first floor, and there's a few familiar faces mixed in with new converts. Theo Valis is here, braving the frontiers of consciousness as always, as is Nicole, the perky brunette from the States who smoked DMT with us out at Alan Shoemaker's ayahuasca church last Sunday.

I feel wedded to the ayahuasca brew that Ron was making yesterday, knowing that it will have absorbed our psychic energy, and the same commitment seems to have drawn back Eliza, who smiles up at me with a mellow, penitent vibe. Yotam, a hip Israeli journalist in his late twenties with a mighty black moustache, and a friendly Irish couple in their early thirties who have been wooed away from beer and the World Cup by our ayahuasca tales back at the Yellow Rose, also turn up towards dusk, with Vance in tow.

We're all waiting now, mingling and chatting and preparing ourselves for liftoff while Ron snaps back into dad mode to give lil' Queto a quick bath. I mention to Ron the conversation Jem and I were having about McKenna's mushroom-ape theory and the evolution of language and consciousness, which triggers his own reminiscences:

"Humans work the soil. The plants take from the soil. But mushrooms break down the soil so plants can use it. They're a highly intelligent race of beings," Ron says, as Queto runs around naked, holding out his little boy penis like a hose.

"Are they from outer space, Ron?" I ask, remembering another wayout sound bite from Terence McKenna's glory days.

"Most definitely," Ron snaps back, without missing a beat. "And the psilocybin in mushrooms is very similar to the DMT in the ayahuasca brew, so they'll go well together. Who knows, maybe mushrooms break down the soil of language, too," he says, with those old, old eyes of his looking right into me.

Ron's getting his ceremonial gear on, a beautiful maroon Shipibo top—a *cushma*—with brilliantly detailed ayahuasca patterns splashed over it, and a pair of brown loose pants. It's an almost double of the same colored ayahuasca top Jem bought from the grandmother *manta* sellers outside the Yellow Rose this afternoon and is wearing now. Seeing these two white Westerners here together in their matching outfits, one wonders which is the shaman and which the student. They both have pale blue eyes and a similar energy, as if they could be brother-monkeys under the skin.

Ron spreads out a large Shipibo *manta* cloth on the wooden dining room table that he has made for his altar space. It has the typical vibrant wavefront patterns of ayahuasca on the base, but in the center of a number of colorful concentric circles is a cross-section of ayahuasca vine split into five-leaf clovers like an archetypal tree of knowledge, small embroidered flowers within each segment.

Ron carefully places his sacred objects on it: his hand-carved, Indian-head wooden pipe, crystals, an old King James leather Bible, wooden rattles, a metallic singing bowl, and some bottles of *agua de florida* and other miscellanea.

Juan places the mushrooms on a broad leaf next to the ayahuasca centerpiece to resonate the symbiosis between the plant sacraments. Above the altar space is a mantle with little wooden animal spirits and totems, and hanging above that is a classic Roman Catholic painted portrait of Jesus with flowing brown locks, dressed in a white robe with a red sash pulled back to reveal his sacred heart, his head surrounded by thorns and a spectral aura, the righteous fire of an awakened one.

Reverently, I hold up a single long-stemmed liberty cap mushroom and place it over the sacred heart. *Come to me tonight, mushroom-monkey spirit, Hanuman-McKenna, share thy tongue, let me speak your truth,* my subconscious flashes up.

"Queto, you've gotta go to bed, there's a ceremony tonight!" Ron chastises the cheeky little monkey as he draws pictures on some scrap paper with me. We're going to be doing the ayahuasca ceremony right here in the lounge room, surrounded by jaguar skins on two walls and a third under me, my spirit-bed, as I write.

To my right, Jem says, "It's crazy, yeah, all those carved wooden creatures up there like totems," pointing at the hand-carved figurines on the mantle above the altar and the shrunken head spirits hanging from the wall near them. "My totem is the shark," he explains, "the great-white shark, to be precise." I bet. Evolution's arrow, the king of the sea for the last eight million years without change.

We talk about it, and everyone's got a totem it seems, including Juan, to my left, whose animal is the hawk, Vance the jaguar, and Ron and I the monkey. All of us readying our beast-forms for the astral menagerie.

"You can come up one by one to drink," Ron says in slow, reverent tones from the altar. "Put your intentions into the cup. There's fifteen minutes to half an hour, usually, before the onset. There's no guarantee whether you will purge or not—it's very probable. Maybe even both ends."

Jem steals a wry smile, like a schoolboy giggling at a fart. The Irish couple look at each other nervously, as if they've bitten off more than they can chew, but it's too late to go back now.

"If you can't make it to the bathroom [outside] then just try to get off the path where no one will walk in it. I ask everybody to stay in the ceremony until it's finished; if it gets intense for any reason ... I will blow smoke around the house to seal it off, so no bad spirits come in. If you're outside you're not in this protection, so if you linger outside for too long a time I'll come looking for you to bring you back to the protection of the circle. We form an energy when we drink together ... and when one of us is gone it's like a link in that chain is broken, and a lot of times I feel that."

"Am I allowed to smoke cigarettes?" Jem asks in his firm English accent. We're all reverting to tourist mode with questions and demands of Ron, who patiently explains the ins and outs of the way he conducts the ceremony.

"Yes, but why don't you try the *mapacho* tobacco on the table? It's pure, no pesticides or anything have ever been used on it."

"Ron, how do you feel about people singing in the ceremony, and making sounds?" Theo Valis asks in a guarded tone, like he's a closet soprano.

I remember him telling me about drinking with a circle at Guillermo's during last year's Shaman Conference, where he experimented with his freeform bells and whistles approach to the mapping of the DMT spaces, trying to recreate what he was hearing and pulling the sonic threads down to earth. Word-shaman, rapping *icaros* into a Western paradigm. After hours of this while high on ayahuasca, every single person sitting the circle wanted to kill him, Theo told me, without a trace of regret.

After my own translinguistic wording experiences I know what he means. At the peak of the aya space the core of me wants nothing more than to roar like Tarzan, becoming pure ur-vibrational frequency.

"Well, that's a good question. Normally I lead the ceremony; if somebody wants to sing—if the urge is really strong... I ask us all to be respectful of each other. We don't talk during the ceremony because it can interrupt other people's journey next to you or across the room. It's a very personal journey inward, so if you get the urge to sing I would just ask that you ask me if you may sing. Many times I will ask after a while if anyone wants to sing. Before I could sing in a ceremony I had to do six months' worth of diets. To learn this work is also a discipline, it's not an easy path to follow."

Theo has a suppressed grin on his face like he's heard it all before but doesn't want to play that game. With over one hundred ayahuasca sessions under his own belt, and as many smokable DMT journeys conducted in his own indomitable anarchistic style, I know he often feels that a lot of Peruvian shamanism is weighed down with archaic dogma. But when in Rome, I guess...

Despite any nagging doubts, Ron is a qualified shaman who's paid his dues. But it's different drinking with a Western *curandero,* and being able to ask him questions in English and receive answers without the translation hurdles. I think a lot of us feel a bit more comfortable with it on one level, though still unsure of this gringo's spiritual prowess on another, like a white man can't be as authentic as an indigenous shaman.

As the lights go out and we all sit in the darkness on the floor there's a few nervous laughs and sighs as we settle into the session. The gentle bass of cicadas melts into a soft whistling *icaro* from Ron as familiar rhythms take hold of me, spaghetti-western/Peruvian mantras . . . Ron *soplars* the space, cleansing it of any negative energy, and then he offers up a prayer:

"Thank you, Lord, for this day, for the work we have completed and for this gathering and this night. For all these people that have arrived to drink. This *cielo* ayahuasca (sky ayahuasca) is very well prepared and originally planted by don Jose, my teacher. There's a piece of *chacruna* that don Jose also planted that I didn't know he had, his secret, and I've used that in the brew also. *Chilisanago,* two flowers of *toé,* and one flower of *toé blanco,* and always . . . *mapacho.*

"Thank you, oh Lord, for all the things in the world. You give us life, you transform energy from the sun, so we can live, and without which no one could live. Special thanks for these teacher plants. To me all plants are medicine, but we just don't know how to use them. And for this many people destroy them. But what is, is. I only change what I'm capable of and I accept all other things.

"We ask for beautiful visions, tonight, and healing. For this whole world is sick. Thank you for the work you have bestowed upon me. May you always be here to guide and protect me, wherever I am . . . Amen."

And then we drink, some of us boosting the vine with a handful of the freshly picked hallucinogenic mushrooms, gritty and fleshy on the palate. The Irish woman heaves uncontrollably into a bucket immediately after her cup of medicine and falls into a light trance. Her partner, a red-cheeked Guinness-loving lad, holds his jungle lager down, as does the rest of the group. Theo Valis seems to have decided not to impose his trip on the group and curls up into a fetal ball, which he remains in for most of the night, silent running through the astral plains.

Ron sings his haunting *icaros*—as fine as any indigenous *curandero*—and one by one we all settle into the ayahuasca fugue, breathing, vomiting, traveling within. Vance is purring lightly to my left near Juan as Ron breaks out the Tibetan singing bowl to intersperse his chants, sounding like a male Yoko Ono thrashing about. The sound of the bowl reverberates through the dark, piercing the skin and flesh, straight into the energy body. *As usual, all the action's on the inside.*

A heavy rain pours down on the outside, the sounds of the storm mingling with the constant beat of Ron's *shacapa* fan and our coughs and hurls, as the sickness comes up and out. It sounds like a room full of drowning sailors.

I'm suddenly aware that I am in the jungle, surrounded by the morphic resonance of dozens and dozens of animal spirits. All of their faces impinge of me now on the canvas of my mind, melting from one to another. I've entered the event horizon of the Great Spirit—here comes the human zoo...

A colossal alligator eye suddenly fills my field of vision, smiling, reptilian. *Do you want this? Are you ready,* it taunts? *Shed your skin and slip into the genomic code, sink beneath the waves of life ... ALL is all is all is One ... The sun, the plants, the insects, the birds, the reptiles, the mammals, the monkeys, the gods, the word, shedding from their skins and melting into— through one another, morphing with the knowledge of the web and the things that bind.*

I'm caught up in this never-ending roller-coaster-Wonka-vision-glass-elevator of becoming, hurtling through our shared genetic memory... Next to me on the floor, Jem is seeing them, too, as he tells me later: "There were lots of stars and I started to see the planets. The colors were magnificent. The snakes on the floor were all flashing colors, it was mad." A snake is right in front of me now, gigantic, rainbowing, and as its forked tongue hisses I'm leaning into it, embracing it, becoming it.

"This one creature, it had the head of a snake, but the face of a man or a woman," Jem recounts to me after the ceremony. "All of a sudden its arms would go really, really long and wrap round me. There was dancing, girls dancing with men... They were all beasts—and humans—but their bodies had all changed, like the pictures you see of Egyptian gods with human bodies and animal heads." These beast-people are morphing all around us, faces elongating and bodies snaking together like a river of animals all caught up in a great current. "And then it would be just be one. I never closed my eyes—they were just there."

Renowned British biologist and author of more than ten books on the overlap of science and new paradigm thought, Rupert Sheldrake, explains the theory of *morphic fields* as "memory... inherent in nature. Most of the so-called laws of nature are more like habits..." In his decades of research into plant development, Sheldrake realized that to understand the development of plants, a "morphogenesis" starting in the genes was not enough. "Morphogenesis also depends on organizing fields," he said, and he further argued that this applied to higher beings like animals. And he's not alone—many developmental biologists have proposed that biological organization depends on fields, variously called "biological fields," "developmental fields," "positional fields," or "morphogenetic fields."

"I suggest that morphogenetic fields work by imposing patterns on otherwise random or indeterminate patterns of activity... Morphogenetic fields are not fixed forever, but evolve. How are these fields inherited?" Sheldrake suggests that these fields are transmitted from individuals of a species through "a kind of non-local resonance, called morphic resonance. The fields organizing the activity of the nervous system are likewise inherited through morphic resonance, conveying a collective, instinctive memory. Each individual both draws upon and contributes to the collective memory of the species. This means that new patterns of behavior can spread more rapidly than would otherwise be possible."

In front of my eyes now there's a primal Kong, a giant gorilla radiating a fierce energy, as clear as day. The Ur-Monkey. And then I realize it has Jem's blue eyes, it's him—he's the *missing link*... And I look down at my own hands, eyes open now, and my hands are long and black, covered in fur, and we are the beasts—and they are us.

Suddenly a primal scream pierces the night, and I know that the vine has kicked in strong and made someone face their dark places. "Ron... I need you..." Eliza whimpers in a low moan. "Roooonnn, help me, help me!!!" And Ron scoots over and starts singing soothing *icaros* to her, adjusting her vibrational body and smoothing her energy down with the sacred songs—which just makes her freak out even more. "Noooooooooooo!!!! This is wrong, it's evil, it's black magic!" she screams. "Rak, I need you, Raaaakkkk..." And the sound of my name carried in the dark wakes me from my trance and has me instantly up and over to her, before—

"I work in the name of the Lord and Jesus Christ his only son," Ron shouts back, asserting his will not just on Eliza's fears, but on the group and the spirits all around. "Rak's got his own journey, we all do, now sit back and trust me, Eliza, this is what I do..."

Eliza seems to calm down at that, and I scramble back to my spot on the jaguar rug in the dark, between Jem and Juan. Later, Eliza tells me that she lost her center, her ability to trust, and she was in some really dark places. I tell her it's okay that she couldn't trust Ron—she couldn't trust herself, and she had to go through the not trusting to burn it out and find that place where she could trust again.

"Eliza really lost it for a while there, hey," Juan whispers later, our mad scientist with his hawk-like eyes. The sound of his purging next to me, long and deep and often was like a backbeat throughout the night. He's been wrestling with visions of the spirit world, alien landscapes like inverted Photoshop jungle lakes, plants merging into the sky and insects and beasts alive with the sweat and pulse of life, all of us caught up in a genomic swirl.

As the ceremony winds down I wander round outside towards the water hole, past the house. A storm rumbles overhead and lightning streaks down to connect heaven and earth. I roll out my tongue to catch the flashes like snowflakes. Suddenly a primal urge to conjugate wells up inside me, a need to let out all the energy into words, to ground it into the world.

"*Watt ta ta ta a ta a ta tat tat tat to da do da dilly dilly billy boo bup BOO!*" I translinguisticize, forward language centers engaged and channeling the spirit of the beasts, minutes of cosmic conjugations where the sound just pours out and the energy behind the sound comes in. Liquid glossolalia spilling out into the night. It wakes Theo Valis from his zone of one, I'm sure, as well as the rest of the crew inside, but I'm sorry, *when the lightning strikes the tongue must speak . . .*

On the rim of the pond I can suddenly feel the tight presence of a slothy white gorilla spirit, an astral "Bigfoot" hanging in a tree, like a Platonian archetype. If I sort of squint my eyes and peer past the branches across the pond where it's sitting I can see the negative space it occupies, the shape of it silhouetted like the spirits I saw on my deep, DMT journeys.

I can feel this spirit-beast looking at me, trying to size me up. I take it in for a few minutes, holding its energetic gaze, then get the hell out of there, scuttling back onto the veranda and into the circle of protection Ron's cast around the house. I feel like I've stared down the *King of the Beasts . . .*

At the end of the ceremony Ron comes around and blows smoke on everybody to close down their energies. "The smoke helps get rid of anything bad, any negative energy in your body where you need protection," he explains.

Like his Peruvian *maestro,* don Jose Corale Mori before him, Ron believes that tobacco is the first sacred plant, and that everything begins and ends with it. As Jem lights up his own tailor-made and we slowly meander out to the front porch to marvel at the stars and the weight of the night, I light my own *mapacho* and let the smoke fill me. Ruco the dog comes round and reads my energy and wrestles me, grabs my head and playfully bites down on my crown chakra . . .

"Your arm looked just like a cat's tail for a second there," Jem says—he's still tapping into the morphic field and seeing visions in his periphery. "Look, I just wanted to say—shit...You know, thank you, man, for this experience. I'll never forget you. I want you to know—that book I'm writing, you've changed...in a good way."

"I had a knowing, in the visions tonight, Jem. You know how we were discussing the missing link earlier...Well it's not the body that you should be looking for, it's just a fossil. It's the word-vibration-soul of the thing that feeds. Spirit comes in and becomes a cat, or dog, or snake, or human...We're all the energy, all part of that wavelength. When you say a word we make the vibration, we mint it crisp, we bring it down. *Look for the spirit, it's the missing link.*"

We go back inside the homestead then, wrapping ourselves in the warmth of the group, all roused and talking slowly, laughing and crying, all of us gnostic *ayahuasqueros* chewing the fat, sharing our lives, our insights on the medicine and the journey we've just shared. I look around and Juan, Nicole, Theo, Vance, Yotam, and the others are all calm and beatific. There is such a centeredness, a radiant calm from us all. I wonder if this is how the early Christians felt, partaking of their sacrament and being in the presence of their Lord.

"You know that Jesus took hallucinogenic plants also?" Ron asks philosophically.

"Yeah, I've heard the rumors," I laugh. "Jesus went to Gethsemane before the crucifixion, he went to the garden where the plants live. Even the cross he carried was made from a tree."

"Sure—and Moses and the burning bush, what the hell do you think he took to make him talk to that burning bush? Some kind of plant!" Ron cries excitedly.

Theo Valis comes around with a Blue Lily herbal cigarette and we all indulge. "How many people are there in the world?" Ron asks philosophically. "All of us make the One. Sometimes I think there's probably the same number of cells in a human body as there are people on the earth." The energy here is so sweet and replenishing; it feels like we are flowers that have opened up to the Source, drinking in the light, the sound, each other.

One of the functions of the shaman is world-bridger/word-bridger, and as always, Ron tells us stories:

"I used to be a butcher," he says lackadaisically. "I'd slaughter lambs. You have to hold them down, tie them out and make a long fast slit down the center, split it right open. Then you reach inside and grasp the heart, and squeeze it shut durn good. The animal is so gentle, it just goes with it then, it accepts and surrenders and it's like cream, the spirit creams and goes back into the great pool all spirit springs from.

"It's the same here in Peru—the body is blooded and gutted and skinned, and within half an hour you've got the meat boiling on the pot and the skins are drying and the animal has spread itself through the whole village, its essence is giving to us all, it just keeps on giving, and it lives on in us, the skin, the blood, and the soul..."

Amen to that, brother, amen. This all feels so divine. Da Vine. *The Vine of Souls*. The visions it brings and the connection it makes to ourselves and all things.

For this, my Lord, I am so grateful.

Part II
INITIATION

"We are not talking about passive agents of transformation, we are talking about an intelligence, a consciousness, an alive and other mind, a spirit. Nature is alive and is talking to us. This is not a metaphor."

—TERENCE McKENNA

14

Shaman School

Pasaje Colon, Iquitos

MONDAY JULY 17–TUESDAY JULY 18, 2006

The three-wheeled *motorcarro* speeds down the dirt road skirting the perimeter of the airport and turns into *Pasaje Colon,* depositing me outside the familiar two-story home of don Juan Tangoa Paima. I breathe a sigh of relief as I look up at the "Sanctum Sanctorium" where I'd had my intense ayahuasca breakthrough almost a week ago, and realize I'm home.

My training wheels have come off; I've said my goodbyes to Bowman, who's heading on to Cuzco, and Vance, who left this morning from out front of the Yellow Rose amidst a flurry of Shipiba women and last-minute *manta* fabric buying. I feel like a medieval monk leaving the world to cloister myself in this suburban tower, preparing to go deeper under the surface of the world with my teacher, to learn the ways of ayahuasca at Juan's shaman school.

This is the second week of the six-week course Juan's running alongside Carlos, his gringo apprentice, and while I'm only here for a taster, to write about the school and get an understanding of what they're doing, I've got some catching up to do to get up to speed—and I'm not sure if my "prior learning" with other *curanderos* will count here.

It's warm and sunny today in the late morning light. The whole family is up and going about their business and they immediately make me welcome as I get settled in the student rooms they've just finished building at the front of the house.

La casa is full of people and bustling with energy. Seven kids, some now adults with partners and kids of their own live here, as well as

Carlos and six gringos who are currently busy with lessons out in the backyard with Juan. The house is new, barely a year-old, built over a simple three-bedroom hut that preceded it. An electric saw pierces the tranquility with a screeching blade as one of Juan's son-in-laws cuts through some long planks of wood, and every few days more banging and construction goes on as little by little the house comes together.

As I unload my backpack Carlos tells me about the idea of this shaman school, which goes under the name of the "Wind Spirit Center for Healing," and how Juan convinced this white boy from Massachusetts to share his dream of a place to train Westerners in the healing arts of indigenous *curanderismo* . . .

"I really feel like he was calling to me, via the spirit of ayahuasca, or to Westerners like me, to come down and help him with the project, because it was something he wouldn't be able to do on his own," Carlos says with a proud smile. He's dressed in a white "Growroom" cannabis t-shirt and shorts, topped off with the red Che Guevara cap that never seems to leave his head. He's amiable, intelligent, a deeply spiritual guy—and an American through and through. He's designed rave flyers, gone through his party phase, hitchhiking the country and following bands like *Phish* all over, dabbled in psychedelics, majored in philosophy, and chowed down on burgers from every fast food chain from coast to coast. He loves his french fries, and yet, he also deals with the world of spirits.

Now at thirty-two he's an archetypal Gen X slacker fleeing the McGlobalized West and all it embodies for the suburbs of Iquitos and a life worth living. The trouble is, the West has followed him down south.

"Westernization has become more and more prevalent in every part of the Amazon and has resulted in reducing the number of *curanderos* because [its] influence is showing young people that there is a different future out there, a future that involves less of a sacrifice of their own hard work and energy and time—and for more reward, more monetary or materialistic reward," Carlos says, adjusting his glasses and lighting a tailor-made cigarette.

"So a lot of children don't want to go through the sacrifice of becoming a *curandero* because it is a difficult process and an enduring process . . . Modern medicine is implying that indigenous cultures are *primitive* and that they are modern and so their medicine is better. And so if people are going to pursue medicine in their lives they're more apt to learn Western medicine.

"So there are fewer and fewer *curanderos*. And there are many, many tribes now that don't have *curanderos*," Carlos sighs, heavy with the ways of the world. That's all good and well, but I wonder how opening a school to train Western healers is going to alleviate the indigenous lack of *curanderos*?

"Well, we aren't just going to be teaching Westerners," Carlos responds to my question with a smile. "The school is directed towards Westerners as a means to bring in money so that the few [indigenous] students that are still interested can study for free without having to pay for their schooling . . ."

Despite the proliferation of shamanistic retreats all around Iquitos, there's nowhere else in Peru quite like this school that Carlos and Juan are putting together, and I'm impressed both by what they're attempting to do and their sincerity. It's no small task they've set for themselves, especially for Carlos, who's left not just his culture behind, but the Western reality paradigm as well. It makes me wonder just what the hell a white boy like him is doing in Peru, apprenticing to an indigenous shaman trained in an unbroken lineage by the jungle tribes. And why does don Juan think a gringo has what it takes to continue the heritage?

"This is really difficult. In fact, most people think I'm out of my mind for wanting to do this," Carlos says sheepishly, and shrugs his shoulders. "I left a house with a hot tub and I drove a great car and had an awesome job. How could I possibly give that up for this?" He exhales cigarette smoke and stubs out his cigarette, carefully putting the butt in his pocket for later disposal. "But I felt like I had no choice and if I didn't give it up, and if I didn't decide to do this, I would be miserable."

I know what he means. Once you've started out on the spirit path there's no real turning back, no matter how hard you might try. But as

I've been finding, the more you accept the call the more synchronicities and opportunities open up, guiding you to where you need to be on the path. And as Carlos leads me out through the kitchen towards the other students in the back yard I feel right at home here among this Peruvian family, so different from the makeshift tourist tribes I've been hanging with on my travels.

Out the back the dogs are basking in the light while a little brown and black puppy circles round looking for love. Leonore, Juan's wife, is doing the washing in brightly colored plastic buckets to the side of the ayahuasca brewing area, as she was that first morning I visited last week, hanging out the family's clothes on the line. A baby kitten plays with the chickens as the dogs sniff the dirt, and then they all curl up and bask in the warmth together.

Juan's in his usual unassuming t-shirt and shorts, lecturing the American students who are gathered round the spacious back yard, which extends almost fifty meters back. There's two outside toilets (one just a makeshift curtain and a board over a small stream that runs through the yard, carrying all the compost and refuse away to some other neighbor), a concrete bathhouse, and dozens of giant trees with mature ayahuasca vines entwined around them, reaching up above the canopy to the light. Seeing Juan walking around with the Americans reminds me of Aristotle and the Greek "peripatetics" and how the philosopher was meant to wander round discoursing with his students in nature . . .

I want to make friends with Juan, but I quickly learn he's busy, and we have the language barrier between us. Juan is, in fact, constantly multi-tasking: instructing the students; performing family chores and helping with the building; preparing for our trip to the jungle next week; doing local community drop-in healings; and a million other things besides. The shock wave of his energy field is electric; he's like a hands-on CEO building a startup company from scratch and personally keeping it running with his own force of will. There's no dead time when Juan's around and the force of his energy and the stress he carries hang with him and colors all his interactions.

I hover round the *maestro* with imploring eyes, trying to find a free second to engage him while he talks to Jolane and Julia. Finally, he looks at me distractedly, like I've interrupted his train of thought, and shakes my hand and says something I don't understand in Spanish. "I won't carry you," he says abruptly in broken English, seeing my bewilderment, and turns back to the other students to continue his plant lecture.

"You have to make an effort yourself to learn," Carlos translates apologetically for Juan, tottering after him. I'm a little bit shocked and hurt by this, our first interaction. I can see he's busy and I respect that, but the bluntness of his manner doesn't leave me with a good first impression.

Like many teacher/student relationships, though, I know that the student has to be humble, to learn respect, and to obey the master. Freud's ideas of *transference* and how common it is to imprint onto an authority figure, and thus overlook any personal flaws, also comes to mind. That goes doubly so when turning on a person to psychedelics (or entheogens like ayahuasca). So it's quite easy to do the same with shamans. You get your favorites and you bond to the good ones, especially the first time you have that breakthrough experience.

For me, that was with Juan, under the gaze of the black puma almost a week ago. But for all my subconscious idolizing, and confusing the map with the territory, Juan's been quick to cut through it all. He simply doesn't have time for sycophants and that hits me like a Zen master administering the "a-ha" blow to the back of the student's head.

Right now we're in the equivalent of kindergarten—we've barely touched the surface of the spirit world and know little of its secrets, much less its rules. "I'm only in like, the third grade," Carlos says seriously, and he's been apprenticing for almost two years and sees and deals with spirits all the time. "Juan says when we get to the end of a long initiation—like the twentieth grade—then, and only then will we be ready to call ourselves *curanderos,* or healers." Behind his glasses his eyes sparkle for a second with a longing, the dream of a gringo from Massachusetts putting himself on the line and trying to make a difference in the world.

As Juan's called off to do a healing on a visitor, I blend in with the other students. There's Len, the friendly long-haired giant from Chicago, whom I'm bunking with in the boys room. He says he's here to further his own spirituality and to "foster the healing ability that's latent inside me." Last Saturday was his first time with the medicine and he's taken to it like a fish to water. Big, infectious smiles break across his face each new time he drinks now, he says, and embraces the flow.

Carina heard about the program from a friend, who drank with Juan last year. "I applied because I had just finished an apprenticeship doing herbal medicine in New York State and I was very interested in coming to South America and learning about alternative healing arts," she explains.

Her best friend, Julia, adds, "I've received a great deal of healing and education from taking the medicine and sacrament of ayahuasca. And I know that my brothers and sisters can also receive tremendous and profound healing and education through this work, and I want to help that process."

Jolane is an American currently living in Bristol, who wears rose-colored glasses and a cheerful smile. At thirty-seven she's the oldest student here, and also one of the most determined.

"I've realized that my path in life is to be a healer of some kind," she says, disarmingly. "So I wanted to try and develop these skills and learn a method of helping people that I knew worked. I know it works because it worked on me."

Last year don Juan purportedly freed her from possession by a spirit and performed an exorcism on her. This year she's learning *icaros* and how to heal herself. "People that think using psychedelics is a shortcut don't know what they're talking about," she says adamantly, "because you're packing so much work into a very short period of time. But I know it's doing me good—*I can feel it.* I can feel layers of stuff being pulled back and cleaned and fixed. It's fantastic."

They all have a friendly and infectious vibe, but it's funny to be surrounded by so many young Americans in their mid-twenties after the global backpackers I've been hanging with at the conference. Still, we're all students in shaman class, united by the vine that binds.

So it is that we all gather in the kitchen that night, fingering and smelling the *mapacho* cigarettes Juan has given us to aid in our dealings with spirits. We're all on a mini-*dieta*, restricting our intake to the small, toothless fish called *boquichico* (which inversely are so full of tiny bones it takes forever to pick apart and eat safely), boiled potatoes, broccoli, cucumber, and tapioca.

The idea behind it is that the toothless fish haven't eaten any other living creature and the boiled vegetables are sugar-free, which will allow our bodies to cleanse and readjust closer to the default settings we were born with, more or less. It's only a three-day diet, so it won't be that full-on, but as we sit here and Len reminisces about his favorite deep-pan pizza back in Chicago, it already seems like an eternity.

Juan's facing us at the kitchen table, singing an after-dinner *icaro* and explaining their importance. He hasn't eaten in almost three days, not since the last ceremony—it isn't necessary, he says—his energy body feeds him. All he's had is herbal tea, a little bit of liquid past his lips. "A *maestro* is like a plant—if he doesn't receive enough light, he shrivels and dies," Juan explains, translated by Carlos at his side. As his words hang in the air he hums another gentle rolling *icaro* as the smoke from his *mapacho* curls around his form.

The family is cooking a normal dinner behind us and two smelly dogs that have rolled in garbage and days old carcasses are gracing our feet while we gag at their smell. We're all talking about our Western food addictions and as I concentrate on the feeling of food, on the spirit of food, I try to draw the spirit essence of each foodstuff into me. I'm feeding my astral body like Juan does—tasting each bit, digesting them till I feel full in the bounty of this spirit kitchen and the magic weaved here.

The thought strikes me that the whole world needs to *dieta*, to purify the global body to make it a better receptacle for the soul. I suddenly realize that the diet fads that sweep the world have got it all wrong, that they're trying to sculpt the body, to shape it to fashion's whims, and the intent is all twisted. And in a flash of the mind's eye I can see *Paris,* and then *Britney,* and the millions of dominos that fall after them, the teenage girls of the world getting into ayahuasca culture and following the *dieta* and the purge. A generation of sassy Western *ayahuasqueras* that Norma could be proud of, all serving the spirit and treading the pathway to higher consciousness...

Juan calls ayahuasca "the Science" because to him it is. He explores, he tries things out and verifies the results, the same as any white lab-coated technician. The "geniuses" are the spirits within the Science, the entities all around that fill the astral ecology. They don't have human functions like we do—no hunger, no sex, maybe no fear or joy, either—that's why they're so attracted to humans and their flesh, to experience these things through us.

The right way to approach the spirits is humbly, with the right heart, Juan says. It's important to figure out whether they're a good spirit or a bad one—and the simplest way to do that is through action. If they attack you, bite off your own etheric arm or try to do you harm, well, that's a bad spirit. If they don't threaten you they're probably good and then you have to develop a relationship with them. Really.

Next, ask them their name, because all creatures—here and there—have *vibrational wavelength-names* they attach to, and to know their name is to have an opening to their power. Then you sing *icaros* to them, wooing them.

"This is the essence of ayahuasca," Juan says, feeding us with his knowledge and the energy that radiates from him.

"Juan is a spirit doctor, and sometimes he goes to conferences in the spirit world to hear what the spirits know and compare notes on new events and developments," Carlos explains from the end of the table. "New problems mean new advice must be sought—but God always has the last word."

It's like this: Juan's been treating the local community for many years. While he has many regular patients with ongoing ailments, like arthritis, there are also new diseases and problems that develop, so new cures must be sought. For instance, Lonzo, a young man in his early twenties, came to see Juan six months ago. Western medicine had diagnosed him with AIDS he caught from unprotected sex. Juan had never encountered the spirit of AIDS before, so he did a quick diagnostic with ayahuasca and it told him to seek out a specific plant, that its spirit could help.

So, in spirit form the good doctor sought out this plant on the astral, and its "genius" transmitted its *icaro,* the special song it held within its heart. With that vibrational string, that frequency locked in, Juan developed a relationship with the plant and used its song to heal Lonzo. He's been coming twice a week for over six months now, and Carlos says that the open, weeping lesions that gouged his skin have gone, his strength has returned, and the AIDS virus within him is in remission.

I've heard all about the "miracle" curing properties of ayahuasca before, but I've yet to meet anyone first-hand that has been saved from a fatal disease with it. Still, as Juan says often, *nothing is impossible with the spirit of ayahuasca.*

"Juan has given himself to the Science [ayahuasca], and it's important that you give yourself to him, and have faith in the Science through trusting him," Carlos says, smiling at his teacher.

I remember the freak-out Eliza had back at Ron Wheelock's house during the night of the beasts, screaming about black magic, the work of the devil, and how my own ego desires led me astray. I agree—you have to trust your master, that's why it's so important you find one you energetically mesh with so no loose ends remain, no doubts to affect your trip.

At the moment though I find myself wanting and trying to mesh like that with Juan, but somehow it just never sticks.

"*Ay la li ay la li ay la li ay la li . . . Ay la li li li li lili lili lili lili li li . . . ay la li ay la li lili lili lili lay . . . ay la lili lili lay . . . ay la la lili lay . . . ay lili lili ili lay la lay la lay la la lili lili la la lay . . .*" Juan sings. "These sounds have a property that helps to cleanse the body when sung," the *maestro* says. "It is very important to know an *icaro,* because it is power, the power to cure. If you have your own *icaro,* or *icaros,* then you will be able to heal yourself."

"Every *icaro* is a power, each one has a knowledge." As Juan sings at the table we're trying to whistle along, to capture those essential frequencies like groupies being fed crumbs from the master. I hum along and try to lock in the groove, but it eludes me. I keep getting Western imprints, theme songs, ringtone tunes, and I realize that's one of the ways our culture keeps us boxed in, with sonic mantras flooding our brain and keeping us on controllable wavelengths.

It's the same with our plants. The tobacco here, *Nicotiana rustica,* has no chemical additives so it's clean enough to connect with and evoke the spirit. Smoking it creates an instant burst of new receptors that flood the brain, spurred on by the intense nicotine rush. That's why native peoples all over the world use it as a sacred plant—not a consumable to feed addictions. The tobacco here is literally *psychoactive* if you know how to approach it, to bless it, and sing to it.

Put three *mapacho* cigarettes in half a cup of water, let them soak and the spirit-essence of the tobacco will come through, Juan says. Then you drink the tobacco juice. "It turns your day into night," he laughs. "It gives you visions and is a strong purgative. If you are threatened by bad spirits you can protect yourself wherever you are with tobacco and blow them away, but you have to know the *icaros* and how to prepare it."

"Ayahuasca can heal, but it can also be used to kill," Carlos continues to translate for Juan, reminding us of the dark side of this force. The key is remaining humble, being a servant of ayahuasca, not a master. "Give yourself to the benefit of others, to God," Juan says, his eyes darting over us, reading our energies. "You must have a purpose to help other people, a desire to help others. If you have a pure heart, a humble mind, and faith in your soul—then the Science will open up to you and show you its wonders."

The potential Western *curanderos* here are a long way off from that level of healing, though. Jolane's about the only one who has locked in a basic *icaro* rhythm, although Len, Julia, and Carina have also been practicing hard each day, listening to Juan sing on CDs Carlos has given them.

"*Icaros* can reduce your visions because when you first learn them it's like changing gears, and your attention or consciousness goes from watching to singing," Juan warns, yawning now, his energy dimming like a flickering candle. "This can reduce your connection with the visions, until you learn to sing the *icaros* like second nature, without splitting your attention. Then you don't even need ayahuasca. The *icaros* are the keys to communication, you must dedicate your life to them."

Juan gets up and collects the cigarettes left on the table and smiles at us with a weary look on his face, winding down from a long day. He's full of secrets, of knowledge and power, and while his class tonight has barely scrapped the surface it's been invigorating, nonetheless.

"I was born in 1951, but my spirit was born a thousand light-years ago . . ." he says out of the blue. "It's the same as with Jesus Christ: he was here for an infinite, infinite amount of time before he came to this planet to be born into the Virgin Mary. Likewise, I am a spirit that has existed for thousands and thousands of years before I was born into this specific body. So if you really want to know the story of how I got involved in *curanderismo* it begins a thousand light years ago . . ."

And then, as if offering us a last little cosmic morsel on our school plates, he stops by the back door and says, "Each planet has an energy, an auric field that envelops and protects and nurtures it, and connects to the rest of the cosmic garden. Each planet's vibration has to be penetrated to enter it, and it takes a strong mind to tune into the wavelengths and work with them. The force of your mind allows you to penetrate these areas and explore the universe with your spirit."

There's a sparkle in his dark eyes as his lips curl back into a smile, and he knows he's got us hooked. And then the kitchen lesson is over, leaving us with new ideas to digest, and a world of spirits to feast on.

It's *boquichico* fish, boiled vegetables, and tapioca for breakfast this morning, as it was all yesterday, and the effects are starting to make themselves known. With all the natural sugars gone from my neurochemistry, the plain state that is left is more open and receptive to frequencies, and I can feel that now familiar theta-wave vibratory frequency settling lightly over my third eye.

It's not just brought on by ayahuasca or DMT, I realize—it's a natural receiver state of the brain that Western foodstuffs dilute and pollute. Fasting has a well-known ability to bring on the visionary state, and we now know that on a neurochemical level reducing the intake of sugars filters off high-end faculties and lowers vitamin uptake, which then removes *nicotinic acid,* a visionary inhibitor, from the blood. Now here in the jungle, after much ayahuasca and a day of the sugar-free *dieta,* my mind is slowly becoming clear, and my receiver of consciousness is flickering with the feather-soft tremble of spirit's wings.

Ariel and Meera are singing *icaros* and hammering up some ayahuasca vine, chopping its body down into shards for the brew tonight. Ariel's bare-chested, with long hair that trails down past his shoulders, a dark beard, and caramel eyes that look right into you and lock and load. He looks just like Jesus would have 2,000 years later, white billowing pants, beard, long black hair tied back—except his sandals are Velcro explorer wear.

Meera, his lover, is small and slim, with long dark hair and black eyes, proud Jewish looks—strong and full of power—and as they sing *icaros* to the vine and hammer and imbue the wood with positive energy, I take an instant liking to them both. *"Ah manyana tiempo . . . Oh ha lana uri . . . malagrade siedam . . ."* they sing back and forth to get the correct words and pitch.

They're a beautiful couple, here learning the ways of ayahuasca. They've been with Juan for two and a half months, dieting, singing, making the brew and tending the fires, cooking for the family, playing guitar, and radiating love. It feels like I imagine a kibbutz would, the energy they bring and connect with, the big family we have all become.

Picking up a thin piece of cut vine, its brown-green skin colored with splashes of milky white, I see the ayahuasca symbol that the Shipiba grandmother manta hustlers sew on their patterns, the seed cross-section that was on Ron Wheelock's altar the other night. It looks like a five-leaf clover, a sacred geometry flower there in the root heart of the vine, all the way through. I know that it all means something, that the outward symbol reflects an inner energy that has shaped it. *The world, she talks to us in these symbols, and as I deepen my shamanic studies I'm here to listen, to learn, and to transmit her message.*

The brew they made last Saturday night was too strong, it was cooked for double the time, and a lot of *icaros* and energy was piled into it to make up for a relatively weak brew the time before. Everyone was floored, unable to find center. The ceremony lasted over six hours as the *ayahuasqueros* flailed about on the floor unable to cope with the intensity. *Bastante*—too much, everyone agreed, too much.

I know this because Bowman went to the Saturday night circle here when it turned out Guillermo wasn't drinking, and by all accounts he barely survived. He said he felt the darkness all around, attracted to his perception of it, his sneaking doubts about the light and dark here. And when the darkness descended and engulfed him he found a strength within himself, an ability to grow bubble-like force-shields that welled up and enveloped and protected him from the dark, dark things.

Monika drank here that night, too, the day after her DMT experience at Ron's. She went to the hell realms, she told me later, shredded on a dark wheel of energy that unraveled her very being.

"Juan gave me a big brew because I told him I had health issues, but now I think at the core it is a psychological thing, a dark memory of something that happened to me as a child. But that brew—I can't do it again, I can't go to those dark places, it's too much. It's like a flood of information and I can't process it, I need a trickle to fill me, to pace myself and learn." Her piercing blue-green eyes were pleading, connecting, transmitting her pain as she shared the memory.

Even don Juan and Carlos were floored; Carlos was unable to move, and don Juan was shaken, disorientated by the power of the vine, Bowman said. It took all their strength to go to the aid of another woman who left her body entirely, and whose soul was in danger of being lost in the unchartered depths of the cosmos. All she could do was utter Shipibo whistles and sounds when roused, like vibrational wind whooshing through an empty house—no mind was left to navigate the journey. Juan stayed with her for a long time and eventually managed to ride back her soul, to sculpt it back into her body and close the door. Just in the nick of time.

So after that hell journey everyone's nervous and wanting a lesser trip as the ceremony begins later tonight. Juan's eyeballing people and measuring out controlled doses, what he thinks they need, but not heroic doses like on previous nights.

There's us six gringos students and the two Israeli live-ins lined against the walls, sitting on straw mats on the concrete floor. Four Peruvians are sitting in the plastic chairs opposite the *maestro,* including Lonzo, the young man with AIDS who comes regularly to be treated, his dad, and now, it appears, his mom as well. We're all settling into the group mind vibe, letting our energies mingle as we drink one by one and find our sacred space within.

Both Juan and Carlos are tired from a long and exhausting day dealing with mundane matters: getting the boat ready for our jungle trip next week; reconciling with Juan's English business partner who's gone off the deep end about their property and access rights to it; and, of course, dealing with us gringos and our needs as students, and the responsibilities therein.

Juan is especially tired, and he tells us so as we sit and wait for the ayahuasca to come on. He also tells us that he is here, as always, and will lead the ceremony and the healing, but it's kind of begrudgingly. I'm getting to know his energy signature and sometimes when he's tired he leaks energy and emotions, his ego and human body's needs and frailties come through. But he is here to heal, he says, this is his duty and responsibility.

"*Juannnn! Juaaannnn! Juaaaannn!!!*" a piercing cry suddenly breaks our reverie. It sounds like a crowd outside, many voices—is this some type of group hallucination? No, it's a group of people that have descended on us right at the beginning of our ceremony—and the timing couldn't have been worse.

Carlos goes out and confronts the crowd in his ayahuasca-bewildered state. A tour group has turned up unannounced, and a group of Germans and English tourists are standing there, all dressed in white. Carlos leads them inside and the local Peruvians are shuffled off to the kitchen to give seat space to the new arrivals. The energy is crazy; we can all feel the energetic disruption of the new crew but we're already loaded and rolling, no time to integrate them before the aya comes on . . .

I can hear sounds, strange liquid burbling noises that pop and rustle and waver and become, like musical burping. My mind seems to sing them at the same time as hear them, as we overlap and become one. Virtual kaleidoscopic spaces open up, the realm of the colors and the light and the underlying sound or vibration, which forms them. *Jaguarflutterbys* are speeding by and melting into the mind's eye, drawing my consciousness to these perceptions, the ability of ayahuasca to open these doors . . .

Watching this screensaver of the soul I cast out my mental net: "*Come to me ayahuasca, my mother, my sister, my lover. Teach me your secrets, show me your real self,*" I whisper in the dark, as her light fills me. And aya shows me herself, her true self, and the screen of my mind is filled with a liquid gold like molten sunlight. It runs up my left arm like a snaking virus, becoming me, infecting me with the light, the yolk of infinite becoming. I grok what she is telling me, the secret of aya: *liquid, intelligent light . . .*

The vine drinks of the light, deep from the Source. It is the receiver of cosmic information and it transmits it to us to become one with the cosmic order. The top of the food chain is the sun, and beyond that, the galactic sun, and so on and so on in infinite regress through the cosmic ecology, the synaptic pathways of the universal brain, each sun a pinprick of neuronal activity on the macro scale. As above so below. The cosmic chicken and the egg, and the timing of it ALL . . .

But as the vision fades I'm pulled back to normal consciousness. There's a lot of blockages tonight, a lot of holding back and a wild energy from the new arrivals that none of us was anticipating, and the overall result is a mild journey that barely scratches the surface of the holy space. But the cause and effect, the timing of these things are never what they seem. Everything is perfect, always.

Aya gave me what I needed, a booster shot to tune me back into the Source, but she also denied me free reign to become in that space. Aya put me in my place as a humble servant of the call. *Patience, she seemed to say. This is day one. You have a lifetime of lessons in front of you.*

When the ceremony is over I return to my room, slightly deflated from the mild journey but also awakened again to the call of ayahuasca. I didn't purge in ceremony, which was a first, and I take this as a good omen for my deepening relationship. But when I sleep... drawn into the dreaming, endogenous DMT rushing to fill the serotonin receptors in my brain and unlocking the world within... Then the medicine, the science starts to play with me and reward me for my patience. Tuning into the sleep, a fluttering frequency fills my forehead over the third eye, and I'm catapulted into deep, electric DMT space...

All through the night and into the morning my dreaming becomes a lucid sheet lightning of totems and energetic connections... Towards dawn, all the thousand and one roosters of Iquitos break into synchronized a cappella hosannas to the light, and the rush, the waterfall, the vast notes of beauty contained in their call become me from the inside out. "*Koo ka kaaa Ko,*" they sing one after the other...

For long hours the roosters crow to the glory of God, they fill the air with their song, the yolk of their becoming. They sing the *chicken icaro* and hint at the secret of the golden light that connects us all in its infinite thread, the molten heart of ayahuasca.

A dog howls. In the room next to me a man is making love to a woman and her muffled cries, the pleasured, rounded ohhhs reverberate over and over through the air, merging with the cry of nature, the chickens and the insects, all of us beasts.

I'm totally connected to the web of life all around me, pulling at its threads and wrapping them into me, and the timing of us all is perfect, complete, and unbroken...

15

Snakes and Ladders

Pasaje Colon, Iquitos
WEDNESDAY JULY 19–SATURDAY JULY 22, 2006

Juan's got the *curandero* blues this morning and he's got every reason to be upset. He gripes about his problems, and they are many. In ceremony in the dark last night I'd heard him tirading to Jessica, Carlos's Peruvian girlfriend. She's been coming to the last few circles and is interested, apparently, in being a *curandero* herself. It was in Spanish, of course, but the gist was he's got problems too, you know, and the life of a *curandero* ain't easy, no siree, and that's plain to see today.

Juan's lucky to earn ten soles a day from the local community, yet he cannot refuse the call of the spirit, or turn people away. On top of his duties as a healer, he's still building his house and school; he has eight kids under his roof and seven grandchildren; and he's the sole breadwinner. People are dropping round all morning to chat, to be healed . . . and to discuss projects. Juan's always on the go but his energy levels can't keep up forever.

He's run down—on Carlos's infrared footage of last night's ceremony he was even falling asleep towards the end. He's not infallible, no matter what his ego would have us believe. He may be a "Sorcerer Supreme," but he's also a man, and the world wears us all down in the end. And Juan can't afford to let his guard down—he has enemies, *brujos* wanting to take him down. "*Brujeria* everywhere," is his perennial refrain; you have to be constantly on your guard.

I'm grumpy this morning, too, a hangover from the electric shock the power point gave me when I tried to recharge the iBook to finish the *Australian Penthouse* article. A full surge of electricity ran up my arm, just like the molten light did in the ayahuasca vision. On the bottom bunk bed across from me Len's busy singing away to Juan's *icaros* and his enthusiastic, high-pitched screeches drive me out into the main room.

I thought I'd just about seen it all by now, but I have to do a double take when I walk by to see Juan whipping a withered, pain-addled grandmother with an *oretga,* or *eshunga* plant, a thorny pain bush. She's like, seventy or so, withered, and her top is off revealing saggy breasts with the texture of shriveled prunes. Sharp sighs escape her as Juan whips her over and over again, across her entire body, dragging the spiny thorns on an angle to better connect with her forehead and cheeks.

"AAHHHH," she screams, flinching back from the master. As he keeps flagellating her shoulders and legs she cries out again from the pain, her eyes trembling and hands shaking. My heart goes out to her but it's a steely kind of a heart, because I know that this too, is medicine.

The *eshunga* brings pain to take pain away. It numbs the body where it's been stung and in this case it's working on a deep, cellular level to remove her arthritis. She's good-natured about it, crying out every few seconds and pulling away, but then allowing Juan to keep working—as if she has much choice by the way he grips her arm.

Later in the day in the bedroom next door I can hear him *soplar-ing* Leonore and his children, the short, sharp *whoosh* ringing out as he cleanses their foreheads with the smoke. He does this regularly with the family, healing and locking down their energetic centers and I suspect it's not just for their health, but their psychic protection from all that *brujeria* out there he's always so worried about. And after what happened to his first wife, well, I wouldn't be taking any chances...

Carlos told me the story that first ceremony night, when we smoked *mapachos* and gently came down from our ayahuasca high. Over the years Juan has traveled extensively, training with many *curanderos* to further his knowledge of *curanderismo.* He found a powerful teacher with the Achuri tribe in northwest Peru, the adjoined tribe of the Shuar Indians over the border in Ecuador. These tribes used to be one, until the government took land and redrew the map, splitting the community in two. Juan stayed with the Achuri and eventually, as the next powerful person after his teacher died, he became their chief.

Carlos tells me that was unusual because he was not of Achuri blood. Juan was the first *mestizo* chief of the Achuris and remained with them until a time came when they, through visions, saw it was important that he leave and spread the wisdom of the Achuris to as many people as possible.

They felt that their tribal culture and people would soon be gone due to the Westernization that was inevitably happening. They couldn't preserve their culture and they couldn't preserve their bloodline, but hopefully they could preserve their wisdom for the benefit of humankind.

Somewhere along the line though, Juan made a lot of enemies, and a group of nine jealous *brujos* got together and decided to take him down. They hired an *achiquero,* a witch that works with specific animals like spiders and snakes, and paid her several thousand dollars in order to attack Juan. But she couldn't penetrate Juan's defenses because he had attained such a powerful level in the spiritual dimension.

However his wife, whom he met in his early twenties when he came to Iquitos, did not drink ayahuasca and was the spot of weakness within him. And so one night while she was sleeping a black centipede crawled inside her vagina and bit her. The black centipede is one of the most venomous creatures in the Amazon. It was too much for her and too much for Juan... and she did not survive.

So when Juan found his next wife, whom he had seen in many, many visions over and over again, he made sure that she drank ayahuasca. He insisted that she build her own defenses and become a *curandera* in her own right. Not to the levels that Juan has, because of her responsibilities to her family, but enough that she would have defenses against an attack of that nature. *Brujeria* all around, you see, once bitten twice shy, and you can never be too careful. *Claro.*

I've read about the painter Pablo Amaringo, whose book *Ayahuasca Visions* has so many spellbinding pictures of the visionary realms. He'd trained to be a *curandero* for many years but rejected the path when it became apparent that he would have to kill another *brujo* that blocked his way, and his is just one *brujeria* story among many. All this black magic and sorcery was starting to feel like an astral version of a Mafia gang war, all those dons revenging themselves on each other.

By coming here and training with don Juan we were potentially opening ourselves up to his enemies, I realized. What the hell had I dropped myself into, I wondered? But it was too late to back out now—even if I wanted to.

Later, still pondering the *brujeria* dilemma, I go to cleanse myself in the washroom out the back of the house. There's a deep stone circular well in the center of the room, and after bathing with cold water in a plastic bucket I hoist myself up over the lip of the well and dangle my feet down into its obsidian depth. I can't feel the bottom. And suddenly, a vision:

I'm surrounded by serpents in a pit of a million snakes, writhing and curling over and over each other like one giant super-organism. The wet, rank smell of fear and death hangs around me. I'm in the pit and the sound of the snakes breathing and hissing is electric, filling the chamber and reverberating into me—and then it's gone.

I pull myself out of the well, shaking. What the fuck was that, I wonder? *Brujeria?* Or a projection of my own fears? It seems an augur of things to come, but am I ready to confront it, whatever it was, to go into the dark place and learn what it has to teach me? Do I even have a choice about it?

Thursday morning Carlos wakes me just after dawn and we go with Juan's teenage son Gabriel to the Belén markets in town to gather food for everyone. The markets stretch on for miles in every direction, thin streets chocked full of the hustle and bustle of life and a vibrancy that is exuded from every person like a pheromone, the hot and sweaty stick of the primal buy and sell.

Belén is divided into sections: fresh fish, meat, fruit, vegetables, spices, clothes, sacred plants and medicinals, consumer items, and the unexpected. The narrow walkways between the wooden stalls are rigged up with plastic tarps and string to create patchwork tunnels for the trade. Walking through the market almost feels hallucinogenic in itself, with the steady onrush of Peruvians with their rounded smiles and life-energy streaming past and into you, making you part of this place.

We pass a spice store and the flash of color is like a rainbow. Dozens of powdered spices and rich liquids are hanging on strings, trapped in plastic bags, brand name noodles hanging behind them. Next to the spices two middle-aged women in blue dresses and aprons are cutting and gutting chickens, right out in the open on the table, dozens of carcasses laid out on a blue tarp and buckets on either side to wash them on the way in and for the entrails on the way out. The women handle their knives with the quick, sure cut of surgeons, skills honed by a lifetime of slicing, as second nature as breathing.

All of the market people have the same unassuming vibe. They're at home here, doing what they do to make a living and they've been doing it so long it's part of them, visceral. And it's not quite Third World, just Peruvian. The locals are getting around in t-shirts and jeans, shorts and skirts, sandals and flip-flops, baseball caps. It's just down to earth, I guess, with no First World pretension.

We pass stalls with shimmering produce from the sea, fish still fresh and twitching in the air, their scaly bodies piled one on top of each other. Like the chickens, the fish are being gutted here in the open, life and death on display for all to see. The web of life is so strong here you can virtually reach out and twang the threads and see the reverberations and drink in the energy.

Like markets everywhere, the stallholders hang in the shadows with an expectant air, like a spider about to pounce on its prey and lay their spiel on you. Three-wheeled *motocarro* taxis cruise by the narrow streets, jostling with shoppers and men lugging huge loads of green bananas on their backs. We pass through the fruit and vegetable stalls and the wash of color is overwhelming, Technicolor, more real than real. At another stall, live turtles are on their backs, struggling for balance in a world turned upside down.

A motorbike taxi pulls up with three giant pig carcasses stretched out stiff in the back seat, hooves and snouts sticking out of the open-air carriage. Their skin is white-pink and blooded, wrinkled like they don't quite fit, or as if they've been shed and re-suited and not quite put on again correctly. There's a slit down their centers from head to toe and they've been partially sewn up again for the journey between worlds, from the slaughterhouse to the market. They look so incongruous there in the back of the taxi, their bodies on the vinyl seats like paying passengers, like they're asleep, all of them, despite their red and gaping wounds.

Still the market goes on and on, seemingly inexhaustible, women with children in their arms, breastfeeding babies, slicing, gutting, dicing, life and death, life and death, the energy of the animals and the plants intermingling with the humans, rubbing off till they are all one strange fruit.

And again and again I realize—we ARE all one, this is the vision that ayahuasca brings, of the unity of all things, energy packets in the waveform embedded with life essence. These individual bodies that contain and frame us are all on display here today, every day in the markets of Belén and the markets of the world. Creatures eating and being eaten, killing and being killed, the free markets that capitalism is only a pale shadow of.

We head up *Pasaje Paquito,* which is perhaps better known by its nickname "Shaman's Alley," the long vertical strip that connects two main thoroughfares of the Belén Market and where all the sacred plants and medicinals are sold. It's popular with the locals as well as the gringos and I'm barely there a second before a woman is calling, "Ayahuassssscca ... Senor, ayahuasca. San pedro?" and shoving a small glass jar of powdered san pedro extract under my nose.

Plantas Medicinales, Curantivos, Afrodisiacos the hand painted shingle above her store says. She manages to communicate in broken English and hand signals that you put the san pedro under your tongue and see visions. Her stall also has ayahuasca vine broken up into wood chips in a bag at the front, *chacruna* and *chagraponga* leaves, *mapacho* cigarettes and cigars, tobacco and smokes of a hundred varieties and dozens of other items I don't recognize. Bottled potions with white handwritten labels line the walls like a wine cellar, but all these brews cleanse, cure, and bring you closer to God.

There are medicinals stalls like hers lining Shaman's Alley on both sides and business is brisk. Mixed in among the bottles are little dolls, herbal love and sex potions, arthritis remedies, candles, soaps, creams, coca, as well as the hallucinogens. This is the end result of legalized drugs—not the shock and awe and crumbling of civilization that the moral majority and the spin doctors have been prophesizing for generations, but the simple integration of sacred plants as medicines available for all who need them, sold openly beside the fruit, meat, and vegetables that also feed us.

Past Shaman's Alley the outer rim of the market breaks and you can see down to the river and the ramshackle wooden shantytowns down by the water's edge where the market people live—the slums of Belén. The whole town is built on rafts and when the water rises so too does the town, floating on the water and the refuse that is carried away by it, the Venice of the Amazon.

"Belén" translates in Spanish as *Bethlehem,* and walking through the shantytown past the market, seeing the families living their lives in the open, their wooden bungalows with no walls and thatched roofs, children playing in the dirt streets, I realize it's entirely possible that this place is a Bethlehem. *Christ consciousness* is on the rise, after all.

Which makes me wonder which house is the poorest of the poor, where is the manger, and when will the Peruvian messiah be born? Ninety percent of the locals are Christians, imprinted with the religion of the *conquistadores.* They wear their crosses around their necks, adorn their buses and *motorcarros* with Jesus stickers with his open heart chakra connecting to the spirit world, and they breed like rabbits from puberty on, eschewing condoms and birth control, which the vast majority don't have access to anyway.

Children are the biggest resource this place has and every family has at least half a dozen kids milling round their shanty huts and playing with each other, filled with the joy of life. They are poor, but happy. Like dustbowl peasants in a Steinbeck novel, all they have is each other, and the poor help the poor. You see them sharing food, looking after each other's kids, huddling together in the rain to keep dry. They are a tribe, a community, and together they are rich.

There's a rainbow over Belén this morning as we return from town and unload our goodies. The others are about to break *dieta* and feast on a meal of rice, black beans, boneless fish, bread, and fruits, and even though my body is tempted my spirit is strong. The *jaguarflutterby* feeling over my third eye has been intense for days now, like I'm developing a new neural pathway connecting me to the spirit world that I'm loathe to flush away with a wash of natural sugars and spices.

Carlos, however, wants me to break diet—Juan is building up our tolerances over time and I'm urged not to deviate from Juan's wishes. I feel like I'm being shanghaied but Juan is the master and I am but the humble student. And that food sure does smell good.

I'm not the only one who isn't up to eating, however—Carina's sick, again, as she has been on and off for the last few days now, so queasy, in fact, that she couldn't hold down the ayahuasca in the last ceremony. She went into town with Julia yesterday to get a pregnancy test and lo and behold, it was positive.

"I feel that everything happens for a reason," she tells us all after breakfast, with a wide smile, as her whole world turns topsy-turvy. Instead of coming here to learn the art of *curanderismo,* the tiny being growing within her has changed her whole center of gravity, and she's starting to see the real reason she's been brought down here is for her own healing.

"The fact that I found out down here was a blessing," she says later. "I feel like I've received so much love and healing from Juan and the ceremony, not only for myself going through this new step, but also for the baby that is inside of me growing. I feel that it is such a unique blessing for it to be experiencing all of this in the earliest stages of life."

Ayahuasca is a medicine as all *curanderos* throughout South America stress, and it's fine for pregnant women to drink. Juan's wife Leonore drank ayahuasca up to her eight month of pregnancy with her last child, but as Carina says, "It's a special case for every woman, what her body is feeling, how sensitive it is—and mine just feels very sensitive."

So no more ayahuasca for her, although she's happy to stay and see out the rest of the course, and participate in ceremonies in spirit, if not in body. As her best friend Julia squeezes her hand and gives her a reassuring smile, I realize I really like Carina. She has a gentle demeanor and funny schoolgirl giggle, and it's nice to be able to share this intimate time of her life with her and the other students.

After breakfast and the breaking of the diet, the *jaguarflutterbys* feeling fades. I can feel the sugars, the natural glucoses, sweet and beautiful entering my body and settling back in the grooves of my brain, bringing me back to baseline. I feel pained, upset, but respectful of don Juan's orders not to stress the body-mind too much too soon, to have respect and patience. So I sit out with Ariel and Meera who are practicing making their own ayahuasca and have chopped and crushed a vine down and washed and tended the *chacruna* leaves gently in a colander.

It's said that every plant has an energy or spirit, and also a male-female gender. The most powerful DMT-containing ayahuasca brews are potentiated by picking only the male *chacruna,* or *chagraponga* leaves, Meera tells me. You can tell the male leaves by turning them over and looking down towards the base where a little bud protrudes, the plant penis. Adding the yang energy of the male *chacruna* leaves to the yin energy of ayahuasca perhaps balances out the brew and synergistically makes its power stronger.

Ariel is playing Hebrew folk songs on his guitar, wooing the spirit of ayahuasca in the metal pot on the fire in the backyard. They sound like Cat Stevens tunes, gentle rhythms that ripple out from him through the air and connect with us all. Both he and Meera have bright red welts over their bodies, marks from the *eshunga* plant they have whipped their bodies with, the same one I saw Juan operating on with the old lady yesterday.

"Wow, that's *eshunga*, right?"

"You want to try?" Meera asks, and before I can say anything she's grabbed a knife and gone over to the little plank bridge across the stream that acts as the backyard waste disposal system, flushed last night by the rain, and picked a clipping for me. She whittles back the sharp, prickly thorns that grace the stem and overflow in smaller spikes on the surface of the leaf, like hairs on skin.

"I can't believe I'm doing this," I say. "Thank you for picking it for me though, for feeling pain for me."

"It's okay, it only hurts a little," Meera smiles back. "You really have to trim it back to be able to hold it and apply it to your body."

"Okay..." Whew. I take a deep breath and invoke the power of this plant, to learn its secrets and energy. *Come into me, eshunga, grant me your strength, your power. Make me strong, so I can be a better vessel for the spirit.*

And I start whipping, the thorns of the plant catching and piercing my skin, over my hands and up my arms, over the shoulders and onto my back. Thick red welts spring up where *eshunga* has touched me and the pain sears in, an itchy, red heat, a wall of hurt...

Ahhhh, my body feels alive, absorbing the pain and turning it into strength. I feel great. I keep applying this plant medicine till my whole body is covered head to toe, then I brush it over my forehead and cheeks, my ears, feeling the power and vibrancy of the thorns starting to fade already, the energy of it in me.

"The plants bring pleasure and they also bring pain," Meera jokes, smiling at me. "But always, you learn about yourself. With ayahuasca, it reflects the mirror of who you are."

Meera's been learning the *icaros* and how to heal and all of the mechanics of shamanism, but her journey, like those of all the students here, is very internal. "I'm working on releasing my fears, my darkness, all of this," she says with a wave of her hand. "You should too."

I look down at the ayahuasca brew on the boil as the deep muddy brown starts to bubble over with green. Meera starts singing the *icaro*, "Ayahuasca . . . ayahuasca . . . ayahhhhhuuuuuuu-asca," over and over again, a Santo Daime song she's learned, stringing away on the guitar and the energy is so calm and content and loving, all of it, all of us and our frequencies feeding the brew.

Ariel uses a leaf fan to bolster the flames, adjusting the wood under the fire and tending to it with a singular patience. I wonder about him—and Meera—two open, loving Israelis, and how they've ended up here in South America learning the ways of ayahuasca.

Santo Daime may have grafted its jungle wisdom onto a syncretic Christian mass, but it could work as a sacrament in any other brand religion, deepening the theology with a working entheogenic catalyst. It's certainly not orthodox, but ayahuasca could revitalize religion as we know it by cutting across whichever surface dogma you ascribe to and connecting you to the planetary spirit pulsing underneath.

"What do you think it's doing—the ayahuasca?" I ask. "Do you vision, and does that challenge your own religion, the Jewish faith you've been taught?"

"No, it deepens it," Meera says. "Through ayahuasca I'm learning to see visually." Where Western psychology would say that the interior visions are triggered by the individual's subconscious, the understanding that ayahuasca brings goes much further. There are independent entities out there, it reveals, but as Meera says, "It's like if I see a bad spirit, it's not a bad spirit—it's me. It's part of me but this part is a reflection because everything is ONE. Even the spirits are a part of me. Of course they exist in the world because the world has many different parts, but when I see a spirit or something that reflects in me, I learn how to work with these parts that are unbalanced, to give them love and to heal them.

"In that way, slowly I feel I am learning to do this with other people, too. It's amazing that the cure, the *icaro,* is really a projection of love, it

249

connects to your heart. And I feel, basically, that no matter how many techniques you have, the basic technique to connect to that place which is so pure, is *love*. There are no other motives. This is what I feel. It's very hard to put into words."

Ariel's still stirring the pot and tending the fire with a cool, collected strength. When he's finished tending the brew he sits down on the white plastic chair next to me and gives me a warm smile.

"The main work for me with ayahuasca now is to know the fourth dimension," he tells me, his pale eyes shying away. "The work I'm doing here is to practice that and be open to it, and also to let other people know about it, to prepare themselves for something that I believe is happening in a few years to come. It's very important. For me this connection is something I was born with, not just something I read about, and it's become clearer and clearer as I went on."

He's a very centered dude, soft-spoken and self-contained, radiating a strong and light-filled energy. He really does remind me of an ayahuasca Jesus—a holy man cleansed by the plant and filled with an inner light from the connection it's revealed.

"My creativity has grown five times," he continues. "Every time I want, and this happens to a lot of people I know who use ayahuasca, you just wish for a song, or you feel like you want to receive a song, or a picture or anything, and you receive it. A lot of beautiful and amazing things come to you that are a part of you, but it's not your ego, your machismo, it's something you think of coming through you. You become like a tube, a radio station or receiver for this world of the self and for the heavens to pour through. It's a kind of unity that I feel is much more perfect."

All of that love is going into the brew that will slow boil all day, and then Saturday night we will fly...

Then the *maestro* sings the heavens open and a wave of healing sound-vibration washes over us. Fluttering dreamspace spirits soaring, calling out to me: *feathers.* Knee-deep in the session ayahuasca brings me a vision of feathers, glistening in the light of mind's eye. They are knowledge-feathers, interfaces to the secret of the *icaros,* the shaman's songs. The living language of creation is pouring into me once more, filling the empty spaces . . . Icarus's wings flying on the surface of the sun. A tantalizing flash of possibility, and then it's gone.

My relationship with ayahuasca is like snakes and ladders, three steps up, two steps back. After that first breakthrough night drinking with Juan I've not managed to get through to the same degree, one cup or two, *dieta* or non-*dieta,* clear headspace or fear-ridden. She is like a fickle lover and I can't get the groove of her, that target window of ayahuasca rivers, the great green circuitry pattern that leads on to the universe within.

I've pretty much returned to the baseline consciousness, back down the ladder to who I was before my deep and transformative peak experience with ayahuasca that first ceremony with Juan. And it's strange to realize that this feeling of being *normal* is no longer the optimum state I wish for myself, that it now feels flat, like a two-dimensional reality sapped of the power and grace of the divine that infused every action, thing, and moment.

Merging with the Godhead and joining its vibrational wavefront was like the drop rejoining the ocean and realizing the true nature of water for the first time. That larger energetic presence not only filled me, it had always filled and animated me and all the living things on this earth. For a brief moment I had the eyes to see it, the ears to hear it, and the tongue to speak it.

Ah, that feeling, that certainty. The awareness that all living things are not just connected, but are animated by the same life force energy that emanates from the Source, that underneath our skins we are all one. It's not an intellectual knowledge—it's a deep-seated cellular surety, as real as the beat of your heart or the air you breathe; you know this for a fact, you feel the energy and you are the energy and it all makes sense, it all threads together. Yet instead of magnetizing the energy towards me, I now felt my desire pushing it away at the same time. What was I doing wrong?

I wonder if that electric shock I got, 220 volts for a good three seconds jolting up my right arm, has energetically sealed me, locked me down in the material flesh of the body. The afterglow from the heavy DMT sessions has faded, a distant echo, and now heaven's gate is barred from my entry. It is ironic if that's the case because in traditional shamanism one of the ways to start on the path is to be chosen by lightning, struck by the bolt which joins heaven and earth. Has my suburban lightning sealed me back to the ground, never to soar again?

Later in the dorm room, when I'm sleeping fitfully in the dark, something enters me, snaking down from above like a current of energy and waking me. I feel it course in like a child on a slippery slide, grooving me, spilling all the way down to my left leg where I'd twisted my ankle days before, and settle there. In the light trance between waking and sleep, that halfway world where you feel things without words, I can feel the spirit in me, its extra energy.

When I marshal that energy and project it up from my bunk bed, the round neon light overhead sparks into life, over and over again, a half dozen times. Who, or what is inside me? My fears and projections? *Brujeria?* A wandering spirit come home to the flesh for a time? And what the *fuck* am I meant to do with the ability to surge lights and appliances?

Suddenly I can feel the cold weight of a spider in my bed, crawling over my feet. I still my fear, slowly getting out and searching vainly for my torch. Minutes later there's another ripple, a plop sound, and the cold weight of another insect presence here inside my mosquito net, right by my shoulder. I can feel it and hear it fluttering its insect wings like a moth caught in the net. But every time I look—nothing. It keeps happening, little etheric droplets washing over me—until I realize.

I'm magnetizing energy here in my mosquito net, spirit forms drawn in by my resonance. By not purging, the ayahuasca energy has been kept down and in me, potentiating it. The energy of the insects is bubbling up from deep within my energetic body, singing to me and whispering secrets...

Much later the bird's dawn call melts into me again, filling me, teaching me their secret language, their vibrational pitch and essence. Their song is like water flowing, becoming, sweet joy burst upon the world. I suddenly realize that before I can sing an *icaro,* I must know the sonic triggers, the ur-sound notes that one plucks to make the song, the particles that make the wave. It's the language of the angels, the secret the feathers have been trying to teach me: *a vast semantic web of ur-language, the raw stuff that the icaros themselves are made of.*

My power lies with words, which may partially explain the glossolalia I've been spewing forth lately. It's the language of the spirits filtering through me, triggering sound where the spirit intersects the flesh.

Nature sings me her song, she bathes me in her knowing and makes me full.

And when I am full the flower blossoms and the sound comes pouring through.

16

Heart of Darkness

Pasaje Colon, Iquitos

MONDAY JULY 24–TUESDAY JULY 25, 2006

I wake to the sounds of gringo shamans, Jim Morrison, and the Doors. I'm drawn out of bed to the good doctor's waiting room, where one of his sons is watching *Apocalypse Now* on the television, a quirk of Peruvian TV programming...

It seems a curious omen, after all that has gone on here in previous ceremonies, of Bowman's warnings of the darkness, Monika's excursions to the hell realms, and my own inklings that the dark is real and exists, if only to counterbalance the light. On the television in front of me the Americans are bombing the hell out of the Vietnamese countryside and all the unlucky bastards who live there in a wall of napalm death.

"We'll use Wagner—it scares the hell out of the Slopes ... and my boys love it ..." Colonel Kilgore is saying on the television as I head back inside, walking as bombs explode around him. He's wearing his black cowboy hat with crossbones on it. The battlefield is their canvas. "Bomb them back to the Stone Age," he says. "Napalm son, nothing else in the world smells like that. I love the smell of napalm in the morning..."

It's the iconic *Apocalypse Now* scene: as the *Ride of the Valkyrie* soundtrack crescendos and washes out the whole world has gone mad and bleeding death and blood and fire and Kali is unleashed, the end times have arrived and the Americans and Vietnamese are all caught up in its black current.

"Shall we dance ...?" Colonel Kilgore says.

Maybe, but it takes two to tango, the light and the dark; it's all part of the great pattern.

Heavy shit first thing in the morning. I feel like a drained battery, like deep in my skull the pineal gland is still producing DMT, not melatonin as it should in daytime, like there's some imbalance in my brain.

Or maybe I just need a coffee—it's been days now without one, or sugar, or greasy Western food, and I can feel myself changing. So I wake up slowly and share a *mapacho* with Carlos out on the front porch in the sunlight, the sounds of apocalypse echoing out from the open window behind us.

"Y'know Juan fought in Vietnam," Carlos says idly, dragging on his cigarette. "I mean, he didn't kill anybody or anything, but he was there."

"For Peru? Like, with the Americans?"

"Sure. When he was nineteen Juan joined the Peruvian army, as almost every citizen does. The Vietnam War was going on and the U.S. asked the Peruvians if they could provide some jungle specialists. So the Peruvian government offered up several battalions, which of course, came from the Amazon. Juan was one of a hundred soldiers in a battalion to be sent off to Vietnam. A jungle-trained shaman smack dab in the middle of a geopolitical fracas."

Carlos has an almost photographic memory of the story and the great love he has for his teacher and his intimate connection with him shines through. Juan's like a father to him, more so than his blood father since their paths have diverged so much. He's like the eldest son of the family, continuing on the family business in the traditional Amazonian way, and one of those duties is to know the family history.

"Unfortunately the U.S. government didn't know what they were doing and decided to drop Juan and his comrades unsupported in the middle of the jungle. They thought the Peruvians would just know what to do. Juan had already been initiated into *curanderismo* and he had *mapacho* tobacco with him. He didn't have any ayahuasca, but he had his tobacco with him and was able to use it to see where the enemies were so that he could avoid them. He also had the tremendous benefit of speaking Mandarin Chinese and so he was also able to communicate on a certain level to the Vietnamese he was fighting against.

"At one point he most likely would have been captured or killed had he not been able to speak to the Vietnamese and explain he was not on the side of the U.S., nor was he on any side; he was simply a young kid who had been sent to the jungle to fight and he didn't want to hurt anyone. Miraculously, the North Vietnamese let him go."

At other times Juan was able to smoke *mapacho* to contact the spirits and learn the location of the enemy. It was this same connection to spirit that lead him through the war unharmed. Out of a hundred Peruvians sent to help the Americans, only nine returned alive.

"After the Vietnam War Juan fought in the Peru-Chile War," Carlos continues. "At one point he was in a helicopter and his copilot decided to commit suicide. They came to a river and he said to Juan,

"'Juan, you've gotta jump out.'

"'What are you talking about I've got to jump out? I'm not going to jump out, we're in the middle of nowhere.'

"'Juan if you don't jump out you're going to die because I'm going to crash this helicopter.'

"'What are you talking about, you can't crash this helicopter, what are you talking about?'

"'Juan, jump now or I'm going to kill you.'

"Juan jumped into the river and a few minutes later the helicopter crashed. The pilot's head landed over on the shore."

The chickens squawk happily in the morning light, the sound of them mixing with the noise of the kids playing around the house and *motorcarros* purring softly in the distance. I can hear Juan speaking in rapid-fire Spanish to someone in the kitchen, followed by the sounds of hammering. Juan walks through the room then, and Carlos pauses his tale like we're two guilty schoolboys gossiping.

Juan's complaining about *brujeria* again and says that he felt some dark energies probing the house last night. Like all good *curanderos,* Juan has a psychic burglar alarm to protect his home. It's probably nothing—this type of thing happens all the time on the astral, he says deferringly.

Carlos continues his tale as soon as the *maestro* moves on to other chores. I'm riveted; I feel like I've stepped into the movie.

Towards the end of his tour of duty in Vietnam Juan received shrapnel wounds to his head and lungs from a bomb going off. Cold hard steel has a way of cutting through even the best jungle magic, it seems. He spent time in the U.S. recuperating, where he got to see modern medicine for the first time, which is very unusual for a native *curandero* to witness. He then spent time recovering in Canada, where he was approached by an oil company who wanted him to join them on expeditions.

Juan agreed and returned to Peru to lead them into the jungle, where he led the oil company onto indigenous land to test for oil. This was a time when there was very little jungle expeditioning going on and it was still a dangerous place—many of the tribes were still cannibals. The Jivaro [Shuar], with whom Juan later studied, taught him how to shrink heads. They were still very much eating people when he came into contact with them.

Then there were the animals—Juan saw two of his coworkers killed by a black panther. He also saw tremendous anacondas, boas, giant snakes forty or fifty feet long eating monkeys they had caught. The Canadians would probably all be dead without him—and it killed Juan too, in the end.

During one of the expeditions Juan was bitten by a poisonous snake. He wasn't able to get treatment fast enough and he died en route to the oil company's makeshift jungle hospital. He died—his pulse stopped. His heart stopped.

Juan later described the experience of his soul leaving the body and how his spirit didn't know he was dead. His friends were crying, his coworkers were very distraught because he had died. He was trying to tell them, "I'm right here, I'm fine," and they weren't listening. So he tried to push one of them, touch them, y'know, to say hey, buddy,

I'm okay. And his hand went right through him. At that point he said oh-my-gosh. He saw his dead body and realized—I'm dead. Wow. He knew these guys couldn't hear or see him and that he couldn't touch them, so there was no point in staying. He just went off into the jungle.

Juan walked for a while until he began to see a light glowing and he followed it till it led to this golden city in the jungle, a giant city of golden light. When he went to the gates he could see his family members—his ancestors who had passed on were there at the door waiting for him. And he thought, well, this must be heaven. This is where I will go. But the ancestors told him no. It's not time for you to come into the city.

They directed him to go to a lake and so he walked for several hours in spirit to a lake. At the lake he saw another light deep within the water. And the light emerged, it rose up and broke the surface and a sphere of blue light appeared. And inside the sphere was an angel in white wings, dressed in a white robe—a woman.

She stepped out of her globe of light and took him on another journey into the jungle, further in until they came to a clearing. At this clearing there were three paths leading on in three directions. And the angel informed him that he was to choose one of the paths. Juan didn't really know what was going on, there was no path that spoke to him or called to him, so he simply chose the middle path. As he started to go towards the middle path the angel placed her hand on his shoulder and said, "No, no that's not the right path. You're supposed to take this one—on the right."

So Juan took the path she suggested and he traveled again for several hours. This path led back to the hospital where his dead body had been laying for eighteen hours. And he got back into his body and came back to life. The first thing that he said was . . . "Agua [Water] . . . !"

The doctor in the morgue came over to him and asked, "Are you Juan Tangoa Paima, or are you the devil?!" Juan assured him it was him, as unbelievable as it may have seemed. After that he spent two months recuperating in the hospital and was as good as new . . .

By all accounts the story is impossible. It's literally impossible, but I know I believe it. Perhaps that explains why nine *brujo* shamans Juan encountered banded together and tried to take him down. He brought the Canadian oil companies in and they destroyed the cultures of the indigenous jungle people. It's the kind of thing that can make you a few enemies, sure, but are they the bad guys or good guys themselves? Where do you draw the impossible line?

Perhaps Juan is a black magician after all, but not in the way it's traditionally understood, watered down to some dualistic archetype. It's not all cowboys and Indians here, Juan's a flesh and blood man as well as a *curandero* and he's made mistakes—we all have.

But Juan has tried to rectify his situation by going back and studying *curanderismo* with the tribes he encountered, and doing the work so as to maintain the lineage of indigenous teaching and wisdom. So it's a very difficult situation. There's an ocean of grief for all involved, for whatever the reason, and the karmic blowback can last a lifetime—or many lifetimes.

Hearing the full story of Juan's past puts a whole new spin on his sensitivity to *brujeria* and the dark forces that hover at the fringes here.

Now I know why he's so cautious.

Throughout all of South America ayahuasca ceremony days fall into the same rhythm—Tuesdays and Fridays, one of the only commonalities between competing *curanderos* (and sometimes on Saturdays, following the Brazilian lead). Juan says that somewhere in the evolution of the science all the shamans realized that by conducting their magical work on the same night it potentiated the ambient energy for them all. All those *curanderos* tapping into the Source, working their juju on the astral, and the psychic overflow creates a great tide that if taken at the cusp leads on to the heavenly realms. Or the demonic, I guess; let's not forget all those *brujos* working their black magic, and the difference between them is often only a matter of perspective.

There's a crowd of fresh arrivals here tonight, all local Peruvians come to be healed. Lonzo is here again, and some friends he's bought with him. Not long before the ceremony starts a young dude arrives fresh from Cuzco—Jack, a boy-sorcerer who had apprenticed briefly with Juan around the same time Carlos joined him.

They used to be friends, but now it appears Carlos can't stand him, you can tell from his body language—apart from a brief hello they don't speak. Juan shakes Jack's hand and greets him familiarly; everything seems fine, although there's an underlying tension in the air.

Jack's thoroughly Westernized in a cool black leather jacket and a bandana. He's smoking a *mapacho* in the waiting room with his girl-friend, a good-looking *mestizo* with long dark hair and beautiful black eyes. They both look like they've stepped out of an MTV video clip.

It's the Cuzco trip—shamanism is quite a business there, I'm told, and quite the "in thing" to do on the global countercultural circuit. All those Western tourists and the dollars they bring have also bought an ultra-competitive edge to the business of shamanism there, and an equal level of battle to the astral plane. *Brujeria* is rife in Cuzco.

When the lights go out we are blanketed by the dark and in that sacred space we are one. Each ceremony is different, according to the participants and the energies they bring and the group mind we build between us. Juan provides the space, he consecrates and sings it into being with his *icaros* to fuel our visions, so we can lock onto the carrier wave of our own consciousness and ride it. But the journey is different every time and tonight, a few *icaros* into the ceremony, Juan's singing stalls, then stops abruptly.

Suddenly the dark is awash with magical darts, *virote* that spread around this sacred space. They explode like a cluster bomb on our psychic wavelength, multi-colored dash-like confetti that shower the room and cover everything. Jack's an astral suicide bomber and these *virote* are a well-established weapon in the *brujo* arsenal. I wrap myself in a second skin of sheet lightning and am blinded by the flash.

Juan launches into a new *icaro* as if to catch the darts or weave a psychic net around us for protection. He's busy summoning his *mariri,* the magical phlegm of the *curandero,* with which he'll build a protection or an *alerta.* The *mariri* is the ultimate defense against attacks on the higher planes and is nourished by smoking *mapacho.* It's a force that is dangerous to use in itself, and has its own drives and needs.

In ancient times shamans were said to challenge each other with their *mariris,* often with fatal consequences. Today, with so many *curanderos* all fighting for their place in the psychic ecosystem it's said that few *maestros* have retained their *mariri,* but that conversely it's easier to attain, and can be passed on from teacher to student from mouth to mouth, where it resides.

My mind imagines Juan on the astral, surrounded by his allies and familiars, the black puma and the green dragon. I can see him towering above Jack, scooping him up in giant hands and imprisoning him in a spirit-vine cage, lockdown. Juan has been in control the whole time, aware of the energies and willing to let them be released and then contain them, following the path of least resistance.

The magical *virote* are disabled but still glowing all around, and I'm not the only one who can see them. Next to me, under the window, Len uses his own psychic energy to gather the *virote* up into a central vacuum and deposit them gently at Jack's feet. I can see what Len's created: a spinning black tube that captures the multi-colored specks, rotating gently in the dark.

Jack makes a thunderous vomiting sound but manages to hold it down till he's made it outside to the front lawn. Juan's stopped singing now and we're all left in the silence without *icaros,* as the sound of Jack's vomiting fills the room, over and over again, primal beast sounds merging with wracking heaves and spit. This is no ordinary purge. He vomits off and on, mostly on for what seems forever, like he's bringing up his intestines, heaving, heaving, and heaving again, all that black magic pouring out of him.

"*Brujo,*" Juan declares, and goes round the circle in the dark and blows *mapacho* smoke on us all, over our crown chakras and down our backs and fronts. When he's finished cleansing the ceremony goes on, though Jack never rejoins us. Halfway through the night I hear the roar of a jaguar and realize he's left, taken off on his bike, both him and his girlfriend, nursing a bruised ego.

And that's a good way to describe my first experience with a genuine *brujo*—it was all about ego. Jack was just showing off to his old teacher, flexing his magic muscles to show what he'd learned, the charms of ego and pride that are so valued in the Western world.

As the lights go on we all rise from our inner journeys and look around sheepishly at each other. The room is abuzz with the drama of what just went down, but Juan's downplaying the whole incident.

"Some people have their own selfish intentions for doing *curanderismo*," Juan says later. "They have not surpassed their own personal desires, and so they take the same ayahuasca and yet they are only looking to help themselves, and thus they are not giving the love out—they actually want to take more in. They think they can help cure someone else or that they're more powerful than their opponent . . . but they are inviting diabolic energy into themselves in an effort to become more powerful, rather than inviting the spirit of light into themselves so they can work for good."

In the language of the Pastaza Runa Indians in Ecuador they call the earth spirits that they encounter a *supai,* an emanation of nature. But when they translate it to Spanish the only word they have for it is *diablo.* They don't see *diablos* as evil, that's merely the word they were taught by the Christian missionaries who saw all forms of spirits as the work of the devil. Similarly, post-conquest Peru has grafted a Christian understanding of the light and the dark to an indigenous perspective of both extremes springing from a central Source.

From an indigenous perspective the West's psyche is itself under the thrall of the beginnings of *brujeria,* encouraging ego development and the cult of personality over the cooperative union of the tribe and the ego-dissolving connection to nature tribal people share. All our archetypes are cast in the heroic mold of good versus evil, heroes and villains, gods and demons. All of our history one vast tapestry of battles and war, life and death, everything in duality and set against itself.

Indigenous people have their own creation stories and mythologies, but ultimately they know that the universe is not an enemy that must be fought, but the mother, which must be respected. Yet as the Westernization of the last tribal peoples continues, the Western paradigm has taken root in shamanism itself, and the Western ego feeds on the seduction of power. As Jack showed us tonight, there are bad guys. And by playing on their level the shamans become the new action heroes, caught up in the never-ending battle. *Here lies the heart of all our darkness, in our fall from unity consciousness.*

"Man, Juan sure kicked his butt on the astral," Len says, dragging deeply on his tailor-made cigarette as we kick back on the bunk beds in the dorm room. "I can't believe the nerve of that guy, coming in here like that. It was totally the dark side of the Force."

It's funny though. I've been as guilty as any other seeker in my hero worship—probably more—obsessed with ego desires, with my own imaginings and perspectives on the spirit world, and projecting myself onto the canvas unfolding before me.

Like Jack, as my knowledge of ayahuasca has deepened, I've let myself become seduced by the power it brings and the abilities it enables. I've tried to capture the essence of ayahuasca. I've told myself that this is the nature of a writer, and one of the roles of the shaman is the *psychopomp,* he who travels the worlds to bring back information for the rest of the tribe—and that's true. But somewhere along the way I've gotten very caught up in this whole shamanic odyssey, playing out my own heroic imprints.

How many other Western *ayahuasqueros,* I wonder, are doing the same? You can still think of shamans as plant Jedis if it helps, but you might as well romanticize white blood cells in your body. Don't confuse the Jedis with the Force. Buddhist teachings have the idea of the "finger pointing to the moon," that there are many paths and ways to the Divine, but the ways and paths are not the destination themselves.

Curanderismo isn't a heroic battle with otherworldly forces, it's more a filtering program that cleanses and defrags the universal algorithm as its code transmits through the frequencies. Our attempts to romanticize it only commodify it, but in the end, maybe that's what is needed to help it reconnect to the Western demographic.

I now have an inkling of the power inherent in ayahuasca and how invigorating that can be, but through Juan I also feel the responsibility it entails and the service to the higher good. It's something he's helped nurture in all of us here at the school as we struggle to see with the eyes of the world, to reconnect to the subtle levels of spirit and the plants.

And that's where the teachings are coming from, the living Source of knowledge: *the plants.* Their wisdom is on tap to use and it's calling out to me now to reconnect to the collective consciousness they share, to go beyond the light and the dark and into the *green.*

That's where our next, perhaps greatest lesson lies—with the plants, deep in the Amazon jungle.

Back to the Source.

17

Return to the Source

On the Amazon River

We cruise along the mighty Amazon in a twelve-foot long wooden *pamacari,* a boat with a thatched palm roof, our little outboard motor puttering along beside the constant stream of canoes and other river traffic. The Amazon isn't the giant here that she is further up towards Leticia and the border with Colombia and Brazil, but still, gliding down her and seeing the vibrancy of life and the energy of the locals bathing and washing by the river, I can feel her power nonetheless.

A little girl in a blue dress stands down by the shore, waiting for her father who's paddling towards her in a canoe in the afternoon light. The waves from our boat engulf the shore as we speed by, rocking long rows of canoes anchored to the muddy banks.

I'm crammed into this ramshackle wooden shell with the two boat men, Juan, his son Gabriel, his eighteen-year-old daughter Flor, who's here to cook for us, Carlos, the four American students, and two friends of Juan's we picked up at some villages along the river, who will act as helpers. We're squeezed in along with our luggage, petrol, water, hammocks, and supplies, and a giant cutting of bananas even taller than Len, fresh off a tree. Juan's at the back of the boat by the motor, looking pissed off as he stares into the water rushing by. Carlos sits further up from him looking hurt, the tension between them palpable.

Juan's been stressed by the jungle trip and the logistics of it all, and he almost pulled out of the whole mission this morning. He told Carlos that he feels he wasn't included in the preparations, that Carlos doesn't know how to organize things and that he's feeling really put out. There's some stress about money and I get the impression Juan's feeling the pinch and resents allowing Carlos to pay for the trip out of the money the gringos have paid for their classes at the shaman school.

The cost for the full six weeks is U.S. $1,800, so with four fee paying students there's money there, but Juan's not in control of it. It's that or there's something else going on under the surface, but the result is a very agitated *curandero* ready to pick a fight, and poor Carlos is copping it. And when your teachers fight, what are the students meant to do?

The day melts into the timeless rhythm of the river, the gentle lap of muddy brown waves and the electric whirr from the motor. One of the boatmen is flirting with Flor, and to show off he nonchalantly grabs a long machete and trims his toenails with it. We drive on in silence, passing small peaceful towns that dot the green banks of the Amazon.

A slow flotilla of familiar thatched-roof boats with Peruvian flags on the back service the towns, unloading cartons of Inca-Cola, passengers, and supplies via canoes and men who wade right into the water and carry off the cargo. Down by the foreshore women wash their clothes with little plastic buckets, their children frolicking around them. As the boat glides past sunlight glistens off the surface of the water, dazzling me.

Later we turn off the main mouth of the Rio Amazonia and onto the Rio Yaniyaku, about three hours down river from Iquitos. We pass *Los Isles de Monos*—Monkey Island—and sure enough, a red-faced baboon with bright orange fur screeches at us from a half-submerged tree by the shore. It's a lot more populated around here than one would think, with small village communities every few miles or so, interspersed with tourist retreats like Amazon Lodge that cater to the jungle tourism market.

In the late afternoon we arrive at base camp, a jungle clearing 400 meters wide and 200 meters deep, with a few half-built *malocas* and one finished central *maloca*. This is Juan and Carlos's healing retreat—the Wind Spirit Centre for the *Ayahuayra Project*—the jungle basecamp at this school for shamans.

The property has only been cleared back a little way—after that it's deep Amazon jungle at its finest, a dense wall of green. Just us and Mother Nature. As if to welcome us the foghorn cry of birds rings through the humid air, and suddenly I tune in on the insects whirring and the sounds of life humming all about. We thread up our hammocks and mosquito nets around the perimeter of the large central *maloca*—our classroom—and get settled. Don Juan still hasn't left the boat—how can we have a school without a teacher, I wonder?

Carlos goes in to talk with him and finally he arrives, in his green St. Patrick's t-shirt and gumboots and starts directing the other men. He inspects one of the smaller *malocas,* checking the stumps and watching the men machete the grass down to clear a path. The commander-in-chief is back in action.

"Well, we're here—for what may be the first and last time," says Carlos gloomily, before explaining that Juan's confessed one of his stresses has been about coming here at all.

It seems that Juan's main backer, the Englishman, bought this land to develop a tourist lodge and he's now saying he wants the ayahuasca program to run to that stream and bring in the big bucks, which is diverging from Juan's dream and intent. It's all coming to a crux—spiritual tourism and the dollars it brings versus the spiritual path of the school. Juan's thinking of pulling out and starting somewhere new, and the pressures of it all have been responsible for his dark mood.

Carlos is worried now about his own plans. He was going home to Massachusetts for Christmas, then throwing himself back into the school, maybe getting a loan and putting all his energies towards this dream. But what's the point if it's all falling apart? Maybe he should stay here.

"I just want to say from my heart that there are very few people doing the work you are doing and no matter whether it's here or somewhere else, I know you're going to do good work," Len says, the big lug, and he gets out of his hammock to give Carlos a hug.

They can relocate, sure—but to where? The modern world is encroaching even here, hours down the Amazon, with a major jungle lodge and tourist attraction only kilometers away. Eco-tourism is booming and the world is getting smaller and smaller. But if the school is to take root it needs to be deep in the jungle, isolated from the world outside.

The plan is for students to train at Juan's home in the suburbs of Iquitos when starting out and if they decide to go on to the more intensive six-month course they will relocate here to the jungle. This is where all the plants are, where the power of the earth is, and where there are few distractions. The great green web of nature breathes all around, feeding and being fed.

In the first three months of the apprenticeship it's planned to have guided classes by Juan, and then in the last three months the students will be on their own here, assisted by a family that will cook their meals and prepare food. At the moment Jolane's not sure she can use the bush toilet—a plank of wood over a stream a hundred meters from the *maloca*—because there's no plastic seat; Carina's been vomiting all morning while Julia comforts her; Len's missing his girlfriend and deep-pan pizza; and I'm trying to imagine my American friends here undergoing a three month *dieta* and staying in seclusion. I'm not sure they—or I, for that matter—would survive it.

Anyway, by then the shamans-in-training would be expected to know how to make their own ayahuasca, preparing and drinking the brew in their own ceremonies that they would lead, developing their own personal relationship to the plants, and learning their own personal *icaros*. Three months in the jungle with just you and the plants, journeying into this ancient vegetal internet.

As everyone gets settled and over the dramas of the day I go down and swim in the river, its muddy brown current cleansing and carrying me away. Small fish flip out of the water and splash down again before the eye can catch them, circling round my legs and nibbling gently. Yes they're piranhas—but they're just taking baby bites.

A hundred meters upriver an Indian drifts lazily along in his one-man canoe, fishing for his dinner. Birds sing their deep calls as the sun begins to go down and the jungle fills me with its essence.

That night we all huddle under the thatched roof of the *maloca* as Flor prepares a meal of rice, some chewy meat I chose not to identify, and vegetables. Everyone's feeling the weight of the jungle on us in the dark, the sounds of the insects and the unknown, and perhaps because of that we're all reminiscing about back home.

"What I really miss right about now is Slim Jims," Len says, and the others murmur agreement. We discuss *Pac-Man,* peak-oil, and Hugo Chavez; we're regurgitating all our current news and popular culture memes, emptying ourselves to make room for the wisdom of the jungle. As the mosquitos come out for their dinner we quickly retire to our hammocks and tell ghost stories by torchlight. Across the river some animal makes a cry to the night as the jungle closes in, enveloping us like a second skin.

Here we are, the "Class of 06," deep in the Amazon, what feels a million miles from anywhere.

Home at last.

In the jungle rainforest, nestled among a dozen shades of green, a troupe of monkeys chatter excitedly, announcing the story about to begin, the energy of a new day. Macaws shriek through the clear blue sky and the deep bass drone of insects layer the air. The bird sounds trigger the plants, who wake up to take in the morning dew as the web of life ripples into action.

It's a new day at the shaman school and today we've got jungle classes with Juan and Carlos, who take us on a short hike into the neighborhood to get our bearings. We pass single-file—Juan and Carlos, Len, and Joland and Julia (Carina's stayed back at the *maloca* for a rest)—down thin trails they've cut through the jungle depths, pausing to look at this plant and that, and some of the towering tree specimens that dominate here.

A giant woody ayahuasca vine has curled itself round and round a tall tree to our left, snaking up above the canopy to drink in the light.

Its smooth brown bark is speckled with patches of white and moss and twenty meters up, thin green sprouts shoot off its body and curl up towards the sun. A smaller, second vine also grips the tree, mirroring the first like twin strands of DNA.

Further up ahead the path goes deeper into the jungle and curves round into a wall of trees and seems to disappear. The colors are more intense here, dozens of shades of green like someone's amped the saturation in Photoshop—and everything seems bigger, better fed, and more potent. This green wonderland is many things: ecosystem, food stock, even hospital. It's from the abundance of the jungle almost all of the Western achievements in medicine and healing are derived, from the plants. I feel like a first year intern being shown around the hospital.

"Every plant is like its own doctor and getting to know the plant doctors is like getting to know doctors as we would, in the same way," Juan explains, looking much calmer this morning. He's dressed in his green St. Patrick's t-shirt again and shorts, topped off by a red baseball cap, and he swings a large machete with a swift, controlled motion like it's his scalpel and he's making an incision into the jungle. "Even then the minor plants are powerful; I use them as well, but I stress that the plants that are the most powerful are the trees."

The vegetal kingdom isn't good or bad, Juan says, pointing out some choice specimens to us; plants have both polarities within them, just like humans do. The *puna* tree, for example, is used in *brujeria* to kill people, but it can also be used to cure—it depends on the intent of the user and the way you look. So too, when looking at nature, the traditional Western intent has been to see it as a resource, something to be used and exploited for our own needs.

The indigenous perspective acknowledges our interdependence with nature and all its creatures embedded in a web of life that unfolds out into the higher dimensions that certain plant interfaces reveal. As we are fed by nature it feeds on us and the energies we discharge, both supporting one another. Acts of mutual cooperation abound and if you look under the skin of classical Darwinism all that natural selection also fuels the web of life. No energy is ever really lost, just shunted across wavelengths for the greater planetary bio-organism.

One of the immediate examples of this is the colonies of leaf-cutter ants zigzagging across our trail. These ants are everywhere in the jungle, long processions of them running up almost every tree, each ant carrying a leaf or part of a leaf like tiny placards in a mass protest march. The leaves are later cleaned and chewed into a mushy pulp that in turn grows a fungus. The leaf-cutters cannot live without this fungus, nor can the fungus grow without the ants tending to the leaves: another perfect symbiosis between nature's children.

Juan goes on to explain the higher dimensional details: "Each specific species of plant has a spirit, and that spirit lives and continues to live in a reincarnated form, so that no matter when the tree dies—the spirit is not in that tree anymore, but the spirit goes into another new tree. So it is the same spirit or archetype if you want to call it that, constantly in its present form, unless a species was to be wiped out by extinction.

"It's the same with us. When we die our spirit is not going to die, either. Our spirit may actually go on into an animal, a tiger or a snake or something, or come back into another body." He hacks away at a low-hanging palm leaf then and looks back at us as if we're slow Westerners holding him back. *Don't you get it?* his expression says? *It's alive . . . all of it, all of us one big thing, and there's no point the head begrudging the heart its nourishment.*

The "great symbiosis" between the plants and animals in the biosphere is constant and primal. It begins with the breath, with plants breathing out the life-giving oxygen that nurtures the animals, who in turn exhale the much-needed carbon dioxide for the plants. It continues up to the seed level, with fruit producing plants being eaten by birds and mammals, who also carry the seeds long distances where they will propagate again. A perfect yin-yang engine of creation, and it's hard to say who's working for who when everyone profits.

Dr. James Lovelock, a research scientist who worked for NASA in the 1970s formulating methods to detect life on Mars, coined the "Gaia" hypothesis (named after the Greek goddess) to describe the earth as a whole organism. In his 1979 book *Gaia: A New Look at Life on Earth,* Lovelock posited that the living and non-living parts of the earth could be viewed as a complex interacting system. He says this bio-organism can be viewed as "a complex entity involving the earth's biosphere, atmosphere, oceans, and soil; the totality constituting a feedback or cybernetic system which seeks an optimal physical and chemical environment for life on this planet."

The theory was first refuted by the scientific establishment but has been finally embraced over the last thirty or so years, and is now more conservatively known as "Earth System Science," or as Lovelock calls it, "Geophysiology." The slow drift of Western science towards a whole-systems understanding of life on earth is something that indigenous cultures have always believed. Amazonian tribes call their Gaia archetype *Pachamama,* or Mother Earth, who oversees planting and harvesting, and is universally revered and prayed to.

But while nature is a great green web, the vegetal network is just one sharing server time on the planetary internet. The wavelength of the stones, the animals, the insects, and others unseen all overlap and connect to one another.

Indeed, the parallels between shamanism and cyberspace have been brewing for a while, and seem to be dovetailing in many ways. The developing technosphere is all based on networks, and bio-mimicry, copying pathways first established by nature. There's even something organic in code itself.

Roy Ascott, a "network artist" and figure in Ars Electronic, an early web-based art movement, sees the hyperspatial dimensions plant sacraments can take us to as equally valid as cyberspace. The only difference is that the plants are the interface, not computer chips. After spending time with Kuikuru Indians of the Brazilian Mato Grosso in 1997 and participating in their rituals ingesting hallucinogenic mushrooms, Ascott developed a theory of three planes of reality, which he termed *Verifiable reality, Virtual reality,* and *"Vegetal reality"*:

"Virtual Reality, dependent on interactive digital technology, is telematic and immersive. Validated Reality, dependent on reactive mechanical technology, is prosaic and Newtonian. Vegetal Reality, dependent on psychoactive plant technology, is entheogenic and spiritual. Vegetal Reality is quite unfamiliar to Western praxis . . . and is often viewed with fear and loathing by those entombed in Validated Reality. Vegetal Reality can be understood in the context of technoetics, as the transformation of consciousness by plant technology and the ingestion of psychoactive material . . ."

One reason for that prejudice by those in the Validated Reality is the paradigm is itself a product of a disconnection from and an ignorance of the plant kingdom on an experiential level. It's no coincidence that the rise of the Industrial Age, when Charles Babbage invented the Difference Engine, the first prototype computer, was also the period where the Western connection to the earth was at its lowest. The knowledge of the sacred mushrooms, mescaline, and peyote had been virtually eradicated along with the Indians that revered them in the Americas, and ayahuasca and other plant sacraments were yet to make it out of the jungle.

Without plant interfaces, the Victorian era made its own tools, and came to see the world as part of a mechanical universe. Humans commodified and consumed more than their fair share of nature's resources, and that concentrated gorging also produced the technological marvels of the twentieth century. The potential energy in the great green web was just redistributed.

While biologists are quick to point out that humans are in a form of seed-carrying symbiosis with the plants, how many I wonder, would be able to see the full tapestry the plants have woven, and how the green web, having activated deeper levels of consciousness in us seed-bearing humans, could be seen to have *seeded the digital web, in its own likeness?* Not many, I'm sure, because the vast majority have yet to wake up to the idea of plant consciousness itself.

Up ahead, Juan's waving his machete round, carving his way through the jungle. The students are following him sheepishly, carefully picking their way past broad, green palm fronds and low hanging vines. High above a monkey swings from tree to tree, a smear of black and gray against the green. I fumble for my camera but nature is too quick for me. Too quick for us all, a trillion untold computations in the planetary mainframe pulsed out with every heartbeat.

There's nothing to do but bask in the Gaian code, or to update the old Leary mantra, "*Log on, tune in, and veg out*" on the plant broadband.

At sunset the jungle comes alive with the insect orchestra, a solid wall of sound that hits me in the gut and threatens to melt me into its vibrational wavelength. I can feel the buzzing, fluttering theta wave state of the hummingbird as it settles behind my eyes, blanketing me like ocean waves and connecting me with the Source.

As I look out from the *maloca* the jungle looks back, hundreds of tiny lights in the twilight, fireflies blinking off and on, never in the same spot twice. Either that or there's an entire village among the trees staring back at me, all of us too scared to acknowledge the other.

When it's dark the ceremony begins. The brew is a bit gassy, and even don Juan's moved by its strong flavor. We drink, one by one, Carina abstaining because she's been vomiting repeatedly all day from her morning sickness. Ayahuasca is fine for the mother and baby—it is the medicine, after all—but she just can't keep it down. Len has been sick all day, too, from food he ate in the market at the port yesterday, and he brings the aya up again almost as soon as it's touched his lips.

Don Juan launches into his *icaros* and as we sing along a group harmonic develops that deepens and enriches us all. We are carried away by the sound and the spirit of ayahuasca, filled by the sounds of the jungle and the deep release of civilization, of the cellular awareness of being here, surrounded by the plants and nothing else.

Well, almost nothing else . . . Suddenly Juan senses something and stops his *icaro*. He leaves the *maloca* and wanders off into the night, the light from his torch coming and going as he walks round the perimeter.

"There is a spirit presence hanging around the camp," he explains on his return. "It's the spirit of a woman who died here," he says somberly, divining her story from some astral communication. "She was brought here, her and her baby. They both had AIDS," he says flatly. It strikes me as woefully sad that a person could be left here like that to die, that she had no one to love her and nurse her, no one that cared.

"But she wasn't ready to move on, she was too caught up in this world and couldn't accept heaven," Juan continues. I can't stop thinking of her trapped out here, starving to death, the spirit ebbing away, her child in her arms and the injustice of the world, the pain we cause each other and how that pain transfers over from one life to the next. Again I'm reminded that energy is neither created nor destroyed, just transmuted through the delicate web of life. We are all connected, even after death.

Hours into the ceremony I leave the *maloca* and stumble off towards the bushes, finally ready to purge. Ayahuasca-drunk, I sit out by the toilet area set up over the stream where a giant old grandfather tree has set its roots down into the earth. In my altered state it appears as the *World Tree* that unites heaven and earth in its branches and roots, the original tree of knowledge.

Vine-tendrils from the ecology in the branches above snake down and tickle my shoulder, welcoming me, teasing me with an almost sensual embrace. I can feel the energy of this being radiating into me, strengthening and supporting, filling me with its wisdom. I gaze up into the criss-cross branch network and see spirits of the wood like Disney faerie folk, dryads staring back at me. It takes a while to realize they're not flesh, that these spirit forms aren't some type of disfigured humans.

They dance around me in the dark of the night, protecting me, showing me the sights and the other spirits out there in the jungle: the boa, the puma, other trees and plants in their vegetal community. As I look back into the jungle and marvel at the spirit-energy in everything, this vast ecology of souls, I wonder how I could have been so blind as to not notice it all before.

The tree dryads take my hand then and fly up the giant trunk of the grandfather, stretching up into the sky. Suddenly I'm getting some type of transmission, in that proto-language before words, the voice of spirit. It's beaming me impressions of a time before time and of the formless void that birthed us all. And the first thing to be borne here is a tree, dreamed into the world by the great dreamer, it says. From its roots grow the earth and all the elements, and from its spirit grows the fire that becomes the sun above. In this way the world was created. A central world tree spinning on its own axis at the center of the universe, feeding and being fed, creating and destroying, and heaven and earth are full of its glory.

Suddenly my vision bursts open with a sea of green as a buzzing vibrational essence fills me: the *Green Lady* herself, the *Queen of the Forest* in direct symbiotic connection. We call them the plants doctors but they all serve the Mother, I realize, she's the one the medicine pours in from.

She comes to me radiating an energy field that shakes me down and destroys me, as we merge our auric fields. Fuucccccccccckkkk, my wavefront is merging with hers, it rocks me, slow and heavy and deep, awesome and full of grace. My vision's flooded with sights and sounds all melting into one another . . .

An infinite orchestra of the birds
The budding of flowers
A trickle of water
and the language of the clouds . . .
La madre ayahuasca, I hear you, I understand.

The vision fades and I drift back to my body here under the care of the grandfather tree, over the shit pit. In the light from my head torch my ayahuasca vision animates each frame of my hand's movement, like cartoon cells streaming, a dozen hands overlapping, like a snake moving through time.

I stagger to my feet and back to the central *maloca*, where the ceremony is winding down and Juan and the others are talking about their visions and experiences, decompressing from their spirit journeys. A single lamp on the floor of the *maloca* gives the impression of a warm, open fire as Juan, Carlos, and the students lay in their sleeping bags around the circle. It feels all homey, like summer camp, or an ayahuasca version of the *OC*. I'm still shaking from my ayahuasca high, trying to focus on the blurring outlines of people as they vibrate multi-dimensionally before me.

"I was drinking in the Santo Daime church in the States for a couple of years before coming down here," says Carina, smiling as I return and sit down on the wooden floorboards next to the other students. She's curled up in a ball with her hands around her knees and staring into the light. "And I never really purged except for my first time. But I've been purging profusely since I've been down here and I feel like my body is just being very sensitive and trying to protect itself from whatever might be going into it.

"So I haven't had many visions because it's been so hard for me to keep the ayahuasca down, or to even take a full dose. But the first couple of ceremonies I had some experiences where I felt very connected to the entire universe, and saw the whole world as this beautiful artistic creation. Every living thing is its own evolving masterpiece of itself, and humans are all like that as well."

Right on, sister. Jolane puts a comforting hand on Carina's shoulder and then gives her a big hug. It's her turn. "Y'know, I've realized that my path in life is to be a healer of some kind. I want to try and develop these skills and learn a method of helping people that I know works. And I know it works because it works on me." Jolane's got a clear connection that comes through in her *icaros,* which she sings, shakily at times, but well. She's been seeing spirits regularly and now she's got the bug—and the bent for it.

It's the same with Len. He's says he's always wanted to help people, and that ayahuasca has helped him connect with that feeling and to begin the process of healing that was needed inside him. "I've wanted to come here to South America for many years," he tells us with a grin, lighting a post-ceremony cigarette. "I thought more in the Andes, but this opportunity presented itself here to further my own spirituality and to learn more about myself. And to foster the healing ability that's latent inside me that I know I have."

Julia sits up on her knees then, composing herself to speak. "Y'know, I've been a participant in Santo Daime for the last five years, and I recently became a *Fardado* of the church, a proper member," she says, choosing each word carefully. She has such a gentleness and grace about her, and an awareness of her movement as she speaks. "I find this work closely related to the Santo Daime work, because the sacrament—ayahuasca—is very similar, although in Santo Daime it's been consecrated." She brushes back a blond dreadlock and looks at us clearly, her face full of a radiant energy as she talks.

"Whereas what we're doing here creates a space for more mystical experiences that reconnect you to the earth. And that's good, because there's also this global situation of social injustice and economic disparity that needs to be addressed by human beings who are whole and healthy. So that's why this work has to go forward."

Carlos totally agrees. "The spirit, or the awareness of the spirit of ayahuasca, needs to get to these spiritually sick places," he says with a frown. "The United States is full of spiritually sick people, and we're doomed if we don't find this power within. But if we do we can change the world for the better. We can all make this world a paradise—the potential is there if we just abandon our mind and listen to our soul.

"There are *brujos* who are against what we're doing here," Carlos continues, confiding with us. "They feel that *curanderismo* and the spirit medicine is something that should be kept within the indigenous population, and by spreading it we're tainting it. And that's something that we have to be very, very careful about . . .

"But the reality is that the Western world is here. We're in the Amazon rainforest, in one of the last places where indigenous cultures live in the same way they always have. Western culture is bringing its own ideas here as well, and ayahuasca and *curanderismo* is fading away."

Carlos looks at us with a completely open heart then, a look of mutual recognition of us crazy gringos out here in the jungle trying so hard to honor the connection we've felt to the Great Spirit which runs through all things.

"It's really up to people like you and me," Carlos says, "to bring the spirit of ayahuasca out to other places in the world." *All of us seed-brothers and sisters, united by the vine.* "Places where Westernization has come full circle, where people want to have the perspective of indigenous culture in them again. Where they want to feel the connection to the earth again."

A silence descends as the sound of frogs croaks into action around us, soundtracking this long night.

Juan looks at us, his students by the lamplight, our shadows cast round the *maloca*. We're a long way from our comfortable Western lounge rooms and computer screens now, but that won't be forever. I realize what he's seeing in us all now: *the potential.*

"We're all students and similar," Juan says firmly, taking turns to look at us one by one in the light of the *maloca*. "I too, am not of pure Peruvian bloodline. I'm a *mestizo.* I studied in many different countries as well and I understand that it's not where you're from—it's what you have inside, who you are that matters. But with you and the people like you, we can spread the wisdom of ayahuasca as far as we can for whomever wants to come and learn it."

It's said there are around 4,000 *curanderos* throughout South America, but soon there might be ten times that many in the West, thousands of sparks lighting up the astral. We're not his first students and we won't be his last, but we're part of the wave, it's here, and the tide is turning.

And now, as the strain we have put on the planet by our cultural over-indulgence reaches crisis point, and natural disasters and extreme weather wrack the globe, the need for a sustainable relationship with the Green Mother has come full circle.

All of us are seeds for the vine, all of history the story of what we did when we left the Garden.

And now the Garden is coming back.

18

The Love Creek Session

Iglesia Matriz, Iquitos

Monday July 31–Wednesday August 2, 2006

The Iglesia Matriz church is a catholic cathedral on the southwest side of Plaza de Armas in the heart of Iquitos. As I walk up to it in the midday heat the lemon and brown colonial-style spires conspire to give it an icing sugar and wedding cake feel, while the Swiss-made clock in the center of the tower seems an authoritarian reminder to the peasants to get back to work.

It's still one of the tallest structures in Iquitos, towering over the city as a stark reminder of the power of religion in this country. The church dates back to 1911 when the cathedral was built to replace an earlier chapel in the center of the plaza, right about where the fountain is now. It used to celebrate the mother of Christ and the feminine, a reminder of the jungle under the concrete and the living spirit of the Goddess that preceded all faith-based religions.

The shaman school had gotten back into town yesterday after a slow boat ride, stopping off at various riverside villages. I'd immediately plugged back into the global databanks at Cafe Cyber on Calle Arica, and found an email informing me that Ronan—a friend from Australia—was dead. He had late-stage pancreatic cancer and his condition had deteriorated quickly in the last few weeks. We knew each other through the local ayahuasca scene and had friends—and a certain woman—in common, and we had also shared a ceremony together only a few months previously.

He seemed so healthy and dynamic then, all of us high on ayahuasca and kaleidoscoping through the jeweled labyrinths and emotional topographies opened by the vine, tucked up in our *doonas* and blankets and dressed in our best New Age white (to be receptive to the spirits, we were told). I had to be doing something wrong, I'd figured, because apart from feeling stoned and energetically blocked, I wasn't having any visions. I kept coming in and out of my light ayahuasca fugue to the awareness of the guy to my right furiously masturbating under his *doona,* enflamed with energy stuck at his base chakra and pumping iron over and over and over. He was driving me *crazy* but I'd lost the ability to speak, or break the ice and I was trapped, cast as a voyeur in this soft porn higher consciousness session.

"You dirty dog, c'mon mate, this isn't the time for that," a guy to his right said. I focused and saw Ronan, smiling sage-like on the other side of the masturbator, who was shocked back into quiescence. We were bunkered down in the womb-like chamber of a white metal UFO, originally built as some low-budget Australian sci-fi prop, now a meditation space here at *Opeia,* an eco-arts retreat outside of Geelong, in the Otways National Ranges of Victoria.

The shaman was Darpan, an Australian whom had trained extensively in South America with various *curanderos* after being introduced to the vine in the early 90s by Terence McKenna. John Bernstein had sung a song he'd learned from Darpan for us at the Estrella ayahuasca disco almost a month ago, all of us across the world entwined together by this most enigmatic of vines, which had now led me all the way to South America and its jungle home. Strange the way things work.

The world really is how we dream it—and pray it, for it's our intention that is the catalyst. Carlos suggested to me that a simple prayer would be better for Ronan than disturbing his spirit with ayahuasca, and he gave me instructions on having this done as part of the Catholic mass. So Monday morning after my goodbyes to Juan, Carlos, and the class I'd packed up my stuff and moved back to Mad Mick's, where Mick and his "wives" had taken me back in with open arms. I was still buzzing from my ayahuasca high. And I had to say farewell to Ronan.

Next to the church entrance is a small store with religious items. The nuns behind the counter help me fill out a book for a prayer to be said for the soul of the departed—the *misa de oro*. You give them the name of the deceased and then they repeat it during the mass, directing the prayers to help that soul who has departed find their way back to God. After filling out the prayer form I step into the church and kneel down on one of the wooden pews at the back. They're hard under my knees, as always, to induce the right level of penitence. *Jesus died for our sins* and all that, a whole religion built on guilt . . .

But there are other ways to see the world and to view religion, which after all, is Latin for *re-connect*. Back in the jungle ayahuasca showed me that re-connection as a vibrant, living presence, the interdependent web of life that births and sustains us. *The Green Mother.*

Above my head nine oil paintings on the ceiling of the church depict various scenes from the life of the Virgin Mary, the Goddess in disguise. I was brought up Catholic, with all the religious archetypes and dogma, but it has always seemed just another mythology to me, as colorful as the stories of Egyptian gods and as lurid as the tales of Krypton from the comics of my youth. I'd never managed to find God here in a church—the idea of having to come to a building to communicate with the divine is a human conceit. Instead, I'd come all the way to Peru and the jungles of the Amazon to drink a plant hallucinogen to find a real, living God, and even then "he" turned out to be the Goddess.

As ethnobotanic commentator Jonathon Ott says in his book *Ayahuasca Analogues,*

"Shamanic ecstasy is the real 'Old Time Religion' of which modern churches are but pallid evocations. Shamanic, visionary ecstasy, the *mysterium tremendum,* the *unio mystica,* the eternally delightful experience of the universe as energy, is a *sine qua non* of religion, it is what religion is for! There is no need for faith, it is the ecstatic experience itself that gives one faith in the intrinsic unity and integrity of the universe, in ourselves as integral parts of the whole;

that reveals to us the sublime majesty of our universe, and the fluctuant, scintillant, alchemical miracle that is quotidian consciousness. Any religion that requires faith and gives none, that defends itself against religious experiences, that promulgates the bizarre superstition that humankind is in some way separate, divorced from the rest of creation, that heals not the gaping wound between body and soul, but would tear them asunder . . . is no religion at all."

There's a dozen or so locals here praying privately:

Dios te salve, Maria.
Llena eres de gracia:
El Señor es contigo.
Bendita tú ere entre todas las mujeres.

Y bendito es el fruto de tu vientre:
Jesús. Santa María, Madre de Dios,
ruega por nosotros pecadores,
ahora y en la hora de nuestra muerte.
Amén.

When I translate it in my head I realize it's the mother they're praying to in another of her various guises, all as equal as each other.

As I look up there at Jesus on the cross, the crown of thorns piercing his head, the nails driving him into the wood, I suddenly remember that time at don Juan's where I felt what I imagined Jesus must have felt, dying and being torn apart, melting back into the roaring vibrational sea of the Godhead. I had an inkling of what it is like to die, or at least, to begin the soul journey to the other side.

In a flash I imagine Ronan, his goatee beard and puckish grin, his warm brown eyes. I see him in my mind's eye and he's smiling, but shaking his head incredulously that I'm here doing this. But as I look up at the image of the Virgin Mary I can see the Green Goddess, the Mother, and I know that Ronan has gone back into her embrace, she who births us all.

So I say a prayer to the Goddess, the ALL, on behalf of Ronan, who crossed over early. Holy Mother Ayahuasca, hear my call. *Blessed art thou and the fruit of thy womb, the Jesus-consciousness in us all. Ayahuasca connect us to the web of life and help us find our place in it. Muchas gracias la madre sagrade . . .*

Godspeed, my brother.

As I walk out into the sunlit plaza the sound of terrified squealing echoes down the concrete streets like an indictment. Rounding the corner I find a Peruvian man dragging a live pig off a taxi onto the steps of the church, its legs bound with rope. As it squeals its death rattle a few locals gather around and laugh, like this happens all the time.

All of us go back to the Goddess sooner or later, they seem to say, so why fight it?

The internet café is an invaluable gringo meeting spot and later in the day I bump into Theo Valis there. He's been gone on a week-long botanical expedition about twelve hours down the Rio Ucayali, then further down a tributary to a remote Mastes village and another five hours trek into the jungle, not too far from the Brazilian border. There, in a crude open hut he did a mini-*dieta* and drank ayahuasca for a week with don Gallindo, a seventy-five-year-old *maestro curandero* who specializes in admixture plants.

Theo says the *maestro* showed him how powerful ayahuasca could be in potentiating other plants—not just ones containing DMT—and that he received an immense healing. During an eight-hour session he says he also received an *icaro*, despite repeatedly telling the ayahuasca spirit that he was not able to remember melodies.

Theo's also spent the last week making his own brew out in the jungle and distilling it down to the clear plastic water bottles like the natives do. Now he's off to Europe and then a trance festival in Portugal, and is selling the ayahuasca for U.S. $200 a bottle to help fuel his trip.

The whole thing leaves a bad taste in my mouth, though. I have this

underlying feeling that the sacredness of ayahuasca is being commodified and diluted by hawking it in the internet cafes alongside the chips,
cola, and calling cards. But that's the business of shamanism, I guess, a
perfect blend of the archaic with the modern. I'd seen worse transac-
tions just minutes before while on the net.

As of July 2006, typing "ayahuasca" as a key word search into Google
came up with 865,000 entries. The forums at *ayahuasca.com* are the central point of the global online interest in the vine, which was itself one
of the main catalysts for Alan Shoemaker to start the Shaman Conference here in Iquitos. There were hundreds of mentions by professional
anthropologists and academics, as well as the web pages of spiritual
seekers and religions like the UDV and Santo Daime. There were pro-
motional sites for all the jungle lodges and healing retreats throughout
South America. And then there was the dark side of the business of
shamanism—the free markets.

You can even order ayahuasca over eBay, I was surprised to see—
"Ayahuasca vine, *Banisteriopsis caapi*, Shaman Drink 500gr," the ad read,
only $24.67 and counting. That's 12.50 pounds U.K. after three bids for
500g of the vine with one hour and six minutes left before bidding closes.
It's listed in the *Home & Garden > Metaphysical & New Age > Other Metaphysical & New Age* section and 164 people had viewed it. Sold from and
shipping only to the U.K. What a clever plant, this ayahuasca, to go from
sacred indigenous medicine to the latest global fad, in a scant fifty years.

After Theo leaves I spot Chuck by the door and catch up with him
for a rare *cerveza* down by the boulevard. Chuck's dressed in blue Levis
and a white t-shirt, topped off by sunglasses and his trademark Andy
Warhol-like shock of silver hair: the all-American gringo. Chuck's one
of the first wave of Western *ayahuasqueros* and he's been staying in Peru
for his summer holidays off and on since '79, hanging with the Indians.
He's a Carlos Castaneda-era Indiana Jones who knows his way around
the scene here, but for all his macho jungle adventuring, he's also a pretty
sensitive guy. You don't do ayahuasca for almost thirty years without it
rubbing off on you.

"I've had a lot of psychic experiences since I was a child and I believe very much in the spirit world," Chuck says, cigarette in one hand and a beer in the other, bearing his soul to me here in the midday sun. "I don't believe it's something that is dreamed up in the human mind. I know there's some other world out there, but usually it's inaccessible."

Tourists and locals mingle along the paved sidewalk of the boulevard, clogged with European-style cafes and bars. Clusters of merchants selling *tourista* handicrafts hang by the marble pillared wall with their wares laid out on blankets before them. On the corner that same determined gaggle of Shipiba grandmothers wave their *manta* veils at passing gringos, but they recognize me and know I won't play the game.

"Ayahuasca opens up that world, but sometimes I become very sad when I take it because it's telling me things of sadness, about what the human race is doing to the earth," Chuck says wistfully, then he looks off at the dance of the *manta* veils as they billow in the breeze and the information grids engrained on them twist and turn like they're alive. "And I'm one of the guilty ones, I don't consider myself outside the guilt as far as what's going on."

He holds up his *cerveza* bottle as if to say, see, here we are consuming, part of the Westernization of the jungles. We might be ayahuasca seekers but we're all still tourists, we all go home after our experiences here, however transformational.

Since the conference ended Chuck's been hanging with Javier, a *curandero* in Belén who's currently treating a thirty-three-year-old mother with eight kids who has a cancerous growth as big as a grapefruit on her neck. The plant medicines have cleansed it once, but it's come back again and Javier's worried about it, Chuck says. He's a master healer and it's a rare privilege for a Westerner to drink with him, so when Chuck offers to take me along to his next ceremony Tuesday night there's no hesitation—for the story never ends.

After a month in Peru I've barely scraped the surface of the mystery of ayahuasca. I've seen the science of *curanderismo* and the business of shamanism from the inside and the out, and the only real thing I understand is that the rabbit hole goes deeper than I ever suspected, and my thirst to travel down it grows.

Tuesday afternoon I meet Chuck outside the Yellow Rose and share a *motorcarro* down to Puerto Bellavista Nanay, the busy main port of Iquitos. We're headed to a little property called Love Creek, where Javier holds his ayahuasca ceremonies. As our *motorcarro* enters the busy port we pass Javier and some of his Peruvian clients standing in front of the marble arc statue at the entrance to the markets and we instruct our driver to pull over.

Javier's wearing non-descript Western clothes straight out of the Belén markets: blue Converse All-Star sneakers, tan canvas shorts with deep pockets, a blue Tommy Hilfiger t-shirt, a watch, and a baseball cap. He's got a classic Peruvian face, rounded and Buddha-like, white plastic rosary beads trailing down over his little potbelly. He gives us a big smile and shakes our hands warmly, radiating a happy, contented energy, like he's just had a Sunday roast and dessert and is about to sit down and have a nap. When he smiles a gold filling in one of his front teeth shines through—his wife is studying to be a dentist, and medicine runs in the family.

With him are two guys on holiday from Lima, where they work for the Ministry of Health in undisclosed capacities, and who will be trying ayahuasca for the first time tonight. They both speak a smattering of English and we exchange pleasantries as we thread through the crowd. The colorful wooden market buildings are bustling with shoppers weaving through the stalls, stopping to sample selections of fresh fish on open-air grills, rice, fruit, and vegetables. Workers cart endless boxes of supplies down to the river's edge and waiting boats that feed the hungry townships along the river.

Along the dirt road leading down to the water pole houses have been built, raised ten or more meters above the waterline. These wooden buildings house bars and restaurants filled with local Peruvian men drinking *cervezas* at any time of the day or night on the sprawling verandas, like a slice of the old Wild West.

As we climb into a local *collectivo* boat I'm fascinated by the number of floating houses which rise and fall with the fortunes of the river, and the families that go about their business from them. Children are jumping into the water and bathing while women do the washing off the back, all of them oblivious to the empty water bottles and rubbish that laps at the shore in a constant tide. It all ends up in Brazil anyway, so why worry about it, one of the boatmen tells me with a wide smile.

Chuck's brought yet another new machete with him as a present for Javier's parents in the village. "It only costs U.S. $2 but to them it's invaluable, they can clear the land and make improvements," he says proudly. Chuck likes machetes, I remember. In the jungle on the way to the ceremony with Percy he'd swung that blade with the glee of a white Westerner cut loose from the bounds of civilization at last.

"He's a bit like an action hero, like Chuck Norris," one of the Peruvians opposite me jokes as Chuck brandishes his machete with a crazed look in his eye, hamming it up. It's no wonder he carries a machete around everywhere—he's been warned of an anaconda in the area and he's got a fear of the giant snakes in him. Javier says the big anacondas have the power to wrap themselves around a tree and just pull it up by the roots.

"Can you imagine seeing that thing on ayahuasca?" Chuck asks. "That'd be the last thing you'd see. Have you seen that clip on the internet where they cut the guy out of the snake?"

"No fucking way."

"Yeah, look at it. They cut it open and pull the guy out, and he's semi-digested. Google it. Maybe something like anaconda eats man," he laughs. "They say they'll get you on the river when you bend down and look like a big piece of meat, like an offering to them, kind of a shaking meatball. They're not real fast, so when you come across one in the forest they jump on you. Imagine the force of hundreds of pounds of movement! Ay yai ya yai!"

It's a short but very pleasant ride across the river to the government sponsored village of Padre Cocha, where the boat docks down by the muddy shoreline. A criss-cross network of wooden planks and gangplanks connect the *collectivos* to the shore and then well-worn pathways thread up through the green hills, past washing hung out to dry in patches on the green grass, to the village up above.

The people here allowed the government to build them concrete homes a few years back when the authorities were trying to upgrade the primitive bamboo huts and *malocas* they lived in. But then the government had the nerve to charge the locals rent. "It's our land," the Indians said. "Take back your walls!"—and it's been a standoff ever since.

It's pretty mellow on the streets, though. A paved footpath takes us through a charming walk and as we pass along the whole village streams to and fro, going about their daily life. Women with plastic buckets balance fruit in them on top of their heads as they walk along. Kids fish in local ponds off the bridge and play soccer on open fields between the houses. Afternoon clouds part on the horizon with brilliant rays of light streaming down—it's biblical. *This is the Promised Land, the vision sighs,* even if it is a semi-urban redevelopment on a tributary of the Amazon.

After a twenty minute walk we arrive at Quahrade Amore—Love Creek, a small, muddy trickle in the jungle. The creek bed itself is only about five meters wide and a meter deep, although it's almost empty now with only a thin sluice of muddy water reflecting the canopy of the trees and the sky. Despite the fact that the water has almost completely dried up, the creek bed itself isn't dry, but a rich moist mud nurtured by the surrounding rainforest.

The area around the creek has been thinned and cultivated and there's three wooden benches spread out every twenty meters or so like a picnic area. A small log bridge crosses the creek and connects with a clearing on the far bank where there's an open-air hut twelve feet across with a single hammock in the middle of it, and a wooden desk on the other side. The floor is covered with plastic bags, gumboots, flip-flops, and various other miscellaneous goods. A large family is huddled under it like contestants in a reality TV challenge to squeeze as many indigenous Indians as possible under such a tiny roof.

Rider, the wiry fiftyish head of the family steps forward to greet Javier and shake our hands. He's bare-chested, dressed in black sports shorts with a red stripe, black gumboots, and a brown baseball cap. Chuck says something in Spanish and presents the shiny new machete to him with a smile. He takes it carefully and inspects it top to bottom, thanking Chuck profusely as he slices at a nearby vine.

Behind him stands Juan, Rider's elderly father, who with his graying moustache and neat slicked hair is a dead ringer for a Peruvian Clark Gable. Next to him is his wife, a round-faced woman with an air of resignation about her; a woman in her twenties with wide eyes and an even wider smile; two older teenage boys; three younger lads; two young girls; and some babies.

Like virtually all the indigenous villagers throughout Peru they're dressed in cast-off Western brand logo clothes, including faded Quick-silver surf t-shirts and imitation GAP pants. They smile and say hello and somehow accommodate us in this tiny space and Rider's wife sweeps the dusty floorboards for us as the family makes us welcome. We sit down and get comfortable, taking off our hiking boots and soaking up the energy of the place.

After a while Chuck rolls some maryjane—Western plant medicine— and the family take a great interest in the plant, the dozen of them leaning in and asking questions about its properties and the spirit involved. Cannabis has been used for over 5,000 years as an oil, a food, a drug, a medicine, and a fiber, Chuck explains patiently to the family. Javier laughs and says he likes to use *toé* in his brews, but marijuana is also a powerful ally.

Javier goes over and gathers his dried datura leaves, wrapped in newspaper, for us to have a look. Toé is like an elegant and beautiful 1920s socialite—in the West this white lily goes under the names datura, Jimson Weed, or Deadly Nightshade. You mix the dry white lilies in with the vine and it induces a rushing hallucinogenic effect when you drink it, Javier explains, rubbing his hands over his belly to pantomime the waves of energy that *toé* releases. You can also dry it and roll up the leaves to smoke, which can coax you to sleep while taking you on extreme spirit journeys, Javier explains with a smile.

As Chuck and I share the joint and sit back the magic of Peru unfolds in the late afternoon light around us. "This place is just so beautiful," Chuck says after a while, looking over at me with heavy, stoned eyes. "I used to do a lot of drugs, back in my younger days," he admits, "but now it's just ayahuasca and marijuana, the plant sacraments, yeah."

After a while Juan, the grandfather, wants to show us something and calls us over to a nearby bench. Languidly we get up and go over to see him holding a magic stone about the size of a football. He found it some years ago in the creek bed here at Quahrade Amore, Chuck translates for us. They're very rare in these parts because the Amazon is full of sedimentary sand and when they find a stone like this it's considered extremely fortuitous. Chuck picks it up and devours it with his eyes, mesmerized by the smooth weight and power of it.

"Rak... I'm not a paleontologist, but this looks like a fossil of some kind. Look right there," he says excitedly, pointing to a rippling indent on one side of the stone. "Doesn't that look like fins?"

Chuck's entranced, squinting through a pocket magnifying glass at the upper rim of the stone, then holding it up carefully for my inspection. It looks like a stone heart carved from a mountain, with two protuberances along one side like eyes, or the stubs of stems where the valves connect to the arteries.

"*El bocca*," Rider says, turning it over to see a row of imprints in the stone like gums without teeth. He cups it in both hands and blows *mapacho* smoke over it, cleansing and blessing it from top to bottom. It called out to him to find it, Rider says, just as one of the plant doctors would.

The earth speaks, you see, but it doesn't speak in words: *it speaks in energy. And that energy manifests in the species that live on the skin of the world as the Gaian collective.* Millions of years ago we lived in caves, womb-like, enveloped by the energy of the stones, and the memory of their voice is still deep within us.

I've been so preoccupied learning about ayahuasca and the plants here in the jungles that I must admit I haven't paid much attention to the stones. There was a stone healer at the conference who brought with him an array of *piedras,* as they call them here, that he used in his own practice in Iquitos. *Encantos* are special healing stones used by the shamans, I remember him saying.

Despite the rarity of stones in the Amazon, their magic is recognized and respected as an extension of the way the plants work. Amazonian *curanderos* believe that the harder the wood of a tree the more power it contains, and so too, the stones have an even more powerful nature inherent in them, if only one can access it.

Not all stones are magic, Juan explains, but you can tell from the shape of the stone, and how it molds to the body what type of power it contains and its healing properties. Different colors also signify varying potentials. White stones *(yura encantos)* made from hard marble, are considered the most powerful, purifying and cleansing the body. Because they can be recharged over and over they also provide an *arcana*-type protection to the recipient. Black stones help repel negativity of any *brujeria,* red *encantos* help nourish the blood, green *encantos* are linked closely with the plants, brown *encantos* speak for the earth. Crystals give a clear vision and connect to heavenly realms.

As with the plants, stones can be used in a variety of ways to connect and divine. One way is to leave them in water overnight to let their essence seep in, blowing *mapacho* smoke over them for cleansing. The intent of the user and the need for healing is focused on as you drink the mineralized water the next day, and the power of the stones enters you. Or stones can be laid on top of a patient, their power healing specific blockages directly.

The power of the stones is old and deep, even older than the plants, ultimately. But once you establish a relationship with the stones, the *encantos,* it is said that they can come to you in your dreams and reveal their wisdom.

To entertain the newfound audience a four-year-old boy in a grubby

Fantastic Four t-shirt shows off his remarkable singing ability, launching into a light trance state as he begins an enchanted song, a tribal story from long ago. He's some natural jungle savant, getting into an auto-poetic groove, the notes of his song falling one after the other after the other in an enchanted melody. Time slows and then stops almost to a standstill, that golden moment of the afternoon when the light captures us all just so.

"*Gracias,*" the boy finishes and instantly the whole frozen tableau breaks and people spring into action; the spell is lost.

Javier sets up string hammocks under the trees and as the sun sets the mosquitos rise in a wave of expectant bloodletting. I fall into a hammock, letting the Gaian web catch and enfold me back into its embrace, preparing for launch. One of the sons gets the wheelbarrow and lifts the young singer into it and speeds him on a ride around the clearing, down past the trees to the creek. The mom keeps sweeping the floorboards as if nothing has happened, and Chuck turns towards me and says, "*Encanto,*" and smiles.

I can feel it beginning again; in truth, it never ends . . .

Tonight Javier's dressed in a traditional ankle-length Shipibo gown with rose patterns on it, the mark of a *vegetalista*. It looks unerringly like the faded 1950s dress my grandmother used to wear when she went shopping up the street—except for the baby monkey skull hanging on a bead necklace and the red bead headband crowning his head. It's the feminine again, the holy archetype, *la madre sagrade*. He sits on an old log surrounded by plastic bottles of *aguadiente* and ayahuasca all marked out in the light before him, Western castoffs holding the holy sacrament.

Javier holds up his *shacapa* fan, rattling it as he *soplars* the area, a long and thick *mapacho* burned down to the stub and hanging from his lips. He's singing Shipibo-style *icaros* which undulate with a sweet, slow tumbleweed roll, and it's then that I remember he was Percy's teacher for a time—that's where I've heard these tunes before, back on my first journey into the mystery...

"*Salud,*" Javier says, holding up a little wooden bowl full of ayahuasca and handing it to Chuck.

"Oh ho hi-o," Chuck grumbles, and burps. One by one we go up to Javier as he smiles at us and reveals his Buddha nature, letting us sip from the holy cup.

Whhhiiissssss...

Whhhiiissssss...

Whhhiiissssss...

The sound of his *shacapa* is like rainfall beating on the roof of me. Whhhiiissssss... whhhiiissssss... whhhiiissssss... whhhiiissssss... I'm going down, down the whirlpool, into the beat, a deep trance state as Javier hits his stride, *soplaring* and cleansing, never-ending, riding the sound into the atomic sea... Whhhiiissssss... whhhiiissssss... whhhi-iissssss... whhhiiissssss...

His music comes alive revealing subtle, infinite vibrational patterns, cascading beats and whirrs and clicks counterpointing the constant rain of the *shacapa*. The surround-sound effect is back again, spatio-distortion, and I have to focus. I know Javier's there in front of me but I can hear him singing as clear as day ninety degrees around from me. I'd swear he's walking round us but he doesn't move from his spot as the *icaros* pour through him like a waterfall.

Beside me, Chuck's lying on a blanket on the ground as he's carried off into the dream. He's opening his eyes and closing his eyes but there's no difference in the visions invading his skull, he tells me later. The two health workers on the other side of Chuck are very quiet, all of us carried away by the force of the vine. I'm rolled up in a cocoon, going in, melting into a familiar sea of archetypes as my subconscious rises up to greet the ayahuasca. Chuck's the Lone Ranger, Javier's Tonto, of course, and I'm the Thunderbolt Kid. I'm melting into the heavenly archetypes as the world unfolds and the Love Creek Session starts getting heavy...

The *chik-chik-chik-chik* of the *shacapa* becomes everything. The rattle is the sound of the cosmic heartbeat, the sacred mother nurturing us all. Later, bathed in Javier's sweet, sweet *icaros,* I can feel the hologrammatic intelligence bleeding through: I can feel our energy fields feeding the web around us, the insects, the plants, the stones, the earth. All of us intersecting, rippling wave forms of becoming lapping up against each other.

Javier comes round to blow *mapacho* smoke over our crowns and down our backs, cleansing us. I'm fully in oceanic bliss, deep in the ayahuasca space. All of a sudden there's a jolt of electricity, a thunderbolt from my third eye like living lightning. Ahhhhhh. *I've arrived.*

I look up through a diamond pattern to see Javier standing there in his spirit doctor form, performing surgery. A galactic homeopathic burst of the medicine hits me . . . I feel like I'm in an astral doctor's office and he's looking over my light body for blockages or problems. So by the way, I've got this thing in my leg, y'know? I've got this pain in my ankle that hurts a little bit, I communicate telepathically. *Could you take a look?*

This is a different type of hallucination than other ayahuasca visions I've experienced—this time I can feel the images I'm seeing having a direct effect on me, like interactive virtual reality, tele-medicine for the soul. The spirit isn't just wavering about outside of me—it's in me, spiraling down the tunnel of my flesh. And *voom!* The energy goes right there, the light of the psychic stethoscope travels down to my ankle as the spirit doctor starts examining it as real as you please.

My ankle is bathed in a warm light which hovers there for a few minutes, then suddenly my whole leg spasms and a small dark snake rises up from my ankle, away from the light. I can see it slithering on the dirt by Javier's feet before shooting out into the night. *Fuck. Me.* I guess I was sicker than I thought.

My woes go deeper than the flesh, though. What I really want, more than anything, is to merge with the DMT-ayahuasca space, to create some permanent but controllable bridge with the freedom to move between it and the baseline reality. To prove to myself this is possible and that I'm not really going mad, drifting into unconscious ego traps. The last time I entertained this idea back at that first ceremony at Juan's house, the ayahuasca space was too strong, too hyperdimensionally powerful to contain and remain myself.

But I know we all have this potential within us, that's what "*Christ*" or "*Cosmic*" consciousness is all about, connecting to the Divine and remembering it within us. Feeding the activated light body that had been switched on in Iquitos. *Curanderos* diet to cleanse their energy fields to be more receptive to the Great Spirit that enters them, but it's a connection we can all share to whatever degree we choose to accept and work with it.

My vision shifts as the ayahuasca brings up images from my data banks again; it's reading my vocabulary and talking to me in my own symbol-language. A parade of archetypes flows past me and suddenly there's Jesus, my big brother and friend, surrounded by happy Hebrew villagers. It looks like a picture right out of the children's Bible of my youth, but it's more likely triggered by my visit to the Plaza Matriz yesterday.

Jesus smiles at me and it's like basking in the sun, but on the inside. He reaches into his white robe and holds something out: a bleeding heart surrounded by a coruscating aura of white light. I eagerly reach out to touch it but it changes and morphs into the shape of the stone heart that Javier had shown us earlier, pulsing with an inner life. Jesus brings the stone up to his mouth and blows on it and the stone heart sings its *icaro*, a haunting underwater-jukebox melody, and the vibrational signature enters my crown chakra and spirals down my head and into my chest, to my own heart.

As the stone energy courses through I can feel the ecstatic frequency of the planetary grid, the collective consciousness of the stones under the plants. The topography of the invisible landscape reveals itself and I can feel everything moving at different vibrational frequencies even though we're all still. I can see energy moving through the flesh of our bodies, our vibrational wavefronts interweaving with the atomic curtain.

Most of all, I can feel the power of this magic stone flooding into me, its special *arcana* entering me, tuning me into the deep, slow wavelength of silicon consciousness. *This is how the stone "sees," I realize.*

And then I'm floating in the sea of vibration again, reading the wave we're all made up of. It feels like my brain is filtering and drinking in the prime frequency. It's pure hologrammatic intelligence, awareness of the universal hologram we are embedded in and made manifest.

All of us are energy fields that collectively build the hologram—we are IT, the IT I couldn't grasp on that first DMT journey at Ron Wheelock's house, the IT of the cosmic overmind: the humans, the beasts, the insects, the plants, the stones, the earth. All of us energy fields, intersecting, intelligent, rippling waves of vibration becoming at all times, each action and thought setting off new waves that affect and change the hologrammatic whole.

The stone has unlocked the knowledge I hid down in my heart that first time I had my deep ayahuasca breakthrough at don Juan's, the awe-ful, raging certainty of the cosmic ecology. What a terrible truth, this naked force of creation, within us all this time.

Why me, I wonder, as waves of Godhead flood in, unlocked by this key-stone. Jesus, what a cross to bear.

Or as Saint Thomas, the doubter, wrote (Verses 19–20 of the New Testament),

> *Jesus said: Blessed is he who was before he came into being. If you become my disciples and hear my words, these stones shall minister unto you. For you have five trees in Paradise which do not move in summer or in winter, and their leaves do not fall. He who knows them shall not taste of death.*
>
> *The disciples said to Jesus: Tell us what the kingdom of heaven is like. He said to them:*
>
> *It is like a grain of mustard-seed, smaller than all seeds; but when it falls on the earth which is tilled, it puts forth a great branch, and becomes shelter for the birds of heaven.*

19

The High Frontier

Calle Raymondi, Iquitos
WEDNESDAY 3–FRIDAY AUGUST 5, 2006

"Tell me, you look like a strapping young man. Would you like to be rock hard in your penis, yes?" says an elderly Peruvian gentleman to my left whose face has broken under the weight of sunken jowls. He's dressed in neat Western clothes and is sweating profusely in the humidity as he pats down stray wisps of hair that hover over his balding head. "Making love to the woman all night long, many times, yes?" he continues, leaning in confidentially to speak mano-to-mano to me in guarded tones like somebody's dirty old grandfather.

In stilted English he explains he's offering to sell me *chuchuwasi* or *maca*, a jungle Viagra used by the Quechua Indians for hundreds of years to boost stamina and sex drive. As he opens his briefcase I marvel at the neat rows of bottles and capsules that fill it, like an Amway marketer doing door-to-door business.

I'd come back on an early morning boat from Padre Cocha for a jungle lodge ayahuasca package I'd booked Tuesday before leaving for Love Creek. Still reeling from the ayahuasca session last night, I now found myself sitting on a wooden bench in the white walled offices of the Refugio Antiplano on Calle Raymondi, waiting for Scott Petersen, the owner of the place, to arrive with the other tourists for our jungle expedition.

I'd had a light sleep and was tired from the ceremony and all the purging after the visions, and this snake-oil shaman next to me seemed to smell my weakness and pounce, expertly cornering me with his briefcase full of performance-enhancing potions.

"Maca makes you very strong in the bedroom, my friend, the women cannot resist it," he says in a thick, hypnotic tone.

Once upon a time *chuchuwasi* was a root extract from a creeping vine that was known to only certain tribes who populated the tributaries of the Ucayali River. It had a whispered reputation as a powerful libido booster, especially for women, so now of course it's peddled as some type of natural aphrodisiac in the global marketplace.

The good doctor drones on for over half an hour, extolling the virtues of the maca root and its history, as well as his own performance under the sheets (which is not a pretty visual). I'm almost convinced it'd be quicker to buy some and shut him up than listen to his long, locker-room commentary in this humidity. Thankfully, Petersen finally arrives and shoos him off and the maca hustler scoops up his pills and bottles back into his briefcase and is out the door, tapping another tourist on the shoulder in the street and beginning his spiel again.

"Sorry about that," Petersen says, shaking my hand. "The old coot's always in here trying to sell some maca, but he doesn't bother me as I don't need any help in the bedroom, I can assure you of that."

Petersen's a tall, goatee-bearded American in his early fifties with crinkly blue eyes. He's dressed in a dyed shirt with tiger-like stripes, blue jeans and cowboy boots, and he carries the authoritarian air of command. As well as being a tour guide and businessman, he's also a trained herbalist and anthropologist who has been studying for over twenty-five years with indigenous shamans. Ten years ago he came to Iquitos to put his knowledge into practice and offer Western tourists a place to relax, heal, and learn the ways of *los plantas medicinal,* with ayahuasca at the centerpiece of his program.

It's paid off big time: the "Refugio Altiplano" (Refuge of the High Plains—he was going to call it a sanctuary but thought it sounded too religious) is now one of the largest tourist centers on the upper Amazon. Petersen has representatives in London, Denver, San Francisco,

Tokyo, and Stockholm that refer customers to him and his website at a steady rate. They get tour groups, packs of six to eight people coming for the jungle tour and, of course, the ayahuasca.

There's an equal number of men and women of all ages, Petersen tells me, with a lean towards people in their thirties, forties, and older. Many stressed-out professionals come to relax and reconnect with nature. They stay on average ten days each, at U.S. $100 a day, and participate in six ayahuasca ceremonies over that time, working on healing their physical and emotional issues, as well as their spirit.

An American couple in their mid-twenties wanders in looking for a jungle lodge and Petersen goes over to chat with them. A beautiful *mestizo* woman, who is also Petersen's lady friend, sits with me at a table behind an amazing wall-sized painting that displays village huts raised on poles, overshadowed by a number of UFO-like craft budding from the hallucinogenic rain.

She hands me a color brochure for the Refugio which shows a sprawling jungle retreat, and tells me all about the usual adventure activities like rafting, kayaking, swimming, fishing, bushwalking, and nature hikes as she reveals a long pair of taut legs and smiles at me invitingly.

Petersen calls himself a "shamanic counselor," not a shaman per se. He's a member of an indigenous shamans' guild in Lima that networks and regulates the craft, but he also draws upon the modern world of medicine, psychology, and salesmanship in his practice. You have to know the mind of the seeker to know how to best guide them, he explains, and by drawing on an indigenous and a Western perspective, Petersen claims to be able to see the issues facing his clients in a clearer way. Right at this moment, however, the main issue is clinching the sale.

"Yeah, so what is this *aya-what-sca*?" the guy says, looking puzzled and flustered in the early morning humidity, no doubt regretting leaving the cool air-conditioning of the Yellow Rose and the coldest beers in town. His girlfriend looks around at the wall hangings and native wooden crafts, taking it all in, slowly.

"It's the main plant ingredient in our shamanistic healing ceremonies," Petersen answers carefully, sizing them both up. "We work with a number of native *curanderos* in a strict indigenous format at our lodge in the jungle. We brew our own ayahuasca—it's a purgative that repairs damage from stress, alcohol, drugs, etcetera. It lasts for a short duration. One of the main benefits of taking it is increased levels of intuition. You become aware of the world around you at increased levels. It helps the mind, body, and spirit to integrate—does that sound like something you'd be interested in?"

"Wow, that sounds like something we'd really like to do, y'know." The couple nod and say "yeah" at all the right junctures during the spiel, but they have no idea of what it all entails, really, and Petersen's deliberately downplaying certain aspects to try and clinch the deal. If the clients don't look spiritual he sells the health and adventure angle; if they do look spiritual, or like a weekend warrior ready to embrace shamanism, he promotes the spirit angle. But he won't push ayahuasca on somebody who's not ready for it—that'd be a stupid and unnecessary risk both for the individual and the business.

Besides, the pull of the jungle is enough for most tourists and the Refugio has that in spades, so there's something for everyone here. If Petersen is the Richard Branson of spiritual tourism, then his signature brand is without doubt *Virgin Ayahuasca*.

A large percentage of the overall ayahuasca tourism market in Iquitos still comes from drop-ins off the street, who are introduced to ayahuasca as part of the jungle adventure package. It's so lucrative that the Refugio Altiplano is only one of almost a dozen tour operators in the blocks around the Plaza de Armas to offer ayahuasca ceremonies as part of their menu for curious tourists.

A cursory investigation reveals A&E Amazon Excursion Tours on A. La Marina; Muyana; Mad Mick's Ecological Jungle Trips; Amazon Lodge; the Jungle Explorer; Orlando's Expeditions; and the Living Light Lodge on Putamayo—with jungle guides waving pamphlets in your face for many more lodges and start-ups every hundred meters around the plaza. A typical billboard outside the Amazon Lodge reads, "Large swimming pool, children's pool and games, 3-floor look-out tower, 20 comfortable bungalows, day & night time canoe rides, full restaurant and bar, ayahuaska (sic) ceremony."

The local tourist broadsheet, the *Iquitos Times,* has a half-page ad for the Refugio on its back page. A letter in the ad, excerpted from the Refugio's guestbook comments, reads,

Dear Scott,

I am in awe that the earth has moved in such a way that I have landed at the Refugio Altiplano. I cannot count the number of shades of green I have seen nor explain the peace that comes from breathing with the lungs of the earth. Each night I drifted into a deep sleep, emersed [sic] in the symphony of nature, covered by a blanket of stars.

These experiences I have gathered here have had a profound effect on my being, and I will surely carry them with me wherever I go.

Carley Humphrey
Team Canada
Global Youth Network

The rise of spiritual tourism in South America has been carefully followed by some organizations, including MAPS, who published the report "Ayahuasca Tourism" in South America in 1998 by John N Grunwell.

"Ayahuasca tourism is certainly unique," the report states. "One would be hard-pressed to find a more evolved and alive form of drug tourism, particularly one with so many apparent benefits (assuming it is carried out correctly). Ayahuasca seems to appeal to people unconcerned with traditional models of life, people searching for the extraordinary, the remarkable and unusual facets of life. That there even exists a tourist industry to serve this population strikes me as amazing. That this industry is heavily advertised and available to anyone with the financial means to undertake a trip, that it is not a hush-hush experience available only to a select few in the psychedelic drug underground, is perhaps even more astonishing."

What most people don't mention, however, is the impact that ayahuasca tourism is having on the environment. "Not only are the people of South America placing demands on the supply of ayahuasca, but with the influx of tourists, sources could be in danger of complete exhaustion. [In Brazil], the UDV now harvests their plants from church-owned plantations, taking away valuable agricultural land," John Grunwell wrote in the MAPS report. And it's not just land, but intellectual property that's also endangered.

There's a well-known U.K. company that charges U.S. $3,000 for two-week shamanistic retreats here in Peru. They used to work with Javier, Chuck told me, but they only paid him on average U.S. $300 to host up to half a dozen or more gringos in four or five ayahuasca ceremonies over those two weeks. What's worse, their website would repeatedly fill with medicinal information gleaned from the shamans they worked with, who would eventually be dropped and a new healer brought in to be milked for his knowledge.

But as I've learned through the conference and speaking to *curanderos* and their customers, not all the effects of ayahuasca tourism are negative. Many lodge operators claim they embed their shamanistic ceremonies within an eco-adventure package so they can control the harm done to the environment and the indigenous people. And the money the ayahuasca tourists bring in promotes the conservation of traditional tribal culture and preservation of the forests around the tribe—or at least, in theory.

There's no guarantee that all that money stays in the economy in the long run, and with more and more Westerners backing jungle lodges and ayahuasca healing retreats, fronting the seed money for local *curanderos,* it's going to make for some happy venture capitalists in the coming boom times. "Globalization 101" is all about supply and demand, after all.

The Refugio, for instance, is set up as a corporation with one owner—Scott Petersen. People can support the corporation by paying U.S. $20,000 which makes them donors and offers a reduced lifetime rate of U.S. $50 per day, or they can pay a greater sum and have a house built on the property for their stay. There's also a non-profit wing of the Refugio set up to buy the jungle land from the locals to protect it from logging and inappropriate development, which you can donate to and receive a tax-free offset.

As well as "assimilating" the jungle, as Petersen calls it, the money also goes towards helping create employment and education for the villagers who no longer own their land. Maybe one day they can work in the floating gift shops down by the river, I don't know.

The American couple eventually chicken out of their chance at jungle enlightenment, and without their numbers we don't have enough of a group to make it worth the petrol costs on Petersen's new twelve-person speedboat out to the Refugio. Unless someone else signs up we'll have to wait till tomorrow when a businessman is flying in from Denver, and head out then.

"They weren't our type of people," Petersen says when the couple have gone, reaching for his *mapacho* and relighting it.

"So just who are your 'type of people' then?" I counter, intrigued.

Petersen leans back in his cane chair and looks me up and down like a well-fed lion deciding if it can squeeze in another morsel. "There's always going to be an element of people that come flying over and just touch on the surface," he says. "Then there's going to be the people who are called to this and it becomes an instrument in their lives and they become shining lights for this type of work. That's the way it goes. For every five hundred people that are interested in ayahuasca there are maybe thirty people who are going to go deep and assimilate it. And those, my friend, are the type of people this type of program really supports. It's like panning for gold amongst the sand.

"We're not just pushing shamanic medicine, what we're doing is basically promoting the human species. That's what we're here for. We're trying to help people evolve. We're trying to help people become more joyful, more powerful, more energetic in their lives. We're not just trying to push a program at them. Our main focus is the person."

Petersen's friendly, but machismo energy takes a lot of energy to match. He runs a tight operation, and you don't want to be the grunt holding up the whole platoon. So I'm actually relieved that our trip has been postponed because I could sure use a few hours' sleep and some downtime to integrate the last ayahuasca session before the next one begins—the spiritual backpacking circuit here is nothing, if not eventful.

As I head back to the Bunkhouse for a well-earned rest I pass four funky young Americans, three boys and a girl in their early twenties, cool kids sitting at a table at the Yellow Rose. It's barely been a month since I arrived here in Iquitos and sat at those same tables myself, an ayahuasca virgin all wide-eyed and naïve, and I recognize that same look on their faces.

"I don't know, Todd," says the good-looking blond girl with a white Shipibo top on. "I'm just not into the *drug* thing, y'know."

"From my experience it's not like other drugs, not even like mushrooms, yeah?" Todd replies. "When you take ayahuasca you can see spirits right in front of you, you're not being paranoid—they're really there. This whole experience is on a different plane than the physical. It's about healing, not escapism."

"Well if it's healing I'll give it a go," another boy says, and as I climb the stairs to the Bunkhouse I know that not only are they going to try the vine of souls, but so will their friends, following in the wake of these cultural catalysts, the forerunners that brave the new.

Wrapped up as the latest healing modality, ayahuasca is on the verge of the becoming the next big thing, for better or worse.

The gold rush has begun.

It's late Thursday afternoon and sunlight glistens off the water of the mighty Amazon River as our speedboat slows to pass locals in their wooden canoes. Whole families look up from their paddling and wave warm-heartedly as the wake from our boat shakes them. We're headed to the Refugio Altiplano, located on a quiet tributary of the Amazon some thirty-five kilometers south of Iquitos.

Petersen's at the wheel of the speedboat threading through the water, expertly dodging tree trunks and the eddies and swirls of the river. He's got the concentration of a professional driver, his hands firm on the wheel as waves break on the windscreen and spill over the lip of the boat onto the deck. Petersen exudes the cold command of leadership from every pore; he's the captain, the leader of the whole expedition, there's no doubting it and he doesn't leave any room for questioning it.

Behind him is Ronaldo, a stocky, fortyish businessman from Denver, Colorado, who works for an international NGO that brings medicinal supplies to the locals. He has a round, puppy-dog face and an amazing phoenix tattoo on his chest, creeping above the open neck of his sweat-soaked shirt. There's a beautiful warm energy about him, an open-heartedness and lack of pretension.

We strike up a friendship as we discover we both have kids almost the same age and I tell him about my journey so far and my encounters with the shamans and gringos around Iquitos.

"I used to be in the Marines," he tells me above the roar of the motor as we cut through the waves at a steady pace, looking back at me with brown eyes and a friendly smile. "But I found I couldn't stay there and maintain a spiritual path. I've been aware of ayahuasca for years through a mutual friend back in Denver that Scott and I share, and I guess I'm curious to see if it can help with my journey."

Across from us are a middle-aged Spanish couple who are here for the jungle lodge and some R'n'R, and aren't interested in ayahuasca. The man's stick thin and has a frail, nervous character. Talking with him later he tells me he's a diabetic and needs regular insulin shots and rest. His partner is a quiet woman from Lima with long black hair and a subdued smile. They're friendly enough but they keep to themselves and over the course of the next few days never seem to ask anything about our ayahuasca ceremonies.

As we pull into dock at a collection of floating shanty huts with tin roofs and beer signs out front at the riverside village of Tamshiyacu, a swarm of young Peruvian boys chatter excitedly and grab our guide rope, tying down the boat with practiced hands.

"They're excited because they know I'll give them a sole," says Petersen as we stock up on some last minute supplies at this river out-post. Ten minutes later we're back on the water and twenty minutes after that Petersen cuts the motor and guides us in to the Refugio wharf.

As we arrive a cluster of jungle huts with conical roofs and long thatched walkways peer over the shoreline. We walk up to the high plains and are greeted by a group of Peruvians who help settle us into one of the dozens of spacious bungalows that are scattered through the sprawling 250-acre property.

The structures have been built with natural materials from the for-est by workers from surrounding villages. Each *tambo* is equipped with its own mosquito-netted bedroom, a living room, balconies overlook-ing the forest, and a modern bathroom with toilets and showers—an unheard of luxury in this last outpost of civilization for miles around.

Everything about the Refugio is grand, like the size of the cen-tral building—an audacious three-story *maloca* called "El Centro," the "Ponderosa" of the Amazon. Down at ground level a few indigenous women from the nearby village are pacing to and fro on the dirt floor, preparing our dinner. It's meant to be a diverse menu of fresh natural food, including fish, fruit, and vegetables from the surrounding region, but it's mainly rice and fish because of our dietary preparations for the ayahuasca ceremony tomorrow night. Outside the kitchen a black rhesus monkey paces nervously up and down the wooden floorboards, dragging on a chain that anchors him to the ground

The middle level, with a large mosquito netted room dominating the back, is eerily quiet. Long tables and dozens of chairs lie unused, and in the deepening shadows it looks incredibly sad in its emptiness. Half a dozen hammocks sway in the breeze on the top floor, with an empty dining table twenty meters down the end, as if a whole tribe of displaced Indians who live here have scattered as soon as they heard the motor of the speedboat. Perhaps they're out there now hiding in the jungle, waiting patiently to come back to inhabit this sprawling, jungle McMansion when we're gone.

After dinner the Spaniards make their excuses and leave Petersen, Rolando, and I ensconced in the hammocks in the dark, smoking *mapachos* and watching the moon. There's an eerie silence for miles around, a heaviness that hangs over the jungle in the silver moonlight. This place feels like what it is: an outpost of civilization surrounded by miles and miles of jungle. Within the compound is the only satellite internet connection this side of Iquitos and modern technology, including solar panels to power the electricity. Incongruously, this whole top floor is lit only by candles, and the whole *maloca* is built from the same simple materials the jungle has provided to the Indians since time immemorial.

"I feel like I've been gone for a week," Rolando sighs as he's enfolded in the deep comfort of the hammock.

"Wait till tomorrow—it'll seem like three weeks," Petersen counters with a laugh from the hammock opposite, lazily rocking back and forth, the master of his domain.

"This was poverty before I came here," he says with a sweep of his hand, then lights a *mapacho*. "Now my workers get the possibility to earn one hundred soles a week and to send their kids to school. It's all because the Refugio is here that they have these opportunities. There aren't really economic options in this country. What are they going to do out here? Make more babies?

"It's the same with the Indians—the real glut here in Peru and in the Third World in general is creativity," he says in the dark, a thin streak of red from the tip of his cigarette the only thing visible as a cloud covers the moon. "Who's creative enough to take a lump of wood and make a sculpture out of it? People are dumbed down by the colonization process and the tribes don't value individualization, they place a higher value on the tribe getting along. *Make something out of nothing*—put form to madness—that's what these people are screaming for, and when someone comes along who can do that they immediately put them on a pedestal."

Petersen has a background as a trained herbalist and has studied psychology, so he takes a deconstructionist view of what's going on out here, and of the larger dynamic of the Western-indigenous relationship. He's also a canny operator and knows how to work the system.

"That's why I get along well with the tribes," he says. "They see me as a savior figure and that makes it economically viable to live and work in a shamanic setting. I bring in the tourists and they bring in the money and it feeds the community."

To the poor people in the communities around here, where the average Indian earns around one sole a day (around U.S. 30 cents) the Refugio Antiplano must seem like the Taj Mahal. And with the prices it charges (U.S. $100 a day) it can afford to be. This is the business of spirituality, after all.

But Petersen holds a lot of power out here, and while he has a level head and a clear business mind, one gets a sense that he also readily enjoys the prestige and gravity his position brings. He is the man, the shaman, the businessman, the leader, and what he says goes. His word could mean life or death for the remote communities spread around the Refugio, who look to it and him as the main source of income, whether working on his property or selling handicrafts or other essential items.

"We're buying up the rainforest so we have a whole empire of free land here," Petersen tells me, explaining the ecological preservation aspect of the Refugio's business plan to buy up or "assimilate" vast tracts of the jungle around the Refugio. They've saved 1,500 acres of land so far and while it sounds noble, all that land ultimately belongs to Petersen's non-profit organization, whole communities boxed in and enthralled by his will. The potential for abuse is huge, but to his credit, Petersen seems to have his heart in the right place and is doing everything above board.

This whole place has an echo of a previous era, of the rubber barons who controlled the jungles a century ago, enslaving the indigenous population, and the Spanish *conquistadores* who came before them. For a moment I wonder if this isn't all some crazy karmic routine he's playing out here in the jungle—that Petersen hasn't been here before in a previous life, civilizing the Indians and building fortresses to strange gods. Tourism, it seems, is now the next step in that legacy of imperialism and control, of enslavement and servitude.

But the Refugio is not just a place of sanctuary from the throes of civilization, it also marks the boundary where the outside world begins, where the jungle meets the lodge. And now, five hundred years after white men first arrived, as the wisdom of the jungle and the plants recolonizes the West, the Refugio and retreats like it are the nodal points of penetration. With such potent jungle hallucinogens fueling this whole tourist boom, you could call it the *High Frontier*.

In the distance the thundering boom of a rifle shot goes off at exactly ten o'clock each night, twice, so there's no mistake about it. In the deep silence of the jungle those shots would ring out for miles, a sign of the power of this place and its master. Petersen's ordered the guards to do it to let all the locals in the area know that they have guns and are protected.

"It's kinda protocol around here," he says, looking at me with a grin. "We have three guards, one for the boat and the port, one for the internet house and the equipment there and one for the main building. We haven't had any trouble in over eight years, but that's because they know we're vigilant.

"Well, gentlemen, it's been a long day and it's time I hit the sack," Petersen announces, flashing that trademark confident grin and putting back on his cowboy boots. He's got ten pairs of them, he tells us as he nonchalantly pisses off the third floor balcony of El Centro. "Get a good sleep, both of you, because tomorrow night we drink the medicine, and you'll need all your energy to face what lies within."

He walks off then, the sound of his cowboy boots creaking on the floorboards in the dark.

Early in the morning a light breakfast is served in my *tambo* by an Indian who leaves a tray with some fruit, bread, and tea. Later, Rolando and I meet up in the hammocks again, surrounded by the sounds of the jungle as a perfect air of tranquility ushers in the day.

Rolando didn't sleep well and he's nervous about the ayahuasca ceremony tonight. "Well, y'know, it's different every time," I tell him, "and describing the experience is a whole different thing from living through it, believe me. But once you know the process a bit and can trust yourself in the ayahuasca space . . . it's amazing, the most holy of experiences."

It's funny to hear myself go on about ayahuasca like I'm some expert; this will be my eleventh session here in Peru, not counting those two DMT intensives, and thinking back now over all the circles and brews and the *curanderos* that led them is like remembering the names and touch of lovers.

Just then Petersen arrives with a white top wrapped around his head like Lawrence of Arabia. He's swapped his cowboy boots for gumboots and is dressed in a modest purple shirt and blue jeans, with a small woven bag slung over his shoulder. He's all geared up today like John Wayne surrounded by all these damn Indians.

We set off on a tour of the grounds at a brisk pace, around the back of the Refugio and across a long wooden bridge with a thatched roof, to the vast botanical garden he's recently cultivated. A flat grassland in the middle of the jungle is surrounded by a muddy central dam the size of an Olympic swimming pool, filled with little plots of over two-hundred-and-fifty medicinal plants revered for their healing properties.

There are grasses and trees and fruit-bearing plants all boxed up in little wooden frames six feet long and two wide, like open-air graves with little blue placards announcing the names of the deceased: *Argo*

Sacha Ludwigia Octovolvis; Ajo Sacha; Machimanso Blanco Eschweilera Broctea; Rollinia Mucosa; Boton de Oro Spillonthes Ocmelle; and a bevy of others.

Along the back of the clearing is a long row of a dozen or so modest ayahuasca vines growing up twenty-foot high pole braces. They're tended to by a group of workers from a local village sheltering from the hot, sweltering sun in the shade, who stand up tensely and break into work as the boss arrives.

Because the ayahuasca vine takes a long time to mature and so much is needed for the ongoing shamanistic ceremonies at the Refugio, Petersen also buys the vine in bulk from local suppliers. "I have good contacts," he says, "and they're always pleased to contract with me to pick up another batch, and they will hunt quite far afield to do that. They'll bring back about ten sacks at a time," he explains.

There's an ayahuasca deposit drying in a pit in the ground near the ceremonial *maloca,* and every time they cook up a new batch of brew, which is about every three weeks, they pull some pots out and mix in some *chacruna.* "I'm more or less looking about ten years down the line until my own supplies of the vine are mature enough to sustain the needs here," Petersen says, smoking a *mapacho* in the shade.

A hundred meters past the gardens we explore a magnificent two-story jungle house, built for families who stay on the property. Another hundred meters beyond that is an amazing five-story tree house of Olympian proportions. It's at least thirty meters tall, and seventy-five steps up into the great green canopy overhead is a Robinson Crusoe-style bungalow with views of the river and the jungle for miles around.

After descending we meander through the forest and stop to inspect a host of other two-story jungle cabanas. "Some people say they don't need houses this big to stay in, but I just ignore them. I build what I want to—I'm thinking in terms of the future, too. And it creates a certain atmosphere," Petersen says.

The Peruvian workers make these houses by going into the surrounding jungle and stripping the area of wood they need—and then they use a power saw to carve each tree down to planks and poles. The loud screech of metal and machinery booms through the trees like the king of the beasts. It's bloody efficient, and Petersen says the workers can do sixty planks in a good day, with only half a dozen mistakes. Thus it is, from the emerald jungle they've built this empire—*the Refugio Altiplano.*

The most they've had at one time here is thirty-five people, which is also the most the ceremony *maloca* can hold—a sprawling building buried in the forest past El Centro. As I wander round the grounds of the Refugio I feel like a tourist in the Disneyland of the Gods—but in the off-peak season. For while each building is a magnificent accomplishment, each one is also empty, bereft of people and furniture, like a showroom or a village that's been neutron bombed and all the people have been vaporized.

"We really have enough land cleared and houses built to handle the amount of traffic we're expecting," Petersen says. "I think there's going to be a wave over the next four or five years, and I don't think this will be a bad thing."

All these empty buildings are here because he's building for the future, for that time after the wave of Western *ayahuasqueros* has broken on the shores of the jungle, when the serious seekers can come and fill this place.

"What we're seeing now in this whole wave of interest in shamanic medicine is a race to the peak. After the peak it will start to hone down to those who are really serious about using these techniques for healing and therapy, and psychic exploration. It's bound to drop out of the backpacker market and go more into the intellectual market. And that's what the Refugio is already positioned for. So we're in it for the long run."

Later, we have lunch back on the third floor of El Centro at a dining table set for six. The tablecloth is adorned with beautiful Shipibo tribal art, ayahuasca river patterns that morph into dogs with teats, like Etch-a-Sketch doodles adorning the cups and plates and bowls.

As we eat quietly in the empty geography that surrounds us, I suddenly feel terribly lonely, and I wonder how Petersen has stuck it out here all this time.

This vast empire, built and waiting, just waiting to be filled . . .

"Because I worked as an anthropologist doing ethnographic studies throughout the Amazon and the Andes, I've seen a lot of shamans who are basically very mediocre or not shamans at all," Petersen confides to Rolando and I inside the ceremony *maloca* as the ayahuasca session begins.

We're in a giant, two-story walled hut with a conical roof that seats up to thirty-five people on the bench on the inside perimeter. It's at least thirty feet across and almost as high up, the largest native structure I've been in anywhere in the Amazon basin. There's only four of us here tonight, though—Petersen and Walter, Rolando and I—and the candles on a wooden altar at the head of the *maloca* throw our shadows into the round depths of this spectacular jungle cathedral.

"The Indian shamans that I work with, however, bring in a very intense understanding of the shamanic medicine from an Indian-Amazonian perspective," Petersen continues, setting out bottles of *agua de florida* and ayahuasca on the altar. "It comes right out of their genetic past and you can certainly feel that in their songs and in their capacity to work. And Walter here is one of the best," he says finally, indicating the hired help waiting patiently behind him.

Walter's a short, quiet Peruvian with sharp slitted eyes and a broad nose, the corners of his lips turned down in a perpetual grimace, an emotional death mask. He looks like a witch doctor from deep out of some Hollywood jungle, crowned with a slick Elvis-style lick of hair. Like Petersen, he's dressed in a white Shipibo ceremony gown, the *cushma,* decorated around the edges with ayahuasca patterns like on the *manta* fabrics, and he's holding a *shacapa* leaf fan with which he brushes down the altar.

Dipping into his bag Walter sets out a mound of *mapacho* cigarettes on the altar, then tips one into the candle flame and begins drawing in the tobacco. No emotion can be read on his broad poker face as he exhales, staring at me dispassionately as the smoke wafts slowly around him. He looks like a dragon basking in the embers of a fire. I get the impression that he gets paid to sing his *icaros;* smiles costs extra.

Petersen's hired Walter just like all the other laborers and workers here at the Refugio, like hiring a gardener or a guide. "Walter first started as an apprentice with an older shaman being the *maestro,* but he didn't know his place," Petersen told me earlier today. "He started telling me to remind guests that they should tip him, and telling me where to sit and what to do in the ceremony, and I thought 'fuck you, buddy,' you're not the boss here.

"A lot of shamans have big egos," Petersen said, "and you have to know how to deal with them—same with a lot of tourists. Finally he needed time off to conduct ceremonies for his own clients, German tourists. I said fine, but when he didn't return by the due date I thought fuck him, I'm not going to put up with this. So I told him not to bother coming back, and from then on I've worked with Walter in ceremonies, letting him do the *icaros* and take the lead. He's great, y'know, he doesn't have an ego about it, and we work really well together."

Reading between the lines I figured that meant he knew who's the boss and how to take orders.

From time to time Petersen brings in other shamans to enhance a ceremony or to balance out the energies. He has scouts in Pucallpa that headhunt for various skillsets, like expertise with certain plants, or shamans that do healing work with difficult illnesses, or have specialties with *icaros.* When he finds someone he likes he flies them in for a few weeks to cater to the needs of any special groups he might have out here, then he ships them out again just as quick, a straight business deal.

Still, Petersen pays well and no one refuses the short-term contracts, but it's clear to all involved who the boss is. One step out of line and they'll never work at the Refugio again.

"I saw that guy one time in the streets of Iquitos and I gave him ten soles and said go get a good meal," Petersen laughs.

Walter's getting antsy waiting around for the conversation to die down, and out of the corner of my eye I see him check the digital watch on his hand, a similar brand to the one Petersen wears. My heart sinks as I feel the energy of money hanging in the air and the empty grandeur of the *maloca*. It all intermingles with my energetic body to create a resistance to the flow, a feeling of unease.

As Walter gets settled in the center of the space in his chair, where he will sing and carry the ceremony, Petersen goes around strategically cleansing Rolando and I with scented water and blowing smoke on the crowns of our head and down our backs. Then he says a prayer and doles out small cups of ayahuasca brew in the flickering candlelight.

Walter begins singing but his voice is dry and hoarse, like a scratchy Tom Waits record. At various times through the night I just want him to shut up. His singing feels awful, not quite *brujeria,* but at least as energetically wrong for me to not want to be here, part of this, done this way. I feel sorry for Rolando undergoing his virgin trip and knowing that he's got two more ceremonies at the Refugio, and that this will be the best he will experience in Peru, not quite the real deal.

After a while I can feel the layers of my body and my energy body awash with the spirit of aya, cleansing, teasing, trying to find a toehold to open the gate, but some part of me is still struggling against it, unwilling to go with the flow. Wave after wave of aya hits me, saying *come on, play, why won't you play?* but the time's not right, I'm not in my power, not here. It doesn't feel holy; it feels like a holiday retreat, an ayahuasca health spa. After Juan, and Javier, and the other indigenous *curanderos* I've drunk with, the tag-team of Petersen and Walter doesn't fill me with confidence, or visions.

I struggle with the ayahuasca and it struggles with me for a few hours, rolling around on the hard wood floor of the cathedral and staring up at the thick poles and beams that support that vast thatch roof. I have a sense of infinite space here in the jungle, of our little outpost of civilization surrounded by a sea of living green. I can see the others in their positions around the *maloca* by the trickle of moonlight, heavy with the calm weight of concentration.

Rolando's quiet, sitting bolt upright on the bench at the front of the *maloca* in a light trance and staring straight ahead. Walter never moves from his singing spot, but as Petersen comes round and tends to us, anointing us with *agua de florida* and other essential oils and massaging it into our temples, Walter adjusts his *icaros* accordingly.

"It's not a very visionary brew," Petersen announces sagely, "but it will still be healing you on a physical level."

Eventually I purge off the side of the *maloca,* sickly sweet vomit raining on the ground below, and even that's not quite satisfying, not the medicine I usually encounter.

And as the thunder of shots goes off in the dark I realize it must be 10 o'clock, and here I am bunkered down on the high frontier, riding a bum steer.

I wonder if it's too late to get my money back.

20

Stairway to Heaven

The Cathedral, Refugio Altiplano

SATURDAY AUGUST 6, 2006

A giant stingray swims above me as plain as day, the mighty wings of its body pounding heavily and projecting it forward through the astral.

I'm stunned, in awe of this spirit-beast as it slices gracefully through jeweled waters, its long tail trailing behind it like a string of faerie lights. I'm lost in a morphing sea of rainbow geometry and Rolando's here, too, ahead of me, both of us adrift in this spirit world. Sigil-shapes form before me like some alien language but constantly slip off my mind's linguistic centers, refusing to be understood.

I call out to Rolando, the vibration of my voice visible as a wave in the shimmering mindscape before me, but he doesn't hear me. I move towards him but just like a dream he's always beyond my reach. Then a rip in the current pulls him far out to sea, and he's gone.

As I hang in this liquid geometry, trying to hold onto a sense of self, a spirit puma stands before me, majestic and proud. It's a powerfully built animal with large paws and sharp claws, tightly packed muscles rippling under a sleek black coat as it walks towards me, radiating power. It's the same black puma that appeared in my vision before I left Australia, that also looked over me during all those ceremonies back at don Juan's. Its unwavering gaze holds my attention, unblinking, peering deep into my soul as it pads towards me. Sidling up close, the puma's nostrils flare and the whiskers on its face twitch as it reads my vibrational imprint, sizing me up.

"I want to find Rolando, he's lost. Can you help me?" I say, but not in words. The puma nods, sniffs the air, and turns to go. As it gallops through the spirit worlds it carries me along with it, pausing under an energetic waterfall that thunders over us, hundreds of square units of energy roaring down with devastating force. I realize that the force I'm feeling is not just the waterfall, it's the puma energy coming into me, making me strong. I can feel my own muscles as I bound along, up the center current of the waterfall and into the sky realms, climbing a stairway to heaven.

In the classic work *Shamanism,* by Mircae Eliade, published in the early 1960s, the anthropologist defined shamanism as "the techniques of ecstasy." By this he referred to the ability of the shaman to enter into ecstatic trance states in which their soul leaves the body and ascends to the sky, or the underworld. There, the shaman is said to talk with and make use of a number of spirit allies, all the while remaining in control of his consciousness.

In the classical, controllable anthropological paradigm this might very well be the case. But as I was discovering, things were very different nowadays with Westerners on the shamanic backpacking circuit. I was way out of my depth here but willing to trust my spirit totem and surrender myself to the process. What other choice did I have?

As I burst through some invisible portal I have the distinct feeling of entering a new vibrational space, like when your ears pop with a change in altitude on a plane. I'm struck by that same feeling you have when you look through a plane window and realize through the dark of the night that you've reached an outpost of human civilization, or in this case, the spirit world.

THEY exist, flitting past, rainbow-arcing angel things, the busy presence of a mass of beings morphing past me; rush hour in this futuristic city in the clouds.

Oh. My. God. Is this ... could it be ...

Fuck me, is this heaven?

❁ ❁ ❁

When my mom met my dad it was at some crazy costume party the summer of '67. He dressed as a priest—she went as Carmen Miranda, with plastic fruit bundled up in her beehive hairdo. The priest outfit was actually his—he'd just come out of training for the seminary—and two of his brothers and different uncles were priests and bishops. Priestcraft runs in the family, so is it any wonder I'm on the path I am, treading between two worlds? The karma of generations of white men grasping for a true connection to the divine lay behind me, urging me on.

If at first you don't succeed, try and try again, the maxim goes. So here I am again, spending my Saturday night braving the shores of consciousness at the Refugio Altiplano, in this vast jungle cathedral that towers imposingly above me. The ayahuasca tastes sweet and smooth tonight, almost sugary this time, with a trace of medicinal alcohol rounding out the flavor. I'm sitting by the altar in the candlelight as Petersen pours me a mug of hot coffee from the blue thermos by his side to chase away the bite of the brew.

He's dressed in his work *cushma* again, the High Priest, but as he sits cross-legged on the bench, a pair of black gumboots peeking through incongruously, he reminds me that the difference between the modern archetype of a priest and a *curandero* is that while both are intermediaries of the divine, in the indigenous job description, the *curandero* is also a healer.

"Since all of the religions came originally from shamanism," Petersen explained earlier, "when they start losing their spark and their effectiveness and their draw, they usually go back to their origins. And the origins are visions and healing and that's how Christianity got started, a really good healer put together a system, y'know. Why was he so popular? Well, because he was a healer. And it worked! In almost every religion you'll find the same thing. The founders are shamans, they're *healers*. That's what people are looking for, some way to upgrade their lives on an energetic-perceptive level so they can start experiencing things."

There were so many rich veins to tap here, a deep reservoir of cultural imprints and archetypes and possibilities that were being continually thrown up by my subconscious as part of my own understanding and healing. Priest-healer-traveler between worlds, my dad would be proud of me.

I've been constantly grappling with my own journey into the world of spirits and shamans and trying to contextualize what I was doing here in the jungle re-connecting to the sacred. It was no longer about a single story; the more I experienced the mysteries of ayahuasca, the more the psychic floor continued to give way and open up whole new levels of meaning to goad me on. The gonzo in me would have it no other way but still, it was curious.

Since the shaman school training with Juan I'd realized that my own *tour de force* through Peru was turning into a classic *shamanic initiation*. And I was far from alone. It was as if some spontaneous signal had been switched on in the gene pool and this wave of ayahuasca forerunners I was now part of was merely answering its call.

There were dangers, of course, and having run one of the largest ayahuasca retreats on the Upper Amazon for almost a decade now, Petersen has seen them aplenty.

"A lot of the New Age kids are wandering around the Third World lost," Petersen had said over a breakfast this morning of fruit and bread. "They know the world they're coming from is flawed, and then they come to this new place, not speaking the language and full of the idea of the noble savage and the Green Mother."

Peru, however, has its own problems, its own paradigms and flaws, and it's not perfect. "These kids get caught up with power tripping gurus and shamans and they get burned, spat out, and cynical. You've got to be able to sort the wheat from the chaff, discern what's going on in the culture, not just take it all at face value. But these kids don't have the training or skills for that—you need to be able to psychoanalyze and have some anthropological training to be aware. Without that you're trapped in superstition and myth."

Yet despite the pitfalls the waves of Western ayahuasca seekers continues to build. Many of the people I've met so far have expressed to me that they are here in Peru seeking healing, drinking with *curanderos* as they search for something they know they need to be whole.

The history of Western culture in the last two thousand years could be seen as the "Empire of the Mind" conquering the exterior world and extinguishing the interior one, with the result that we have atrophied our spiritual connection. On a deeper level then, the thousands upon thousands of Westerners coming to Peru to be shamanized could be seen to reflect an equal need in the larger populace for a spiritual healing and a reconnection to the earth. And as the seekers return to their communities across the globe, their presences may yet prove strategic.

Sitting back down I take my space on the bench that trails around the right hand rim of the *maloca,* making sure I get my bearings for later. One of the locals is behind me; Rolando's up front taking his medicine, with Petersen to the left of him. This morning after his first ceremony Rolando told me he felt an increased empathy and a "sense of closure; of dealing with my emotional issues and healing them," and the presence of a force "that was very loving, very embracing." Which is to say he barely scratched the surface of the raging hyper-dimensional flux, but tonight is to be very different.

I didn't really journey either last night and I'd been blaming Petersen and Walter for the ayahuasca not working, but that was just projecting the blame elsewhere. I'd been thinking about it all day and I'd realized it was all about *me.* The ayahuasca was doing some deep healing on a physical and emotional level to smooth out blockages and disturbances. And now, Petersen suggested, doing ayahuasca a second night in a row would be like a booster shot building up our astral immune systems. It should be all the easier to access the higher realms because the spirit of ayahuasca was still in us.

Walter's on the floor in the direct center of the cathedral, underneath the apex point of the thatched cone roof, soaking in the energy of the stars and radiating it out into our psychic atmosphere. As he smokes a thick *mapacho* as big as a cigar in the dim shadows of the candlelight, the orange smolder of the tip trails through the air and carves faces and shapes that seem to taunt me.

I'm not as intimidated by him today and I'd even managed a stilted conversation with him earlier about the origins of ayahuasca, translated by Petersen:

Walter's tribe, the Shipibo-Conibos, have a legend of a wise man from long ago called Oni, who was said to know the names and properties of all the healing plants of the jungle. Oni was the first to recognize ayahuasca and combine it with *chacruna* for fabulous visions. He learned so many things that he kept on drinking the brew to the exclusion of all else. No food or water passed his lips, nor did his body stir from the jungle floor it sat on, chanting day and night.

As time passed and he grew older and older, ayahuasca ropes started growing from his fingers and tangling round his legs as he merged with the forest. Finally he became one with the jungle itself, which is why ayahuasca is called Oni in the Shipibo tongue, or *rope of the dead (souls)*. When Oni's wife died her body was tied to the foot of a tree and from it she birthed the *chacruna* plant as a complement to the ayahuasca.

Still today, the Shipibo believe that spirits and gods live in the sky, and that ayahuasca is a stairway that joins heaven and earth for the spirits to pass along. The Shipibo call these spirits *yoshinbo* and warn that one must constantly be on guard against them, a belief only reinforced by the Christian missionaries that have imported the concept of "devils" to the natural equation.

Likewise, the Shuar believe that their ancestors had a rope that connected this world with that of powerful spirit beings. These beings appeared to the Shuar as people like them, but they could transform themselves into any form they desired. Then one day a Moon-man who was jealous of the Shuar cut the rope and severed their connection with the spirits. Since that time ayahuasca has been the only ladder they have to connect the worlds above and below, the stairway to heaven.

The idea that at some distant point humans have had a direct connection to the spirit world is an old one, deeply entrenched in the belief systems of indigenous peoples around the globe. The West, however, has taken a while to catch up, and even when it does touch on the matter it does so in a mechanistic and reductionist sense.

Psychologist Julian Jaynes, in his influential book *The Origins of Consciousness in the Breakdown of the Bicameral Mind,* argues that as recently as three thousand years ago the human brain was configured with a bicameral mind, in which cognitive functions were split between one part, which speaks, and another which listens—and obeys. This schizophrenic-like state was what allowed ancient people to hear "the voice of God," a historical trait that crosses all religions and cultures.

Jaynes went on to argue that as verbal and written language was embraced it changed the bicameral brain state and accelerated the ego's development. Some "gifted" individuals retained a connection to the other side of the brain, which Jaynes concluded could explain the oracles and seers of the ancient world. Divination and prayer became cultural bridges that filled the gap left as the "voice of God" disappeared.

As Western *ayahuasqueros* venture into the indigenous world, sifting metaphor from dogma and focusing the knowledge they gain through a Western perspective, they are, in a very direct way, jumpstarting something like the bicameral mind back into life.

Now the "voice of God" is speaking through plant sacraments like ayahuasca and filtering into the archetypes of the global unconscious. But unlike Jayne's mechanistic viewpoint that the bicameral mind is simply another part of our brains talking to us, with ayahuasca the West is now learning to open up and trust in a spirit world *outside* of ourselves. Our very survival may depend on it.

Petersen claims that having a Western viewpoint as well as an indigenous perspective "gives you more breadth of adjustment and also more breadth of interpretation . . . Most of the Indian shamans that I work with," he told me, "have a belief system that we would describe as 'magical thinking.' They'll perceive things coming from *outside,* rather than from *inside,* as being coordinated from forces outside of ourselves. And I see that as a fact, but at the same time these forces have a counterpoint inside, so it just depends on which end of the elephant you want to look at first."

To heal properly you ultimately have to acknowledge the reality paradigm of the person being healed, Petersen says. "There is no use saying, as some shamans do, that this will heal you so shut up and accept it. Everyone has a belief system deep within that makes them work. You have to work with that, not against it. And anyone who doesn't respect that is just a head-fucker."

Since Jaynes first published his theory in the late 1970s, however, other researchers have disputed his claims. In commentary on Dr. H. Steven Moffic's rebuttal to Jaynes's theory in the *American Journal of Psychiatry,* Drs. Assad and Shapiro wrote, "Jaynes' hypothesis makes for interesting reading and stimulates much thought in the receptive reader. It does not, however, adequately explain one of the central mysteries of madness: hallucination."

An indigenous perspective would call them *mareaciones,* and honor the ability to receive visions, and sift prophetic meaning from them. *Curanderos* themselves gain their power through being able to navigate through the visionary world on behalf of their patients. By continuing to define these altered states as abnormal, however, Western culture not only diminishes the consciousness it may have once held, it elevates the "back end of the elephant," as Petersen would say, to prime position.

As the ceremony begins Petersen says a Christian prayer in Spanish to consecrate the space, and then he smudges the four cardinal directions to cleanse the area of any bad spirits. Then as Walter begins *soplaring,* Petersen comes around and bathes us with *agua de florida,* tuning us in. I can feel his subtle energies working on me as he massages my temples lightly, and suddenly an internal vibration wells up within me like the roar of a waterfall, carrying me away.

I'm plunged into a deep theta state, my eyes rolling back in my head and eyelids fluttering rapidly as the beat of the hummingbird's wings hits me on my third eye over and over and over again, brainwaves lapping at the shores of consciousness. The beat increases as the vibration spreads across my entire face, like I'm wearing a mask made from the hummingbird's motions and it is my browser onto the world. While my body lies hot, sweating, and convulsing by the floor my spirit soars.

Somewhere deep within the vibration bursts open and rises up to envelop me. It's like a womb-sac, a bubble of pure heart-space that nurtures and protects, filtering out any negative energy. It wraps itself around me like a soap bubble, rainbow light swirling and coruscating on the oily surface. I remember Bowman back at don Juan's, singing these bubbles to protect himself from the dark, too, and realize this is something we all have within us, like an airbag of higher consciousness.

The roof lifts off the back of my head then and I'm seeing in all directions at once, without physical eyes. It's disorientating and I have to accustom myself to a whole new way of being before I can even focus on navigating this space.

Suddenly I'm hurtling down a tunnel, through loops and coils and round corners with soft edges like a body, but it's the cosmic body. And the ayahuasca rush of it, the bright, spiraling sparks of light that pulse their meaning at me as I hurtle by... *Infinite majesty. Jewels.*

I'm surrounded by colors and the silhouettes of the spirits as they flit about, as if through an unfocused lens, or looking at them from the corner of my eye. I know they're spirits because they have a gravity and a weight to them, a presence that I can feel that makes the hairs stand up on the back of my neck and a fine bolt of lightning snake down the chakra staircase along my spine. I make little hand signals, finger rolls to signal accelerate and decelerate to the spirits, drawing them in then pushing them back with the movement I learned on that first 5-MeO-DMT journey, so long ago now.

Suddenly my bubble bursts and I have the unbearably real sensation of being skinned alive, of coming to grips with the cosmic ecology outside of our flesh suits, the *intense G-force of the Godhead,* outside the 4D constructs we've made to protect ourselves from the raging hyper-dimensional flux. It's as if our spirit bodies are one large muscle that has never been exercised, and now, thrown into the deep end, I'm trying to work that muscle while being bombarded with the energy of this place. I feel like I'm drowning as the waves of energy flow through me and fill me from the inside out. I can't breathe; I'm panicking, hyperventilating, losing it in a big way. *Wipeout...*

The sound of vomiting draws me back to reality as I open my eyes to see my shimmering, iridescent wire-mesh body spun around the edge of the *maloca,* and a million bright jewels blossoming from my throat and cascading out into the night.

By a single candlelight I can see Petersen standing over Rolando at the head of the *maloca* with his bottles and potions, rattling on his chest with the *shacapa* leaf fan.

"Why don't you try leaning on your back," Petersen says to Rolando, putting one hand behind him and helping him recline on the bench. "Let's breathe together for a while," he continues, sitting down next to Rolando and taking him through some deep breathing exercises. "Relax, there's nothing to worry about, you're okay," he says, but Rolando's sweating and burning up.

He's been pulled out into that dimensional rip I wiped out on, man overboard on the astral seas, deep in the cannonball rush of it all. There's no off-switch from what he describes later as the "going insane space," that torrent of kaleidoscoping beauty assailing his raw light body.

"Rolando... Rolando can you hear me?" Petersen's shouting now, standing over his body slumped on the bench. "Shit. Walter, you'd better get over here." Rolando's eyes are open and he's staring straight ahead—but the vessel is empty. While Petersen does some polarity therapy on Rolando to smooth out his energy field and help him to ride it out, Walter begins singing a new *icaro* to help guide him home.

I can feel another wave of the hummingbird's wings rolling over me, taking me back out to the swirling *Sargasso* sea that Rolando's lost in. Each part of it is like a fractal, the visions spiraling out through an endless infinity, overwhelming me.

Over breakfast this morning Petersen explained in detail about the Amazonian pantheon and the four main spirits that shamans call in to help with their healing work. One is the black puma, which relates to the heart center and the attribute of courage. The other is the black boa, which corresponds to kundalini energy and bringing the energy from the lower chakras to the higher chakras. Another is the electric eel, which deals with the coordination of the neurological system through the whole electrical system in the body, which allows for readjustment of imbalances and so on.

And lastly there's the stingray, which brings the electrical field of telepathy and intuition into play, and allows one to extend beyond their body, into the area of astral travel. These are, according to Petersen, basically metaphors and symbols. The spirits of these animals have a counterpart in the neurological system of the human being, so they describe functions that are part of us and help invoke these functions.

So I invoke the black boa, the kundalini energy that connects the base chakra to the crown chakra, and I can feel it snaking through me, becoming me, bringing me up higher. I invoke the electric eel, that connection with my body and my energetic self, to smooth out all rough edges and to find equilibrium and balance. And I invoke the stingray, letting it blanket me in its organic, unfolding, connecting essence—which is when this bright hallucinogenic metaphor explodes in front of me, leading me full circle to find Rolando, then lose him on the shores of heaven.

I'm sorry to say there's no grand vision, no man with a white beard that whispers a magic word in my astral ear. I'm still too new to this whole shamanic odyssey, still winging the whole thing and stumbling across dimensional spaces like a squatter trying out doorways and looking for a place to crash. I can't control the visions enough to slow them down and interact, and the heavenly city starts to fade as I continue to tumble through hyperspace.

Eventually I descend and enter a murky gray cloud dimension that writhes about like an anaconda. I'm lost in this fog, marooned on a sea of fears. This place feels like somewhere souls go to rest, or where they're lost or trapped, a purgatory realm lower down the harmonic scale.

Spirits appear in the space before me and I'm instantly petrified. I make my mudras, little hand signals to roll back the spirits and *soplar* them with the *sooouuuu* sounds don Juan taught me, shooing them away. They hover just out of my reach, like they're waiting for some gate to open and to enter my flesh, but that's not going to happen. The way to survive this zone is to accept it, I instinctively realize, to let it pass through me like all the realms, and all the experiences therein.

The key, as I learned at Love Creek, is keeping an open heart. The heart chakra represents unconditional love, and when I open that it connects me to the astral. Once I'm in my power of unconditional love it becomes the navigator, the rudder of my hyperdimensional vehicle. When I've got that unblocked and ready to blossom I can connect to it ALL and it's much easier because I'm not holding back or struggling against it. *An open heart is like a homing beacon in this space, sending out a pure signal.*

Just then the black puma gallops through the fog, dragging Rolando's spirit body behind him. Rolando's eyes light up and he seems to recognize me, but he's holding on to his sense of reality by such a slender thread there's no way he can communicate. We're both lost, tumbling through a dream behind the spirit puma as he thunders through the worlds, towards our bodies.

In the peripheral vision off to my left a vast "Star Destroyer" made from living shadows hangs silently, each black pinprick containing a vast entelechy of souls. It feels unspeakably dark and cold, this giant shape that fills my vision, yet I have an urge to dive into it, to become it.

Before my eyes the puma strays towards its gravity field and starts to unravel like a loose thread that pulls apart a garment. It's sacrificed itself for me, I realize, and just in the nick of time I pull back. My energy field can't stay here, it's not synergistic or healthy. There are some things that you just can't accept into you, that must be kept beyond.

Suddenly there's this sound that I also see as light, a rippling, pulsing, geometric flower that blossoms through the fog. Some part of me remembers the sound: it's an *icaro,* the slow tumbleweeding roll of vibration accompanied by the eternal beat of the *shacapa.* It's Walter, I realize, he's like a lighthouse in the dark, the sound of him guiding us back from this dark netherworld. His song pierces the night and touches us intimately, personally, filling us with light. *His song is magnifico.*

All that first ceremony I was so caught up with a lack of connection and a lack of magic, and that was how all the fears entered me. Then Walter's voice had sounded rough and cheap, all Tom Waits-like, and I'd thought that Scott Petersen was a charlatan. But all that was a projection of my fears and lack of connection, because without a connection you're empty. The opposite of fear is joy, and as ayahuasca connects and brings awareness, it can also bring joy at your role in the grand scheme of things.

Walter's song is like a light, leading us home. Rolando and my spirit form melt into the geometric patterns endlessly morphing and becoming in response to our understanding of them. As I direct my intent towards it the song-light guides us out the netherworlds and back towards familiar ground. We drift down, past endless vibrational levels of being and *kerthunk.* We're back.

I open my eyes to see the cathedral in all its majesty, lit up by the light of the candles. My gaze takes in the bend in the wooden floorboards, the weave of the thatch as it climbs to the apex of the roof, and the feeling of great majesty that now fills this space. The night is hot and the electric buzz of insects surrounds us as always.

Petersen's there on the bench surrounded by shadows with Walter to his side, crooning his *icaros,* both of them standing over Rolando.

Rolando sits up and opens his eyes sheepishly, like waking up from a dream.

"Welcome back, gentlemen," Petersen says, and a wave of relief floods me. But at the same time I know that once you've bungee-jumped into heaven there's no real coming back. The ayahuasca world is as real as this; indeed, maybe more real.

In the ayahuasca way of seeing reality, *we'd come back into the dream.*

21
Down to the River to Pray
Sachamama, Km 18 Iquitos-Nauta Hwy
Tuesday August 9, 2006

I sleep for two days solid and I dream and dream and dream of heaven and earth and all the things in-between. In the dream I'm wandering through an *Alice in Wonderland*-like jungle, looking for Afra, my daughter, and the sense of spirits hangs heavy in the air.

This fades to a giant book-screen like a cosmic dictionary, with long, scrolling vertical words all framed by an infinite golden thread. I can't recognize what the words mean or the alphabet they're formed from, but the sense of shining, golden language is overwhelming nonetheless. It's like the secrets of the universe, *the source code of the Divine* showing itself to me and it's so real, so intense, that I know I'm being led back to the path, to the great vine of the spirits, *ayahuasca . . .*

I wake with a sense of urgency, a need to participate and reconnect with the medicine after a few days off the path, recovering from my experiences at the Refugio. But tonight is a ceremony night, and by the time I've opened my eyes I know that I will drink at Sachamama, out by Kilometer 18—the thought enters my head like a command. Sachamama is one of the last places I wanted to visit before leaving Iquitos and heading down to Pucallpa. I had just over three weeks left in Peru and I was determined to push deeper up the Amazon to continue this shamanic odyssey all the way to the end.

I'm changing—I can feel it—and it's thanks to the ayahuasca and the dieting I've been doing between ceremonies. Both of these are catalysts for the pure state of consciousness that we all hold the potential for, that

we're born with. Is this how babies feel in their freshly minted innocence, still connected to the infinite splendor of creation? I suspect so.
So much of the *dieta* is to cleanse the body and the mind, to restore it
to the default levels we were born with before decades of sugar, spices,
and oils changed the configuration.

I remember don Juan saying how "our own humanity is what holds
us back," and now I think I understand. Nature has an intelligence
behind it; it designs its creatures to connect to the Source. *But it can't
stop us from crashing the operating system.*

I have an early breakfast at the Yellow Rose—which has been feeling
lonely and empty without the conference *ayahuasqeros* in town. Still, Iquitos is never empty of seekers and I bump into my seed brother Rolando,
who's talking to a balding French guy in his fifties called Sigmaa.

It turns out that Sigmaa's friends with Jan Kounen and helped as a
translator on his Shipibo-shamanism documentary, *Other Worlds.* He's
in town to drink with Guillermo at the Espirit de Anaconda for a few
weeks—which we both, coincidentally, call the "Club Med of Ayahuasca." Our conversation drifts to the Indian "saint" Amma, whom he
met working on Jan's second documentary, and about the spirit that
connects us all. Just thinking down these pathways seems to reenergize
me, and something that was empty inside me starts to fill again.

Just before midday I walk down to the bustling market stall circus of
Belén, melting into the sea of people that crowd its streets. As I walk my
holographic awareness kicks in and a river of visual language flowers all
around me in semiotic detritus. The words on the overhead billboards,
the lettering on shop windows, logos on clothes, numbers, letters, they
all pop out at me in a "magic eye" landscape of hidden meaning. Key
words catch my eye and I know intimately what they mean, all of them
referring to the ceremony tonight and my imminent ayahuasca journey:

POWERFUL flashes off an aspirin advertisement to my left.
GRAND JOURNEY off the travel agent sign to my right. Up ahead,
the word DEATH stares down hauntingly off a billboard—and then I
have to stop looking.

I'm fully aware that on one level Western psychology would say these insights are mere ego delusions, or evidence of schizophrenic thinking. The problem is that all forms of altered states have at one time or another been labeled schizophrenic, psychotic, or epileptic, precisely because the Western point of view is so ethnocentric and guarded in defining "ordinary consciousness." The hologrammatic awareness level of consciousness would definitely be perceived as schizoid precisely because it disintegrates individual ego into a *planetary-level distributed consciousness* where everything is naturally referring to everything else.

So in integrating the possibility of this awareness back into the material world I'm flirting with "madness," but consciously so. I'm aware of the neuro-feedback loops I'm creating and exploring the meta-narrative possibilities by accepting this information on one level and remaining objective on another. Or, to put it simply, *I'm wandering the streets of Belén lost in a sea of language, the hero in a "choose-your-own-adventure" multi-path narrative of the soul.*

The game is on.

I dodge the taxis and buses that swerve across both lanes of the street and the stray dogs with the unloved eyes and the children with the hungry faces, and finally find an autobus headed for Nauta, along that vast highway that connects Iquitos with the satellite towns.

In the hologrammatic universe there are no coincidences. Like the words leaping off the billboards, more signs and omens crowd in on me. The autobus is, of course, loaded with Jesus sacred heart stickers and a Jesus hologram by the gearstick has a bleeding heart that is glowing with the light of heart chakra activation.

I bundle into the small, cramped space with a dozen locals and we head off down the highway, past familiar *ayahuasquero* haunts—Ron Wheelock's turnoff near the Questacocha Zoo at Km 9, Guillermo's drop off point at Km 14.5—and just under half an hour later I'm dropped off at Km 18 by the side of the road, where the bitumen meets the jungle.

Half a dozen locals mill about under an L-shaped open air hut with a thatched roof and stick picket fence that sits ten meters in from the road, a two-story hut attached behind it to house the roadmen. The sign outside reads "Jardin Botanico. Museo Galeria Sachamama. Iquitos—Peru, Km 18." *The word on the street calls this place shaman central.*

Established in 1991 by don Francisco Montes Shuna, an indigenous *curandero* and visionary artist, Sachamama was the first shamanistic health retreat of its kind in the area, and in many ways it has set the template for all the retreats that followed who cater to Western audiences. Don Francisco writes on his website that "during an ayahuasca ceremony, I had a vision of a man and a woman with snakes on their heads. They came towards me from the southern part of the land (on which is now built the ceremonial house) and told me that one day I should found a botanical garden to be named Sachamama (the mother of us all)."

Fifteen years later the legend of Sachamama has it that this place has the strongest ayahuasca brew in all of Peru, and thousands of Western seekers have passed through its doors.

Don Francisco has done the hard yards, building up this place from near poverty. He was routed with his family down in Pucallpa by members of the Shining Path, who demanded protection money before burning down his house and original ethnobotany center. When he came to Iquitos he worked as a banana transport laborer and an ice-cream vendor before getting a job as a gardener, close to the location of what would eventually become Sachamama. Over the years Francisco has been strategically placed to take advantage of the trickle of Western seekers and ride it as it became a wave.

Don Francisco's young cousin, Jose, a hip twentyish Peruvian with sideburns and a goatee, greets me at the roadside way station and walks me the half a kilometer or so down the jungle trail to the retreat itself. It's not really a road, more a dirt track surrounded by an endless sea of trees and dense green foliage that envelops us.

We pass through the enthnobotanical garden where more than 1,200 species of native plants and trees are growing. The garden is spread over sixty hectares of mature, secondary rainforest in a designated conservation area. Ayahuasca vines the size of anacondas curl around ancient trees, spiraling up into the heavens. A strong, powerful energy, old and deep runs through this place like an electric current, almost palpable in the air.

We arrive at the main building, a large square *maloca* where ten students from around the world are sitting at a long wooden dining table, laughing and smoking cigarettes. The white tablecloth has kitsch icons of pineapples, bananas, oranges, and apples straight off a slot machine.

The *ayahuasqueros* stop talking as I enter, and for a second it feels like I'm the new kid at school in the cafeteria at lunchtime, being stared at by the established pecking order. Many of the seekers here are good-looking and dressed in hip Western brands, smoking cigarettes as they while away the day. Four of the students are French, three women and a man in their mid-to-late twenties.

A long, sullen, dark-haired dude with a black goatee beard sits at the end of the table, lording over the place. He's from Buenos Aires and has been brought here by his girlfriend, Luce, a slim, attractive woman in her mid-thirties who sits by his side. Luce has a strong nose, like a younger Meryl Streep and a kick-ass attitude to match.

I light a *mapacho* myself and sit back, explaining that I'm a journalist writing about ayahuasca and sharing some of my experiences so far. The constant sound of hammering echoes through the room from a few hundred meters away, where workers are busy building an extension to the student dormitories.

"The ayahuasca here is very, very strong," Luce tells me as she smokes her clove cigarette. "Francisco uses a lot of admixtures in his brew: *toé, chilisanago, chiricsanango, chacruna, wambisa, mapacho*... very strong, but then we have nothing to compare with. We've been here in Peru three weeks and we've not visited any other *curanderos*."

Unlike the casual *ayahuasqueros* I've encountered in my travels, the crew here at Sachamama all seem to bunker down for extended stays and intensive diets with the plant doctors, often isolated in their jungle huts.

A monkey at the end of the table smiles at me, baring its teeth and bounding over in a flash to lick the sweat off my hand. Then it tears through a *mapacho* someone's left on the table and sifts through the tobacco. Frantic, it leaps a few spaces down the table at a young Peruvian boy of about seven, biting at his hand as he jumps to his feet, crying and backing away. One of the French guys shoos it away as a Peruvian woman comes over and comforts the child.

I drift off from the table to examine the *maloca* and a room to the back past the dining area, where round wooden medallions advertise *Museo Galleria; Una Vision Hecho Realidad; Spirituales/Cultural/Educativos.* Inside an antechamber I pass long glass cabinets along the walls which hold dried leaves and samples of plant medicinals, with little handwritten cards explaining their functions. Passing through a bead curtain I enter a large gallery space with dozens of pieces of ayahuasca-inspired art hanging on the walls, painted by don Francisco and one of his daughters.

Francisco is a cousin of the one-time *ayahuasquero* and renowned visionary painter Pablo Cesar Amaringo, whose book *Ayahuasca Visions* has helped communicate the visual nature of the hallucinogenic spirit world the vine reveals. Like Amaringo, Francisco brings back a little bit of that world in his art, grounding in the inks and oils a vibrant tapestry of interdependent life that extends beyond our everyday senses.

Each painting is like a doorway into another world. One canvas shows a giant towering World Tree with thick ayahuasca vines coiling around it. At a vagina-like opening at its base a *curandero* in a striped *cushma* sits smoking a pipe and shaking a *shacapa* leaf rattle at two men in Western clothes before him, sitting and kneeling on leaf pillows. One is smoking a pipe himself while the other holds up a glistening power stone towards the *curandero*. All three are surrounded by interlocking layers of leaves, vines, and jungle spirits that hover among the hallucinogenic canopy. Owls, parrots, and jaguars stare out from the tableau, their forms melting into the sea of green. Behind the tree the light of an inner sun is eclipsed by the thick trunk.

A second painting shows a tree with a host of winged spirits like biblical angels blossoming among the leaves. Surrounding them are pulsating energy blobs representing young spirits, which would make this some type of nursery. A dozen single eyes open in the air around the tree and look out. In the root system under the tree trunk a grandmother spirit is curled up. Her long elongated hands push up out of the ground and become vines, with *chacruna* leaves sprouting along their length. Next to this painting is another showing these same *chacruna* leaves in close up, dancing with little human arms and legs.

A third painting, and perhaps the most beautiful, is signed Robert M O, Pucallpa, 08-04-2006. If Salvador Dali were to drink ayahuasca in the jungles of Peru this is what he would see:

A proud red parrot melting into a rainbow caught by an outstretched hand that itself turns into a serpent. Two jaguars with open mouths hunt the spirit forest, surrounded by plants and low hanging lianas that open to reveal geometric lattices within. Faces and eyes sprout from the geography and melt into the undergrowth. The green gives away to blue as sea-spirits frolic in underwater cities, passing ships adrift on shifting vistas, vast organic machines with cogs and blossoms that keep turning one into another, no beginning and no end to this pulsing web of life . . .

Woah. I'm triggering a synaptic imprint just looking at it.

José comes back with Javier, a tall, skinny bald-headed guy who's incongruously wrapped up in a heavy denim jacket in the afternoon humidity. Javier's a global traveler who migrates around the world's festival circuit, DJing, partying, and spreading the knowledge and practice of plant medicines. He was born in Switzerland to Spanish-speaking parents and he also speaks French and English, a real boon here in this global ayahuasca retreat.

As we talk I tune into the open, almost tender energy Javier carries about him. He has his arms crossed and grips his jacket close to him like he's cold. He's wearing blue jeans and a white t-shirt with a skull in the top center, surrounded by two ravens looking in at it, their beaks touching like a scene out of an Edgar Alan Poe story.

I hold my hand out to shake but he looks at it like I've offered up a dead rat, explaining he can't touch another person while he's on *dieta*. It's the energy exchange, you see, he's too sensitive to other people's energies. He came here for a month last year, and then again for five months in the winter where he dieted and connected with the plants, including toé and ayahuasca.

"On *toé* there are many places I have no recollection of whatsoever," he says in a slow, pronounced accent, like there's a time lag between his thoughts and his ability to speak them.

For the last three weeks he's been dieting extensively with *chiricsanango,* a small root often called the cold plant, to balance out his hot-cold perception and his sensitivity to extremes. He's planning on moving to Cuzco where he will conduct san pedro ceremonies and there's no way he can face the cool climate of the Andes without healing his imbalance first.

"Dieting puts you in another dimension," Javier says, "one in which you are not distracted by colors and flavors. Food just becomes a matter of sustenance, and not something to distract yourself with. Dieting leaves more space for you to tune into other realities, subtler realities. If you were not withdrawing from all these things then the plant diet would probably be too subtle to feel."

We sit down to chat about his experiences while we wait for don Francisco to get back from town. Javier said earlier that he's seen me at the Yellow Rose and had gotten a flash of a young David Bowie . . . *ch-ch-ch-ch-ch-ch-changes* . . . I get the impression that Javier's psychically sensitive; you can see it when he talks to you, in the way he's looking through you into the energy fields, reading your aura. He pauses in conversation often and lilts his tones, choosing his words carefully like they're on a cosmic teleprompter and he's simply reading the cue cards.

"You're a doctor?" he says finally, reading my mind.

"Of sorts," I reply. A *Doctor of Divinity,* U.S. $40 from the Universal Life Church in California. Best Christmas present I've ever bought for myself, but this wasn't the time or place to get into all that.

Like all dieters Javier is staying here in one of the *tambos* built on the edge of the jungle, withdrawn from the world and in the solitude of the forest where the energy of the plants can feed the soul. Sachamama has grown from only two diet *tambos* around five years ago to over a dozen kitted out in a simple style for the *ayahuasqueros*. Part of the increase is due to the unprecedented publicity Sachamama has garnered in the Western media.

Author Graham Hancock stayed here for six weeks and devoted a section of his bestselling book *Supernatural* to the mysteries of ayahuasca he was inducted into, and Alice Munroe, a Canadian writer, devoted much of her book *The Green Labyrinth* to her stay here. El Mundo Magico, a U.K. tour company, has been promoting ayahuasca tourism at Sachamama through its website for many years, and the retreat's word-of-mouth on the spiritual backpacking circuit here in Peru is without equal. On the way back from my first ceremony with Percy, our bus had picked up a gorgeous woman named Andrea who had raved about the magic of Sachamama with the spark of one who knows. If Guillermo's Espiritu de Anaconda is the "Club Med," then Sachamama is the Hilton of ayahuasca healing retreats. It has a reputation for *five-star shamanism*.

Just then another of the dieters arrives, Pedro, a skinny, easygoing thirty-something from Sweden with a boyish charm, brown hair, and a neatly trimmed beard. He's dressed in a gray t-shirt with "ARMY" stenciled on it, khaki camo pants and sandals, and as he puffs away happily on his small wooden pipe and tells me his life story, I feel like I've known him all my life.

Pedro's been dieting and studying here at Sachamama for some years. He started as a regular ayahuasca drinker and has progressed into an apprentice role with Francisco, singing *icaros* and blowing *mapacho* smoke on those needing healing during ceremony. His dietary practices have led him to strong relationships with the plant doctors and with the spirits themselves, which he tells me he hopes to take back with him into his healing work in Sweden.

Pedro shows me around the grounds while Javier has a rest in his *tambo* before the ceremony later tonight, and as we chat I discover that they're both friends with Kevin Furnas, who trained here for almost two years. I'm not surprised as they all share the same mellow, stress-free vibe of seekers who have attained an inner peace.

As we walk Pedro points out a large building past the art room that houses the dormitories for casual guests. There's a hammock out on the veranda with mosquito netting surrounding it and six individual rooms and two showers inside. Half a dozen Peruvians are hammering away building a whole other wing as big as the existing rooms. There's no electricity here or in the dieting *tambos* further on, although the steady hum of a generator is coming from somewhere nearby.

I leave my day bag here and continue on through the property with Pedro, who sings me beautiful sweet *icaros* he has learned from dieting with the plants. We thread down a narrow pathway with snake-like tree roots pushing through the earth, leading through the jungle to the ceremony *maloca* a hundred meters away. A local Indian worker busily sweeps down the dirt path after us, brushing away leaves with an earnest diligence and the karmic acceptance of one who knows that more leaves will inevitably fall, and that his work will never end.

The forest here is full of old, mature specimens that radiate their presence. They all have names: *yanacaspi, remocaspi, waisacha, sacharuna, chuchuhuasi, cumaseba* ... And like people, they have distinct characteristics and personalities that you get to know once you've dieted with them and learned their song. We pass a giant ayahuasca vine two or three feet wide that wraps around a thick *osookaweiyo* tree, which shoots up dead straight into the sunlit canopy above.

"*Osookaweiyo* has a sweetness to taste," Pedro tells me. He's dieted with it recently and describes the different flavors of spirit relationships each plant diet has. "When I started to diet with *remocaspi* it was the hardest diet I'd ever done," he says, laying a hand on the broad trunk of the great-grandfather tree that towers above us. The *remocaspi* roots are flattened into graceful, broad fins almost two meters high at the base, like the tails of whales lashed together. The spread of the fins carves out a two or three meter clearing for the *remocaspi* from the other trees in the forest, like an elder claiming space.

"I call in *remocaspi* and he gives me counsel and even more stability and strength. He's like the general; he brings you through the battle," Pedro says with a proud smile. "He brought two tons on my shoulders and my mind was pitch black. I didn't see any light in my life at all. I thought I was finished—that I was leaving this place. I'm not cut out for this shit.

"And then he gave me a song that goes—*hum dada ree dada ree da, rum dada ree dada ree dee,* and I just thought it was a joke, y'know. He puts all this weight on me then he gives me a song that's like, 'go out marching with all your friends!' But now I understand; it's like in the old times when they went into battle, they had war chants. This is like a war chant. Grab your energies and go for it, keep on walking. And that's the energy that *icaro* has.

"The plant I dieted with before, *cumaseba,* he's a very noble tree. He's like a king. He has a very noble sense but he's much more soft… *Remocaspi's* hard. He needs discipline. I love him so much because I've been spending so much time with him. But he is hard and he has a sharpness. *Cumaseba* for me was like a big, strong bear that took you under his arm and went grwwwwlll, c'mon fight with me a little bit, y'know."

From there we take a trail past an open-air *maloca* with a thatched roof where the ayahuasca is brewed in a giant black cauldron on a fire pit, and swing by the dieting *tambos* where Pedro shows me his room. Finally we pass by a little stream where Francisco often does flower baths and cleansings, and where Pedro has had encounters with elemental spirits. The density and maturity of the plants and trees around Sachamama has resulted, it seems, in an equal density of frolicking spirit forms that test each dieter.

"When Kevin Furnas was doing diets with *cumaseba* he became a little bit too serious about it, y'know, doing diets with the king, the king of the forest," Pedro relates. "So one evening we were sitting in his *tambo* and *cumaseba* came to him in a vision. He saw this person with a baseball cap and a boom box playing hip-hop music, *boom cha cha cha* and it was *cumaseba* coming to play a joke on him, to say 'don't be so fucking serious, y'know,'" Pedro laughs. "The plant spirits are funny tricksters and sometimes we need it. And then they will play a serious trick on us if we need that, too, to keep us straight."

Finally we arrive at a rather simple ceremony hut where Francisco conducts the sessions, often accompanied by Javier and Pedro, or other students who have mastered the basics enough to be able to function in the altered space and help out with the logistics. The ceremony *maloca* is a square hut about fifteen meters long, with a dirt floor, a thatched roof, and half walls to support long wooden benches that run up each side. "It's simple—when you want to vomit you just lean over and purge," Pedro explains. "No buckets, no problems."

At the top of the *maloca* is a wooden altar *(mesa)* covered with the usual paraphernalia: half a dozen candles, a skin drum and a tambourine, wooden pipes, little Catholic statues of the Virgin Mary, Jesus, St Francis of Assisi (curiously, with two faces on either side of his head) and others, crystals and power stones, *mapacho* cigarettes, and four bottles of *agua de florida* and scented potions, including some small perfumed bottles with fragrant waters. It looks like a well-stocked jungle bar.

Francisco is a *perfumero,* one who heals through the use of scented plants and essences. Towering above the perfumes are three large plastic bottles stained over time with the dark brown residue of the vine, a quarter liter of thick, honey-like ayahuasca tea fermenting at the bottom of each bottle.

"Ah, there is magic here, my friend," Pedro announces, puffing away on his little pipe and remembering all the ceremonies he has undergone here. "Here we learn how to work the medicine. We learn to sing the *icaros,* to manage the *shacapa,* and to work with the perfumes. But at the beginning—I've never sung my whole life, maybe in the shower, but suddenly Francisco asks me to sing a song in ceremony and it's like— there are ten people there and I had to sing! He was pushing me and it was scary, but I love singing now... I have a bunch of *icaros* now and I'm learning more and more..."

We meander back to the main building to discover that Francisco has arrived, sitting talking with the Westerners. He's a non-descript Peruvian with short black hair cut in a plain bowl-shape, and his only affectation seems to be the small square of facial hair growing directly under his nose, a miniature version of Hitler's infamous moustache. He's in his mid-fifties but like so many of those who drink ayahuasca regularly, and diet, he has a healthy glow and vitality about him. He's dressed in a leather motorcycle jacket with a plain white t-shirt and blue jeans underneath, and as he shakes my hand with a friendly air he grins cheekily.

Francisco stares at me with a slightly unfocused gaze and an amused smile like he's seen many journalists here and he knows that no matter how good we are that words alone cannot express the central mysteries he deals with. But he's happy to talk, and even happier to help promote Sachamama—and the work of *curanderismo*. As he says, "I never had any thoughts about teaching or healing Westerners originally; the only thing I cared about was protecting the plants here and then sharing my knowledge and being able to maintain it." But as more and more Westerners have come, the legend of Sachamama has grown, and now it is one of the largest retreats in Peru.

What's it like, I ask him, to have had all these Westerners pass through here, bringing money as their currency of energy and receiving spiritual knowledge in return?

"Maybe we are losing a bit in the exchange," Francisco says, with a canny understanding of the relationship shamans have with their Western students.

"Westerners are getting healing and understanding, and we are getting paid for that, but it's also making the art of *curanderismo* more money driven. Many *curanderos* aren't interested in healing their fellow people anymore, they just want to work with tourists now because they bring the money. So *curanderismo* is losing out as well, that's the downside of it.

"But I'm very pleased to receive people and to share with them the knowledge I have of the plants and of *curanderismo*," Francisco says as he makes a wave with one hand, indicating all the students at the table around us. "It's also good to know that those people will transmit this knowledge with even more people in faraway places. But there's no sense of preference or ego, everyone who comes here does so because they want to learn, and everyone who comes here with that in mind is welcome."

Francisco comes from the Capanahua Indians on the Ucayali River, outside Pucallpa. Like the neighboring Shipibo-Conibos tribe, the Capanahua have retained their belief in the art of *curanderismo* and the healing it can provide. His family has a long heritage of producing healers, and his grandmother—Trinidad Vilces Peso—was a renowned *banco muraya* and *curandera*. She chose him when he was three from among forty-eight grandchildren to pass on her shamanic knowledge, bathing him in flower essences and giving him plant remedies to drink. There was no ayahuasca at this stage, but she was preparing him for stepping into the role. When he was six he drank ayahuasca for the first time.

His grandmother died soon after—at one hundred and eight—when she was lost under the waters and, it is believed, joined the dolphins as a *suniruna*—a shaman who knows and can control the spirits of the water realm. "I was there," Francisco tells me. "She fell into the water in the river and at that moment there were a lot of dolphins about the boat and circling the spot where she disappeared. Later she came to me in a dream to say she's not a dolphin, but she's directing the dolphins, she's like the mother of the dolphins, living with them in the water.

"When I was thirteen or fourteen I first started working as a *curandero*, but it wasn't till I was twenty-two that I became a disciple of the plants. I had some experience healing people and things like that, but mostly I was still a student of the plants. It was only when I reached the age of thirty-three that I reached the level of *maestro* and could consider myself a fully-fledged master *curandero*."

He looks at me with that defocalized gaze, looking through me and then breaking into a broad smile, and I remember the sacrifice he has gone through to be here now, and the need for more healers like him.

As if he too, was reading my mind, Francisco replies, "I see humans connecting with the spirit of ayahuasca all over the world. And just like the
world is turning and moving, so too, the spirit of ayahuasca is moving.
Shamanism is becoming like a world-wide religion, it's transforming
into a global religion and it's growing faster than we realize."

Like the vine itself, I can feel myself growing, thirsty for the light.

That night in my dormitory room I flip through a few pages from
Carlos Castaneda's *The Teachings of Don Juan: A Yaqui Way of Knowledge*
by candlelight, one of the dozens of books left in the dorm library by
travelers as they pass through. I feel like a prisoner waiting for his execu-
tion, his time to die, and just before eight o'clock Javier arrives to lead
me back to the ceremony hut. The moon is full again tonight, with a
stunning rainbow ring around it and a sea of spectral clouds lit up by
the light. The sound of the jungle is electric, with frogs, cicadas, birds,
and the odd screech of howler monkeys.

In the dark of the *maloca* there is light—three candles sit on the altar
blanketing us in shadows. Francisco sits up at the head of the altar with
Rachel Willay, a French woman with short boyish hair in her early
forties who's been here for almost two years. Rachel was a singer back
in France for many years, but she felt that there was no way for her to
explore her spirituality in the commercial music business there. Pedro
tells me she has a beautiful singing voice and often takes point singing
icaros in ceremony.

Francisco has so many apprentices, in fact, that they quite often do
most of the ground level work in ceremonies, guided and overseen by
the *maestro*. Francisco is a bit like the bandmaster or a symphony leader
in a big band—he sets the tone and drives the current, carries the wave
along and transmits the energy that travels on it to the students.

There're ten of us lined up on either side on the benches like football players at half-time. A sweat-lodge or locker-room energy hangs
in the air as the seekers cough and shift nervously on the hard benches,

which throw me back to La Iglesia Matriz in the Plaza de Armas. *I am yet again in a church,* I realize, but this is also the bridge, the control room for our flights innerspace.

There's Javier and Pedro, Luce, the dark-haired dude from Buenos Aires, the three French guys, and a smattering of Americans including Jonah, a young kid in his early twenties with a crew cut, glasses, and a nerdy appearance. He looks like he should be a lawyer, but he's planning on studying at the Californian Institute of Integral Studies next year to study psychology. He says he's had a rough time of it with the brew totally knocking him senseless, and he's not alone. Some of the women are having their periods tonight and have come to be in ceremony, but not drink.

Before administering the ayahuasca Francisco comes around to us one by one to judge and weigh our energies. He puts his hands on my forehead, asking pertinent questions that are translated by Javier at his side: How are you feeling? What experience have you had with the brew? Etc. He reads me like a Geiger counter, what I can handle, what the spirit says is right, and then blows *mapacho* smoke on my crown and down my back. Then he says, "Tonight . . . tonight you will have two-quarters of a cup," a roundabout way of saying half a cup. From my previous experiences with the vine nothing less than *two cups* seems to ever suffice, but I don't know how to tell him this without seeming disrespectful to the master. But as so many *ayahuasqueros* have told me, Sachamama has by far the strongest medicine in Peru, so maybe I should err on the safe side after all. The DMT-*chacruna* content here is reputed to be upwards of 250–300g.

Once the doctor has made his house calls round the circle he calls us up one by one to the altar to receive our medicine. We drink from small wooden cups and the brew . . . the brew is *thiiiccckk*. Thick like foam, the bitter liquid phlegm marshmallowing down my throat . . . It glugs down and coats my insides, seeping into every nook and crevice till a sphere of warmth spreads through my belly.

We sit on the benches coughing and spluttering as the medicine snakes through us. Time elongates in the dark and after a while don Francisco, Pedro, Javier, and Rachel take turns singing beautiful, spellbinding *icaros* that cascade through to the quick of me, until I lose myself in them.

Francisco starts with the slowest, most mellow *icaro,* rolling tumbleweeds on the horizon and the beat of the *shacapa* slowly edging its way from this world to the next. It's one of the same *icaros* that don Juan sang, and maybe Percy and Javier, that archetypal spaghetti-western Shipibo-style anthem of the ayahuasca scene I've heard so often throughout my travels: *An da lay li lee la li li, an de lay la li li . . .*

The *icaros* lap at my consciousness as some of the other drinkers come online and begin humming along, the sound of us all rolling out into the night. As each singer joins the sonic web the healing power and vibrational essence contained in the *icaro* enters them.

As the brew comes on I can hear Pedro off to the left at the top of the room, like the prize pupil, making a deep, contented *"aahhhhhh"* sigh, and I know he's arrived into the DMT spirit zone. *He's come home.* I know that feeling, that sense of welcome and completion, the return to the Source, and I envy him.

As one *icaro* ebbs and flows and stops the sound of prodigious vomiting fills the air. *"Burrrrrrhhhh!"* someone vomits—I immediately think of Jonah—then *buurrrrrrghhh* again, wet sounds hitting the floor outside the *maloca*. It sounds like something's trying to come through . . . wave after wave of vomiting . . . *"Uggghh . . ."* the voice sounds again between wracking heaves, and another purge, waves lapping at the core of him. *Uhh. Why me,* the voice silently screams.

Holy fuck, how much can one person heave? He's vomiting over and over for ten or fifteen minutes, and as the others all come in and out of their own purges I remember we are all sick Westerners being healed.

"Westerners have different needs than locals," Francisco said earlier today. "You have different problems—maybe they're worse. For example, with drugs and addictions—cocaine, heroin, cigarettes, alcohol, and the effects of these on the body, lots of cancers and the like. A lot of people come here to work on their health issues with things like cancer. And spiritually Westerners are very bitter, you feel very low, very bad."

Pedro lights a *mapacho* and *soplars* it on the bench before launching into a song. There's a confidence in his voice as he sings, *"Hum de day hum de dum de day…"* going over and hitting people with the *shacapa* fan, or administering perfume. He sings and then he vomits himself, quick and sure, and spits out any residue, one, two, three blows, like a native with a dart gun.

Later, Javier tells me he's seeing a column of light miles across surrounded by darkness, rising up to the heavens like a celestial laser.

Alex, one of the French students, is muttering to himself, *dat da da daaa, whoo sa cha cha,* riding the vibrations in the inner worlds and breaking out into sound as he goes, my translinguistic spirit brother. A few of the other *ayahuasqueros* start humming along primal ur-sounds themselves here in the dark, and I know that they're having a conversation with spirit, losing themselves in a river of sound. To hear my brothers and sisters speaking in tongues, the liquid jungle glossolalia of our voices melding together feels like coming home. *My seed brothers and sisters are all flowering into angel-speak.*

We are just conduits for these sounds to come through, I realize, and I have a flash of what William Burroughs was on about with all his deconstruction of language. It feels like the conceptual *Logos* is an organism, or a part of an organism, and that whole wave frequency of it is ingressing here now as vibrational waves. *All of us are living language, a library of sound and intent.* In all of Peru I haven't met anyone else who speaks in tongues in ceremony like me, but here, tonight, three, four, five seekers on the bench opposite are alive with the fire of the Logos in them.

All of this is like sensory rainfall falling about me, sinking into the core of me. It's like I have no off switch, no way to block out the sounds of the jungle and my brothers and sisters around me. I drift off, letting the ego go. And for the first half an hour or more nothing is really happening and I'm starting to curse Francisco's paltry "two-quarters of a cup." My budget was dwindling and it wasn't cheap to attend a ceremony here. I felt like I'd wasted my best shot at the Sachamama experience. All this way, all this expense, and no ayahuasca visions...

As Rachel starts to sing a haunting *icaro,* her voice like a lighthouse across a dark sea... *VOOM! It hits.* And it's not like a segue, or a slow dissolve, or a cross-fade coming in slowly. The ayahuasca brew hits me like *lightning,* like a shockwave and I'm at the ground zero of its force.

In a split second I'm catapulted into the deep DMT state, that turbulent sea of geometric spirit... And it's deep... and raging all around. All my being, all my essence is locked down tight, trying to hold on to my sense of self and praying for this disintegrating torrent to calm down, for it not to be so intense. I am skinned alive by the force of this place, more so than ever before, like every ayahuasca trip I've ever done in Peru boiled down to a concentrate and blasted at me.

Some liken ayahuasca to a river. But this Sachamama brew... she is the Amazon at its deepest and widest and I cannot see the end of it as it opens and swallows me whole. It absolutely destroys me on a sea of primal madness. *Bastante!* Enough, please it's enough. I want it to stop, I just want it to stop, it's too much. I've been plunged into the heart of a star, a molten furnace and the pressure here is unrelenting, unbearable. I'm being shredded to bits by the vibratory waves of the inner bardos of the Godhead. *Nothing human can survive here, only the purest of spirit, and I'm not pure enough...*

The river has overwhelmed me: I can't breathe or move my head, much less make a sound as the ayahuasca utterly destroys me. The relentless pulverizing lasts the whole three or four hours of the ceremony, only tapering off slightly towards the end. I feel at least a dozen levels in, deeper than I've ever gone before, totally up the harmonic wavelength of the hyperdimensions.

I spend the whole night pleading with mother ayahuasca for mercy, for a slight reduction in the unbearable intensity of her naked grace. Like a junkie dying for a hit, I'm desperate for a sense of the flesh, of structure, for thoughts and the safe, fleshy comforts of being human. Day-night-boxes-rooms-normal.

I'm grasping at straws, pulling at the threads of reality but I can't hold a thought for more than a split second. I'm a drowning man in the seas of the Godhead and every time I snatch a breath of fresh air I'm hurled back under again into the overwhelming pressure of this cosmic ocean.

I have fears of death and of dying, and of being in this state, this overwhelming ocean-non-stop-raging forever. *Eternity.* The pain is unbearable. I just want to be born again, to incarnate back into the flesh... *born again, born again... back to the lower frequency world. This is why we reincarnate so quickly, to escape the pressure of heaven.* I no longer have a fear of death—here now, in this torrential vibratory ocean, *I have become death.*

And then... something deep within says to let go of myself, of who I think I really am. *Shed your skin and let's get started. Remember? This is where we come from, where we go back to.*

I have visions through the night, a raft of spirits that flit by like morphing psychedelic postage stamps, but mainly I just have that over-whelming rainbowing, kaleidoscoping morphing *intensity*... I can't open my eyes and I can't close my eyes... there is just no space for me to just be. *I am destroyed.*

Eventually I marshal all my strength, every fucking erg of energy that makes me human. I gather my spirit about me with a Herculean effort and pull myself up off the bench to purge over the *maloca* wall.

The vomit comes out of me in a spray, long and deep and guttural as a primal scream escapes me, beast-like, and I cough up wads of phlegm and fluid. The whole time I'm vomiting the medicine is holding on to me, not relenting from its vibratory grip. I'm having a DNA flashback, rushing through the genetic lines that build the vehicles of our flesh and snake through time. There's an explosion of geometric patterns: snake eyes, jaguar skin—the language of the beasts floods through me, a visual language with floating dot trail matrices like Aboriginal art. This whole realm is alive with color and intelligence, like being inside a rainbow, shifting like a patch of oil on water in the sunlight...

The key is remembering to stay conscious, but I just can't focus on anything. I forget how to make protective bubbles as I'm ripped apart and stripped to the bone. My whole body is energy. I'm twitching and fidgeting constantly, burning up like I might self-combust. I can't stop moving, playing with my hands, forming mudras with my fingers to name and channel the energies, and still the onrushing mercilessness of it ALL bombards me in a tsunami of higher consciousness.

I begin rubbing my hands up and down my face, the feeling of skin, the warmth of my hands and the blood pulsing through them the only respite from the intensity of this cosmic ocean blasting me to bits.

An arc of emerald light curves from lower left to upper right past my field of vision and I have the sudden knowledge that I'm in the presence of the *night doctores,* the *plant maestros* themselves.

Their spirit essences flare up against the sea of green, each spirit surrounded by a halo of light. I can hear-feel them talking to me directly for the first time, a dozen or so of these grand, ancient vegetal intelligences, like a parliament of trees before me.

They're "talking" in the sounds of the jungle, the glossolalia of the birds and high-pitched sonic chattering, a sonic menagerie opening up and bearing itself to me. It feels like that first wave of dawn's light as it passes over the land, waking the animals and birds one by one. *An awakening.* And the song they sing is the thread to connect them to the connection ... The emerald jungle opens up and ... "Good morning Vietnam..." it's like talkback radio, the plant doctors and me going one on one ...

Before I know it I can feel-see these spirit doctors hovering above me, on some weird Escher angle to my head and silhouetted against the kaleidoscopic jungle. They're way back in the periphery of my vision where a whole room opens up in the corner for them to operate. That's what this is: *an operating room.*

The doctor to my right is doing something to my head ... *Oh Jesus* ... I can see the spirit doctor on a ninety degree angle as he operates, so his head and my head overlap in psychic brotherhood. No time/all time goes by. I can't see what he's doing . . . what is he doing to me? *Jesus Christ what are you doing to me? What are you putting in my head?*

There's a glint of light like a reflection off a crystal and then something is plunged deep inside me. Then I'm thrust back into the center, back into the current of the rainbow river.

Don Francisco comes round through the storm, gently tending to us shipwrecks with the sweet warmth of his smoke. Javier begins his round of songs and his energy is beautiful and open, very sensitive and giving. The healing is immense as the song resonates through me. I'm tapping my toes, whistling, making mudras, and surfing the waves as I breathe through it all . . .

And at the end of it, totally rejuvenated and rebalanced, Javier sings the soundtrack to our chain gang of the soul, his voice deep and clear:

> As I went down in the river to pray
> Studying about that good old way
> And who shall wear the starry crown
> Good Lord, show me the way!
> O sisters let's go down,
> Let's go down, come on down,
> O sisters let's go down,
> Down in the river to pray.

22

The Hero's Journey

Blue Morpho Offices, Calle Moore, Iquitos

THURSDAY AUGUST 10, 2006

A hero ventures forth from the world of common day into a region of supernatural wonder: fabulous forces are there encountered and a decisive victory is won: the hero comes back from this mysterious adventure with the power to bestow boons on his fellow man.

—THE HERO WITH A THOUSAND FACES,
JOSEPH CAMPBELL

Hamilton Souther arrives at high noon on a slick red Falcon Turbo, effortlessly slicing through the crazy cross-traffic of families balanced on motorbikes, rickety backfiring buses, and zigzagging three-wheeled *motorcarros* to slide his bike up onto the sidewalk. He's six-foot plus and as he removes his motorcycle helmet to reveal a short blond crew cut and piercing blue eyes, he flashes me a confident smile.

"I'm Hamilton Souther," he says, as if I couldn't tell, and extends his hand. For a second I almost lose my cool in the aura of this suave alpha male. He's the captain of the football team, the high achiever, the guy who gets all the girls—the all-American hero. With his classic Hollywood looks he's the Tom Cruise of the Amazon on his own personal *Mission: Impossible.*

I've been trying to contact Hamilton for days—he's the young American shaman that was recently written up by *National Geographic Adventure* magazine, but he's so busy running his ceremonies at the Blue

Morpho lodge out by Km 53 and facilitating all the traffic that article, and a previous travel feature in the *New York Times* Travel section have generated, that he's impossible to pin down. I've visited the Blue Morpho tour offices twice and left messages for him but I feel like paparazzi chasing an unwilling star. It's not as if he needs any extra publicity.

Nonetheless, after seeing him glaring down at me in visions the other night at Sachamama I felt compelled to meet him, so there was something karmic about spending a few hours late Thursday morning sitting in a doorway just down from the Blue Morpho offices, waiting for this elusive shaman to arrive.

His reputation, of course, precedes him. Journalist Kira Salak, in the now-famous *National Geographic Adventure* article, described him as "blond-haired, blue-eyed, exceptionally good-looking. But talk to him for even a minute, and his striking appearance quickly fades before his most obvious quality: his unconditional acceptance of everyone. You cannot make him angry. You cannot seduce him. You cannot offend him (though it is extremely tempting to try). He is like a mirror, always reflecting back your own ego, showing you your attachments, your fixations, your fears. If you end up liking him, that's great, but if you don't, it's unimportant."

As we stand there with the sun beating down on us directly overhead, casting no shadows, it feels a little like two gunslingers facing each other off. There's a second of guarded recognition and then Hamilton leads the way upstairs into the office, which is decked out with computers and a stereo and all the mod-cons and beckons me to sit on the couch in the lounge behind the computers.

Sitting here mano-to-mano in the coolness of the Blue Morpho office, as one seeker of the mystery to another, we talk about shamanism and our ayahuasca experiences. After my Sachamama trip I had a lot of digesting to do, and I was crying out for help from someone like Hamilton who had already treaded the path.

In retrospect, having had the time to integrate what went on to me during the ceremony at Sachamama, I can find only one conclusion.

My whole body was shaken apart by the force of a hurricane on the inside, shaking loose all my vibratory grooves and scars, all my memories, pains, and hurts. *The magnetic tape of me was erased by the storm. That "two-quarter" cup of thick foamy sludge killed me when I drank it, and I had been put back together more than I was before.* It's "Classic Shamanism 101," but I had lived it.

Now in the cool dark cave of the Blue Morpho offices I was wracked with a warm nausea and shaking gently with waves of sensitivity. Last night I'd had a three-course meal as well as a large coffee and chocolate cake at Ari's Burgers, trying to ground back into the body and the pleasures of the flesh. I knew it was just part of the ups and downs of consciousness the baseline world buffered us with and that one must be constantly on guard lest old patterns and beliefs creep in, eroding the new. But I was paying for it today with some sugar-sick energy grounding out the new energetic pathways the Sachamama rebirth had created.

Hamilton sees my distress and fixes me an ice-water from the fridge. And as the cool, calm water enters me, soothing my energetic imbalance, he tells me his not-so-secret origin, and how he came down here to Iquitos to become a shaman:

The spirits told him to come, of course, during a dark night of the soul when he called out to God. With no prior grand spiritual leanings, the spirits just switched on a psychic radio broadcast and barraged him for six months before he caved in and took the giant leap from upper-middle class America and a strict family background to the wilds of the Amazon and drinking hallucinogenic brews with indigenous medicine men.

And he's not alone. I remember Ron Wheelock and his call to the path, Kevin Furnas, Carlos, and all the other gringos that I had met that seemed inexplicably drawn to reconnect with the planet and themselves via ayahuasca shamanism. It was a well-worn path and I was now a fair way along it myself, I realized.

We all fitted the template Joseph Campbell elaborated in his seminal work of comparative mythology, *The Hero with a Thousand Faces.*

In that text Campbell mapped out the archetypal journey of the hero across cultures in what he called a "monomyth." The first stage of this heroic journey is the "call to adventure," which is often precipitated by an initiatory sickness, which comes on suddenly, or can be part of a progressive behavioral change.

The Campbellian hero myth is a thread back to the shamanic lineages of indigenous cultures, a map of the innerspaces almost extinguished in the New World but now reseeded throughout the global village by the Hollywood meme machine.

In Campbell's heroic model the initiate undergoes many tests and ordeals, often undergoing symbolic death and rebirth and meeting with gods and goddesses that grant boons to help on the journey of self-discovery. The hero-shaman traverses worlds and gains knowledge on his magical flight that he then brings back to aid his tribe, proving himself the master of two worlds.

Hamilton's aware of this, of course, since he has a college major in anthropology from the University of Colorado. But what's interesting about him is that he didn't stop with the textbooks. Westerners often have a raw mental drive to succeed that's drilled into us by the competitive nature of our culture, but to survive in the jungle, to master the secrets of the plants and the spirits, to stretch the paradigm of the way the West sees the world and to then be accepted by the spirits themselves—this is a significant achievement.

Despite the fact that dozens, even hundreds of Western shamans were currently practicing their wares around the Amazon and throughout the world, there was something magnetic about the singular example of Hamilton Souther, as if his case spoke for us all.

So permit me, then, to jump ahead and quote from a later 2007 public forum on an ayahuasca thread on *Tribe.net,* an internet portal where Hamilton expounds at length about his entry into shamanism:

"Shamans live and are taught through lineage," Hamilton explains. "Each lineage is different from another and while they may share similarities they will also have many differences. In our case our center is based on the lineage of shamans formed by two different families, Don Julio Llerena Pinedo, and Alberto Torres Davila."

The legendary don Julio Llerena Pinedo is an eighty seven-year-old *maestro* of the "old school" who is locally considered to be one of the "greatest living shamans." Hamilton and his pals have affectionately nicknamed him "Yoda."

"Julio was taught by the doctor spirits directly in the forest, while Alberto was from a lineage of shamans," Hamilton continues, "passing down the heritage from father to son for many generations. Alberto began working with the spirits at the age of eight under the tutelage of his grandfather. He lives with the spirits and has guided me through the same ancient traditions in which he learned. During the time the pact was formed Julio headed a *mesa* of over eight *maestros* (master shamans) that included Alberto, his father, and grandfather.

"I traveled to the remote area where Julio lived in October of 2001 and began participating in ceremonies," Hamilton says. "After a year, I was accepted by Alberto and Julio as a formal apprentice to follow a formal traditional apprenticeship. I was accepted into their lineage, which covers generations of master shamans and very powerful healers. Throughout the course of apprenticing Alberto, Julio, and I formed bonds for life agreeing to support each other shamanically and to work together.

"In December of 2004 I received the title of *maestro,* given to me by Julio and Alberto . . . At the time I began my apprenticeship, Alberto and Julio had no apprentices despite efforts to teach other family members. They had not made it through the rigor of apprenticeship.

"[Since then] I have worked to bridge the tremendous gap between traditional Amazonian practice and the needs of our guests. This form of shamanism takes years to understand, and I have tried to present it to our guests in a way that helps them be able to receive the greatest benefits from the ceremonies . . . We are working to maintain and preserve these practices for the future during a time when local interest in their shamanic tradition is dying out."

Back in the office, Hamilton looks at me with those pale blue eyes, and I feel a strong affinity with my fellow traveler. "You don't need to learn from books, the spirits just transfer their knowledge," he says, explaining about the cosmic hierarchies and the way the spirits engage with us humans on a continual basis. As teachers go the spirits are the best, "continually pushing and prodding you, finding your weak spots and exploiting them to make you stronger." And then they use the material world, the consensual hologram we're in, "orchestrating events and placing hurdles to shape you," he explains.

But at least the spirits don't try to kill you. "The indigenous shamans don't like gringos learning the art of *curanderos,* not really. They'll take your money and take you so far, but they don't like their knowledge being mastered by outsiders," Hamilton confides.

To enforce their will, many shamans use *brujeria* or witchcraft to strike and take down other shamans they see as enemies. When Hamilton became too strong, too good at what he was learning, his enemies became jealous and tried the great shakedown. They manifested a real snake that bit him on the face during a ceremony and almost killed him. His face was paralyzed for almost a year. On the second occasion *brujos* manifested two burning spears in the spirit world and brutally pierced him with them. Crippled with real, physical pain, he barely survived.

Needless to say, Hamilton now works with local shamans of his own choosing, as well as almost a dozen gringo apprentices that are flocking to train with him.

"I thought I'd be a professional golfer," he guffaws when I ask him what he wanted to be when he left college. "I had no idea I'd be up here, doing what I'm doing now." Yet here he is, twenty-eight years old, in the prime of his life and running a very, very successful shamanistic tour company which is bringing in the spiritual tourists as fast as they can fall on his doorstep.

It's a hands-on business and like any new startup, Hamilton is at the helm almost constantly. He makes himself available for one-on-one discussions with up to thirty participants who drink at any one time on his seven-day jungle retreats, and he's always there in ceremony, doing his spirit work and monitoring their wellbeing. It takes an enormous amount of energy and knowledge to hold the space and gain the trust of the Western seekers, and Hamilton has been running himself ragged doing it.

He has a rotating number of American apprentices to look after, as well as six other staff members and the running of the camp itself, yet he manages it all with the focus and wisdom of a born leader. Or a hero. Indeed, many of the mainly American audience who flock to Blue Morpho seem in awe of the charisma and presence he radiates, and describe him in glowing terms:

"Hamilton and don Alberto are my heroes. Real living super heroes ..." a blogger named Alan said on the *Ayahuasca Tribe.net* thread. "Trust me, these guys are the real genuine deal ... The genuine super fucking powers these dudes have and share ... I went in there a post-existential linguistic hedonist and I came out a cosmic fucking warrior. This is the adventure of a lifetime. I'm here to tell those skeptics and the unsures to go to Blue Morpho. Why? Because it helped me ... Hamilton is THE PIMP and Don Alberto is the GRAND MASTER PLAYA."

Adam, an ayahuasca drinker at Blue Morpho, says on the *Tribe.net* thread that he "kicked two years of serious drug dependency in three ceremonies. During my most difficult ceremony, my first ceremony, Hamilton Souther stayed awake with me for eight straight hours, until dawn, holding my hands, praying over me, encouraging me, and pouring love onto me."

Angelito, another poster, says, "Hamilton is a regular guy with extraordinary wisdom. He doesn't go walking around in yoga pants humming 'We Are the World.' He tells jokes, is easy to talk to, and can share a TON of information regarding what your learning. [sic] Aside from being a regular guy, this guy's the REAL DEAL, A TRUE MAESTRO."

Peggy, a "fifty-four-year-old high school teacher who has been on the path for decades," says that her "entire [ayahuasca] experience was terrifying, and I can't explain the relief I felt the moment I initially saw and met Hamilton. He is clear. He is strong. He is fearless. He has walked the walk. He is contained in light. He has done, and continues to do, the work. And most of all, I knew he would protect me. He simply knows the spiritual world. He understands ayahuasca on a very personal, intimate level."

Now, looking into Hamilton's all-American eyes, I know that he has walked this path before me and that what he has seen has paved the way for us that follow. In Hamilton the twin streams of the indigenous shaman and the Western hero myth have become entwined. That legend of the Eagle and the Condor wraps around him like a second skin, the superhero emblems of two worlds united.

And I realize that Kira Salak was right about one thing: *in Hamilton Souther, seekers find a reflection of themselves.*

After my meeting I head down to the grassy foreshore of the boulevard to gather my thoughts and plan my next move. The constant roar of *motorcarros* soundtracks the afternoon as I sit on the grass under a tree and smoke a *mapacho,* watched by dozens of local boys hanging onto the railing. I feel like a thousand years have passed, that I've been through a massive initiation as a prelude to the next stage of my journey. Yet the path of knowledge has a price: *transformation.* My shamanic odyssey had constantly led me beyond the safe constructs of my own body and mind and out into a cosmic ecology full of spirits and intelligence.

My very sense of self has been changed and I have felt what it is to die, to have the ego obliterated and to transcend to the realms beyond. Again and again I have smashed myself open on the shores of heaven, and now after multiple experiences of merging with the Godhead, *what the fuck else was there to do?*

In indigenous shamanism once the initiate has undergone death and rebirth they are reborn into the role of the village *curandero,* with all the subsequent duties and responsibilities. Yet despite all I had gone through I didn't consider myself a shaman by any means, merely, as Jan Kounen had told me back at the conference, an *ayahuasquero*—one who drinks ayahuasca. Yet here on the spiritual backpacking circuit I was starting to feel like a rat in a trap chasing the same old cheese down familiar synaptic pathways. There are only so many ayahuasca sessions you can do without reaching some plateau, where the healed soul then pieces the new knowledge together and does something with it.

My ayahuasca peak experiences, however, have provided moments that transcend my cultural imprints, allowing me to see new pathways and possibilities in myself and in the world at large. And it is through repeatedly dying and being reborn, I am beginning to understand, that I am constantly refining this new perception, sharpening the blade of the soul and laying down new templates for my own growth. As don Francisco had said to me yesterday morning, over a light fruit breakfast as we all summed up our experiences of the ceremony the night before:

"Even though you were in the rough of it you were supported by a host of spirits all around, cheering you on. You are never alone. Have you ever done a diet?"

"No," I replied, not really counting my three-day, aborted *dieta* at don Juan's.

"It would greatly help. You already have such a good connection with the plants. It would potentiate everything. You are on the right path. Your very energy is leading you to it."

Once more I have been reminded what that "*it*" was and why so many of us Westerners were being drawn to it. The traditional shaman role wasn't one we were being called to play, or rather, it was the traditional role of healer, but the expression was different.

In typical Western style the hereditary, lifelong duties of the shaman have been fast-tracked to focus on the spark of spiritual awareness within the self and to facilitate personal healing. In this way a network of *shamanauts,* if you will, has been activated with the ability to journey into the spirit realms and awaken others to the truth of their own divinity. A million heroic journeys all leading to the same collective awareness.

I was starting to think of it as *Gaian Viral Networking*—a distributed mode of healing passed on from one seed to the next. For just as a village needs a proportionate amount of healers, in a community on the scale of the global village (six billion people and climbing) a one to one hundred ratio would mean sixty million healers are needed across the planet right now. And what's more, in the gestalt ghettos of our globalized world, each healer will need to fit new and rapidly changing environments, looking to the past to learn how to make sense of the present, and to better survive the future.

The hero's journey was all our journeys, but after almost five weeks in Iquitos it was time for me to move on. I had vague plans to head down to Pucallpa and the heart of Shipibo-Conibos *curanderismo,* but I needed some guidance.

"Please Great Spirit, help me find my path, I'm a bit lost, I need your help to know what to do next . . ." I called out, then trundled back along the promenade, open to spirit's call.

I felt like I needed some company, someone to cheer me up, and as I neared the Gringo Bar I spotted Tessa, the blond healer who had been hanging with the original group that had formed at the conference. She was hard to forget, what with the cosmic spacescape tattoo on her left forearm and her penchant for stones and crystals. A few days ago I'd bumped into Chuck and Monika in the street, all dressed up and going off to Tessa's wedding to a young Peruvian toyboy.

"Hi there, still in town?" I say, threading my way past the row of motorbikes in the gutter outside the Gringo Bar and to the spare seat opposite her. Tessa is in her early forties, with thin, wavy blond hair, a piercing stud below her bottom lip, and a hedonist's body language— always with a glass of wine, a cigarette, or a man in her hands. She radiates a strong presence and she knows Chuck, and Kevin Furnas, and a few other *ayahuasqueros* I know, so I trust her.

"Congratulations, my dear, I hear you got married. Do you mind if I sit down?" I ask, pulling back the seat.

"No, please," she says, motioning me to sit. "Thank you. It was a beautiful wedding, we had it out at Love Creek in a shamanistic ceremony."

"Ahhh . . . with Javier, yeah, I went out there with Chuck. Great guy.

He—or rather the old guy, Juan, has that amazing healing stone they found out there."

"Not any more, they sold it to Chuck," she says, smiling. Just then her husband, a young, good looking Peruvian who looks about nineteen, but is twenty-six I find out later, with a short black crew cut and high cheekbones, comes back from the toilet. "Have you met Walter?" she says, gesturing towards him.

"Hi, I'm Rak," I say, shaking his hand.

"Brad?"

"Rrrraaak," I say, "like the sound a frog makes," or at least that's what Javier told me, back at Love Creek.

Walter smiles and repeats my name back. "I'm Walter," he says with a big smile, "but my nickname is 'Fish,' because I love the water."

We settle into an easy conversation and are joined by Juan Francis Moldarno, a fiftyish, friendly tour guide with the nonchalant look of a Peruvian Burt Reynolds. Juan practically lives at the Gringo Bar when he's not taking tourists out on personalized jungle retreats, and he regales us all with tales of indigenous mythology interspersed with his own colorful adventures.

"So have you been doing more aya circles?" I ask Tessa finally, after ordering the ayahuasca diet special from the Gringo girls.

"I'm a healer—I'm just not into the ayahuasca," Tessa says, looking at me with an intense gaze. "I heal with a touch, or with a word, or oils, or with my stones and crystals—whatever the spirit calls me to do, it's easy. I don't need to be going on all these retreats and workshops and all that shit to do my healing work.

"Kevin'll be mad because he wanted me to do a diet at Sachamama, but I just didn't feel like it. I like don Francisco, I do. When I first went there to check it out he said he's had a dream saying the bright bird was coming, and then another saying I wasn't coming, and then when he saw me he said, 'finally you've arrived.' But I couldn't stay, the heat's too much for me." She wipes beads of sweat off her forehead with a napkin, emphasizing the point.

"Ha, yeah, it was like that with me, too," I reply, motioning to Dian, my gringo girl-wife for a papaya juice. "He said something along those lines and made me feel very welcome, very at ease. I was out there Tuesday night doing a circle. Very powerful stuff. I might go back there Friday night, or I might just go straight to Pucallpa."

Tessa looks at me squarely with those intense blue eyes of hers. "Yeah, well, I have to get out of Iquitos before it drives me crazy," she says, running her fingers through her hair. "I can't stand this heat. You can't do anything, there's no hot showers, and all my energy is drained. I'm dying for the cold, for Cuzco. I own four bloody ponchos and I didn't bring any of them with me!" she laughs. "I left them with my daughter—she's fourteen and is off in France now with my bloody mobile phone, racking up a huge debt! I'm going to kill her!"

"That's funny, I'm headed to Cuzco after Pucallpa and drinking with some more shamans down there. And I guess I want to see Macchu Picchu, too."

"What's the cheapest flight you've found to Pucallpa?" Tessa asks guardedly, then lights another cigarette.

"U.S. $77 dollars, flying LC Busre, leaves every morning at 8:30 a.m., but it's one of those little planes—only a twelve seater, and you can only have ten kilos of luggage or they charge you two soles per kilo over that."

"Hmm..." she says, and looks at me like a cat who's found a particularly choice mouse crossing its path. "I want to work with more power stones to heal people, especially people that have been fucked up by ayahuasca," she confides.

"Some shamans take tourists out and blow their minds but when it's all over a lot of people don't know how to put back together the pieces. They need time to integrate. They need to work properly with the spirit of ayahuasca, to set out their intent beforehand and then integrate afterwards to see how it manifested—if there's to be any proper healing.

"Juan Maldonado's told me there's this village near Pucallpa where they sell stones, magic stones by the banks of the river. I want some stones from there to heal with, but Pucallpa's hotter than Iquitos and I'm over this bloody heat, it's frazzled me. And we've got to go to Lima to sort out Walter's visa, and I really don't want to pay for two flights to Pucallpa and then Lima, then Cuzco. If you went and got me some stones, I'd pay for your flight."

"Really? I'd love to, I mean, that would really help me out, I'm pretty broke."

"No, that'd be perfect. I'd teach you stone magic, too. I really need them, I have to do something with myself or I get destructive … I used to be an international madam," she says, without batting an eyelid. "And then I became a healer. When I'm good, I'm good, but when I'm bad, I'm bad. It's like the more good things I do, the more bad things I have to do to balance them out. I'm a Libra, you see."

She's full-on, but I'm used to full-on people, especially full-on women. I seem to attract them like moths to a flame, not as lovers, more like lionesses that adopt a stray cub. She reminds me of my sister Nicole, who, coincidentally, is nicknamed "The Madam." It's all getting holographically resonant, this manifestation-on-demand from the universe. The spirits are calling again, I can feel them drawing me to Pucallpa…

Juan arranges to take us straight to a friend of his who's a stone healer. Tessa has a plan to see some stones and find out if I'm comfortable with the path that's manifesting for me. We take two *motorcarros* and head off into the Iquitos suburbs on the edge of town, and lo and behold we end up at the house of the stone *curandero* who was at the conference, who coincidentally used his stones on Tessa during a demonstration.

Victor Ventos is in his seventies and has the slow grace of an elderly monk. His proud and wistful face is framed with chunky sixties glasses frames that he hides behind, like a little boy peering out at the world. He's not feeling well tonight—he's been sick with a sore throat since the conference, so Tessa lays her hands on him and does her magic, sucks out his illness and flicks it away with her fingers, one healer healing another.

I'm waiting next to Fish by a long table, fingering a bed of beautiful polished stones, when I have the flashback. One of the stones has an aquatic bony appearance and long white tendril markings with a gouge in the center like the eye of an octopus. It's an *encanto* magic stone very reminiscent of the one Chuck now owns from Love Creek.

Then it hits me. Yesterday, walking out of Sachamama, I had a flash memory of a stone I own, a smooth gray one a few finger lengths thick, curved like a boomerang, which made me think of another specially carved one with a Nepalese third eye on it a friend gave me. That triggered the image of the fist-sized stone with the eyes and face like a Mayan glyph on it that Victor had at the conference, a psychic chain of events coming full circle tonight among all this stone magic.

I reach down into the bed of stones and there is that exact stone I was thinking about, surrounded by dozens of others, smooth to my touch and manifest, made real, back in my life and moving me forward. It's all getting hologrammatically heavy, mirrors turning in on themselves, and I know this is my path, where spirit wants me to go. There's too many coincidences not to.

Over red wine at La Sala, a few doors up from Hobo's Hideout, Tessa waits till Fish is at the bar, then confides in me again: "*I'm a witch, you see. I trained with a witch in England, I apprenticed with her. And sometimes in my magic work I shape-change. I become a wolf, my whole body morphs and changes and I see the paws and the snout, my whole spirit becomes the wolf. I also have a white wolf named Lupo at home in Tottingham and he visited me in a ceremony once, even appearing to the woman next to me.*"

I'm getting flashbacks to the first chapter of the Carlos Castaneda book I read the night right before the aya circle at Sachamama, where Carlos talks about shape-changing and becoming a coyote, how it's a *brujo* skill. In that book he records how the last *brujo* who became a were-coyote was killed back in 1943 in Mexico, and how they're not meant to exist anymore, but of course … *Brujos,* like other shamans, train members of their family, and are entrusted to pass their skills and powers on.

"And so we were making love the other night," she says, pointing at Fish. "And I had a strange premonition. He changed right in front of me and he curved, towering over me. He became a dolphin right in front of my eyes, and there I was making love to a bloody dolphin! It was the most amazing thing and it was real, right in front of me."

There are legends of these things happening—*Bufeo Colorado* the Peruvians call them—dolphin lovers. They're meant to be evil spirits, like the pink dolphins in human flesh that lure men and women into the water and have sex with them, where they drown in the water. Or they take human flesh to seduce men and women and steal their souls. Like the villagers in the Castaneda book who shoot the were-coyotes on sight, the Peruvians reportedly shoot the dolphins and kill the evil spirits. Days before I'd read an article by Norma Panduro in the *Iquitos Times* talking about the legends of the dolphin lovers and now here was this witch-woman telling me they were real.

The resonances are escalating; this was becoming dense and I'm starting to feel uneasy with the idea of black magic and *brujeria,* even though I trust Tessa and get a good vibe from her, and her connection with Kevin.

"He gave me this ring for our wedding," she says, showing me a silver sun and moon ring on her finger, "and the only one I could find that fitted him was a silver one with a dolphin on it. And his nickname's Fish. Can you believe it?" she laughs.

"I'm married to a bloody dolphin! Maybe that's why the sex is so good."

So that's how I came to work for an ex-international madam turned witch who has sex with dolphins ... And start down the path of stone magic, in search of my destiny. For when the spirit of ayahuasca guides me I go where it leads...

On the hero's journey ...

Part III
RETURN

"I see ayahuasca as all vines. The vine it starts growing on something and it just starts trying to take over everything. And ayahuasca is also a vine. And through us, every *ayahuasquero,* we're like another limb on the vine. And she's trying to embrace the world."

—RON WHEELOCK, IQUITOS, JULY 2006

23

Secret Women's Business
Pucallpa
Saturday August 12, 2006

When I get off the plane in Pucallpa I go against all go the guidebook wisdom and throw myself at the mercy of the first taxi driver competing for my business, getting into his *motorcarro* even though it's unregistered and traveling to the Plaza de Armas in the center of town (every town large enough has one).

The guidebooks will tell you that Pucallpa is a dusty frontier stop on the Ucayali River (Pucallpa translates from Quechua as "red earth"), one of the major tributaries of the Amazon, but that's only half the story. After the paved, clean-in-comparison streets of downtown Iquitos, the busy roads and hot concrete blocks of this place have a heavy urban feel. Vast blooms of giant satellite dishes cluster from rooftops, billboards scream their incessant desires, and—worse—cars clog the dirt streets and kick up dust alongside the *motorcarros* and bikes. This could be anywhere in Peru or a dozen other places around the world that were hot, noisy, and blanketed in exhaust fumes.

With a population of around 200,000 Pucallpa is a fair bit smaller than Iquitos, but the real difference is the roads. Traffic comes in daily to and from Lima, bringing goods and people, as well as culture and change. When the 846 km Lima-Pucallpa highway was completed in 1945, Pucallpa went from being an isolated town with no paved roads to the only Amazonian river town linked to Lima by road. Yet it is the boats and the river that sustain this place. Steady streams of Indians and local *mestizos* flood in from villages along the Amazon, looking for work in the city. Hundreds of tons of goods go up and down the river each day in boats big and small, supplying the villages with rice, water, and Inca-Cola by the crate load.

Pucallpa was one of the first modern parts of Peru to be exploited by Western companies for its raw materials. It has long been defined by its main industries—petroleum and lumber—and still today it is the end point for a seventy-six kilometer-long oil pipeline from the Ganso Azul oilfields in the southwest of Peru.

Part of the sick atmosphere that hangs over the city is due to the fact that so much of the surrounding jungle has been carved up over the decades and the felled trees stripped and shipped down river. Slash and burn clearing is widespread in the area, with thick columns of smoke often hanging over the skyline and adding to the general gloom.

I'm so underwhelmed by the prospect of this dusty concrete jungle that I ask my driver to take me directly to San Francisco, a little village outside town that's also rumored to be the epicenter of shamanism in the area. I've emailed Rama, the French-speaking anthropologist I met at Guillermo's who is staying there, with whom I hope to scope out the scene in the few days I have to stay.

My driver is very happy at the extended ride and in English so broken it will never stick together again he intimates that he will give me the grand tour of the city on the way. I immediately protest that "no tango mucho denaro" (I haven't very much money), a term Javier had taught me at Sachamama when wrangling with don Francisco over the bill. My driver shrugs with the nonchalance of someone for whom "not very much money" is an everyday fact of life, and sets off on a meandering itinerary that takes us from the port to the fields, stopping for a minute or two to take in the sights.

We travel the potholed roads out of Pucallpa towards the outer district of Yarina and then cut in on dirt roads with gaping wounds dotting their length, heading towards San Francisco. It is the most painful ride of my life. The three-wheeled *motorcarro* dips in and out of huge holes in the road, jumbling me to and fro and hurling me up and smashing me down so hard that I can feel the organs in my chest and stomach and my intestines hitting my rib cage. I suspect I may have punctured a lung.

Finally, after forty minutes of this Peruvian taxi-torture we pierce the idyllic country scenery and putter into the sleepy little village of San Francisco, on the shores of picturesque Lake Yarinacocha.

The dirt streets are strewn with local villagers lazily ambling along in the morning heat and the occasional dusty flume from another *motorcarro* or a communal taxi car passing by. We head down the main strip, past an open-air market where Shipiba women in their green tops, patterned blouses, black hair, and gold teeth sit at tables and along the ground, their wares spread out before them for a handful of Western tourists. They're doppelgangers for the Iquitos *manta* hustlers and in classic Puto Mayo style they look like they've just stepped off the corner by the Iron Building and are making a beeline for the Yellow Rose and the gringos there.

There's only one shop in town and next to it the lone public telephone that connects San Francisco with the outside world. Under the drooping thatched roof of a café next door to the shop the striking circuitry maps of the Shipibo ayahuasca patterns creep out like hallucinogenic graffiti. The same patterns adorn houses here and there and shine out from a marble statue commemorating the Shipibo a few blocks down.

It's a reminder of the ubiquity of ayahuasca in the culture here and the intrinsic connection the people have to the vine. Per capita, San Francisco is said to have the highest concentration of *curanderos* in all of Peru, perhaps all of South America. And like that *other* San Francisco it's a rich cultural melting pot for spiritual exploration. I can imagine a few wide-eyed sixties hippies walking around with flowers in their hair, carefree and grokking on the vibe.

The tourist dollar depends on it, in fact, because despite appearances, San Francisco is caught up in a no-win culture war with the globalized world, and ayahuasca tourism is at the heart of the battle.

My driver deposits me a few blocks from the main strip at a modest *pueblo* next to a two-story building which houses the local women's arts collective, where they do the finishing touches on the ayahuasca-inspired embroideries. It's the home of *la familia* La Stenia Bardales, the address Rama has given me where she's staying. The family comes out to greet me on the steps as the taxi driver finally stings me thirty soles for what would have been a three sole journey by *collectivo.*

The family look on with amusement as our altercation drags out and, as I finally pay the scoundrel and get my bags, they welcome me inside among a swirling tide of small children.

Senorita Bardales, the matriarch of the house, is away in Argentina selling the Shipibo pottery and woven fabrics they make here and her husband Julio is also absent, busy with village council business. The eldest daughter, Natilde, a cheerful woman in her early thirties, greets me warmly.

There are so many kids and teenagers here that they can't all be siblings, but cousins in the extended tribe: Amelia, a vibrant little three-year-old; Madelina, another three- or four-year-old; Mariella, who is twelve or thirteen; Lizzie the baby, who's just starting to walk; Niels, a young boy about six; Josie, an older girl in her late teens; Toby, about the same age as Niels, but half-a-head shorter; and Patricia, who's fourteen going on fifteen in November.

Patricia speaks a little English and helps me get settled in the open-air room above the arts collective where Rama has been staying. It's pretty basic, with bare floorboards and mosquito nets; a desk near the stairs scattered with what looks like anthropology textbooks, in French; a hammock by the far wall; and some of Rama's gear by her sleeping bag on the floor. But it also feels clean and safe, and for a new arrival to the area it's just what I need: the security of a family and the familiarity of a friend.

Rama is also away, doing some translation work in town, but she's due back this afternoon. I leave my bags, glad to be free of all my possessions, and Patricia agrees to take me on a tour of the town while we practice our Spanglish.

San Francisco is a clean, modern village, with a population of 1,154

Patricia tells me, and it's the type of place where you'd know about any changes to those numbers. It's clear and sunny but the laconic serenity is pierced by constant messages from loudspeakers strapped to poles every fifty meters or so, threaded throughout the streets of the entire village. They are, I find out later, messages for the community to orchestrate group events like clearing land, helping out on projects, or personal messages like, "Mrs. Pedro your taxi driver has had to cancel and can't take you to the party as arranged because the party has already started and he's having a good time." Hola, hola, hola ... they squawk over and over again, as each person's message is broadcast through town and percolates into the collective unconscious ...

Still, there is such a sense of presence, a sense of being here now in this place, like this is some secret village paradise that has fallen off the *Lonely Planet* radar. It seems imbued with an inherent sense of what the West has so recently realized it has lost: *community.* The kids play in the dirt streets and the men and women all hang out the front of their *casas,* in the shade from the heat of the day. Everyone's just ... *being,* going about their business, and here I am careening into town with my stressed-out media-vibe and trying to sniff out the heart of shamanism before lunch.

Time, you can never have enough of it, and with barely three weeks left in Peru, and with the jewel of the Aztecs, Machu Picchu, and the Andes still before me, I had such a short time to see San Francisco and make it up river and back that it was starting to stress me out.

I could learn a thing or two from the locals. The Shipibo have been in this area for over a thousand years, according to archaeological digs that have found similarities between Shipibo art and the Cumancaya-style that peaked in the ninth century AD. They were originally a matriarchal culture that worshipped the spirit of the monkey—they were even called "the Monkey People" by other tribes. Tiny skulls of baby monkeys threaded into beadwork necklaces are very popular now at the handicrafts market, I notice, as we meander past on our way down to the lake.

Today is *Sabado*—Saturday—and like all days, the village women are in the concrete *mercado* selling their wares: the familiar Shipibo woven blankets and textiles with the ayahuasca markings on them, the intricate lines and rivers of psychedelic detail mixed in with beads, jewelry, and carvings. The prices are the same as in Iquitos, the broke tourist in me notices, but there's much less hustle and push.

The Western world first contacted the Shipibo in the seventeenth century, and during the Rubber Boom years of the nineteenth century they were employed en masse as wage laborers, feeding the insatiable Western appetite for rubber. Rubber gave way to oil and lumber, religion and tourism. In came the electricity, the radios, the made-in-China brand label t-shirts and shorts, and the hand-me-down baggage that goes with cultural acclimatization. The streets are clean, the buildings are modern, but the whole economy is now intrinsically tied to the outside world and whatever income they can scrounge for a living, and at the heart of that is tourism and the sale of their ayahuasca-inspired artworks.

The colonized have now become mass exporters themselves, textbook evangelists for the Free Trade agenda. But just twenty years ago the jungle surrounded the village and provided an abundant source of food and goods for the community. Patricia tells me the Elders speak of that time, still in recent memory, when the lake used to be clean and overflowing with fish.

Patricia takes me down to the *la cocha,* a serene lake a few hundred meters wide and a few kilometers long, with one or two boats in sight, quietly floating on the water. There's a dozen *niños* down by the dock and playing at the edges of the water, looked after by their slightly older brothers and sisters. The water is warm and inviting and as I plunge in for a refreshing swim, small fish nibble at me with puckered mouths and make me jump in fright.

Patricia tells me they're honest-to-God piranhas...."But you will be alright," she says. "They just bite gently, unless you are bleeding somewhere and attract a lot of them..."

Up above in the sky two birds are flirting with the breeze, climbing higher and higher in darting spurts and then coasting down the same distance, playful and alive. I have a psychic flash of the DMT consciousness, *the awareness of the inter-connectedness of all things and the way the world speaks to us through us, its creations.*

For a few brief moments I can see meaning in the parting of the clouds and the streaming of the light, in the way the birds fly and the water laps against the shore. The world is stirring and talking to me again in perfect harmony and grace, as if after a long hibernation.

Walking back to the village we come across a grove of trees off from the shoreline all entwined together, and I have a flash once again of family, of the togetherness that this village engenders.

Back up near the main store Juan, a young French guy with a big Rasputin beard says hello, and we do the obligatory two-Westerners-thrown-together-in-a-small-second-world-village exchange. He tells me he's drunk with Don Mariano, a local *curandero* seven times here in San Francisco.

"He's good, and he's also a doctor. He will heal you, he heals everyone," Juan says, stroking his long beard as he rattles off the names of different *curanderos* in town and their pros and cons.

I can feel the snake stirring at the base of my spine and the spirit of aya as she climbs my chakra staircase, like the touch of a lover after a long absence. *Tonight the dance begins again, and my soul aches for it . . .*

After our tour of town the familia graciously offer me a lunch of rice and eggs, which I share with them in the silence of our language barriers. The two six-year-old boys in their World Cup shirts dig into the rice with their bare hands while the baby, little Lizzy, cries in the background. I take a nap in the hammock upstairs in the spare room, and an hour or so later I wake to the sound of Rama's voice drifting up from the kitchen down below, and gingerly head down towards her.

"Ah you made it," Rama says with that delicious, lilting French accent I remember so well.

Her face is lit up with a large smile revealing a perfect set of white teeth against light-brown skin. She's wearing a simple blue skirt and tanktop, native beads around her neck and long amber earrings that accentuate an already long and noble face, her frizzy hair up in a bun. At six-foot-two Rama looks like an African queen, with an air of authority and respect that short-circuits any underlying sexual tension. But she is a beautiful woman, and her beauty is more than skin-deep, with a familiarity I can't quite place.

She's busy cooking pancakes with the girls, heaving a heavy frying pan up into the air to flip the pancakes as she cooks them. "I used to be a pancake chef back in France," she tells me with a laugh. "When I was seventeen I wanted to come to Peru but I had no money or job, so the government paid for me to learn the art of the soufflé, non, the art of the French pancake. I was also a model for a cellular phone company," she adds with another smile.

"It was funny, y'know. I said to the universe that I just wanted to be recognized for being me, for myself, and then this part came up and before I knew it my face was all over France. It's funny how the universe works," she says, looking me deep in the eyes till I have to look away.

"It speaks to us through the other players in the game," I say, "the coincidences and the resonances."

"I too, have felt the call of spirit," she answers, eyes darting at me over the flow of eggs and flour she's mixing in a bowl at the table. "I've been coming here to Peru since 1998, but it's all been very academic. Now I'd like to work on my own book, and write about my experiences here." Rama's currently on a Fellowship for a French Academy doing her post-doctoral work in anthropology on the Shipibo culture, with a focus on women's issues.

After the pancakes Rama takes me around town in search of a *curandero* to drink with tonight, and I ask her some basic questions about the role of *curanderismo* here.

"Are there shamans in town?" I ask, testing the waters.

"Si, many. Many," she says, explaining that it is because the Shipibo have such a strong cultural identity that they have also retained the old ways of shamanism. But how is it, I wonder, that so many *curanderos* have clustered here? If the role was still hereditary they couldn't all be from the same family, could they? And do they mainly serve Westerners, or the local community? The journalist in me wanted to know, but poor Rama was struggling with condensing complex sociological issues down into bite-sized English answers.

"Lots of people use ayahuasca here, but traditionally locals only come on Friday or Tuesday, and the shaman is the one who drinks," Rama explains. Legend has it that the Shipibo have traditionally never drunk ayahuasca themselves—that practice came from other Indians. "Suppose they might come with a baby who is in need of healing," she begins.

"They present their case and baby to the shaman to examine and he drinks the ayahuasca to diagnose the problem and find a solution. *The patients don't drink.* Some are drinking to see something more clearly, to understand a situation, but traditionally the people of this village don't drink, they just don't do it like that. It's only the Westerners who come here to San Francisco, they are the ones who drink ayahuasca with the *curanderos.*"

We walk about fifty meters up the street and turn right at the three-story concrete water tower, then go another hundred meters or so down another clean dirt street, where Rama points out three shamans' houses all within a stone's throw of each other, and another just a little further on. "The shamans in this town are all political," she explains with a shrug of her shoulders. "This one is good, this one is no good, they all say about each other."

"One . . . two . . . three . . . four . . . Four *curanderos,* all on the same block?" I ask. "That's crazy!" and she giggles at my incredulousness.

As we walk along past the telegraph poles lining the street, running commentary of the local Saturday soccer match blares out over the loudspeakers. The better roads, water, electricity, and many of the amenities are paid for from the money the ayahuasca tourists generate, Rama tells me, and have been installed as recently as eight years ago.

As for the gringos, the vast majority are here for one thing alone: the experience of ayahuasca and the take-home handicrafts that document it. San Francisco wasn't built on it, but as the jungle recedes the town has definitely been sustained by the spirit in the vine.

First we visit Don Mateo, one of the main chieftains, but he's away in Lima till next Sunday. Rama says he is very good and well respected in the village. "He has his set price for the ceremony and after that he won't ask you for anything, you know..." she says with that wide smile of hers and a tilt of the head, as if, you know, you've been round the block with a few shamans up in Iquitos and you know how it can be.

There's a set price for your ayahuasca ceremony, and some dodgy operators might only ask for twenty or thirty or fifty soles before it begins. A part way through they may say they need something more and ask for another donation before they will continue. Mateo's not like that, Rama stresses, he's a good man and well respected in the village, so it was a shame to miss him.

We continue our laconic walk and Rama shows me another large building with a thatched roof twenty meters from Don Mateo's house, a shamanistic retreat catering especially to Westerners. Rama tells me it's pricey—up to a hundred soles a circle, too much for my ridiculously dwindling freelancer budget, and there's no one around at the moment anyway.

Rama casts me a sideways look as we turn another corner that seems to say *just how broke are you, anyway,* but then it subsumes back into her gentle smile. I could show her the ongoing costings list in my diary meticulously documenting the fact that even living at the level of the locals, eating and sleeping at their prices, I still won't have enough to last my last three weeks here in Peru. And there's no monetary reprieve from back home, either—but that's a bridge to cross when I come to it.

"How long will you be 'ere?" Rama says in her delicious French accent as we walk along, past locals pottering in their front yards in a strangely 1950s white-picket fence paradigm.

"I'm not sure," I reply, as I grasp for the right words to describe my unusual predicament, my knight's quest up the Amazon in search of the magic stones for the Madam... "I originally wanted to spend a week in Pucallpa, but this friend of mine from Iquitos, she's convinced me to go to this town a few days upriver on the Amazon... She's a stone healer and she wants me to go get her some magic stones... It's a town called *Orellana,* have you heard of it?" I don't expect her to have; Juan Maldarnado had to draw it in on the map of Peru I had printed out from the internet before I left Australia.

"Orejana?" she says with a little shake of her head.

"Yeah... something like that... Well, the stones are somewhere outside the town... It's a bit vague, I know, to be going hundreds of kilometers up river with only a napkin map drawn over lunch and some written instructions from an Iquitos tour guide with little sense of pertinent detail, but that's the plan. *Mad, isn't it?*

"My *Lonely Planet* only has like, a paragraph on San Francisco and next to nothing on Orellana, so I'm not sure of the distances and cost, and I'm getting low on time and money. But I wanted to see if I could get the boat to Orellana and maybe stop off at some villages along the way and drink with more *curanderos* as I go... I want to continue to explore ayahuasca, that's what I'm here for..."

"Surely. But in Iquitos you were only interviewing shamans, or you were drinking with them, too?" Rama asks.

"No, I drank with them, too," I say with a grin.

"With twenty different shamans!" she exclaims, then laughs a care-free girl-woman cry, as if I'm being too try-hard about it, but still there is some gumption in the path nonetheless...

"Well, I interviewed about twenty shamans and some apprentices, and drank with about twelve of them... I like it," I laugh. "It feels natural, and I've got an affinity with the spaces it reveals..." And then I remember Rama telling me she has only drunk twice, with Guillermo, and doesn't feel the need to drink again because the memory is still so strong within her.

Maybe that's what it is, that flame of activated awareness that I sense within her that is within me, the remembrance of another *ayahuasquero* . . .

"I know another shaman," Rama says. "He is old, but still good. He is the father of the husband of the wife I'm staying with, and he may be cheaper, do you want to go see him?"

"Surely," I reply, and Rama turns around and leads me to a property directly opposite the retreat. The contrast is startling: no large Westerner targeted building with creature comforts here, just an open air, run-down bungalow that is the home and workspace of an old *curandero* in-residence, one of the original village doctors.

Don Leonardo is short and squat like a gnome, his face peppered with gray stubble and deep creases, framed by an old pair of glasses. He's in a stained khaki t-shirt, navy shorts, and bare feet and he looks like an old, poor man. I remember Hamilton Souther nicknaming his elderly indigenous teacher "Yoda" and realize the analogy fits so well with this *curandero* that he will be my Yoda, too.

Leonardo's been looking after his sick wife, his son Ernando tells Rama in a soft Spanish drawl that she translates for me. "She doesn't want to live anymore," Leonardo explains with a sad look in his eyes.

Rama says Leonardo doesn't usually set a price, but tonight there are unusual circumstances with his wife and, apparently, his daughter both ill, and because of that he seems to want a higher rate—fifty soles for his wife and fifty soles for his daughter, or one hundred soles for the whole ceremony. I respect this, but I'm also very aware of my own financial limitations.

A bit of haggling ensues but in the end all he's asking is, *how much can you afford?* I tell him and after a final round of negotiations we agree to meet tonight at 8:00 p.m. He smiles, looking down, slightly forlorn. It's his duty—a true *curandero* cannot refuse the call to help, but even *curanderos* need help themselves, I suspect.

"How many times?" he asks me in broken English.

"*Non entiende?*" I don't understand.

"*Mareaciones?*" he demands. Visions?

"Whooooppamamasshaashhkalilllybobobidoooooo!!" I reply. "Mucho."
"Bueno." Yoda nods wisely, then laughs at my youthful exuberance.
His teeth are worn down when he smiles but his face has an honesty
and integrity to it that I trust.

Then he shows me his bottles: brown dyed plastic water bottles with
a thick aya residue lining them, and he asks me if they are okay. I smile
and nod my agreement. The birds twitter above us in the trees.

We understand each other.

In the late afternoon Rama takes me off with Natilde, her sister-in-law
Cortelia, Patricia, Lizzy, and the two boys. I'm going to watch them
boil up mahogany bark for the rich brown dye it exudes that colors the
cotton fabrics they make their embroideries from.

We all set off along a dirt road, Natilde and Cortelia carrying a giant
metal pot between them stacked with rough shards of wood and bark
inside it. It's the exact same size cooking pot that I've seen at so many
curandero's houses that it immediately makes me think of the similarities between the two rituals, and the common thread of ayahuasca that
connects them.

In Shipibo culture the man receives the visions but it is the woman
who transmits them, I realize. It is the women who have the duty and
care to make the Shipibo textiles, to do the painting and the embroidery that is needed to map the ayahuasca journey. Girls are initiated at
a young age by their grandmothers and taught the secrets of the weave.

Writer Howards G. Charing talks about these origins in an article,
"Communion with the Infinite," published in the British-based shamanistic magazine *Sacred Hoop.* Charing quotes a Shipiba woman who
says, "When I was a young girl my mother squeezed drops of the *piripiri*
(a species of cyprus) berries into my eyes so that I would have the vision
for the designs. This is only done once and lasts a lifetime."

Elsa Raimonda Merlinda, a charmingly coy elderly Shipiba who
works the *mercado* selling her fabrics and crafts, told me earlier today that

her grandfather would see the patterns she now sews while in visions on ayahuasca. There are ten levels of consciousness, he told her, and that as one diets and does more intensive work with the vine the deeper into the fields you go, and the more there is to map.

It's only at the last level that one sees the ayahuasca patterns that are passed down to the *manta* fabrics, although many *ayahuasqueros* I've spoken to say they see flashes of jungle circuitry and the "ayahuasca rivers" quite early in their journeys, when their consciousness is just dipping into that great pool of unbroken spirit.

Either way the idea of levels to consciousness is a fascinating idea that has been paralleled many times by researchers in the West and in the Eastern traditions. The Sufis have their "Fifty thousand layers of Godhead"; the Tibetans their "Upper and Lower Bardos"; and even Tim Leary pronounced his "Eight Circuits of Consciousness." But if there are ten levels of consciousness, what then is beyond that? Is there an eleventh dimension, or a twelfth?

And why stop there? Some of the ayahuasca patterns I've seen have a central circle or square surrounded by a web of energy, but other designs have infinite and equal geometries. Sometimes the circle design is offset like a lens or a window onto the pattern within, which goes on into infinity. From my own journeywork I was interested in understanding the essence of what each dimension was, not necessarily how many there were.

The Shipibo designs provide an intimate knowledge of what the West is just beginning to understand about energy, and also a map of the higher dimensions that far outstrips the most delineated quantum frameworks.

Some designs have lines like street grids with blocky nodes setting out the houses and squares, just as if you'd flown over a city at night in an plane, or were sketching out a crude circuit-diagram. To my Western-media mind it all looked very *Pac-Man,* each blocky pathway like a 16-bit old school Atari graphic. But ultimately, I realized the *manta* fabrics offered us a unique snapshot of the vibrational wavelengths of consciousness perceivable with ayahuasca.

The level these patterns appear on is like a clear canvas, but that canvas is itself a vibrational wavelength. The patterns can be thought of as neural pathways on top of the canvas, or consciousness output. To stretch the metaphor, when ayahuasca takes you into the Overmind or the Mind of God, these patterns are the thoughtforms, the ideas or consciousness flickering on the surface of the brain... *like coral reef of the Divine. And beyond that invisible canvas, then, lies the final unknown...*

Shipibo legend says that the ayahuasca patterns were taught to their ancestors by the Inca themselves. The Inca people were named after Inca the king, and the king was himself named after Inca the God, the one from beyond the stars who gave them all the knowledge they needed to make and do things in the world. Whatever the origins, the intricate patterns the Shipiba women sew onto their fabrics are a direct transmission not just from times past, but from places deep within.

They're fundamental blueprints, but does that mean that there are no new patterns to perceive? Were new embroideries being made that mapped more recent iterations of the ayahuasca vibrational space? Or was the secure product rollout of the traditional patterns on the tourist handicrafts blocking the creative flow of new designs? Elsa told me that the "interior landscape is changing," but beyond that the dynamics of *entheocartography* and capitalism were lost on her.

Still, if the *manta* patterns were maps of consciousness and the thoughtforms of the Divine, then it made sense that those thoughts would be changing, too. Science already measures the "heartbeat" of the planet—the fluctuations of the earth's magnetic field are called the "Schuman Resonance," which has apparently increased in recent times from 8 KHz to 11 KHz, causing many a hippie to declare imminent planetary transformation. *Can MRI scans of the Divine be far behind?*

After a short walk we finally arrive in Cortelia's backyard where there's a large open clearing and a dugout fireplace set up for the pot. Natilde's camera shy and she has reason to be: she's not just facing me taking the occasional photo of her for the record, Rama is also filming today, getting some footage for her studies. Natilde spreads out a blanket on the ground and sits there with Lizzie sorting out different seeds to crack open for additions to the dye. Every time she looks up either Rama or I are there with our cameras poised until she looks away again, shyly.

Cortelia's on the ground on a dusty plastic mat with a company logo on it, breastfeeding her baby. She hands the small square dyed cloth to another woman who continues the work, her own baby daughter playing by her feet with a yellow plastic ball and staring up at me with wide, open eyes. Around us some of the older girls sit on the thin wooden benches and gossip. They're all busy making the *manta* fabrics, breastfeeding, cooking, always cooking, washing babies in the sink, organizing the arts co-op, and running the business.

"Perhaps this is the equivalent of the shamans," Rama only halfjokes, motioning to Natilde as she gets up to stir the fabric with a long wooden pole, and I know she has seen it, too. I remember Scott Petersen's theory he expounded back at the Refugio, that male shamanism might have evolved as a reaction to women holding the real magic power—that of childbirth—and I think Rama is right . . .

It's the women who hold the key to San Francisco, not the men. The important thing is not that there are ten male shamans or so in a few block radius peddling their psychic wares; it's that the ayahuasca patterns that have passed down from mother to daughter for generations— the art of the craft that is the public face of ayahuasca tourism—is women's business.

And so too, is spirit.

24

The Prime Directive

San Francisco, outside Pucallpa

SATURDAY NIGHT AUGUST 12, 2006

At eight o'clock sharp I leave the house of La Familia Bardales and walk down the dirt track to don Leonardo's home around the corner. The night is still warm and villagers throng the streets chatting amiably and clustering around their front doorsteps. It feels totally natural to be going off to see the village shaman now, amidst this festive atmosphere, and I realize how important it is to have this work culturally accepted and supported.

How different a feel to taking "drugs" in the West is this path of shamanism that I am now on, and that so many Westerners like me are treading. Here in San Francisco the entire community revolves around the shared experience of taking ayahuasca: their language, songs, clothes, and their way of seeing the world were all originally shaped by the aya-huasca vision, and have only recently been Westernized. As I walk along the dirt road in the moonlight I feel like I'm walking through a dream, that I could reach out and push over the cardboard house fronts with a touch of a finger to reveal the multidimensional spaces behind them.

I find don Leonardo down the back of his property past the main bungalows, in the sleeping hut: a long rectangular building with two layers, an outer thatched one and a ceiling-to-ground mosquito netted interior decked out like a peasant's Bedouin tent. A slim mattress and another slimmer piece of foam lie on the floor. In the center of the space is a low wooden table and on it are a candle, a piece of chain, a dozen *mapacho* cigarettes, and a drinking glass. The ayahuasca is in a typical two-liter plastic bottle, but only an eighth is full with the dirt-colored liquid.

Leonardo smiles with the cheeky grin of a child when he motions to it, and swirls it around and around to settle the brew. Past the altar he shows me other tools of his trade—two pan flutes, a voodoo-like doll of a rough man-figure made from clay, and some wooden bowls. A blue plastic vomit bucket lies between us and the table.

I'm expecting his sick wife and daughter but for long minutes don Leonardo and I sit there by the candlelight, alone, and exchange pleasantries in our respective stunted languages. Leonardo is dressed neatly in brown pants and a white shirt rolled up at the sleeves, his hair slicked back like a suave gentleman as he chuckles away to himself. As I look at him by candlelight any apprehensions I might have had all melt away. Tonight Leonardo will be my *own personal shaman, my village Yoda;* it's just him and me going into the aya space, and that takes away some of my usual stresses dealing with group energies, of holding back or pattern matching.

Leonardo starts whistling the Shipibo *icaros* gently under his breath, the short sharp *whooshing* and *shooo shooo shoooing* of his *soplaring* cleansing the area of bad spirits—and when that doesn't work he just uses his fingers to pluck them from the air and flick them back to whence they came.

He pours me a third of a cup of the dirty brown fluid and it has the whiff of an alcohol base in it—not fresh, but not off, either. After my last devastating session at Sachamama I'm not keen for an overwhelming experience, but I trust my teacher to pour my dose, to let him take the lead. I focus my intent on contacting the spirits and the plant doctors, on communicating with them and hearing whatever message they have for me tonight.

After pouring my cup Leonardo swigs directly from the bottle and we both settle back onto the mattress, sitting upright and staring at the candlelight gently flickering on the altar. Back at Sachamama Pedro had taught me a trick to center myself in the aya space when it morphed too much, too quickly. Stare at a candle he had said, to practice your centering, your ability to find focus in the flux. So I watch the little flame and ponder on its light while we wait for the ayahuasca spirit to fill us, sharpening my spirit blade as I go.

Leonardo offers me a *mapacho* and I accept, having grown used to the spirit in the tobacco and the calm energy it brings. We spark up in unison with our identical transparent yellow lighters, chuckling at the connection, and blow streams of smoke into the night air.

Leonardo begins talking then, chatting away, and I swear I can hear a second voice, or he's responding in another lower voice, or the spirits are talking... Leonardo engages in a long dialogue with the spirits, invoking and enchanting, questioning and answering, a *tête-à-tête* with the other world. He *soplars* again, making his whistling wind sounds and *shoo shooing* more bad spirits away, cleansing the air.

After twenty minutes or so, gently whistling his Shipibo *icaros* the whole while, he motions me to lie down and get comfortable, signaling that he is about to extinguish the candle. He grips it between his fingers and blows, smothering the flame, and we are plunged into a cool and relaxed darkness.

Faint sparks and liquid images start building and rolling over me. I can feel the aya in me, gently spiraling into my core. It's a small dose, no *toè* or ravaging energies, just the smooth, calm healing of the medicine in me. Leonardo launches into his *icaros* then, the familiar spaghetti-western tunes that I've heard so many times before, and I remember how powerful a magic they are. He sings well, gently, staggering out his breaths and elongating the end of each chorus to gain breath for the next stage.

The *icaros* wash over me as the aya starts to build. I feel like I'm on a slow spinning wheel inside my head as my spirit starts to move and shake loose from the flesh, like a boat being lapped at by waves.

Leonardo sings and sings and sings, carrying me away as the hummingbird visits, its wings beating me into a deep dream state as the visions begin. And it is so gentle, so perfect a reintroduction to the medicine after my fears that I would not be able to handle it again that I know that mother aya is reading me and giving me what I need.

Minutes pass by in this fugue state, enveloped by sound and healing. After a while Leonardo asks if anything is happening and lights the candle and administers a second booster dose before plunging us back into darkness. I lapse into a light sleep, awake but in delta, and in my slumbering cocoon the ayahuasca finds a window deep into me.

Suddenly I'm in the presence of spirits, or rather, a singular spirit, one of the *night doctores*.

I'm letting him heal me for a while before I even realize he's there, and when the conscious brain kicks back in I have to open my eyes to ensure what I'm feeling can be seen, to check it's not Leonardo himself working on me. In the dim moonlight I can see Leonardo sitting upright in the same position across from me, still singsonging his *icaros* and blowing *mapacho* smoke.

Yet I can feel this spirit with the weight and gravity of a real person, a thin man of medium build. He's above me, holding my head with a hand on both sides, centering me as the medicine does its work. The feel of him, the reality of it is unquestionable. The spirit-doctor, or maybe it's Leonardo in spirit form, or whoever, is still over me, invisible but tactile, healing and smoothing out my energy body like the current of a stream steadily beating down on a rock.

Soon the doctor himself slips inside my body—I shake at his entry, rattle and rebalance myself as he finds his way deep into me. I can feel the same stream of energy lapping around my mouth and jaws, moving like electricity through my energetic body, unmistakable. I'm taking the idea of possession really calmly, no fear because I can feel the integrity of this spirit. It's amazing the tactile solidity of his presence, but as I wake from my deeper delta state the equilibrium is lost and the visions begin . . .

Flickering morphing kaleidoscope images assail me with a green organic edge. Waves of green flame interspersed with white flame cancel each other out; vegetal images and consciousness, a calm, controllable plant realm ride. Slo-mo snapshots of trees appear before me: one, two, three grandfather trees that stare down at me, offering support. I instantly realize they are the same trees I contacted at Sachamama, old elemental beings that grow in the enthnobotanical garden there, and that my link with them is strong, even though they are far away.

Leonardo's singing *Yodaram shamar yodaram shamar...* or something that sounds like that over and over again, and in my hallucinogenic interconnection the word-sounds of his song are hitting me, impressing on my mind like ripples on an astral pond.

Later in the ceremony Leonardo's son, Ermundo, comes in under the mosquito netting to be healed and Leonardo spends time singing healing songs for him and blowing *mapacho* smoke on his crown chakra. And in the still of the night we fall asleep, enveloped by the dark and the spirits, safe in their embrace. And we dream of them and they of us, as the two worlds become one.

It's this merging of the two worlds that makes San Francisco so special: the masculine and the feminine, the indigenous reality with the capitalist blueprint, the ayahuasca world and the tourist theme park. Yet I'd decided if I was to do this mission up the Amazon I had only today to explore it before leaving from the port tomorrow on the fastest boat I could find to Orellana.

So after Sunday morning breakfast with *la familia,* Rama takes me to see Brian, an American anthropology student who's been living here for some years now, to get a better fix on the local ayahuasca scene. We find him a few streets away at the house where he's staying with his local Indian girlfriend and her family, ten of them all under the one thatched roof *maloca*.

Brian's about six-foot tall, skinny as a beanpole but well muscled from working hard in his permaculture "hard-grow" garden plot. He has crew-cut dark hair, glasses, and earlobes with large holes where they've held mock-tribal jewelry in that new-primitives way long popular in the cool hoods of the global village. In his shorts and Western "Ecology" t-shirt with a Shipibo necklace dangling down over his chest, he's the very picture of the student anthropologist gone native.

He doesn't have much money, he tells me with a smile—he's so broke he doesn't even buy his *mapacho* tobacco from the store for a sole. Instead he buys raw tobacco and rolls his own, lighting his cigarettes with Venezuelan matches that have a picture of Hugo Chavez on the box. What little money he has saved he's put into his new family's home, building a new outdoor bathroom and walls for the open-air family *maloca*. But what he does have in abundance is knowledge, the type that could transform this little village—if only they'd let him.

As Rama leaves Brian takes me through his garden, explaining the village projects he's been involved with in his three years here, and the wall of cultural indifference that he keeps hitting. First there was the waste recycling initiative (which encouraged recycling plastic bags and bottles as the base material for mud brick houses).

That all fell apart when the locals lost enthusiasm with mud brick houses because it wasn't their tribal way—the Sierra tribe make mud brick, the locals told him, and they're a long way away from here where it's dry—the rain here isn't the best when it comes to mud. Undeterred, Brian turned his hand to permaculture gardens and the living example he's created here in the front yard of his girlfriend and her family.

His girlfriend's grandfather was a *curandero* himself many years ago, but he gave it all away when he was converted by the first wave of Christian missionaries to come through here. It's slightly ironic, then, that a few generations later Brian is here, full of youthful enthusiasm and walking that fine line between an objective Western anthropologist and a human being that can't help but get involved in the affairs of the people around him.

He's a living example of the fact that our presence here changes things, and he's conscious of that and trying to do the best he can with the skills he has—but so were the Christian missionaries. Most cultures expect they're doing the right thing when it comes to other cultures, but by the time anyone can tell any different, the damage is done.

In *Star Trek* they had a rule called the "Prime Directive"—that higher civilizations were never to interfere in the development of more primitive races. Kirk broke the rule all the time, of course, because it's the American Way to get involved and believe you can make a difference. And it's not the same when it's a closed system on a planetary level. Those "other races" are us. But still, there are cultural firewalls that kick in when the Prime Directive is breached, no matter who's responsible or what their intent, and the ripples are felt by both the contacting culture and the contactee.

"They're going to have and receive what they want to receive, y'know," Brian tells me with a broad sweep of his hand that takes in the entire village. "They can have so many things but it's so hard to offer them the right thing for the right reason. You can offer them a responsible option but it's usually the irresponsible option that's more enticing. It's instant gratification," he says with a grimace, looking down at the permaculture garden by his feet and no doubt bitter that it too, was rejected by the villagers as something too hard, too different from their traditional ways.

"They all want Big Macs over enlightenment, huh?" I say as a condolence. "The villagers here and elsewhere in Peru are becoming Westernized, but surely, some Westerners are learning the ways of indigenous knowledge and getting back in concert with the earth. So there's a karmic balance that we can still take heart from, isn't there?"

"Yeah…" Brian says half-heartedly, looking at me with intense eyes and a tight smile. "But I'm not sure of the equality of that balance, it's not so easy to measure the way the cultural transaction works. Like, lots of Westerners come here and stay a while doing ayahuasca…"

"Rama tells me you did an apprenticeship yourself… what do they call it here?"

"An *alumno*. I suppose you could call it an apprenticeship. I called it that. And to this very day don Mateo still says when he introduces me to people, there's Brian, mi alumno . . ." Brian takes his glasses off and pinches the bridge of his nose. "That was a period in my life," he says, "where I was looking for my connection to the natural world and to the planet. I thought, that's what I want to do, I want to help people and be a *curandero*." He glances at me suddenly with a look that says he's just let out a secret and it's too late to get it back again.

"I don't know if it's because I'm paranoid, but I don't like doctors. I don't have much confidence in Western doctors. It might be the culture, but when I've gone to them they make me doubt them, their intelligence and everything . . . Good *curanderos* look for what causes [a problem] and they look for how to solve that problem. Why is there this wound? How can we make it better? It's a microcosm of all of society, how we just keep putting band aids over problems. Like poverty—we're not curing the cause of the problem, we're not curing that, just alleviating the symptoms."

Brian's a pretty cool dude: young, impassioned, still free enough to be striving for a better world and idealistic enough to believe one is possible. We sit down at a long wooden table in the shade and while away a few hours discussing shamanism, the business of shamanism, and the indigenous–Western dynamic here in town. As I find out more of Brian's story I wonder if his experiences on ayahuasca have led him to this purist approach, or if it's something in him, and in seekers like he and I that leads us to the vine and the spiritual world it opens up?

"The people who come here to San Francisco come for the ayahuasca; the secondary reason they come here is to look at the jungle. No one comes here to see nature," Brian tells me with a wry smile. "If you come here for nature what's there to see? You can come to my house and see the garden and walk through our secondary forest . . . but there's no jungle. Around here there's just a lot of burnt trees . . . Ayahuasca is the most lucrative thing you can do in town, hands down, without a question," he says, looking down at the ground with another grimace.

"There might be between ten to twenty [*curanderos*] in San Francisco, maybe fifteen proper *curanderos*, to be more conservative. But then the question is: are they real shamans? Because there are people with knowledge who want to help people. Then there are people with only a little bit of knowledge and aren't quite as wise. The majority of people here have knowledge of healing plants and the properties that make you hallucinate, but the thing with ayahuasca is it's a little bit different because you can drink it and not have anything happen to you. These people, maybe they know a few *icaros* and they know how to cook the vine, and they see that it's brought in a lot of money. And so people see it as a job, it's big business.

"In the last three years there has been a steady flow of tourists here from Italy, Europe, and the United States," Brian says as the hot afternoon sun beats down on us and we smoke *mapachos* in the shade. In the trees above us birds flit to and fro and sing to the sound of *motorcarros* thundering along back streets in the otherwise quiet afternoon air.

"I've seen a lot of people who have come to drink here," Brian continues, fixing us a *mate* tea in little wooden cups. "Last year there was a group of Europeans that all came in the middle of the day. They got on the loudspeaker and called for Don Martin [one of the other village *curanderos*] because they wanted to drink ayahuasca. In middle of the day—they just showed up wanting to drink ayahuasca!

"Martin wasn't there but one of his *alumnos* was, and he was like, okay, I'll drink with them. He was pretty much the only guy in town who said yeah, I'll take their money, I'll go against our taboo about drinking during the day and just give it to them and earn my money. So they drank and maybe three or four hours later they were wandering through the streets, a little bit spacey, enjoying the nature with big smiles on their faces. And they just got back on the boat and went back to town. It was so weird," he says, shrugging his shoulders. "How can people do that?"

It's that instant gratification again, pass out the Mickey Mouse ears and the *shacapa* leaf rattles. If the ayahuasca experience can be successfully commodified in this way, and by all accounts it can, then what the West *gains* might be something far less than what the indigenous culture here *loses.* In fact, that's just what happened with pretty much every other holy sacrament that has been revered by indigenous peoples across the world.

Tobacco, for instance, is still honored here as the mother of all plants, but used without the proper intent it's just another addictive kick to peddle from the roadside stalls. Maria Sabina, the famous Mazatec *curandera* that introduced R. Gordon Wasson to the sacred "flesh of the gods," or "magic mushrooms," later bemoaned divulging their existence to the West.

"From the moment the foreigners arrived, the 'holy children' [magic mushrooms] lost their purity. They lost their force, [Westerners] ruined them. Henceforth they will no longer work. There is no remedy for it," she said towards the end of her life.

The other sacred plant of the Mazatecs, *Salvia divinorum,* is now a pop fad on YouTube where the plant, still legal in some states in the U.S., is smoked and the initiate filmed in full loss of motor coordination during their holy journey. Many of these videos, which are quite popular on the site, are labeled "comedy." These videos are heartbreaking to watch, as naïve Western teenagers get off with no respect for set and setting or proper intent. Without elder guidance and the proper understanding of why and how to use these tools, the West reduces the sacred to the profane again and again.

Then there's the question of what the tourist demand is doing to the quality of *curanderismo* here, and the shoddy operators springing up to take advantage of the demand for shamanism. "A lot of people who come here are searching for a lot of things, and [some of the shamans] are like, okay, this guy, we know how to work this guy to make him think what he wants..." Brian explains. "I know people in town who have a lodge; they receive a lot of tourists. I have a feeling that they utilize tricks... They'll come and ask you, how's your cold? Like, you don't even have a cold but they'll ask you how's your cold, maybe to start thinking about it. Then they'll say, hey listen, whenever you want to come over we've got medicine for you.

"So I think these bad shamans are out there as well as the good ones. They manipulate thoughts and they manipulate the organism to act in a certain way, and possibly even to make them hurt a little bit more. It may be a thing like Western doctors where they say oh, just take this pill, buy this, and it doesn't really cure it, so further down the line they have more problems and more money goes to the doctor...

"On ayahuasca you really open yourself up. You're susceptible to more influences. It all depends on how strong you are personally or internally. With some people a shaman could plant a thought or an idea in their head during a ceremony and it will grow inside of them and they will continue with this idea. There's a possibility that you could consider it like brainwashing, if you wanted to put some tacky term on it."

It is true ayahuasca has the potential to change everything and allow you to see the world in a different way. It's just that from within the perspective of the person undergoing the changes it's also hard to discern which bits are fantasy and which bits are oracular insight. That's part of what the shaman is supposed to be there to help you figure out.

"When I've drunk ayahuasca it's always been a cleansing for the body and then a cleansing of the mind," Brian says. "I go through and methodically organize all my responsibilities and reexamine each responsibility and each relationship with everybody that I work with and all my family members. I think of all the different things that I could do—it's like my head is just flooded with all these thoughts. There are some wonderful ideas, it's like genius. I should do that, and then at the end it's like whoosh, oh my God, that's so much, how many [thoughts] can you do?"

I know what he means. In many ayahuasca ceremonies when I've thought of my friends and family it's not that the spirit has been saying move mountains, it's always been more simple, like tell a person that you love them, or be kind about this, or clarify that relationship, or whatever... "Ayahuasca brings up a lot of issues to face," I say, "but I believe it also allows your spirit to speak to your conscious mind. If you do the things it suggests it can help clear up your relationships, and if everyone did that it could really clear the air with the culture in general."

"Yeah. Maybe you just take the motivation you get from that experience and realize that there are so many possibilities in this world and then you just go and do what you can. And I feel fine doing what I can," Brian says, looking out on the village with a smile.

Bugger the *Prime Directive*. It strikes me that since the 1960s mentality of cultural sovereignty the globalized world we now live in is like a *Hadron Supercollider* smashing cultures together at an astounding rate. And a good way to integrate the rapid cultural acceleration is through a psychic lubricant like ayahuasca, or a plain open heart that relates to people as people no matter what culture they're from, and treats them all as one big family needing love and nurturing.

In the end there's no easy demarcation line that says all indigenous *curanderos* are doing good work and all Westerners are infecting the noble savages with WWF wrestling and imitation Nike label t-shirts. Each side is affecting the other as their cultural memes rub off. It will be another generation, perhaps, before we see what the rapid globalized melting pot that is San Francisco becomes—but if the tourist dollar holds out it's sure to involve ayahuasca.

I just hope it also involves genuine heart and soul, and that against the odds, the mystery and majesty of ayahuasca can survive the consumerism of the West.

25

Up River

Pucallpa

MONDAY AUGUST 14, 2006

Pucallpa's a hot, sweaty, dusty city with nothing much going for it, which is good since I'm only here to get out of it.

The port is surrounded by a bustling shanty *mercado* that screams Third World: food, textiles, plastics, clothes, toys—a lifetime of crap bought and sold by the locals who ply their trades and eke out a living with their fellow hustlers by the littered shores of the Amazon.

On the river a vast flotilla of boats cruise about, bringing their loads down from Iquitos and up from the towns below. Giant cargo barges pushed by little motorboats carry the bodies of once proud grandfather trees of the forest, neatly stacked row upon row, destined for some processing plant to be spat out as floorboards and furniture. Dozens of shirtless laborers pour over the logs like insects picking at corpses.

Rama's come with me to say goodbye and show me round the markets while I get some essential supplies. She's been a gracious host and my guardian angel during this leg of the stay, and through her and la familia Bardales I've got some connections, however tenuous, up river.

"It has been nice to meet you properly, Rak," she says with a sisterly smile. "I hope the research for your book goes well up the river. Certainly you will be the only gringo aboard," she adds, leaning down to give me a hug and wish me on my way.

Orellana's about three hundred miles away as the crow flies, but as the river twists and turns it could be almost double that, and as Rama has so tenderly planted the thought in my mind, I am probably going to be the only gringo in a few hundred kilometer radius. Just me and my daypack, filled to the brim with my camera, MiniDisc, and an odd assortment of expensive media gear that could feed a family for a year if they were to steal and hock it in the city.

I wish my Spanish was better, but it's nothing compared to my sense of *practicality* going all this way in search of *encantos*—magic stones from somewhere in the middle of the Amazon. I'd emailed Tessa this morning from an internet cafe but hadn't heard back from her regarding meeting up in Cuzco.

This whole mission was looking extremely dubious and was held together by a shoestring: I had about two hundred soles in my wallet, vague directions from Juan Maldonardo as to the location of the stones, and an equally vague promise from an "ex-international madam and psychic witch with a lust for life" for compensation should the mission by some stroke of fate be successful.

But as I walk along the edge of the cliffs overlooking the river, dodging merchants loading the boats anchored down below, a sense of great adventure fills me, drowning out all doubts. *I'm going up river, up the Amazon, and that's all that matters.*

My boat—*Jacobii II*—is a thirty meter long wooden cargo driver packed to the brim and beyond with Inca-Cola, Real Cola, toilet paper, rice, bananas, live chickens stacked in wooden cages on top of each other, eggs, luggage, boxes, large striped plastic carry bags, more bags, more boxes, and people. At least twice the amount of people any legal boat in the West would be allowed to carry with the same amount of space. Passengers keep streaming in all afternoon and filling every nook and cranny with the carry-on pieces of their lives—luggage, books, clothes, food, etc.—tied up with string and wedged between hammocks and bodies until everybody's intimately connected, like it or not.

The early arrivals also sling up their hammocks—an indispensable item for long boat journeys. Rama's lent me a lightweight string hammock that I manage to squeeze in among other hanging bodies near the middle of the boat. The entire deck space is steadily filled by an endless canopy of colorful cocoons that blossom at varying heights, so two or even three hammocks can virtually occupy the same horizontal space, and other passengers can sleep on the floor beneath them to make sure all available areas are covered.

I'm locked in side by side with my neighbors, so close our elbows touch. There must be fifty people down here in the hold with me, mothers with children nestled in the hammocks with them, babies being breastfed, bodies down below them doing the same. I know my bags are safe down there because a mother and her baby child are sleeping on them for cushions. *Here I am going up the Amazon in the local equivalent of a Greyhound bus, piled in with the masses—and loving it.*

We're hours late taking off—which I'm soon to find is standard business, but with a full load of cargo, both human and consumable, we're finally ready in the late afternoon. The people are friendly, down to earth, dressed in shorts and t-shirts and cheap Western gear, the children of the villages that dot this mighty river who have gone to the city seeking their fortunes.

Up on the prow of the boat a tired, middle-aged man in a baseball cap stands guard over a television set in a cardboard box, while another well-dressed man sits on the stairs next to his crate full of chickens. As we shove off from the port I find a wooden box at the nose of the boat half-full of ropes and crawl inside to take in the view.

Sunset comes in brilliant streaks of pink that grace the darkening sky and reflect on the waters off the prow of the boat as it slices through the waves. Once we putter out of Pucallpa we stick to the right hand bank a few hundred meters out, and the dark silhouette of the jungle stretches on and curves round, hugging the river for as far as the eye can see.

The night air is cool and the moment is calm and serene, with the faint shriek of howler monkeys here and there in the far distance. As the boat bobs to and fro on the waves and cuts slowly and steadily forward, a common air of expectation hangs over us all.

It's another story in the middle of the night when I suddenly need to go to the toilet—which happens to be on the top level of the boat, right at the back, almost as far away from where I am now as is possible to be. I literally have to extricate myself from the elbows of my companions in the hammocks surrounding me, find a foothold on the floor among the littered bodies, get down on my belly and duck under the hammocks and then crawl between the people asleep on the floor towards the stairs. On the top level I have to do the same in reverse—but it's even worse. The top deck is more popular and about a third more people are squeezed in up here. An old woman sitting on the floor curses me as I crawl past her and the other human debris on all fours, weaving under the hammocks towards my elusive goal.

When I finally get there I find the back landing is empty this time of night, so I just piss off the back of the boat, holding onto the guide rail and marveling at the three-quarter full moon and the lap of waves as we putter steadily down the mighty Amazon. The gentle rocking motion almost puts me to sleep as I crouch by the rail, and for a few timeless moments it's as if I'm back in the womb.

"Where are you from?" a friendly voice asks in English as I return to my spot in the hold. A few hammocks over there's a middle-aged Peruvian with a friendly smile who appears to be up for a chat. It's a minor miracle to have anyone speaking English on the boat, I figure, so I'm willing to give it a go. It turns out my new amigo's name is Juan (of course), and he's a thirty-seven-year-old English teacher from Pucallpa who's en route to Contamana, one of the larger towns between here and Orellana, where he's due to begin a two-month teaching round.

"I saw you in Pucallpa with Rama," he says. "I know her from San Francisco—I taught art and painting there." Ha. It's a small world. Even smaller, I find out, when I tell Juan I'm studying ayahuasca. Not only has he taken it twice, he took it at Sachamama in 1999 and drank with don Francisco, who is a friend of his who shares his love of painting.

Going alone up the Amazon, this feels like a good omen, that *madre ayahuasca* is still looking after me on this crazy quest of mine. I don't need faith to feel the connection ayahuasca brings, but it's nice to have these coincidences nonetheless.

As our boat slowly cuts through the water and I fall asleep in my hammock, surrounded by my new family, I feel less like a gringo and more a member of our floating tribe, one collective organism interconnected at the elbows as we float downstream . . .

The next morning the sun rises over the horizon casting brilliant hues of pink and blue. A fine mist clings to the surface of the water like candyfloss as a pod of gray dolphins crest the waves and chase alongside our boat, playful and free.

Just after dawn more people disembark and we take on extra cargo—the whole front prow of the boat is now filled with greening bananas destined for further downriver, guarded over by a sunken-jowled Shipiba grandmother in traditional embroidered dress. There's a lot less people now so our elbows have some breathing room, as well as our lungs. In the light the survivors of the night all get a good look at each other for the first time, and of course, as Rama had told me at the port, I am the only gringo on board.

I don't have long to get used to the new dynamics, though, as by early morning we reach the small village of Canaan, on the outskirts of Contamana. Before leaving Pucallpa yesterday Rama had introduced me to Pierre Urban—a French author on ayahuasca—and Romuald Leterrier, another anthropologist who had shot a DVD with a local *curandero,* and who recommended it as better ayahuasca territory than the larger town. Contamana was full of *brujeria,* the anthropologist had said, and ego-based shamans chasing the dollar.

I didn't fancy the sound of that, and anyway, back in San Francisco, Senor Bardales had also recommended Canaan to me, giving me a small strip of paper with the name of Alberto Rodrieguez—his friend or relation or something, who lives here.

I'm dropped off at the shore, or as close to it as the rickety *Jacobi II* can come, and I wade through the shallows and reach dry land. Everyone on the boat watches me as they pull back out, some smiling and waving like we're one big family: *adios amigo.*

As I wave back I'm swamped by dozens of local kids who are hyperexcited to see a gringo in town. I'm swept up in their tide of curiosity like a movie star let loose at a suburban mall. My Spanish is still atrocious, but saying the name of the senor Rodrieguez over and over rings a bell, and one young boy leads me up the hill from the river and through the outskirts of the village, to senor Rodriguez's house, dozens of giddy kids and adult neighbors in tow.

Alberto's wife and kids are home but senor Rodriguez himself is in Contamana on business. Still, with the large crowd abuzz behind me, senora Rodriguez and family kindly take me in, followed by a smaller horde of neighbors who spill into the house, staring at me endlessly like a man from the moon.

Out come the trinkets and handicrafts, Shipibo-style, but cost-price, I note, as the dance begins. I buy one baby monkey skull embedded on a bead necklace with red and brown seeds and also five fine ayahuasca embroideries as small as placemats. The woman who sells them to me smiles a wide smile, as if there's not very much business down here and she couldn't be more pleased. La familia plonk me down in a hammock and barrage me with a million questions that I cannot possibly answer. Sadly, my *Lonely Planet* Latin American phrasebook is sorely not up to the task, nor am I.

While we wait for Alberto, one of the neighbors who speaks a little broken English takes me around and shows me the medicinal gardens growing down by the river. Both Canaan and Contamana are still Shipibo territory, and the locals still use ayahuasca, especially since Western medicine doesn't stretch too far out here, even when it is available.

We reach the medicinal gardens and my guide points out a cluster of small ayahuasca vines growing in neat rows, tended by an elderly man in Roy Orbison glasses who smiles at me, revealing missing front teeth.

A group of young girls are washing clothes in the river as a light rain begins to fall, and my guide slices off two large palm fronds with his machete for us both to use as umbrellas from the rain. Then and there in that instant I understand the way to a sustainable culture: Take what you need and only as much as you need, and the planet will keep growing its abundance to take care of you.

In the late afternoon Alberto returns from town. He's a fiftyish man in a striped shirt, navy shorts, and a maroon baseball cap, who can't stop smiling at me in a paternal way. I tell him in guidebook Spanish, "*Alberto's amigo et San Francisco—Julio—pensar je pode encontrar et curandero aqui et Canaan? Je buscar tomar ayahuasca la noche? Que et curandero's nombre? Donde est vivir?*"

Alberto manages to digest my intent and promises to line up an ayahuasca session for me tonight with the local village *curandero*. But that's hours away still, so he invites me to join him now at a town meeting that's about to begin.

Cows plod aimlessly through the dirt streets of the village as the rain continues to fall. As we pass by modern houses with bright blue roofs and traditional thatched roof *malocas* I see women cooking inside, others cleaning and making crafts on their verandas, no different than a thousand years ago except for the electric light poles and loudspeakers that line the streets.

And the pumping dance music from the odd radio—Shakira, of course, whose current track "Hips Don't Lie" seems to be the unofficial national anthem everywhere I've gone in Peru (probably because the World Cup Soccer use it as one of their signature songs). The salsa-dance-techno rhythms are infectious and children are dancing to her music in the dirt streets.

Up ahead a group of teenage boys are playing soccer; whole families are bustling about under their front porches and spilling over into the rain. All of them have a calm gravity, wrapped in their tribal bond and sharing their lives together. Like San Francisco, Canaan is one of those charming villages slowly entering the twenty-first century. And like

San Francisco, the mysteries of ayahuasca are still central here—as is the business of shamanism.

Don Augustine, the local village *curandero,* arrives at dusk and sits with senor Rodriguez and I as the shadows creep in and night takes hold. He's a mean-looking man in his late forties who stares at me with bulging eyes. He looks like a civil servant: small and slender, in a neat shirt and slacks, a watch on his left wrist, his dark hair slicked back and a pencil thin moustache gripping his upper lip.

Augustine seems incapable of smiling and all his energy is focused through his eyes, which size me up and down and up again. It's as if he can almost hear the chink chink of dollar signs in the air. All of a sudden I realize I'm hundreds of miles from anywhere, with strangers, and I'm about to hand myself over to another stranger and take a *mind-altering substance* with him.

"*El precio es 150 soles,*" Augustine says suddenly, and Alberto leans over and rolls his fingers together in the universal sign. In case I still don't get it, Alberto says, "Money."

A-ha. It turns out Augustine will conduct an ayahuasca ceremony for me, but he expects the same top dollar *curanderos* in Iquitos and elsewhere charge—150 soles or about U.S. $50. I offer him 30 soles in return, take it or leave it, and I stare him down, saying "*En estoy pellado,*" or I'm flat broke.

The thing is, I *am* almost flat broke. And this isn't one of the big tourist spots, it's a backwater village that rarely gets a gringo. Augustine discusses it animatedly with Alberto for a few minutes, glaring at me like he wants to go at my throat with both hands and just take my wallet here and now. This is the first real *curandero* I've encountered that hasn't been directly referred to me by someone, and all those horror stories I've heard from other *ayahuasqueros* about problems with bad shamans start to make sense now.

All this talk about money really blows any spiritual vibe, and as if to punctuate that mood Augustine suddenly drops the handful of coins he's been rubbing in his right hand and they rattle onto the floor in the dark. One coin rolls into a crack in the floorboards and disappears, and Augustine curses out loud. I feel a tightness in my stomach—I don't trust this guy. Yet here I am about to drink ayahuasca with him, and at this late stage in the game he's the only trick in town.

Finally, almost regretfully, Augustine agrees to my price and I wave goodbye to the gracious Alberto and family and trundle along in the fresh night air behind my new *curandero*. We walk past the cliff edge that leads down to the river and skirt the waterfront to arrive a few hundred meters away on the other side of the village.

Augustine's home is a small, walled *tambo* where he and his Shipiba wife and their four children all live with another elder daughter, her partner, and their newborn baby. Seeing them all here in the one little home makes me a bit sad for my kneejerk reaction over money; Augustine, too, has many mouths to feed.

I'm a bit surprised, though—are we going to conduct the ayahuasca ceremony here, with the family? I guess that's the traditional Shipibo way, but after the incident with the money and Augustine's brusque manner in general, it just seems like another barrier to a truly spiritual experience. After some of my intense journeys with the vine, the thought of full hyperdimensional engagement here in the family home, with the baby and kids sleeping around us, seemed inconceivable.

I sit down on the hard wood floor, propped up against a wall as the family go about their business and settle in for the night. We make small talk in broken Spanglish and hand signals, and I take photos of Augustine, his wife, and the family, and promise to send them copies. It's a nice little bonding ritual and it takes some of the psychic pressure off as we laugh at the kids' poses for the camera.

The adults take it very seriously, though, and Augustine's wife puts on her good skirt, the white one with the ayahuasca embroidery, and asks me for some special shots of her and her children. Augustine and his wife stare straight ahead, unfamiliar with Western cues, looking off into the distance like ghosts caught in my camera lens.

The kids ask me if I have any other electronic goods, which really tells me where their heads are at, and I bring out the little pocket radio I'd bought back in Iquitos and give it to them as a present. The kids squeal with delight as they tune it in, scrolling past Spanish talkback, classic samba beats, and, of course, *Shakira*.

Augustine is still wearing his classic poker face like a death mask, which makes for some fun family snaps, but we both have a lighter air between us now. He makes a point though of asking me how much the radio cost, not, I suspect, because he thinks I've given them something expensive, but to gauge how much money means to me and if I'm really as loaded as it appears. There seems to be some subtle tension still hanging in the air, and then I figure maybe he's mad at me because offering this gift has checked his next move of hitting on me for more *dinero*.

Eventually it's time to drink. The family stays put, with only the elder daughter, her partner, and baby going to bed in another room. The rest of them—the wife and four kids—lie on a blanket opposite Augustine, while I stay in my power spot against the opposite wall. Augustine launches into his *icaros* by the candlelight, *soplaring* into the ubiquitous plastic bottle half-full of a muddy looking ayahuasca tea. His voice is raw and croaky, screeching out into the night. As he pours the brew into a small glass cup and hands it to me, his shadow sprawls across the wall and ceiling behind him like a giant praying mantis, flexing its elongated arms.

The ayahuasca tastes foul—there's an alcohol base to it and a grimy film that sticks to the surface of the tea like a skin. Leaves and twigs swirl around the brew like he hasn't had time to strain it properly and remove the waste bits—but maybe this is just the custom here, too. Perhaps it's because in the local Shipibo tradition the *curandero* is the only one who drinks the brew, and he doesn't mind the chunky impurities. *Or maybe he's just a mean bastard at heart.*

Augustine sips half a cup himself and as the lights go out and the family settles down I still feel a bit weird about everything. Augustine's quiet now, as we're enveloped by the darkness. I wait for something to come on, and wait, and wait ...

Augustine lights the room with a *mapacho* every fifteen minutes or so, giant *mapachos* the size of cigars that have a fantastic nicotine kick that is almost psychedelic in itself. He blows smoke over the family one by one, blessing and cleaning their crown chakras and down the back of their necks. When it comes to my turn he instructs me to self-service myself, blowing my own *mapacho* smoke. I try my best, *soplaring* the smoke down my chest, neck, and crown chakra. Perhaps I should have grown my own ayahuasca, too, I muse—it probably would've been more effective.

I sit there in the dark for what seems like hours, feeling abandoned by my *curandero* and trying to entice visions and a deeper connection to *madre* ayahuasca.

Eventually Augustine asks me, in a quick and light voice, "*Mareaciones?*"

"*Non,*" I reply, shaking my head, and I know nothing is going to happen tonight but I must still create some space for the magic, just in case. Augustine makes no move to work on me, to sing *icaros* to bring any visions, or indeed to do any healing or energetic work. *It's like bad sex*—all this expectation and effort, yet the act doesn't satisfy. It feels like I'm lying on the floor next to the local village doctor, humoring his poor interpersonal skills while he blames me for being sick and then packs me off home with an aspirin.

"Normale?" Augustine says, and in the dark I can almost feel his energy, slightly concerned that he might be asked to refund the money as he passes me a second cup of his foul ayahuasca brew. I chug it down, bring it half up again, and then manage to keep it fully down. It doesn't make much of a difference, and after a while Augustine gives up any pretense of holding the space, singing *icaros,* or doing any work at all. You're on your own, his actions say . . . and don't I know it.

I feel quite small and alone here, unloved, on some hard wooden floor in a village far away from anyone I know. I'm no longer sure why I'm here, or how I found myself in this strange land, having these most peculiar experiences. I'm missing my daughter and my family. And I want to go home . . .

As if to comfort me, *madre* ayahuasca gently flutters into life, reeling out images of the river, long Amazon riverscapes that fill my mind's eye, interspersed with canopy skylines. Don't use your eyes, a voice from deep inside me says, as I soar along the river's edge, the vision crystal clear and bright the more I focus on it.

Become the river, the voice says. Give yourself to the Amazon and let the *drop rejoin the ocean* ...

The next morning Augustine gives me a lift into Contamana with his wife and some of the kids, all of us packed into a narrow little canoe with an outboard motor that slices through the bobbing waves. Contamana's a nice, clean colonial town, but I only stay long enough to grab some breakfast and supplies and then head back to the port, where dozens of small boats are tied up, their weather-beaten wooden frames and gaudy color schemes giving them the appearance of oversized kids' bath toys.

I find a berth on another cargo boat traveling further up river to Orellana, another few hundred kilometers away. I'm left with a lot of time and nothing to do but watch my fellow passengers and the river, and marvel at the amazing assortment of *crap* that is transported up the Amazon. Crate after crate of Inca-Cola, Real-Cola, toilet paper by the slab—another tree product come full circle. *Is this the essence of civilization that we feed back to the natives: sugared water drinks and something to wipe your bum on when it all comes out the other end?* Sadly, it seems so.

As we stop off at remote villages dotting the banks of the river the locals line the shores by the dozen, waiting for our precious cargo. The men wade right into the water, peppered, if not littered, by plastic bags and bottles and other prepackaged castoffs, the detritus of the West's capitalism, to carry their booty up cliff faces and through the jungle before slaking their thirst for the white man's magic.

I'm constantly surprised and distressed at the level of rubbish that litters every village port that we come to on our journey, but that's probably the cultural elitist in me. Recycling and environmental awareness is still so recent in the Western mindset that I can't be expecting the indigenous Indians here to have a developed appreciation of it—or can I?

Back in Iquitos, Kevin Furnas had told me that in the Amazon everything is based around nature, and after you pluck and consume the fruits and vegetables it's only natural to throw away the remains. The difference, he argued, was that the plastic goods the West has introduced aren't natural and can't be composted. Then I remember Brian and his recycling campaigns in San Francisco, and the knowledge that a culture can only be *guided* to awareness, not have it *forced* upon it . . .

So I'm on a boat—the *Super Kerrly's II*—for yet another day of my life, adrift on the river.

Tommy, in the hammock to my left, is a mild, middle-aged Christian who reads the bible endlessly, then writes out select passages in a little black notebook. He's here caring for his elderly mother, who's wrapped in a blue blanket like a mummy in the hammock next to him. She's very infirm and he has to wipe her spit and give her water constantly. His pure service and devotion to her is beautiful, mirrored on my right by a young mother doing the same for her newborn babe.

At lunchtime Tommy gets his mother and I a bowl of the *motelo,* or turtle soup (made from a fresh turtle that the boatmen have caught off the back of the boat) and then smiles at me unselfconsciously, like a saint.

Sitting on the ground beneath our hammocks are a six-piece Peruvian boy band, the "Master Boys." They've all got matching blue t-shirts with white figures on them and glitter on their faces and arms that shine in the afternoon light in an electro-glam-punk style. An older member of the band, or maybe their dad, sleeps next to a Yamaha K-series keyboard that's still in its box. Their mother sleeps next to them on the floor with their two younger sisters. On the roof of the boat they have, curiously, four black wooden frames in the shape of coffins, with the band logo emblazoned on the sides in a white skater font.

Throughout the day I spot dolphins surfacing to play above the water before diving back down into the depths. But they're all gray fins, and I'm starting to think the legend of the pink dolphins is just that—a legend, a myth spun for the tourists to spend endless hours searching the water.

Then suddenly I see it—a flash of pale pink the color of bad bathroom wallpaper arcing up out of the water, chasing the boat and playing in our wake. A pink dolphin about six to eight feet in length... *erect like a penis*... and suddenly all those tales of Peruvian women impregnated by pink dolphins makes complete sense.

Spruce, Schultes, Razam—I'm following in the footsteps of all those who have come before, the botanists and explorers who mapped the mysteries of the Amazon and stoked the embers of the West's imagination. Yet unlike the great explorers of yesteryear, I know I'm just a *forerunner*, part of the first shock wave of the *great ayahuasca tourist boom* that's inevitably on its way. How many years until the wave of seekers burgeons out from Iquitos and Pucallpa and is pushed upriver by their unquenchable thirst for something fresh, new, and authentic? How many years before the last Amazonian tribes greet the visitors with t-shirts and two-for-one deals? Or is it already too late?

Eventually I go up to the prow of the boat in search of the toilet, again. I linger beside the captain's room, hovering in the doorway of his little cabin and seeing the river as he sees it.

The Amazon is about half a mile across here, with flat floodlands on one side and green cliff faces on the other, dotted with the occasional thatched roof hut and clearings where a village sprouts from the jungle. Perfect white fluffy clouds whip the sky and on the horizon a single shaft of light pierces a cloudbank and settles on the verdant green below like a spotlight from heaven.

The light off the water's edge is mesmerizing and as I fall into a light trance I'm hit by the raw power of this mighty river, and the archaic beauty of these decrepit, overloaded cargo boats that are the only point of connection between the villagers who live out here and the outside world.

Floating down this one river, eternity rolls out before me.

All time is no time, and the river, *she accepts all...*

26

When Stones Dream

Orellana, up the Amazon

THURSDAY AUGUST 17, 2006

Did I mention that I have a map? It's drawn in pen on a napkin from the Gringo Bar by Juan Maldonado ... It consists of two lines for the Amazon River, a rectangle for the town of Orellana, and upriver from the town some dots for a path, with a square to signify a stone hut and some lines for the inland tributary where the hot springs are. Bumpy scrawls represent the Canchahuayo Mountains to the right of the hot springs, giving me some directional foundation. *Around 600 kilometers up river with nothing but a napkin map and a dream to lead the way.* I'm tilting at windmills, I know, but I have the faith ...

The *Super Kerrly's II* arrives just as night falls and the lights of Orellana twinkle out over the river like Christmas lights. There's one main strip of shops that form the backbone of the town and a dirt road that leads from the port to the street. It's packed with throngs of locals out and about on this warm night, hovering around with not much else to do.

Orellana has a frontier western feel—the wooden shop fronts just need a few saloon doors and some cowboys hanging out on the front porches, but instead of cowboys the town is filled with Indians.

Hundreds of local Shetbo Indians sit round on the promenade that overlooks the river in the main square, a large concrete block fifty meters wide with the obligatory statue of Francisco de Orellana, the first European to "discover" the Amazon river in 1542. History has it that Orellana was a Spanish explorer who floated down the length of the river with his party when separated from the rest of the expedition.

At one point they were attacked by native female warriors who "fought as hard as ten Indian men," the Spaniards claimed, which made Orellana think of the Amazons of Greek myth. That's why he named the area the Amazon, and eventually the name trickled down to the river as well.

Tonight under his statue a stocky woman is selling cigarettes to passersby. Dozens of street-stall sellers litter the strip with their goods on display in boxes, lit by enclosed candles like a midnight fairy garden. The crowd, however, has the caged energy of a mob just before it erupts—there's a large majority of young teenage boys with built up testosterone and nowhere to express it, mixed in with some families taking in the night air. The funny thing is as the only gringo in town everyone's got their eyes on me. *Well, what else is new?*

I walk past the main square towards a blue, weatherboard Adventist Church. Twenty meters on I stop at a decrepit, rundown little hostel on the rise of a small hill that looks straight out of Tombstone. The proprietors sit on stools under the wooden veranda out the front and begrudgingly rouse themselves from their idle to show me to a tiny, box-like room with no ventilation, a stone floor, and a wooden bed without a mattress. The manager hands me a small sheet with a wheat logo on it that looks like it was once a sack of some kind. A cockroach scuttles across the floor and darts under the bed, letting me know who's the boss around here. All this for only five soles—and a lock for my door—*perfecta!*

The next morning I check out of the hostel and wander town in search of coffee, and Senor Sayes, the contact that Juan Maldonado has given me for Orellana. Scrawled next to my primitive map Juan has written a three-step fast-track program for success:

1. *Fosiles. Encantos—or piedras antiguas*
2. *Rio de Aguas Calientas*
3. *Two tunnel made by the man.*

From that I gather I'm searching for old and precious stones in the hot springs, but that bit about the tunnel just throws me. I did grill Juan for details before I left Iquitos but his responses weren't exactly matching the reality on the ground. Part of me still can't believe I'm here doing this—but then I remember the stone heart of Love Creek that was shown me in ceremony, and I feel the overlapping resonances with stone magic after my rebirth at Sachamama, and the mineral pull of Pachamama, the spirit of the earth herself, strong within me. Perhaps I believe that I am guided here by the stones to fill the absence of any other real plan, but my heart feels like it's following the right path, and surely all else will fall into place...

After three false starts looking for coffee I stumble into "La Brisars," a small café behind the main plaza, and lo and behold one of the customers here speaks a little English. He hasn't heard of Senor Salles but he asks the staff, who say that Senor Salles moved to Pucallpa a while back.

Emilio Ramiez, the graying owner of the café and an entrepreneur always out for a buck, says he knows the Rio de Aguas Calientas well, and he will take me there for a price. Emilio is short and squat with large dark circles under his eyes like a bloodhound, but he also looks sincere. And with Senor Salles gone, what other choice do I have? Emilio says it will cost twenty soles for petrol, ten soles to hire the boat, and fifty soles for his services to guide me there. It's not a lot really, but it's almost half of all the money I have on me.

Still, I can't complain, and as I follow Emilio around town as he gets the boat and supplies ready a surge of gratitude hits me, and amazement that the help I so sorely need is manifesting so easily. About an hour later we carry our wooden canoe down to the muddy beach below the promenade, where dozens of locals are washing and bathing amidst the usual plastic bags, bottles, and refuse that have been so carelessly discarded. Two or three old wooden boats lie beached on the muddy shoreline surrounded by large carrion birds that fossick among the bones and scraps floating by the shore.

Emilio fixes the outboard motor to our skinny wooden canoe and I sit in the middle and hang on for dear life, balanced by my bag with my camera and recording gear in it as we take off down the river. Emilio sits at the prow of the boat, hunched over like he's resigned to his task.

The day is hot and the sky is blue and peppered with creamy white clouds that roll far above us. Emilio's got a baseball cap that protects him from the sun and I whip off my t-shirt and wrap it round my head to block the heat bearing down on me. We meander past a few other boats and the occasional cluster of huts that break the foliage near the shoreline as we slowly head back down river, towards the Canchahuayo mountains and the hot springs that lay nestled nearby.

After a long while we arrive at a point that looks just as green and barren as the other cliff faces along the river, but Emilio recognizes as the path to our destination. We tie up the canoe and head inland, hiking into the jungle and roughly following the map Juan Maldonado has given me. After about half an hour we come to a clearing where a little wooden hut sits on stilts, surrounded by a few dozen cattle grazing idly in the sun. The hut belongs to Julio, a farmer friend of Emilio's, but he's not home.

We find him a few miles away at the top of a hill overlooking the entire area, cutting down a huge tree with a power saw that cries out a deafening mechanical roar. That saw is the king of the beasts around here—from our vantage point I can see endless rolling hills on large tracts of land the saw has cleared for the cattle to graze on. Off in the distance is the Rio Ucayali, a tributary of the Amazon and a slow cargo boat on its way to Iquitos, a long voyage up river.

Julio leads us further up another hill where we stop and eat fresh papaya from a tree. The sweet fruit fills my mouth and the warm golden juice trickles down my face. Julio points off to his right and there is the hot springs—a cluster of rocks spewing forth a trickling burble that meanders down the hill at a steady pace.

I dip my hand in the warm water and let my fingers feel the silt and rocks at the bottom. They're all sedimentary stones that crumble in the air, not the hard, fossilized *piedras* that hold the magic of millions of years of water that have run over them, hot from the depths of the earth. Tessa had instructed me quite specifically on the properties of *encantos,* and I'm sad to say that for the length of the stream there is no magic to be found... *unless you have the eyes to see.*

416

Emilio shouts out an exclamation and clutches above his head a smooth, brown stone as big and the same shape as a packet of cigarettes, with rounded edges. He hands it to me and instantly the power of the stone floods through me like a jolt of electricity.

It glistens in the light like the skin of some amphibious creature, awash with a changing mix of browns, umber and black hues. Turning it over I notice that one side has a distinct face: a dark indent for the eyes, a light streak of white for the nose, and a finely curved indent for the mouth. A little Inca glyph carved in stone. Pedro—I somehow know its name is Pedro—is without doubt an *encanto*. But he is the only one here.

Emilio quizzes Julio on the matter, and Julio is of the opinion that there are no more *piedras* of this type in the area—the land is too wet and sedimentary for that type of hard rock. Julio explains he knows of another spot on the other side of Orellana, an hour from town by *motorcarro*.

But that will mean another day's adventuring, with added costs for the hire of the car, petrol, and Emilio's services. That will pretty much wipe me out financially, leaving me with no *dinero*, trapped in Orellana where there is no bank, no money, and no way out.

Jesus Christ, why did I ever think this would be easy? And why does it always take a crisis to bring out the best in me? The stones were testing me. This was, I knew, some type of initiatory quest that I had accepted, and the road was bound to be full of pitfalls and obstacles, because that's how you grow. But did I *really* need to lose the plot halfway up the Amazon to further my spiritual development?

The Westerner in me is holding on to all that I have, all that I know, my little sense of identity that is buffeted on the waves of this mighty river. The world, she is stripping me back to my bare essentials and I'm struggling against the process the whole way.

The day is getting on and as we head back to town the clouds close in on us like gray curtains. Emilio's at the prow of the canoe again with his shoulders hunched over, looking as sad and lost as I feel, probably wondering what to do with this crazy gringo who's come up the largest river in the world looking for magic stones and searching for needles in haystacks.

Magic. *Ha.* I could sure use some of that right about now.

Before dawn I wake from the most marvelous dream of my life, a fractaling vision of heroes and villains engaged in an age-old play with no beginning and no end. It's not the content so much as the context that piques my interest: the dream is showing me the effect that every action has over this, and many lifetimes, as elegantly as twisting a kaleidoscope and watching the patterns intersect.

I'm more than lucid; it feels like deep within the aya space, that same fullness of consciousness that engages me on all levels and the deep beat of the hummingbird's wings on my third eye.

I'm looking at the web of life and watching it constantly reverberating with the Heisenberg ripple of us all.

The dream leaves me with the utter certainty that there are not just alternate realities, but that the cause and effect of long ago, right now, and the future all echo across the skein of life and into these dimensions, rippling and becoming without end.

It's the quintessential ayahuasca paradigm as the natives see and understand it: Our world is a dream constantly shifting and quantumly adjusting itself to the parallel processes at work across infinity, and every day when we awake we are no wiser to the change. Everything affects everything because it is all one big multidimensional whole, a cosmic "Rubik's Cube" being played by us, the pieces in motion.

I remember what Brian said back in San Francisco, how the very nature of the culture there was shaped by ayahuasca and the perception of reality it facilitated in those who drank it, and I understand that now on the most intimate level.

I wake in a cold sweat despite the heat, and realize that I'd fallen asleep last night with Pedro resting coolly on my forehead. I'd been feeling pretty low—the enormity of my situation was sinking in—and

I'd called out to Great Spirit for strength and support. I was ready to call out to just about anybody for help but I was pretty much cut off from the outside world, or at least the Western world, for any aid.

And now this dream had come upon me, this deep visionary state of mind, so familiar from ayahuasca mindstates, like a response from the beyond.

When *stones dream* their vision is older and deeper than those of us mere mortals. I cannot put in words the elegant spiritual depth that the vision showed me, but it reinvigorated me with hope and wonder at the larger forces involved in my quest, and gave me the one thing I needed: faith.

For my hero's journey was deep in the initiation phase now. The cosmic seed of my own awakened awareness was blossoming from the pressures I was under. I was on a physical quest for the magic stones, yes, but in truth there was another journey occurring inside me, a quest for self-remembrance, and a need to piece it all together.

I had to abandon myself to the moment and trust in the journey, in myself, and my guides.

I knew now that I had to reconnect to the expanded awareness of unity that ayahuasca had first shown me, but this time without the medicine. The stones, like the plants, have much magic in them, the depth of which was only now starting to seep through to me. I've been so caught up in my ayahuasca quest, and learning about the vegetal world, that I'd been blind to the other layers of Gaian intelligence. The stones were older and deeper than the plants, and had even more subtle energies to connect with.

And my fate was now in their hands.

I rise with the dawn, removing gear from my backpack to make room for the stones I'm sure I will find today. I meet up with Emilio at 7:00 a.m. outside his café; he's still looking tired and haggard, but part of me suspects he loves the adventure, nonetheless. Escorting crazy gringos into the boondocks of the Amazon has to be better than pottering around the kitchen listening to the same old stories from the same old regulars.

Over coffee Emilio tells me the bad news: we can't take the *motor-carro* as planned because the rains last night have swamped the roads. Instead he herds me towards a *collectivo* boat going back to Contamana, patiently repeating the same unintelligible phrase in Spanish that does little to assuage my fears.

I can't figure out what's going on. I have no other choice but to trust Emilio, but just in case I'm being sidetracked I run back to the hostel and repack my bags, taking everything I own with me. My best option may be to just stay on the Contamana boat, I reason, and call this whole crazy mission off.

After ten minutes or so the sky cracks open and a heavy rain pours down, blanketing the boat in a wall of water and slowing it to a stop. Everything appears to be going wrong—despite the prophetic feel of my dream—and when the *collectivo* lurches roughly to the right and the engine gives out struggling against the current, well, I figure we might all drown, or maybe I could just swim to shore and live like the natives do.

The boat pushes through the waves and the crew manages to kick-start the engine before trailing slowly by the shoreline, dropping us off at the same point we started from yesterday. As I plunge past my knees in the mud a surge of adrenaline flows through me, and for the first time on this long river journey I feel engaged, hands on, like I'm driving and not just a passenger. This is the call to adventure that sets the game in motion.

Emilio and I walk through the jungle, past Julio's hut and the cows, but this time he takes a parallel path to the river, through the woods towards *la cocha,* a small inlet lake that Julio told him about yesterday.

The lake is full of sedimentary rocks like the hot springs that crumble when you touch them and we fossick about for a good hour or more without finding any *encantos.* The rain continues to fall around us and Emilio has just about given up when we spy a running stream that meanders down from the hills, a tributary of the hot springs far above.

I drop my backpack and jump straight into the warm waters, feeling the power of Pachamama flowing hot around me. The hard, smooth touch of the stones press against the soles of my feet as I stare down through the tumbling waters and precious jewels shine back at me. I plunge my hands deep into the glistening water and pull out *encantos*— flat, circular, smooth stones worn down by millions of years rest here in the riverbed, absorbing the deep prana of the earth. Their energy radiates from them through the palms of my hands and into my body, connecting me with the earth and on into the cosmic ecology.

This is it: the mother lode. Thank you, *la madre sagrade*.

As if in response the rain starts pouring down hard again, washing the earth. I take off my shirt and fossick up and down the stream, up to my knees in the mud and feeling out more jewels with my toes. I can't help but marvel at the sheer number of beautiful, hard stones in the water here, hundreds and hundreds of the precious niños: grays and brown, burnt umber, magenta and cream shades glistening in the light.

But then it hits me not to let my excitement overwhelm my sense of respect and sovereignty for the magic of this place. This is sacred space, and I am humbled by it, the water tumbling past me and the storm drenching me with its essence overhead, cleansing me.

Each stone is a precious gem that I kiss and bless and thank for letting me hold it. I pick the best ones, some bigger than my head, others tiny heart-shaped beauties that fit in the palm of my hand, magic stones all. Soon there are too many to fit the bag—a cheap striped plastic number I brought back in Pucallpa at the port—and I have to put some stones back and start sorting by weight and color. I feel like a kid in a candy store trying to squeeze in as many precious things into my bag as possible.

It must weigh fifty kilos or more, and I still have to carry it out of the stream, an hour back through the jungle to the river, and hitch a boat back to town. After that I have to travel two days on the river back to Pucallpa, and then via bus to Lima and on to Cuzco, deep in the Andes. Guestimating the distance from the one map I have of Peru, printed off the internet, it could be up to 1,800 km by boat and road, lugging my precious cargo as well as my full backpack and media gear. But I'll deal with that challenge when I'm out of this stream and the torrential storm that is still raining down on me.

A wave of relief floods me, and validation that I am doing the right thing. I wonder if Emilio sees me merely as another cultural plunderer, an extreme tourist coming to this sacred spot on the river to steal these stones. It doesn't feel like that to me, but if anyone else said they'd gone to the Amazon and carried off a bag full of precious stones it'd sure ring warning signs on my cultural radar.

But the path I'd taken getting here was too synchronistic, too mythological not to harbor larger forces. The chain of events that brought stone magic into my life and the unfolding of the mission for Tessa all fit some larger pattern, I could feel it in my bones.

Suddenly something Ron Wheelock said to me back in Iquitos about the plants—and the stones—working through us humans comes to me . . .

"What I have seen with ayahuasca—we're all doing exactly what we need to do, subconsciously. We're not aware that we're doing these things . . . When I went to the Smithsonian Institute . . . I [was] walking around the museum observing all these precious stones, [and] these stones start coming through me in other languages. I started understanding things in other languages these stones were telling me:

"People have brought us here to observe our beauty, but they really don't understand we're very powerful. They've gathered us all up here and we're waiting for the right time to release all of our energy, and we could not have done this without man's help."

The Gaian intelligence knows exactly what it's doing, of course, and the stones need humans to move themselves into the proper configuration. In a direct experiential way I believe these Amazonian stones have chosen me as their emissary, as naturally as a burr chooses an animal to carry it across a forest. There's no ego involved in this, but a humble recognition that I am engaged in a greater process, that I can be of use to the stones in bringing them out of their berth and disseminating their power into the world.

How strange to think that these holy stones will now travel from the steamy heart of the Amazon jungle to the center of the Andes mountains, to Cuzco, where the Inca empire once held court. But then, after the kaleidoscopic dream Pedro had brought me, I seemed to sense a connection between the stones and the ayahuasca patterns the Shipiba women still sew on their fabrics, as if all the threads of the mystery were being tied together as the tapestry of my journey inched towards completion.

Emilio picks a few choice *encantos* for himself and as the rain pours down we prepare to go. My bag strains against the bulk of the stones but the seams hold and I slip my arms through the handles and take the weight onto my shoulders and back. With a Herculean effort I struggle up the slippery mud slopes of the stream and gather up my other backpack and sleeping bag, cursing the fact that I've brought all my luggage with me and now have to carry the full load, as well as the stones, in this torrential rain.

Each step is a miracle, but there is no other way but forward. Slipping my bags over my shoulder I take measure of this, the weight I am to bear in the world. It takes every erg of energy I have, but somehow it stops right at the edge of my ability to do it, no more or less. I am being sorely tested but I can do it, and the stones know this, too. I stagger out of the stream and back into the jungle, letting the rain pour over me.

I follow Emilio back through the muddy jungle track and we take refuge at Julio's *tambo*. He's still not home, so we take off our wet clothes and dry them on the porch while we wait for the storm to pass.

"Musico?" Emilio says with those big puppy dog eyes of his, pointing at my MiniDisc.

"Yeah, um, Shpongle—*magico electronica*. Do you want to listen?" I ask, and he nods and accepts the headphones. He's in a cheeky mood, wearing my sunglasses, and when he does a happy little dance to the music he looks like Tom Cruise in *Risky Business,* sliding along the floor. For a brief while the heaviness he usually carries with him lifts, and he has the energy of a little boy at play. It's beautiful with Emilio here, just us and the quirky relationship we have forged, two adventurers in the service of a higher good.

We eat plantains—bananas—and papayas and I smoke a *mapacho* and lie in the hammock as the weight of our mission leaves me. Emilio doesn't smoke *mapachos*—"Loco" he says, making swirling motions with his fingers to express the heavy nicotine rush they bring.

It feels like we're a million miles from anywhere, outside the bounds of civilization. And out here on the perimeter I am stoned immaculate...

"*Contento?*" Emilio asks, smiling at me.

"*Mucho contento,*" I reply.

"*Bien?*"

"*Muy bien. Encanto piedras mucho bueno. Grande bueno. Muchias gracias Emilio.*"

He smiles then, happy that I'm happy, that he can finally give up farting around the jungle in thunderstorms and return to his little café, because after a day of this, well, maybe the same old customers with their same old stories are all right, after all. And Emilio will have a few new stories to while away the days.

When the rain stops we take our precious load through the brush and across the rickety wooden bridge, over to the river and down to the muddy foreshore. It's only mid-afternoon but I feel well and truly spent, and my luggage is getting heavier and heavier as the adrenaline wears off.

I'm flushed with the thought of success though, and happy that we've found the *encantos* Tessa was after. I'm also conscious of the fact that there was no way in hell she would have been able to do this herself. It really was providence that I was guided to her back in Iquitos, and through her to the stones.

But what a fucking mission... I know you have to trust that everything happens for a reason, but in the dark moments when you have so little you cling to whatever it is you have left. You close off to the flow and become a little death. But there is so much bounty, so much abundance for us all if we only trust and believe in it, and share...

Now all we need is for a *collectivo* to come by and take us home to Orellana, but as the hours pass none of the passing boats respond to our desperate waving. As we sit here on the riverbank I joke with Emilio that I'm thinking of going to a Shetbo shaman tonight and trading an *encanto* for some ayahuasca, stone magic for plant magic. He laughs uproariously and tells me of the time he drank ayahuasca in Contamana—"*brujeria*" he says with a stern face, and makes a whooshing sound with his mouth and pantomimes throwing a dart.

"*Virotes?*" I ask. Magic darts, *brujo* weapons.

"Si, *virote.*"

Ha. Of course, the ayahuasca connection is still looking after me, even way out here in the middle of nowhere. Emilio is part of the network of the vine, this middle-aged restaurateur cum magic stone guide.

We look at each other and for a second there is a slow bloom of recognition on our faces, then we laugh.

"*Mareaciones?*"

"Si. *Whoopobbooboobooboo-cha...!*" I cry, making spiraling mudras with my fingers. "*Madre* ayahuasca told me to come here and *buscar* [look] for *encantos*," I say, as I realize how much I have been led and guided to this place.

Finally, just as dusk lowers on the horizon a lone *collectivo* boat putters our way, chasing its way to shore. Emilio and I take off our shirts and wave them through the air to attract its attention in the fading light, hollering and shouting over the sound of its engines.

And just like that we're rescued, right on time.

As if there was any doubt...

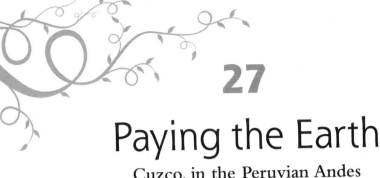

27

Paying the Earth

Cuzco, in the Peruvian Andes

Thursday 24–Friday August 25, 2006

I've been five days now in transit: two days by rickety overburdened boats back to Pucallpa, breaking down in tiny riverside ports every few hours, then a grueling twenty-four hour bus ride to Lima, and then another equally perilous and challenging journey through the barren no man's lands of the Ica desert, past the dusty Nazca lines and their totems pointing to the stars and across the break-back mountains of the Andes, dragging my bag of magic stones along with me.

Everything you hear about travel on the Andean back roads is true. The roads are a pock-marked collection of holes originally designed for mules and llamas, and never really upgraded to carry giant, overcrowded buses laden with families, luggage, and animals. The twisting, turning tracks are littered with little crosses marking the spots where previous vehicles have left the road, and if I wasn't so exhausted by the journey and the ordeal that preceded it, I'd probably be petrified by the sheer cliff drops that roll out below my window as we career through the mountains and the stark power of the landscape shines back at me.

The contrast between the jungles of the Amazon and the mountains of the Andes couldn't be any more stark: I feel as if I have stumbled into a canvas of slumbering giants covered by the folds of some gargantuan skin. Here, without the covering of the plants, Gaia has laid bare her curves and she is mesmerizing in her naked glory.

My eyes scan her terrain like a lover, feeling the folds of the earth and taking in the way the shadows dip into her hidden crevasses. Her body undulates out with an intimate beckoning, inviting me to walk upon desert sands that seem to extend out forever. There are no living creatures visible in this arid horizon, and as we hurtle past small weather-beaten villages boarded up from the winds, it seems improbable that humans could survive here, either. But regardless, or perhaps because of the vast sense of space, there is also a sense of immense spirit, free from human cultivation.

There are few plants in these flat desert wastelands, but I spot sporadic clusters of cactus on the mountains, where the sacred and hallucinogenic san pedro grows so abundantly. As with the jungle, everything is alive and holy, but you have to look a bit deeper to see the magic. Without the concentration of vegetal life it's the stones and rocks that are the dominant force here, with all the power of the sun and earth imbued in them. The plants and the stones are day and night, working on different parts of the soul, engaging different energies. One is of the jungle, one of the mountains, where *curanderos* believe the spirits, or *Apus* reside in their firmament.

All up the Andes is South America's longest mountain chain, without doubt: it's between 200–300 km wide and over 7,000 km (4,400 miles) long, with an average height of about 4,000 m (13,000 ft). Like so many things in South America the origins of the Andes name is lost to history. It resembles the Quechua word *anti,* which means "high crest," but another theory says it derives from the Spanish word *anden,* or "terrace," which fits with the vast terrace farms cultivated in the highlands by the Incas, which allowed them to feed hundreds of thousands of people in such seemingly inhospitable territory.

Finally the bus crests the last mountain and there, stretching below us is the vast valley of Cuzco, peppered with ancient adobe homes with tiled roofs. The streets are clogged with cars and buses, smoke and pollution, billboards and traffic: the classic mix of old world and new. It's a long way from the original capital of the Inca, who thought that the entire universe was an endless realm of sacred corners—*Tahuantinsuy*—that centered here on Cuzco, the navel of their world, right where the Plaza de Armas is today, lined by Spanish churches and gift shops. Twenty-first-century Cuzco has a population of around 300,000 which has tripled in the last twenty years, and it's one of the top tourist destinations in South America.

Cuzco was built by Sapa Inca Pachacuteq, the first Incan king, sometime in the twelfth or early thirteenth century. Legend has it he planned the design of the city to be shaped like a puma: the main plaza was the belly; the river Tullumayo the spine; and the hills of Sacsayhuaman were the head. The puma is the Amazonian spirit totem that connects heaven and earth, and after my own experiences with the spirit of the puma back at the Refugio Altiplano, galloping with it through the heavens, the idea of a whole city sculpted to these sacred geometries was mind-blowing.

Yet it was indicative of the way the Inca saw the world, intrinsically entwined with an appreciation of energy both on earth and in the heavens above. It was also intimately similar to the ayahuasca-inspired perception of the unity of all things, and the multidimensional reality of the cosmic eco-system.

The bus drops me off a few miles out of the historic center of Cuzco and I take a taxi, bargaining the driver down to only fifteen soles this time, and I get dropped off in the winding, centuries-old streets of San Blas, just past the church. Burdened with two backpacks and the heavy bag of *piedras,* I struggle up narrow, cobblestone streets, awash with enthusiasm for this fresh, clean city, full of other gringos and the friendly faces of locals dressed in their Andean blankets and clothes.

Looking back down from above San Blas, the towering baroque architecture of the Jesuit church, Iglesia La Compania de Jesus peers majestically over the skyline. Yet under all the tourist trappings there's a dark story that runs through Cuzco and bears witness to the first wave of Western contact here over five hundred years ago. Each grand and ornate church was built with the blood of Indian slaves, who constructed over the remains of the old Inca city, replacing their time-honored temples with Catholic churches and their palaces with mansions for their masters.

The Spanish invaders had arrived at a most propitious time: the Inca empire was overburdened with the sudden weight of its own borders, and a war was raging between two brothers, Huascar and Atahualpa, sons of the previous Inca, Huayna Capac, for control of the empire. What's worse, smallpox brought by the advance wave of European explorers had cut a deep gouge into the population and was showing no signs of abating.

Change was afoot for the Incas, and curiously enough their own prophecies foretold it. Their legends spoke of the return of *Quetzalcoatl,* the "white god," whose arrival was timed by their calendars for the very day that Pizarro's boat arrived. Pizarro sacked Cuzco in 1535 and the Spanish instigated a brutal repression of the indigenous people and their culture, enslaving a member of each family throughout the land into the *mita,* or public service system, where they were worked until they dropped, mining gold and silver for the Spanish.

What's worse, when a family member inevitably died after a year or two of service in the mines, the family was forced to then send a replacement, an assembly line of death to feed the conquerors' desire for riches. *All of this history embedded in these streets, built with the blood of Indians, welcoming me home.*

I check into the Casa de la Gringa, the new age hangout recommended to me by Bowman as the san pedro connection in town. It's a lush hippie oasis full of light, comfy couches and cushions, polished floorboards, Andean clothes and textiles for sale, free internet access, and a TV room! Moreover, for the first time in two months in Peru I'm staying somewhere classy enough to have hot water. And there, in the lobby, a whiteboard with, "Next san pedro session Thursday 10:00 a.m. Participants: Javier, Anna, Bill . . ." Finally free of all my bags I set out down the narrow alleyways to soak in this new city and all its delights.

Leslie, the ageing hippie matriarch who runs Casa de la Gringa, and radiates beautiful white light everywhere she goes, gives me a basic rundown on the state of play here, then sends me down to One Planet, a backpacker specialist travel store near the Plaza de Armas, where her sons work. As well as the run of the mill Machu Picchu and Sacred Valley tours, One Planet also displays brochures for its san pedro circles, which are run by Leslie, or, when she is too busy, by another of her staff.

Her son has a South African accent and is a stocky lad with a ruddy face in his mid-twenties, who looks like he'd be most comfortable at an Irish Pub downing some Guinness. "It's a full day ceremony, it's a ten hour journey, or you can do it at night," he explains, pointing at the brochure as if it's just another tourist attraction to experience like the ruins of *Sacsayhuaman*. "Rock the Casbah" by the Clash is playing in the background and I feel like I should be doing shots of Jaggermeister and flirting with blonds at the counter.

"What's better?" I ask him. "The daytime because of the visuals, or the night?"

"San pedro can really connect you to the earth," he replies, "so it's often done during the day or in the forest, up in the hills behind Cuzco, in nature. We often conduct ceremonies up at the Temple of the Moon, an Inca site. It can get tiring at night, but it depends what your timing is..." The san pedro tourist experience has been running strong here for over fifteen years and they get dozens upon dozens of gringos coming to try it each week, at around U.S. $60 a go.

Very lucrative for the tour operators, but Leslie and her staff have the right attitude, growing their own cactus and slowly cooking it in boiling water for over eighteen hours, nurturing the spirit in the plant. "You know you're doing it with the best," he finishes, hoping he's clinched the sale. At U.S. $70 for the full day ceremony, or U.S. $90 for the night ceremony, you'd certainly hope so.

There's nothing wrong with his sales pitch and he does take the time to explain as best he can what the experience will entail, but it's so short an explanation—and done as part of a sales transaction—that it leaves me feeling sad. Sad not just for the way the san pedro experience has been diluted down to just another commodity, but for the people taking it in this context. It's not so different from the ayahuasca retreats in Iquitos and the commercialization of the sacred there, but Cuzco has been at it longer and has such a more robust tourist market that everything seems more extreme.

But still, *do the plants care?* If the humans are still having the experience, making the connection with the planet, does it matter to them if they come to it via an EFTPOS transaction in a brightly-lit travel shop that plays Top-40 pop music, or via an indigenous *curandero* trained in the subtleties of the art that only accepts cash? The difference, as I'd learned with ayahuasca, is the *intent.*

Bowman rhapsodized to me about his recent san pedro experiences here a few weeks ago, in an email he'd sent after he'd left Iquitos. Unlike ayahuasca, which can be a bit hit-and-miss, delivering healing but not the visions that the Western seekers are often chasing, san pedro delivers a mescaline-fuelled hallucinogenic space, every time. Or as Bowman said, "*The hills had eyes.*"

I step off the busy tourist-laden footpath of Calle Triunto and into a cool little courtyard housing the "Shaman Shop"—an indigenous crafts and culture business against the far wall, with long totem poles and drums adorning them like a clutch of cacti. A real potted san pedro sits proudly just before the door, where a puma, an eagle, and a snake are carved into the logo above the entrance. Wooden facemasks adorn the doorway, with information brochures on sweat lodges and ayahuasca ceremonies filling the last available space.

The wood-and-glass cabinet on the wall to the left has a noticeboard for the shop, with a picture of an Indian overlooking Machu Picchu, a smoke figure forming in the bowl before him. "Esoteric Tourism" the slogan reads:

> Peru is the new cosmic and spiritual centre of the earth
> where the new spiritual way born "Septrionismo"
> that will guide humanity
> in the millennium of the light

Under that it lists the shaman's email, cell phone, and landline phone details, and wait, there's more:

SPECIAL SERVICES

Share the experiment in the drinking of Sacred Plants
(Ayahuasca, San Pedro and Others)
Get To Know Ancient And Religious Places
Of Ancient Peru and Live Shamanic Experiences
Grest [sic] At The Apus (sacred Mountains)
Energy At Magnetic Places (feel It)
Icaros (Shamanic Singing) Pichay Ceremony
(Purification) Meditation And Camp Fire
Payment To Mother Earth Chacchar
(Coca Leaf Chew) Mother Moon Ceremony
CONSULT YOUR FUTURE WITH THE SACRED COCA-
LEAF OF THE INCAS

Andean pipe music wafts through the inside of the shop as bored counter staff look up at me expectantly. New age aphorisms hang on the walls alongside crafts, t-shirts, and other paraphernalia that hint at the spiritual nature of Peru and indigenous shamanism. This could be a chain-stall with branches in Camden Market, San Francisco, Byron Bay, and hip, New Age villages across the globe. I feel like I'm at a fast-soul restaurant, feeding on the prepackaged food of the gods.

There are dozens upon dozens of shamans and neo-shamanic practitioners here in Cuzco, the vast majority of them catering to the gringo dollar. Tourism fuels Cuzco, and shamanism and indigenous spirituality play a key role in that. After five hundred years the competition is fierce, and the *brujeria* is rumored to be even fiercer.

But since San Francisco I've largely made my peace with the spiritual tourism industry. No one argues about the need or appropriateness of greengrocers selling fresh fruit and vegetables. As long as the shop is clean and respectable, well, you can choose organic, you know. And locally grown. Ultimately the intent of the consumer will be matched by the intent of the seller. If the intent isn't right with shamanism, perhaps the free market will regulate it, as well?

Still, there's something holistic in the supply-and-demand flow chain that connects North and South America. How uncanny that the Inca legends foretold not just the return of the white god five hundred years ago, which signaled the end of the classic Inca civilization, but also that the great-great descendants of the Spanish conquerors would be foremost among those now coming to sample the spiritual practices their forefathers almost extinguished. The elders say that the eagles of the North cannot be free without the condors of the South, and their prophecies predict that now, when the eagle of the North and the condor of the South fly together, the Earth will awaken.

What an elegant understanding of the current global paradigm embedded within the ancient Inca prophecies. And what potent times we live in, with massive earth changes already afoot, just as predicted.

It's not enough to say that the resurgence in global shamanism is fuelled by a deep-seated need for the materialist West to reconnect to the planet—under the surface there is a larger karmic force at work healing the imbalances between old world and new, the earth-based culture and the technosphere. As the prophecies say, *neither side can be free without the other.*

In a similar way, perhaps with spiritual tourism we're not quite clear on what's really going on, filtering the changes through own our limited paradigm. Perhaps, as indigenous cultures are saying, the earth isn't just reacting to what we've done to it; perhaps it is awakening.

Perhaps we all are—tourists, seekers, and planet alike.

Later that night, at a small cheap restaurant next to Jack's Bar, in the main tourist strip, I meet Luco, a dark-skinned local in his mid-twenties dressed in Andean winter wear: an alpaca beanie, jumper, black beard, and a smile.

"Where are you from?" he asks in the eternal spiel of someone who wants to be your friend and sell you something.

"Australia," I say, "and you?"

"Iquitos," he replies, and I warm to him immediately. "Do you want to buy some weed?"

"No thanks. But hey, do you know where I can buy some *mapachos?*" I say, motioning for him to come eat at my table. "I walked all over town today for a couple of miles and couldn't see any anywhere at the usual roadside stalls. In Iquitos they're everywhere—as I'm sure you know." I size him up and decide he's on the level—or as close as I've met thus far in Cuzco—and I decide to open up. "I didn't smoke till the spirit of ayahuasca told me I would have to get to know *mapacho,* if I was to learn the ways of the vine . . ."

Luco smiles as he joins the table. "My father is a shaman in Iquitos, near Nauta," he says. "Have you been there?"

"No, I didn't make it to Nauta, the furthest I got was about Km 48 at another *curandero's* retreat."

"Who did you drink with?" he asks as he drags on his cigarette.

"I went for that shaman conference in late June. Touristy, set for Westerners, but it was a good introduction, a starting point, y'know? I drank with Guillermo, Norma Pandura, Don Juan out by the airport, and after the conference with Javier, this local *curandero* who treats the community—very good—and at Sachamama, of course, and with others."

He nods. "You can get *mapachos* out by the san pedro markets," he says. "No one smokes it here much—they call it *brujeria*. It's too strong for them, it affects their mind, a bit like weed. You sure you don't want some?"

"Nah, thanks. It's ayahuasca and *mapacho* all the way for me. And maybe now san pedro, I dunno, it seems like that's the thing to do here. Do you know any good *curanderos* in Cuzco?"

"The san pedro ones are common," he says, and for a second he has that same black glint in his eyes as Guillermo had, the condor eyes. "It's better, you know, than ayahuasca. The ayahuasca is not safe here. I mean, it is the spirits the ayahuasca connects you to, *they* are not good here. *Too much bloodshed,* you know what I mean?" he says, holding out his fingers and making the shape of a gun with his forefinger and thumbs, like in a Hollywood shoot up.

"Too much history, too much Spanish murder. The spirits here are angry, and dark—you don't want to do ayahuasca here, my friend." And with that he's finished his meal as well as his spiel. Luco smiles and we shake hands and that's it, he's gone, off to hustle weed to another tourist, I suspect. But his words linger long after he is gone.

I'm very tired and it's been a long day, so after a quick internet fix at one of the numerous net cafes that dot the side streets around San Blas, I head back to Casa de la Gringa for an early night. I've left a phone message with Kevin Furnas letting him know I'm in town, and yet another email for Tessa telling her that I had the stones.

There had been no word from her since Iquitos, and I wasn't sure she was even coming. I was perilously low on funds after topping up in Pucallpa after my Amazon mission, and I wouldn't be able to actually do anything in Cuzco and have enough money to get to the airport in Lima exactly one week from today if she didn't come through with her promise for reimbursement. Once again, all I could do was trust.

Back at *la casa* I lay there in my warm, clean bed, surrounded by blankets on the walls decorated with framed prints of indigenous Indians and wolves against hallucinogenic desert backgrounds. On the far wall is a framed poster quoting the Cree Indians:

> "Only when the last river has been polluted, Only when
> the last fish has been caught, Only then will you find that
> money cannot be eaten."

Ironic for a tourist hostel, but indicative of the spiritual tourism dynamic that I've seen so often throughout Iquitos and Pucallpa, and now embodied in this ancient and yet cosmopolitan city around me. It was also another direct reminder from spirit not to worry about money.

It's been a long, long journey, yet despite it all I can't get to sleep. I clutch Pedro, my magic stone, over my heart, and again I implore it to help me on my path, to unblock obstacles, and to bring me knowledge and strength. The stone is cold on my skin—even through my jumper—and it takes time to equilibrize with me, my energy entering it and its energy entering me.

Eventually, after an hour or so of being awake with closed eyes, I dream.

In the dream it's the same as before: the fractaling kaleidoscope of cause and effect, populated with avatars battling each other in the perennial struggle between good and evil, yin and yang, order and chaos. Again the awareness fills me of the pattern they-we make with our lives: lifetime after lifetime unfolds before me in colorful karmic explosions—rainbowing vibrational wavefronts that interact and affect each other, rippling like a constant stream of stones dropped into the surface of the world pond, or magnetic tape being overwritten again and again. *The phoenix rising from the ashes of its own desire.*

It's an exact analogue of the DMT visions, those kaleidoscoping lightshows that are visual representations of sound and the vibrational wavelengths of innerspace. The stone is showing me energy patterns, but this time it's more personal, and instead of watching from a distance, I'm caught up in the thundering whirlpool of it all.

This is no mere dream, I realize, not twice, not from the same stone. This is the thing behind all my plant and stone visions, behind the game of us all. The vast cosmic blueprint that underlies creation is visible now, tantalizingly real and showing me its secrets, and it's so simple it's almost hard to believe . . .

The secret that cannot be spoken is offering itself before me, but words fail me in describing it. I feel like I'm seeing myself one pixel at a time from within the universal photo. And a particle can only know the reality of the wave for a second before the crest of consciousness moves on.

Yet in truth, somewhere deep within us, where some essence of cosmic awareness lies, you know this as well as I. But if we say it, IT changes the rules, *and the mystery must remain a mystery.*

One thought comforts me as I lose my grip of self-awareness and tumble deeper into the dream, then sleep:

It's not about the knowing.

It's about the being.

The next morning there's a gentle knock that wakes me from my sleep, and I open the door to the grinning face of Kevin Furnas, dressed in a brown alpaca poncho with cream stripes and a straw hat.

"Hello my friend," he says in a gentle tone, his hazel eyes sparkling out at me with a warm energy. "I hope I haven't woken you . . ."

"Well, actually . . . no, it's fine, it's great to see you, you got my message last night, then? It's just . . . ah . . . y'see, I was just having this intense dream . . . it's hard to explain, but I think it's this stone . . ." I say, showing him Pedro.

He takes it carefully and runs his hand over the smooth surface, closing his eyes and tuning in on its energy.

"Mmmmm . . . uhuh . . . uhuh . . . yeah, okay," he says, as if listening to it. Then suddenly his clear blue eyes are open and staring at me. "This is a very powerful stone, my friend. And it tells me it's a long way from its home . . . You've been on a big mission, haven't you?"

"You could say that," I smile. "Y'know, I went halfway up the bloody Peruvian Amazon in search of healing stones for Tessa, but in the end I think it was the stones that drew me there for their own reasons. And this one," I say, as Kevin passes Pedro back to me, "has twice now transmitted these very ayahuasca-type dreams to me . . . I feel like I'm playing out some karmic role in this enormous cosmic drama, some sort of *game that we're all in on . . .*"

Kevin smiles at me as he adjusts his poncho and sits down at the edge of the bed, casting his eagle eyes around at the posters and décor. "Ha. That's pretty much it, my friend," he says. "This is the University of Life, and I'm here to pick up where your stone teacher left off," he laughs. "I dieted with the stones at Sachamama, y'know. You bathe them in hot water to cleanse them and drink the water, or meditate on the stone. Most people get hooked on the energy of the plants, like ayahuasca, and they overlook the fact that the stones can be just as powerful," he explains.

Kevin crooks his head on a funny angle then, as if he's looking through me, not at me, reading my energy or something, then he smiles. "Listen, I know it's early, but I've got to head down to the markets and get some things, and I thought you might like to come? There's a group of us going out to the Sacred Valley tomorrow, it might be a nice introduction for you. And you can buy a poncho. In Cuzco, even the spirits wear ponchos."

"Sure, I'd love to."

The *mercado* is a sprawling, bustling hub of food, spices, plants, clothes, locals, and tourists all mingling together. Two middle aged men with tired faces trade notes between the stalls as a heavy-stocked woman behind them thumps a steak over and over on a wooden board, tenderizing it. Children play *futbol* in the rows between the stalls while local Peruvians stream up and down, shopping for their fresh fruit and vegetables.

Kevin and I stop at a sandwich bar and sit down next to two thin, caramel-skinned Peruvian girls in Rolling Stones t-shirts showing big Mick Jagger lips, nursing their lattes. Behind our stall a fruitier drops some onions and scrabbles for them on the ground, then bumps into a local woman who has her hands tied up with shopping bags, sending them both sprawling.

Suddenly each moment freezes in an elongated staccato montage like some DMT-flashback. It's a subtler version of the same type of time dilation that I experienced back at Love Creek, that awareness of vibratory patterns reflecting and interacting with each other. It makes me think of the two dreams I've now had showing me those Level Ten ayahuasca "brainwave" readouts, and how similar they were to the intricate alpha waves that ripple across the Shipibo vibratory canvases.

Here now, watching everyone to and fro-ing in their beautifully mundane roles, it strikes me that the waves we create are just like those

Shipibo patterns, that we may be the physical manifestation of those same energetic blueprints, *the thought forms of the Divine.*

Seen from above, this city and its people, or any populated region on earth is the same: buzzing with the vibratory patterns of sentient life. And the fractaling pattern of us all changes with different cultures and peoples, according to their collective level of consciousness, but there is always an underlying pattern.

"It's funny that you brought all those stones from the middle of the Amazon to here, now . . ." Kevin says, turning to me and breaking my train of thought. "This time of year is celebrated by the locals with a custom called *Hagga La Tierra*—or Paying the Earth. You put stuff inside a package that is representative of the four directions or the four elements, the different metals, vegetal stuff, some stones, some food— usually corn is considered sacred, so you put that in. Basically it's making an offering to the earth.

"The custom goes way back, before the Incas, I imagine. People used to make *manta* fabrics, or weavings, to put their offering to the earth in, and then burn them. Now it's a little bit commercialized, I guess. Most people just go to the store and buy a 'pay the earth packet,' and its full of little plastic things," he says, laughing at the kitchiness of it all.

An offering to the earth, huh? Well, that sure would explain those stones I'd brought back all the way from the Amazon, and the intuition that I'd been doing the earth's bidding in transporting them. I knew then that this was what I had come to Cuzco for: *to pay the earth.*

But first I had to pay two deeply wrinkled old Peruvian grandmothers for this beautiful handmade cream and brown-trimmed Alpaca poncho, which Kevin managed to haggle down to about sixty soles because of a small hole that had been badly restitched on the back.

And with my physical armor now as equipped as my spiritual armor, we head back from whence we came, two amigos blending in with the crowd.

❈ ❈ ❈

Kevin and I pass some time mingling with the other tourists, then head towards Paddy O'Flanerhy's, the Irish pub in the center of Cuzco. We walk up the creaky wooden stairs and into a saloon decked out with Guinness posters and Inca skulls, wooden floors and big tables, occupied by homogenous gringo tourists with mainly British accents.

Kevin's friend Mira, who's from Slovakia, is working behind the bar and greets us with a smile, pulling back her long dark dreadlocks from her cherubic face, adorned with a ring in her nose.

"So…" she says in her thick European accent. "What's the news, has she arrived yet?"

"No, but she rang and is meant to be here after three," Kevin says, and she steals a glance at the clock which is getting onto four. We both share that smile that says we know what the Madam is like and we'll both go with the flow and when she turns up she turns up, if indeed, she does turn up at all.

It's not really Kevin's environment, so after introducing me to Mira he heads back to his home up on the Inca Road, above San Blas. Mira tends the bar and talks to me between serving punters. She helps me navigate a path into Machu Picchu for my mission a few days from now, following a trail Kevin has shown her.

It's a bush track just before the entrance that skirts around the side and enters up over the lip of the mountain, bypassing the exorbitant gate fees that I simply can't afford. It seems like a plan, and just as we finish that, lo and behold, a flash of blond hair streaks into the bar and a tattooed galaxy-arm rests on my shoulder, and Tessa gives me a big kiss.

"Rak! I just got your message, I can't believe you're here, I thought you'd probably given up on the whole mission!"

"Not bloody likely," I say. "I've got something special to show you back in my hostel when you're ready." After a brief reunion with Mira, the Madam and I take to the streets to go back to Casa de la Gringa, stopped literally every hundred meters by someone Tessa knows saying hello and catching up as well.

Finally we get back to my room and I lug the plastic carry bag with the stones over from the base of the bed and unpack them one by one, placing them on a large ayahuasca *manta* embroidery I'd bought back in Pucallpa. There are twenty-six stones in all, covered in dried mud, flashing through with streaks of pink, aqua, and marine like veins.

"You must've been Superman!" Tessa cries at the sight of them all laid out, glittering their magic. "I tell you what, you must've had some divine help to get you through, that's all I can say, because this is just not physically possible . . . You're not that big!"

"It was at my limits," I admit, "but not beyond. And I was happy to do it. It was a grand adventure."

"Look at this one, the mud on it's twinkling," she says with a laugh. "Unbelievable . . . This is real Pachamama mud, yeah . . . amazing . . . This one's perfect for the solar plexus," and she grins as she holds a thick teal stone against her stomach. "And this one will be good for healing work on somebody's arm. And this one," grabbing a head-sized fossil with two openings either side like mouths, "this one is whistling at me. Oh, my . . . I just can't believe you managed to bring so many of these back with you!"

"Well I know that no other gringo has been to where I've been, and gotten what I've gotten. And been *allowed* to by the spirits. I felt like I didn't just do it—I was the messenger and the intermediary for what spirit wants to be done in the world, and now you've got that same mission, Tessa. So I think it's time you pull back those blankets you say you hide under all the time, and get out of the bloody bed. There's work to be done."

Tessa laughs, nervously but happily, and I know I've got under her defenses and that my message has gotten through. *The stones' message* has gotten through. She launches into a traditional Shipibo *icaro* then, whistling the slow-mo spaghetti-western notes into the end of the stone with the two mouths.

"I think this one is a *timekeeper*," she says finally, looking at me intently. "They call them *Goddess stones* or *witch stones* in England. It's an instrument . . . but I can use it to scrye, to divine . . . These are tools for me, and now I have to get to know them.

"Look at the layers on this one," she says excitedly, like a little girl. "That's the spiritual journey, isn't it? Peeling back the layers. You never know till you get all the way back to the foundation how strong you really are." Tears form in her eyes as she runs her fingers lightly over the spread of stones.

"Oh, I've got to give one to Kevin," she cries, nursing a gray anvil-shaped stone that fits in the palm of her hand. "This one is a dream stone . . ."

"Yeah . . . it'd be good to share them around. I've received a strong knowing from these stones that each one has its own destination. They've all got somewhere that they're meant to go, and that's why I was allowed to bring them here, to you. And through you, the others . . . It's a *responsibility*, Tessa. I've brought them this far, and now it's up to you. This is how we repay the earth for what she's done for us, do you *understand?*"

"*Oh my . . .*" she begins, as the power and responsibility of the stones dawns on her. "Of course . . . *Hagga La Tierra . . .*"

And the mission is complete.

28
Talking with Kevin
The Sacred Valley, Ollantaytambo
SATURDAY AUGUST 26, 2006

Ollantaytambo is an ancient Inca fortress/temple nestled in the Uru-bamba Valley, surrounded on all sides by languid mountains that break against the sky. The base of the mountains are strewn with plantation terraces made from finely cut stones, with ruined forts, temples, and battlements further up the incline that hint of the mountain civilization that existed here in its prime, almost three thousand meters above sea level. Some ruins are perched on such isolated juts of rock that it seems as if they must have sprouted there organically, for surely no human hand could build them on the hips of these towering giants. *But the Incas did.*

Ollantaytambo was built over pre-Inca ruins during the reign of Pachacuti in the mid-fifteenth century. By the time the Spanish *conquistadores* sacked Cuzco in 1535, Maco Inca, the emperor of the time, retreated to Ollantaytambo, where he used its strategic location, including the fortified gates and guard houses and the naturally steep slopes and vertical walls, to temporarily hold back the Spanish invaders.

Five hundred years later, the invaders are unstoppable, decked out with sun hats, video cameras, water bottles, and backpacks. Constant streams of *touristos* pile out of a fleet of supersize tour buses that have pulled up in the car park, only to swarm around the central square, with its potted trees and neatly cultivated beds of grass. There must be hundreds of people here all desperately looking for some relief from the late morning sun, studying their maps and guide books as they prepare to brave the cobblestone-street gauntlet past all the handicraft sellers and head down towards the main section of town to really get their ruins on.

"Ollantaytambo was basically the Andes' connection to the forest," Kevin explains as we get off our rickety local bus and gather on the sidewalk. "It was the main connection point between the jungle and Cuzco, so there were Incan ideas being passed to the forest, and ideas from the forest were working through up here..."

I'm here with Kevin, Mira—the cute Slovakian girl from Paddy O'Flanerhy's—and Ricardo, a Peruvian in his forties with sharp eyes, bushy black eyebrows, and puffy cheeks. He tells me he's originally from Puno, that he's been drinking with Kevin for some months, and that he's discovered a latent ability to shape change, taking on the form of a *puma*.

I talk to stones and Kevin talks to plants, and I'm sure Mira has her own spiritual idiosyncrasies, so I'm inclined at this late stage in the game to take what he says at face value. And he does have this feline quality about him, slinking through the crowd like a hunter stalking prey...

We're surrounded by tourists on all sides so we bunker down in the small enclosed square to get our bearings, under a ten-foot statue of Maco Inca himself, his finely cut profile looking down on us commandingly. Interestingly enough, his shield bears an Incan symbol that reminds me of the ayahuasca patterns: squiggly energy lines radiating from a central square. As I'm analyzing the entheographic cues in the indigenous art, Kevin wanders off and starts talking to a drooping *toé* plant in a fenced off enclosure. He stops and sings the *toé icaro*, concentrating on it intently for a minute, then turns to us and says, "Ha... they're always surprised when a human, and a gringo at that, sings their *icaro* to them. Like, where'd you learn that, y'know?"

If this was any other person I'd think twice about talking to plants in a car park—but this is the Sacred Valley, and as well as being a gringo, Kevin is a shaman—he's meant to talk to spirits. Even though it felt like a scene from a shamanic version of *Seinfeld*, I knew that this must be what it's like to walk in two worlds at the same time.

For Kevin had followed through on the path that I, and other *aya-huasqueros* like me, were just beginning to tread. He'd meshed the *cos-movision* of the indigenous world with the Western paradigm in ways that I still struggled with. But still, here, in the car park? Part of me has to wonder: Is he just fooling himself, listening to voices in his head? Or is he so sensitive that he hears and sees what we don't?

One thing I do know: Kevin has had lots of practice talking with plant spirits. When he trained at Sachamama he didn't have Francisco or a human teacher for most of his time there. For twenty months he dieted exclusively with the plants and they were his teachers, in the time-honored Amazonian style. A *toé* plant in a car park then, was right up his alley. As Kevin wrote in his 2005 essay, published on *ayahuasca.com,* "Plant Sentience as Seen Through a Shamanic Worldview," "Once the perceptual barrier is breached humans can easily interact with sentient vegetative life forms [...] an individual begins to hear the voices of his teachers and thus learns to communicate telepathically with plants [...] Generally speaking, humans are considered to be on the *receiving* end of this relationship and knowledge is bestowed by plant teachers who are thought of as wise elders and are often referred to as parents or grandparents."

In the essay Kevin goes on to say, "In truth, once we even garner the possibility of plant intelligence, we are invariably forced to question our own deeply entrenched views about the natural world and our roles in relation to it. Fear has prevented any real inquiry into the matter, for if such a Copernican idea was to be accepted the repercussions would alter the very fabric of reality as accepted by the modern world. Has Western thought strayed so far from its moorings in the scientific method that it now trembles at the possibility of a new hypothesis?"

Well of course it does, but as always, Kevin's too nice to really rock the boat. Accepting *plant sentience* would be a monumental world shift that could obliterate everything we hold dear. All that comfort and glamour, built on a pyramid-marketing scheme as old as history—all that would have to go. A good glimpse behind the curtain would reveal the workings of the play forever more, and after that the lights would go on and the real work would begin. *Is there anything more threatening to the globalized lockdown of the mainstream paradigm?*

I tell Kevin this and he smiles at me wryly. I've been experiencing a sustained shift in consciousness these last two months in Peru and the dimensions beyond, a deep cosmic perspective, but to integrate it into my conscious self and put it into practice it really helped to have someone like Kevin around. He was only a year older than me, and was quickly taking on a big brother role for me in this newfound world of *Apus* and Incas.

I could tell from the way Mira stared at him sweetly that she was smitten as well, and I remembered all the women who flocked to him back at the conference. But as well as being an *ayahuasquero* heartthrob, Kevin is also a role model to a lot of Western students of plant medicine. Like the other Western shamans I had encountered he was a *seed brother,* and in his example there was a burning promise that if he could bridge the worlds, we all could. The cultural firewall that kept the shamanic reality separate from the Western paradigm could be lifted.

During the bumpy, rattling public bus that we caught out from Urambumba this morning, Kevin gave me the download of his life, and how this sensitive, new age soul ended up talking to plants in Incan car parks. Strangely enough, it's a pretty archetypal story:

He was born into a normal, respectable family in San Francisco, but rejected the trappings of that life. Like many seekers, he spent his late teenage years searching for a meaning the mainstream culture couldn't provide. In his early twenties he traveled the world for ten years, on the spiritual path, herding yaks across the Tibetan Himalayas, ingesting *teonanacti,* the magic mushrooms in remote Mexican villages, and ultimately tracing the roots of ayahuasca to Peru, where he trained as a *vegetalista,* one who works with healing plants.

In those same ten years I'd worked for a small-press electronic music magazine, had my own spiritual awakenings at outdoor roof parties and grappled with the Divine, had a daughter, a relationship break up, founded a website or three, and been enmeshed in the mainstream corporate nine to five, all the while harboring a secret desire to learn more about shamanism and connect to the magic of life, of which I had experienced brief snatches.

Our paths, while superficially different, led to the same source, and here we were now in the car park of what used to be the most sacred of sites in the whole Sacred Valley.

"So what's the plan?" Ricardo says as Kevin leads us into the center of town, then hangs a sharp right on one of the main cobblestone streets. The high walls of the buildings each side and the long straight streets trimmed by guttering create the feel of a labyrinth, herding us forward.

"I thought we'd avoid the usual tourist traps down by the terraces and the Temple of the Sun, and climb old Pinkyuylluna hill up here," Kevin says, pointing towards the majestic towering leviathan above us on our right, on the edge of town. "Look, can you see the face?" he cries, pointing towards the side of the mountain.

I have to shield my eyes from the sun and squint, but yeah, there on the lower edge of Pinkyuylluna there is a face, and a body as well, towering hundreds of feet high like a god of old. It's one of those optical illusions that once pointed out you can't help but see all the time: the lighter colored rock face on profile, the strong Inca nose and craggy brow, the beard.

"The locals say it's *Viracocha*, their creator God. He came down to earth on a little island in the center of Lake Titicaca called the Island of the Sun. And everywhere he walked he created form, imbuing everything with his essence. He made humans from the clay, and they built the temples here that trace the path of the sky god as he walked across the mountains to the sea and back again, creating the Sacred Valley. And there he slumbers in his firmament, watching over Ollantaytambo and his people."

"Amazing," Mira says, taking a swig from her water bottle then passing it on to me.

The face of Viracocha, which the locals call *Tunupa,* is a natural phenomenon, but the mountain also has man-made mysteries. Pinkuylluna

Hill has notches carved into it to catch the first ray of sunlight on the summer solstice, June 21. The ray shines down on what is now a field under the hill, subdivided in lots to create the shape of a pyramid. That exact spot where the light hits once served as—according to who you believe—either a storehouse of some kind, or the so-called *Pacaritanpu,* the *House of Dawn:* the house where men became God when bathed in that first light. One of the translations of Ollantaytambo is "storehouse of the gods," although most people just think of the massive plantation terraces and the ruins of the granaries on the mountainside, focusing on the material.

Peruvian archaeologists Fernando and Edgar Elorrieta Salazar argue that this type of intricate terraforming was par the course for the Incas, who sculpted their world in microcosm of the heavens above. As with Cuzco, Ollantaytambo was one of the key Incan sites in the ancient Sacred Valley. This Peruvian holy land stretched from Cuzco, towards Machu Picchu in the north, which has only in recent times assumed its role as a key tourist site; and to the south, beginning at Lake Titicaca, which at four kilometers above sea level is the highest navigable lake in the world. In the sacred landscape of the Incas that mirrored the heavens, Lake Titicaca, where Virococha was said to have landed, was also the zero point for galactic center.

It was because of their sun worship that the Inca colonized the mountainsides and tops, aligning their temples and buildings to be closer to the sun. History has it that human sacrifices, usually those of small children, were also made at the summits of holy mountains, feeding their life forces up to the sun, and from the sun onto the galactic sun, and so on in the cosmic food chain.

Father Bernabe Cobo, a Jesuit priest who journeyed through Peru in the seventeenth century, described in his book, *The History of the New World* (1653), "In the human sacrifices that were most frequently made, they offered the children that the Inca collected by way of tribute throughout the kingdom. [...] they were given plenty to eat and drink before their lives were taken. And the small children who were too young to eat were allowed to breastfeed with their mothers. It was said that they did this so that the little ones would not be hungry or unhappy when they reached the place where the *Maker* was."

Benabe went on to say that there were two main benefits of these human sacrifices: One was to "thank the sun for the trouble it took in giving light to the earth, and in helping the earth produce food for mankind." The other result was to charge the sun with enough strength to continue to do these things.

That the universe could be so reciprocal as to need our energy to nourish itself is something usually glossed over by anthropologists, while at the same time embraced by scientists groping towards a Unified Field Theory of everything.

Human sacrifice is also beyond the pale of Western acceptability, but some Occidental scholars, like John Major Jenkins, an expert on Mayan and South American Indians, suggests that the West could do with a long hard look at what it means by "sun worship," and asks us to understand why so many cultures across the earth did it, from the Egyptians to the Inca.

The reason, Jenkins believes, is that *Galactic Center,* situated in the middle of the Milky Way, is the origin, or goal, or both—of the soul. And the reason he believes that is because the Maya say so, and the Inca, and the Hopi, and the Dogon, as do the root myths of almost every indigenous culture on earth, going all the way back to the Dreamtime and beyond. In Incan cosmology, liberating the spirit from the flesh on top of sacred mountains lined up with the stars was a one-way ticket back to heaven. Some new age chroniclers, drawing upon science fiction metaphors, have called this practice "opening a stargate."

"Y'know," says Kevin suddenly, looking up. "Wise men throughout history went to the tops of mountains to talk to God, from Mt. Sinai to Mt. Olympus, to name but two. But to the Incas, this mountain itself is a living God."

"That won't make it any easier to climb," Mira jokes, whacking Kevin playfully on the shoulder, as we turn and begin our ascent.

❋ ❋ ❋

We walk single-file up a gentle slope at the edge of town, following a narrow path that blends into the rocks and grass, but is still used by tourists and goats. We're climbing up Pinkyuylluna in the midday sun, Kevin leading the way, followed by Ricardo, clambering up the mountain with all the skill of a puma, then Mira, and then me, trailing behind and suffering with the steep incline and thinning air.

As we slowly rise up the girth of the mountain I'm having a hard time of it with only a small daypack on my shoulders—how in heaven's name was an armed *conquistador* ever meant to get up here, much less conquer the mountain, I wondered? Looking back, I can see the town spread out peacefully down below me, and the terraces on the mountains opposite. Everything is so fresh and clear up here, and the wide-open space makes me feel unanchored to the earth, like I'm a bird flying through the sky.

A few kilometers further up is a three-story ruin embedded into cut terrace stairs. It's a large *qolqua* or granary storehouse about fifty meters long, used to house the crops of maize and other produce that were cultivated in the agricultural terraces down below. Storing the harvest in a fresh and well-ventilated place not only protected their food supply from outsiders, it elevated it closer to the sun, allowing for maximum reciprocal energy exchange. And it was from these mountain *tambos* that the best corn and grain was sent on to the Inca king himself in Cuzco, for use at his court and in rituals.

Kevin reaches the ruins first, following the flat path of the terrace and climbing through the open doorway that leads onto an open, roofless room full of tall golden grass. With his black and red poncho slung over his shoulder and sun hat on, he looks like a native from another time.

"You thought I was a nice guy, yeah, but I've lured you all up here to this mountain to do away with you," he jokes, as we all catch up to him. "They call ayahuasca *the vine of the dead* for a reason!"

"Ha. You are no Clint Eastwood," Mira hits back, and Kevin pulls a big smile.

It's been a steady but sure climb and we can all do with a breather, so we break out the water bottles and tobacco pouches and take stock of our surroundings. There's a sense of timelessness that descends on us as the sun beats down and the silence of the mountain envelops us, and the weight of history reaches out with its invisible gravity to embrace us.

Mira sits in the doorway of one of the upper-level *tambos,* rolls herself a cigarette, pulls back a stray dreadlock from her face, and writes silently in her diary while staring at the mountain opposite. Ricardo and Kevin chat quietly to each other, discussing the ruins as the sun beats down mercilessly from the royal blue sky overhead.

I'm buzzing off the raw energy all around and I feel like I'm rubbing shoulders with the ghosts who undoubtedly linger here. After dozens of ayahuasca ceremonies, and the long river journey up the Amazon and back, which had physically cleansed me, I feel like my soul had also been purified. I am like a cup, as sturdy and strong as stone, ready to be filled with the raw essence of the sun itself. And what better place to drink in the light than here?

Somewhere in the back of my head I remembered that tests done recently proved that the area around Cuzco had the highest levels of UV radiation in the world. Even the sunlight here was cosmic.

"*Mapacho?*" Kevin says, breaking my reverie and holding out a cigarette.

"Sure," I reply, still basking in the light. "So this is it, huh: the 'storehouse of the gods.' I tell you, I can feel the energy of the mountain ... I can't believe how sensitive I've become to energy itself in the last few weeks, ever since I left the jungle ..."

"Right. Well y'know, all a visionary plant is doing is taking the filters off the chakras so you can see directly," Kevin begins, launching into another spiel. "This can be done without visionary plants. It's like you were saying with your stone and the dreams it brought—it's not ayahuasca that brings the visions—you're just seeing reality the way it is. Ayahuasca helps you, and it will be different from magic mushrooms or san pedro, it has a different effect. But if you're seeing energy, you're seeing energy, whether it's with a dream, or a plant, or with nothing at all—" he cuts short, pointing at a faraway bird as it crests the mountain opposite.

"The Amazonian system is much more entheogenic based and visionary. You have a great variety of plants used for entering altered states of consciousness. Here in the Andean system that's not so much a part of it all. If you talk to the Q'eros—the Keepers of the Ancient Way of Knowledge—they don't traditionally use san pedro, or ayahuasca or other plants. The system they use is raw—they see energy without tools as interfaces."

I've heard about the Q'eros—back at the conference Sayre Tupac claimed to be descended from them, and he even had a retreat around Urumbamba somewhere, if I remember correctly. Myths that have developed over time about the Q'eros suggested that they were old sorcerers, *alto misayoc* or *pampa misayoc,* the "ones that have a special connection to the natural world." They were said to have lived in the highlands of Peru for thousands of years, and they hadn't been defeated by the pre-Incas, the Incas, or the *conquistadors,* so their culture was intact. Hidden from view, the Q'eros lived in *anyi*—in balance with nature.

Funny, my journey had led me all this way up a sacred mountain to remind me that the finger that points at the sun is not the sun itself. Ayahuasca, the stones, all the shamanic accoutrements, all those were powerful allies indeed, but they were just activating what we all have inside us all along: the innate ability to see, and connect with the energetic grids of the universe.

"The energy ayahuasca and the stones connect to is here—it's everywhere, isn't it? It's the energy of the planet and the stars and the infinite . . ."

"Riiggghht," Kevin says, smiling at me warmly and smoking his *mapacho.* "The Incas call it *Kausay Pacha:* the energy universe. The ability to perceive this invisible world means that your heart chakra and your third eye are connected on an energetic level."

"Hmmm, that's interesting. When I was in San Francisco, near Pucallpa, I was investigating the Shipibo patterns, the *manta* weavings they do that are supposedly energy maps enabled by their ayahuasca visions," I explain, shading my eyes from the light and feeling a bit dazed from my own *mapacho*. "I was told that there's ten levels of energy and that the Shipibo patterns are the tenth level that you see, the visionary level. And someone else also said that those original designs were inspired by the Incan culture in Cuzco. And, that the original Inca king got them from some *celestial source*..."

"Well ultimately everything is celestial," Kevin responds. "Basically, there are different hierarchies of spirits. There are *earth guides,* who are being overseen by *celestial guides,* who are being overseen by higher level guides—and it doesn't end. I don't know, some people say there are ten levels of ayahuasca, or whatever; I think this is just words. What I find with ayahuasca is that having visions of grids, the energetic grid of patterns, energetic mosaics, this is just the first level for me. Then you start moving into more complicated stuff. It's just perspective.

"But there might be some truth to the origin of those patterns. The Incas chose the Q'eros as their weavers because the Q'eros women had such fine, small fingers. And those 'maps of energy' as you called them, were handed down from the visions of the *alto misayoc* high priests, then preserved and transmitted through their art to the Empire."

It was all fitting together: from the tops of the mountains the Q'eros activated their stargates and brought down maps of the hyperdimensions they experienced, and maybe even created dimensional anchors to those spaces themselves. This wasn't art like we think of now, though—each *manta* pattern is said to leave an imprint on the subconscious mind that views it. It's the same with Australian Aboriginals and their Dreamtime art. The map or art somehow grounds the energy of the territory, imbuing it with spirit. The map is a microcosm of the territory, and *hologrammatically mirrors* what's above, below.

"Hey gringos," Ricardo says, padding up to us silently through the long grass, "Mira and I are going to climb a little higher—to that battlement on the ledge up there." A few hundred meters up on the left is a squat block on the edge of a bluff, a little ruined fort balanced precariously on the edge of the abyss ... directly above Viracocha's stony head.

"We're coming," Kevin says, and holds out his hand and helps lift me up. "Are you feeling okay?" he asks, flashing me a concerned look with those sparkling hazel eyes of his.

"Yeah, no, I'm fine," I reply. "It's the air up here, and the *mapacho,* that's all. And the downloads. I'm still buzzing from the energy."

"Ha. They say that the stone spirits are the first spirits, and that they've been around the longest time. *Tread lightly, my brother.*"

And with that we continue our climb.

"Man, this just blows me away," Mira says, steadying herself against the walls of Viracocha's crown and peering down into the endless free fall of the valley below. Ollantaytambo spreads itself out beneath us like a lover, the rolling fields unfolding one into another, hugged by mountains. I understand then, what the Incas must have felt, the living presence of the earth itself, which they called Pachamama. The wide-open space of the Andes was a very different environment than Cuzco, or the crowded ecosystems of the jungle. The more I tuned into it, the more spatially aware I became of the open landscape as a living organism, connected to the clouds and sky and up into the heavens above.

Mira sits down next to Ricardo and Kevin in the doorway of the fort, half-covered in shadow from the afternoon sun, a portal to faraway places. I begin thinking of the stargates again, and our own light bodies activated by our shamanic training. I was just beginning to digest this understanding, which was at the core of the Incan identity, underpinning their whole relationship to the cosmos.

The idea of a light-body was even embodied in the name of the King, the original "Inca." Like the original meaning of "Christ" in

Hebrew culture (an "anointed one"), an "Inca" originally meant one who "shines or glows," a "luminous one," or "child of the sun." The Inca was also believed to have the power to step outside of time. Unlike Jesus and other avatars, however, the Inca was not only the Son of God, but one among many. His power and connection were available to all through his example. It was in us all, the Incan cosmology said, to reclaim our divine nature.

What better place to be digesting these concepts, to be feeding my own light body, than here on the crown chakra of good old Viracocha, the creator God?

The sun's beating down mercilessly now and there's not a cloud in the sky to break the solar connection. I take a long hard gulp from my water bottle and look around at my newfound friends, drawn together from across the globe, and take a second to marvel at the weave of fate that has drawn us all together.

"Hey, I just wanted to say how good it is to hang with you guys, to get a real feel for this amazing place."

"It's a long way from Australia, huh?" Ricardo says with a raspy voice, lighting up another cigarette. Nicotine receptors activate adrenal glands, I remembered, and set off all types of physiological changes. The more he smoked, the more he smelt like, and reminded me of a puma.

"Yeah, a long way geographically, I guess, but the energy of these wide-open spaces is very similar. The Aboriginal concept of the Dream-time is a close analogue of the Meso-American understanding of the energetic nature of reality..."

"And of time," Kevin adds. "All indigenous cultures have a per-ception of cyclic time because of their relationship to the earth, with its changing seasons. But it's funny how similar the prophecies of the Q'eros are to the Hopi, the Maya, and the Inca themselves, y'know, all the Meso-American tribes. The Q'eros prophecies specifically say that a great change is now upon the world, which they call *Pachacuti:* a time in which the world will be turned right-side up, and harmony and order will be restored."

According to the Q'eros, the last Pachacuti occurred over five hundred years ago when the Spanish invaders conquered the Incan empire, breaking the celestial connection woven across the land in their temples and shrines, and chaos reigned. Patiently the Q'eros have waited for the time their prophecies predicted, nurturing their secret knowledge for when it is needed.

"Do you really believe the world will be turned 'right-side up'?" Mira asks, accepting a cigarette from Ricardo, who offers me one, but I decline.

"Don't you?" I ask.

"Yeah, I know what you mean," she replies sheepishly. "After the tsunami and everything, and all the wild weather…The planet's shifting, I think we can all feel it, yes?"

"*It's awakening.*"

"On an individual level that's why we've all been drawn here," Kevin says sagely. "Our energy bodies are awakening to a deeper understanding of the true nature of reality. This is the first time in recorded history that we're moving towards cosmic awareness as a species, y'know, and it starts with individuals like you and me, from every type of background, treading the shaman's path…

"Down there," Kevin says, pointing towards civilization below us with a grand sweep of his hand, "we're in normal, physical reality consciousness. We have filters that adjust our perception, and this is why every culture in the world has different views on how reality is.

"The path of shamanism is like climbing this mountain: basically what's going on is that we're accessing some of our higher self, we're moving up. That's how we get a better perspective on our life, y'know, and that's why we see things more clearly, like oh, that's what happened. We're moving on up into the spirit world, moving towards who we really are.

"This world is a school, but life's not just about learning: it's about *remembering*. At one time we knew everything, but when we come down here they blank out your memory. When you take the filters off with tools like ayahuasca you see the greater reality. But there's always that monkey-mind part of us throwing on the brakes, struggling to remain in control. It's too much. The animal body will die one day, but your soul won't. It's just the fear.

"The key is to remember, remember, remember…"

And I do: Beneath the flesh is a spiritual body that comes, like the Inca, from the sun, but not the sun up there in the sky. There is another sun that lies within, and it burns with the fire of spiritual light. Our souls are like emanations from this central Source; it's where we came from, and where we will go back to.

"Is our collective remembrance part of the Eagle and Condor prophecy?" I ask, snapping back to here and now.

"A lot of people have heard about the prophecy of the Eagle of the North uniting with the Condor of the South, but there's another prophecy that might be even more appropriate. Andean prophecy foretells of the *Taripaypacha,* or 'encounter with the universe,'" he says, leaning in conspiratorially towards us. "It refers to a new golden era in the human experience, the age of 'meeting ourselves again.'"

A warm smile breaks across Kevin's face, as he looks me deep in the eyes. "Imagine, then, that it's not just about the descendants of the Spanish and the New World relearning the shamanic perspective: it's about the remembrance that after five hundred years of being cast across the earth and reborn in different bodies, that it's time for us to come home."

With that he leans in close and draws all our foreheads together, like a football huddle out in the middle of the scrum.

"Y'know, the Q'ero had mastered the art of *anyi,* or the sacred art of reciprocity or exchanging of energies. They had a special ritual called the *Anyi Karpay,* in which initiates exchanged their power with each other, directly through their auras. Right now all of us are connected together in a golden circuit of energy. Everything we know passes between us now."

I look up and Mira and Ricardo are focusing with their eyes closed, smiling, holding the circuit, willing to believe. I realize that any vestigial voices of scientific rationality had finally given way beneath me as well, and that in my heart I was willing to trust, and to accept the universal process that is unfolding, no matter what labels we give it.

Through the gateway of Viracocha's crown, far off in the cloudless sky, I suddenly spied two birds sailing through a sea of blue. Two eagles, perhaps, or condors, or both—they're too far away to tell. But either way, I can read the omen clearly:

The time of the prophecies is upon us. These are the times, indeed, when all the binaries converged: north and south, eagle and condor, old world and new, heaven and earth, past and future.

And we are all part of it—*part of the universal awakening.*

29
Illuminated

Aguas Calientes
MONDAY AUGUST 28, 2006

Machu Picchu has been called the "Eighth Wonder of the World" by zealous tour operators, the "Crown Jewel of the Andes," and one of the "most mysterious places on earth." It's a UNESCO World Heritage site that attracts over 500,000 visitors a year and is the most-visited tourist attraction in all of South America—which is conversely why it's also on UNESCO's list of endangered sites, as well.

There are no roads leading into Aguas Calientes, the tourist town that lies near the base of the mountain on which the Incas built their lost city. No, there's only the train, which rattles slowly tonight, past mountains that tower majestically either side of the tracks in the dim moonlight, threading through the upper Sacred Valley.

Each carriage is priced on a sliding scale of exorbitance, with the most expensive U.S. $500 a seat. All I could afford was the "backpacker special"—the last two carriages of the local train, set apart for gringo budget travelers and the locals themselves. But even then the ticket price had skyrocketed three hundred percent in the three years since my *Lonely Planet* guidebook was published, and as I had grown so used to in Peru, I was almost broke.

After Machu Picchu I'd arranged to have a last ayahuasca session with Kevin on Wednesday night, which would leave me a day to reach my flight to Buenos Aires, and from there the connection back home to Australia. It also meant that half of the money Tessa had given me was taken. I had five hundred soles at the start of the day, but only two hundred after my plane fare to Lima. The train cost over a hundred soles, leaving me nowhere near enough to actually get into Machu Picchu and still make the plane.

Which was fine, because I wasn't planning on paying. I respected the energy of sacred sites, but the heavy, karmic money vibe that surrounded them nowadays didn't sit right with me. The modern urge to spectate and consume spoiled the sanctity of the place tourists came to see, and as Kevin had warned me, nowhere was this more apparent than at Machu Picchu.

Yes, I was a bad tourist, the *estoy pellado* gringo looking for spirit under the soles, searching for meaning and wisdom in a sea of cultural merchandise. Sitting back in the hard upholstery in the almost deserted back carriage of the night train, juggling the numbers in my head, the staggering sense of scale that Machu Picchu commanded hit me. Ten thousand tourists a week, well over a thousand tourists a day—and at U.S. $40 to get in, or one hundred and eighteen soles, that's like, U.S. $100,000 a week or over U.S. $5,000,000 a year. Machu Picchu was the single biggest money-maker in all of Peru—after the exit-tax, and someone was rolling in it, but it certainly wasn't me.

So why did so many Westerners flock to Machu Picchu, and sacred sites like it all over the world, I wondered? Why did they fossick about in the ruins of homes and temples, picking at the bones of indigenous cultures that lived closer to the earth, and knew a deeper relationship with it? Somewhere deep inside, I suspected we could all feel the power of these places to activate our own spirit, to connect us to people and times past, and of different ways of seeing and being in the world.

Rediscovering the sacred was the point of the ancient pilgrimage, yet the Newtonian-capitalist paradigm has left us with a detached understanding of this ritual, diluted into a passive consumer groove that simply pampers the senses. Spending money is substituted for physical and spiritual sacrifice, and the transformative nature of the journey is safely commodified.

Like the *ayahuasqueros* I had met in Peru who were hungry for an authentic connection to the Divine, so too, were millions of mainstream tourists, whether they realized it or not. Sublimated in their package holiday deals and two-for-one coupons was a modern version of the pilgrimage, of leaving the familiar behind and undertaking a transformative journey.

At 10:00 p.m. sharp the train pulls right into the center of town and grinds to a halt in the middle of the Avenida Imperio de Los Incas, one of the two main streets, and nestles itself among the shops either side. As the passengers disembark a cloud of hotel hawkers descends upon us like a pool of piranhas in a feeding frenzy.

Aguas Calientes is clean and well signed, with advertisements for spas and up-market hotels, as well as backpacker specials. Groomed upper-class Americans in Ralph Lauren polo shirts and sunglasses clench their jaws as they're rushed past vulgar natives hustling their wares, on their way from one first-class hotel to another. After hanging with locals and their goats on cramped mini-bus *collectivos* from Cuzco to Urumbamba, Aguas Calientes feels like the Beverly Hills of Peru.

Illuminated by the light from my head torch, I start walking down the backstreets straight out of town, following the dirt road that parallels the Urubamba River, which has the officious title of the "Hiram Bingham Highway." There's a crescent moon out but it's quite dark—and then it starts to cloud over and get even darker.

The dirt road stretches and turns like a fast running stream before me, shouldered on either side by huge, magnificent mountains, stone colossi as steady as the hands of God when he carved the world. Even under the cloak of night the scenery is breathtaking. I'm in awe of these mountains as I walk along over bridges and follow the river to the base of Machu Picchu, about five kilometers out of town.

I'd succumbed to the insidious temptation of a Snickers Bar at one of the little kiosk shops near the train station, the much-needed sugar flowing into my body and giving me support for the long moonlight walk. It felt like a guilty pleasure after months of lowered sugar intake, and a very Western indulgence, like that whole forgotten part of myself was stirring again.

But the mountain was another matter: the road wound up around the base of Machu Picchu for eight kilometers, and for that I would need some extra help. Luckily, I'd bought a few supplies back at the *mercado* in Cuzco: some fruit and nuts, as well as fresh coca leaf and limes. The coca leaf is a sacred plant to indigenous peoples throughout South America. It gives strength, stamina, and endurance, and it was also said to help acclimatize to altitude sickness. The Peruvians also believed that coca leaves were an offering for safe passage. An old lady at the market told me in pidgin English that you take three good sized leaves and hold them in the palm of your hand, over your mouth, and pray while inhaling.

The three leaves correspond to the three worlds: *Ukhu pacha,* ruled by the snake; *Kay pacha,* the puma; and *Hanaq pacha,* the condor. After saying my prayer to the mountain I roll up the leaves and press them into a loose bud on the inside of my left cheek. A lovely numbness overtakes my mouth and soon I am enveloped by a warm, active energy that spreads through my entire body.

A light mist descends and as the clouds cover the moon I'm plunged into near-perfect darkness. As I pull my new poncho tight around me, fleeting streaks of fireflies dart about chasing each other, their light trails streaking into short bursts of order like the aisle lights on an airplane, guiding me home.

And they're not alone: glowing, luminescent caterpillars also litter the side of the road. It seems that the Incas weren't the only ones who cultivated their light bodies, and as if to confirm the point a burst of sheet lightning flickers across the night. The bursts are small, not like a far-off storm; rather the air itself feels charged with electricity, buzzing from the ionization of the mountains.

I feel like I'm in a storybook straight out of myth and prehistory, walking through the clouds. Climbing the mountain is like a prayer in itself, I realize. All my thoughts, my hopes, my energy are going into the climb, making it a sacred act.

I wonder if this was how Hiram Bingham, the Hawaiian-born, Yale- and Harvard-educated historian and explorer who rediscovered the lost city above me, felt when he walked this path almost a hundred years ago. In 1911 Bingham was leading an expedition through the Urubamba Valley, searching for the last two capitals of the Inca, Vilcambamba and Vitcos. In his bestselling 1948 memoir, *Lost City of the Incas,* Bingham says,

"I had entered the marvelous canyon of the Urubamba below the Inca fortress. Here the river escapes from the cold plateau by tearing its way through gigantic mountains of granite. The road runs through a land of matchless charm […] In the variety of its charms the power of its spell, I know of no place in the world which can compare with it. Not only had it great snow peaks looming above the clouds more than two miles overhead; gigantic precipices of many-colored granite rising sheer for thousands of feet above the foaming, glistening, roaring rapids, it has also, in striking contrast, orchids and tree ferns, the delectable beauty of luxurious vegetation and the mysterious witchery of the jungle. One is drawn irresistibly onwards by ever-recurring surprises through a deep, winding gorge, turning and twisting past overhanging cliffs of incredible height."

Bingham met Melchor Arteaga, a local farmer who told him of ruins on top of the ridge where Bingham's party had camped. He called the mountain simply "old peak" in Quechuan, but to Bingham's ears Machu Picchu sounded just like the *Lost City of the Incas* he was hoping for. A city in the clouds, which at almost 8,000 feet above sea level, was nearly as close to the heavens as the Incas got.

A sixteenth-century land title only uncovered in the 1980s confirmed the fact that Inca Pachacuti, who also founded Cuzco, ordered the construction of Machu Picchu in around 1450 AD. It was mysteriously abandoned almost a century later, when the Spanish *conquistadores* arrived in Peru and started taking over. It remained hidden for almost five hundred years until Bingham came along, revealing a historical enigma that has refused clear definition by successive generations of archaeologists viewing it through the Western paradigm. This may be in part because unraveling the secrets of Machu Picchu would reveal the core raison d'être of the Inca culture in general—and the West is only now becoming ready for what it might find.

Regardless of all this, millions of Westerners had passed this way, in what could be seen as a mass pilgrimage over the last few decades. What had they learned? The Incas had an astounding aptitude for astronomical observation, and could predict eclipses, the phases of the moon, the position of the stars, and the workings of the heavens, that much is agreed. *Why* they wanted to know this, and what they did with that knowledge, however, remains tantalizingly beyond Western comprehension.

Nowhere is this more apparent than in Machu Picchu. Was it a country retreat for the Inca, a strategic "Fort David," a religious site, a prison, or an intentional community of sun-worshippers? All I had to go on was my trusty *Lonely Planet* Peru guidebook—and such matters weren't canvassed there.

After hours climbing through the patchy mist the road peaks and widens and a bright shining five-star accommodation hotel straight out of another world appears on the left. I smoke a *mapacho* by the edge of the hotel, about fifty meters in front of the entrance, fronted with turnstiles and high walls—a Disneyland of the gods, indeed—and ponder my next move.

To the right of the entrance, on a lower-level plateau is a small hut, beyond which a set of stairs leads down the mountain. I take out the map that Mira has drawn me of the way Kevin has shown her, a secret seeker's path into Machu Picchu. I'm worried there might be guards so I subdue the light from my head torch and stumble quietly through the brush and bracken off from the stairs, searching desperately for the way forward, a dirt track that leads in, into the holy mountain. But after two or three false starts crawling around in the underbrush I give up on Mira's map and take the steps down, past the hut.

Eventually I find a dirt path leading off from the left of the stairs. This must be it, I think, but it keeps going down, towards the base of the mountain, not around and over. I stumble across the next bit of the path and then it peters out into a dead end, or a narrow goat trail to nowhere, and before long I'm lost. That's when I start to really panic, and the flight-and-fear response takes hold. I force myself to take a deep breath, *soplaring* my fears away. I have to let go of control, this is what ayahuasca has been teaching me. *Let go of the path, of the plot, let go of the holding on, let go of the eternal stress of being . . .*

I reach into my pocket and take out Pedro, my magic stone deep from the heart of the Amazon, from that other aguas calientes, and I beseech him. I rub him on my forehead and feel the *jaguarflutterbys* tuning in, the energy of the mountain sparking into my field of awareness like fireflies in the mist. Please, Pedro, is this the right path, I ask? A strong, deep voice says "yes."

So I continue, even though the way seems to be going down and away. I let go of myself here on the skin of the *Apu*, giving myself over to spirit and letting it guide my way...

Ten, fifteen minutes go by... and the path splits. Another dirt track develops and I follow it. But in the dark of night it's hard to tell what is a path and what's just undergrowth, and before I know it I'm lost again. I start climbing one trail that seems to lead somewhere, and then suddenly I'm hanging off the ass-end of Machu Picchu, on a ledge that leads out to my doom... I can see a few faint lights down below where the Machu Picchu museum resides, and in the distance, the fairy-light glow of Aguas Calientes. And a voice inside that thick-skulled head of mine says, *fuck! What the FUCK have you done this time, Razam!? You absolute idiot . . .*

Eventually the path peters out again, turning into a sheer rock face that towers a hundred meters up, with no holds. I've got to go down, on the skinniest little trails that aren't really even trails at all, but patches of dirt and grass—the body hair of the mountain. I turn to go back the way I came and the way I came seems to end in the clear precipice. One foot dangles off the bleeding edge for a millisecond, and I can see a sheer drop down the side of the mountain and I'm *fucking freaking out here, how the fuck did I get into this mess again?*

Think about it Razam, just hold tight till dawn and the tourist buses will come and they can get some Peruvian search and rescue squad here, or at least you'll be able to see the paths. What was I *thinking,* climbing Machu *fucking* Picchu by dark moonlight? It's all gone horribly wrong.

I can't go down—so I have to go up, skirting around the towering cliff wall and finding another path off to the right, just big enough for a skinny goat. With no other way forward I continue up, through the brush, up and up and up for another twenty or thirty meters, grabbing plants by the handful and hoisting myself beyond them. In the shadows it seems like I can find the top of the mountain, but the top just keeps becoming another top, and another, until eventually... I break through... to a dirt path wide enough to fit three, four people safely.

Huuhhh. *Thank you, God.*

I follow this path up through the brush, following little trails, and eventually I see bits of trash; someone's tied some toilet paper on a twig, to say it's the right way, and a stone path develops. And then—there's a staff leaning against a rock, at a dead end on the path. A shaman's staff, a wooden rod with a red Inca cloth wrapped around the handle. I'd heard rumors of "the shaman of Machu Picchu"—I wonder if this was his?

I keep moving up and around, past the trash and toilet paper hidden here on the backside of the "Jewel of the Andes" and over the lip of the last outer wall. I've arrived at Machu Picchu, finally, through the toilets, right in front of the caretaker's hut near the front entrance.

I can't believe I just did that. That was one of the closest brushes I'd had with death, but there was more to it than that. It felt like the whole ordeal was the mountain's test for me, a way to humble me before it. The mountain didn't want my money but it almost took my life, and in doing so it brought me a whole new respect for it, and for the essence of the pilgrimage itself. Yet again I'd been *initiated.*

And now my current problem is this: it's a crescent moon, clouded, almost pitch-dark, and there's no light. I don't dare use my tiny head torch in case a guard sees me, and the only illuminated sign is near the entrance and says, EXIT. Here I am, the *estoy pellado touristo,* breaking into the most visited tourist attraction in South America and walking through the ruins, alone.

As I gingerly make my way down a path I can see the shadowy outlines of some large stone houses or other buildings here and there, the living history of a lost race. I sneak a brief burst of red light from my head torch to guardedly look at my *Lonely Planet* map of Machu Picchu, but I can't for the life of me find any path in the dark, and I've only gone a few meters when I have to stop and take a deep breath again, and center myself in the here-and-now.

I take off down the grassy strips of the plantation terraces, which have the flat, manicured spread of a mini-golf course, and lead into cul-de-sacs. Just as I reach the end of one terrace and barely clamber over the five-foot stone walls I find myself in another flat plantation grassland, which ends in yet another wall, and so on. This is crazy—I feel like I'm in a midnight "Rubik's Cube," shifting and turning about me on all sides. If only I could figure out which end was up I might have a chance of getting out of here.

The terraces finally end in a stone walkway that leads forward, the cobblestone main street of Machu Picchu. The Incas used mainly polished dry-stones to build their structures, fitting the stones together without mortar, but with such precision that they were virtually earthquake-proof. This lost city was connected by a maze of pathways and stairs with passages between them, which allowed the citizens to clamber over the top of the mountain and utilize as much of the space as possible. The sacred geometry of the buildings even forms a truncated pyramid layered over the mountain top itself, which was indicative of Inca religious structures and gives credence to the theory that Machu Picchu wasn't a city at all, but a *giant temple to the sun and earth*.

Yet now, in the dark, the shadowy outlines of the buildings have a menacing feel. A perfect silence hangs over Machu Picchu tonight, and apart from a few llamas on the terrace flats there are no other living creatures here. The dark weight of the ruins radiates a cold, dead energy, as if I'm in the presence of lingering ghosts.

After my immersion into the shamanic world I know that spirits are real, and if any Incan ruins are likely to have active spirits, I figure Machu Picchu will. Still, gathering my courage and holding Pedro tightly in my hand, I decide to brave the ruins, and take a peek in the cluster of buildings off to the left.

Cautiously I walk down a set of stone steps towards what is called the "royal tomb," where mummified bodies were once stored. At the bottom of the stairs I can see a cave-like room, which houses the tomb. The energy here is intense, and as my fears kick in a chill goes down my spine. I pass a waist-high terrace-like step on the right and the round curving wall on the left and take a quick look with the red beam of my head torch: it's a small room with what looks like walled-up window niches, which I guess is where they put the bodies.

But whose bodies were they? When they say "royal," do they mean kings, like the Inca himself? And were the bodies dead, or simply resting while their owners traveled out into the stars in their luminous forms? A deep shudder passes over me then, like the spirits are here, so I move on quickly, past the tomb and up to the nearby Temple of the Sun.

The Incas had temples they dedicated to the sun in all their major ritual sites, but the one here at Machu Picchu was built on top of a large polished rock, with a semi-circular wall curving round it. As with the site at Ollantaytambo, where grooves in the mountain aligned with a temple down below to capture the solstice light, here two windows in the curved wall are said to capture the first rays of morning light at the summer and winter equinoxes, and be aligned with the star constellation Pleiades. There is also a great table, or altar here where the virgin sacrifices, those young girls with the purest and most cultivated energy, were given over to feed the stars.

Early forensic analysis of the approximately one hundred bodies found at Machu Picchu suggested that around seventy-five percent were women. That led to a theory that suggested they were priestesses, or "Virgins of the Sun" that performed religious rites here, including sacrifices, although modern osteological examinations have shown an equal ratio of male bones in the remains.

Dr. Johan Reinhard, who is an Explorer-in-Residence at the National Geographic Society, has theorized that Machu Picchu was selected as a site precisely because of its position to the rest of the sacred landscape around it. The mountains surrounding the "old peak" are said to be in alignment with strategic astronomical events like the solstices and equinoxes, and this perspective would be in keeping with the Incan understanding of the sacred geometries of heaven being reflected on earth.

Reinhard has led hundreds of climbs into the Andes and discovered over forty Inca ritual sites at altitudes as high as six thousand feet, at which he has recovered the remains of human sacrifices. His most famous discovery was that of the famous "Ice Maiden": a frozen Inca girl of about fourteen found inside the summit crater of Mount Ampato. Tests confirmed that the girl had died between 1440 and 1450, around the same time Machu Picchu was being built, which lends weight to the hypothesis that ritual sacrifices were still commonly practiced.

That hypothesis still stops short of asking why, which leads back to the basic premise of Incan cosmology: the belief that the human sacrifice transmitted the soul back to the stars, and the *Maker* that lived there. To the Inca these weren't sites of murder and evil, but altars for their love of life itself, and mountains were their launching pads.

The organic, intelligent web of life connects the stars and the energy of us all in an infinite engine of creation, that was the not-so-secret truth at the heart of ayahuasca, and it was the same knowledge that the stones had shown me. All of us were staring down the celestial food chain, fed and being fed upon in one macro-cosmic biomass bigger than human comprehension. Another shudder passes through me and I grip my poncho around me tightly and move on.

Pedro, my magic stone is buzzing like a Geiger counter as I meander along in the dark, making my way along a narrow path to the raised platform that hosts the *Intihuatana,* or the "Hitching Post of the Sun," the sacred center of Machu Picchu. Climbing the stairs I take a quick peak with the heard torch, which shows a quadrangular, waist-high granite altar with a stubby pillar jutting out of its center: the *saiwa* or *sukhanka* stone, whose shape mirrors that of Huayna Picchu, the mountain peak that rises behind the ruins.

The altar is also called the "sundial" because it is believed it was used to measure time, using the shadows of sunlight to calculate the solstices and equinoxes. At midday on March twenty-first and September twenty-first, the fall and spring equinoxes, the sun stops over the altar, leaving no shadow. The Incas said that at this moment the sun *sits with all his might upon the pillar,* and can then be "tied" to the rock, symbolically in ceremony, uniting the sun and earth for a few brief moments.

The Incas had hundreds, if not thousands of sacred stones like this across their empire on strategic ley lines where earth energy was concentrated, creating a kind of circuit breaker to absorb and channel the energy of the sun across the seasons and anchor its energy in *anyi* or perfect balance.

The *Intihuatana* is one of only a handful of these energy points that were not destroyed when the Spanish invaders razed the Incan culture, which the Incas believed broke the circuit that connected with the stars and ushered in the age of chaos. The *Intihuatana* survived the *conquistadores,* but in 2000, during the filming of a beer commercial at the site, a thousand pound crane fell onto the stone, breaking a corner and the last relay to the heavens.

Incan myth also says that when a person who is pure of heart touches their forehead to the *Intihuanta,* the stone opens their vision to the spirit world. *What the hell, I think, I'll give it a go.*

I hold Pedro to my forehead as I have so many times before, invoking his spirit power. Then, by the red light from my head torch, I step over the rope barrier and place the stone against the smooth skin of the rock. I close my eyes and lean forward, feeling light-headed, and kiss the pillar, touching my forehead to the rock.

Instantly a vision floods my being for a third time, and a sea of kaleidoscoping hyperdimensional energy unfolds before me, *Kausay*

Pacha: the energy universe. And I finally realize what this is, the vibrational imprint of us all: past, present, and future fluctuating through ten-dimensional space. I can see the atoms of creation vibrating across the spectrum, how the light condenses, slows its vibrational rate, and organizes itself into matter forms.

I can see my aura glowing with the million-beaded drops of light that make up my energy field, radiating in coruscating orbits. A warm sun expands out from me and I feed my light to the world, and am fed back in return.

I am illuminated.

Suddenly, above me, a sound is born. There are no birds; they're all asleep, if they've made it this high at all. Even the llamas are sleeping on the terraces. But there is this sound being birthed fifty feet above me, hovering in a stationary orbit. It sounds like a bird mixed with a human voice, but speeded up on an old tape player from 33 to 45—the vibrational rate is maxed out. It stays above me, mystic in the night, speaking with me and giving me its blessing, talking the language of light.

Then as suddenly as it arrived it's gone. I fall off the rock and onto the ground below, and am plunged back into the darkness of the night. It's cold on the stone floor, and it's time for me to move on. I feel spent from the vision but rejuvenated at the same time, buzzing with a clear light template like after an ayahuasca ceremony. I gather Pedro and my bag and slink off into the dark once more, making my way back to the grasslands of the main square, and beyond that down towards the trail to Huayna Picchu, at the far north end of the city.

Somewhere there on the edge of the mountain I find a small alcove behind a mossy rock, just big enough for me, and I lay down and rest my weary bones, nestled under the warmth of my poncho.

I sleep till dawn, when the tourists begin trickling in, and I walk around on the misty terrace greens, mingling with the gringos and marveling at this sacred city in the light. The scale of this place staggers me, the intricate stone terraces that layer the curve of the mountain; the labyrinth of stone buildings that seem straight out of the Stone

Age. Behind it all Huayna Picchu towers majestically over this lost city, wrapped in a cloak of mist and cloud.

Suddenly I'm confronted by a guard who asks to see my ticket. The *estoy pellado touristo* doesn't have one, of course, and as the irate guard gently escorts me out through the turnstiles, against the steady stream of pilgrims flooding in, I realize my audience is at an end. But that's okay, I have what I came for.

The mountain has spoken.

30
Final Flight
Cuzco
WEDNESDAY AUGUST 30, 2006

"Can you see the puma?" Kevin asks, pointing to the twinkling lights that stretch across Cuzco at night from the Plaza de Armas, up towards *Sacsayhuaman,* forming the shape of the beast.

"Yeah, I see it. Pretty amazing, isn't it?"

Kevin and I are on a small concrete balcony outside *K'uychi Wasi* (House of the Rainbow in Quechua)—his tiny brick studio below the Temple of the Moon on the Inca trail, up above San Blas. We're smoking *mapachos* and shooting the breeze on this cool August night, killing time till the ceremony tonight. Kevin's busy pouring a big jug of ayahuasca from a stone container into a number of two-liter plastic bottles, the preferred method of transportation for the brew in the twenty-first century.

"In Spanish they call the puma *el doramo,* you know. A lot of Amazonian tribes are really scared of them because they're so smart. If someone's walking in the forest a puma might act like they don't see the person, but it does, and it will follow them back to the village. At night it will creep in and take out an entire family, putting its fangs in silently, and going along to each person one by one and sucking all the blood out of them. The victims don't even wake up," Kevin pronounces, looking at me intently.

"Don Francisco said this happened in his village down near Pucallpa, and the whole village left. Only one family stayed and they had a gun, but when they checked on them the next day everyone was dead. So for a lot of shamans they see the puma as clever and powerful—a good ally to have."

"Keep your friends close and your enemies closer, eh?" I reply, watching the twinkling lights of the city dance across the night. The puma was a common symbol of the shaman, and it seemed fitting to be seeing it now, at the end of my own shamanic journey, shaped by the Cuzco skyline.

As always of late, I'm wrapped up tight in my poncho, just as Kevin is in his, like two peas in a pod, and yet again I'm reminded how similar we are, like brothers. It seems fitting that he will be the *curandero* conducting my last ayahuasca session, both of us Westerners on the shaman's path. And what a path it's been.

I'd told Kevin of my amazing experiences at Machu Picchu and my final initiation on the mountain. He replied by telling me how the Q'eros have another term for these end days of the old paradigm: *take onkoy,* which means the "gestation of the luminous body of the world." They say that the more we tune into the subtler frequencies and find ourselves in *anyi,* or reciprocal balance with nature, the more the light collects and transforms us.

Achieving this state, which the Q'eros called the *kausay poq'o,* or "luminous body," was said to be the preferred form of consciousness, free of the blocks of perception and able to see and shape the luminous nature of existence itself. And the ultimate goal of the shaman was to cultivate this light body as a host for consciousness, to transcend the death of the physical individual and enable the illuminated one to move on to the next world, or the worlds above.

I can't help but feel a bit melancholy at the thought of leaving Peru, and the source of shamanistic power I have tapped into on my journeys here. The role of a shaman was often dangerous and difficult, but one that I now believed was vital to the integration of the West back into *anyi,* or balance with the earth. And through *anyi* would blossom the rediscovery of what we really are, and our place in the cosmos.

"Y'know, the only world I fear now is the material one," I say only half-jokingly to Kevin, as we look at each other by the light of the stars, and the burden and joy of what we know passes between us. "It's funny, but even the hardest moments of my journey seem to pale next to the thought of returning home, and the challenge of maintaining this cultivated consciousness amongst my old imprints."

"I feel that way every time I go home to San Francisco, and see my family and the world I left behind," Kevin says. "But you have to remember that you've changed, and you've gained a perspective that can't be lost."

I know that, but somewhere in the back of my head I still doubt my ability to integrate the shamanistic awareness back into the baseline world. I know that Western culture, our diets, and our mental distractions set up a dissonance that doesn't allow the subtle energies of the plants and the stones in. The spirits are still there, but modern culture can't hear their message because it's too busy plugged into iPods and downloading ringtones.

Yet if the West is ever to heal its split with the natural world, that's just where the healing must take place: in the cities and urban archipelagos, in the suburbs and in the hearts and minds of the global village.

Traveling to the jungles of the Amazon in search of indigenous knowledge is just the first step, and if the next involves using sacred plants to pierce the higher dimensions from my lounge room, or backyard, then I was just going to have to get used to it. *We all were.*

"Some people, they ask me, why do I work with ayahuasca in Cuzco?" Kevin says, as a shooting star streaks across the night sky above us. "You know, it's from the forest, and a lot of people don't think it's worth taking ayahuasca anywhere else. But that view seems very, very limited in its perspective. Ayahuasca, I would argue, is not even an indigenous medicine. I don't recognize any patents by any one person on ayahuasca. It's a plant that is opening a door within us by taking off the filter on your chakras so that you connect directly with the universe. So for me, it's beyond Amazonian tribal culture, it's beyond the Amazon itself. *It's a doorway, a human-vegetative connection,* and you can experience that anywhere—even back in the West.

"In the same way a lot of people think it's very important that someone be indigenous. Back at the conference there was this one healer from Lapland. He came up to me and said, hey, we're kind of similar, we both have long hair, y'know. I was like, okay... But then he said, 'you're not indigenous.' And I said what do you mean? As far as I'm concerned I'm indigenous to my country. How am I not indigenous to North America? Oftentimes people use earth-based logic. So the bloodline of my physical body in this lifetime is not indigenous, or whatever. Whereas I remember living lives in every single culture on earth, and on other worlds.

"So this doesn't seem to be important to me at all. I've lived lifetimes as an *ayahuasquero* in Peru. And I would hope that if this life is a school, that in this lifetime, because I've progressed further, I'm a better healer, even though I chose to be a North American, y'know. The physical body seems irrelevant.

"And the way we learn this is by incarnating again and again and again, in different realms and zones as different people and beings, the infinite hierarchy of celestial creatures in the school of life... Until eventually we become everything, the good and the dark, and we remember that we have always been IT."

Kevin's words ring true: this was the same vision I'd had from the DMT, the plants and the stones, the eternal battle of the "Tao" at play and the multiplicity of beings that make up the whole. That was what ayahuasca and all the Gaian interfaces were teaching us: not only are we all connected, we are all manifestations of the same Source, and we are all of us headed towards a common goal.

"Kevin, I just wanted to say, y'know... thanks."

"For what?"

"Ah, you know, for being here, for listening—and understanding. And for treading the path before me and helping me find the way. It means a lot. *Muchas gracias mi amigo...*"

"*De nada,* my friend, it is nothing. *Noqa kan kani:* you and I are the one." He smiles, and an ocean of understanding passes between us. "Don't be scared about *going back,* Rak, that's the purpose of the hero on his journey. It's not just about undertaking the transformation yourself, it's about bringing back the knowledge you find to share it with your tribe, for their own healing."

"Well that's just what I plan on doing, y'know, with the book." I mightn't be a shaman in the indigenous sense, but as a world-bridger between Western culture and the indigenous world, I knew I was playing a shamanistic role. *Language was my medicine* and with it I would do my best to record my awakening and help heal with my words.

"What will you call it?"

"*Aya.* It's my love song to her."

"Ha. I'm sure *madre* ayahuasca will like that," he says with a smile, gathering up the ayahuasca bottles he's prepared and bundling them into a bag. "C'mon then, my friend, let's go talk with her directly, and you can say your goodbye."

I take a deep breath and steal a last look over the puma cityscape before me. A light twinkles out right where the puma's right eye would be, as if the spirit of Cuzco itself is winking at me.

One more ceremony to go, it teases. *The journey isn't over yet.*

Kevin's original plan was to hold the ceremony at *K'uychi Wasi,* just the two of us. But at the last minute some Australians who work at Jack's café down in the tourist bit of Cuzco asked to sit ceremony, so we've switched to their house, a lush, two-story building sunk down into a hill in a nice part of town.

Strange as it seems, I find myself in a modern, suburban kitchen talking to Jane, an attractive blond woman in her late thirties, who coincidentally, turns out to be from my hometown of Melbourne. Jack, her partner, is a tall, lanky man with a friendly smile and a gregarious nature. Both of them are chain smoking, nervous about the impending ceremony.

And to be honest, they don't quite seem to be the core ayahuasca demographic. Some of the Cuzco mystique must be rubbing off however, because despite all they have heard about the vine, they're still keen to give it a go. A friend of theirs, Melanie, a dark-haired woman, turns up after a while, and nervously holds conversation, and before long a dinner party atmosphere develops.

Kevin announces the ceremony is beginning and lays his Inca blanket out against one wall, in front of a makeshift altar where he sets out the ayahuasca bottles and some *agua de florida,* his rattle and *mapachos,* and other tools of the trade.

We're in the basement lounge of the house, surrounded by wood paneling, polished floorboards, maroon painted walls with woven tapestries, and mood lighting. Behind our backs is a wall of bay windows mounted by heavy curtains, with a six-foot mirror taking up the entire space along the other wall. Vomit buckets are laid out at the base of the couch and by the mattresses on the floor. Upstairs I can hear the relentless pacing of a large dog, anxious, as if he senses a storm brewing.

Kevin explains the nature of ayahuasca and what the ceremony will entail as Jack, Jane, and Melanie chain smoke like they're about to jump out of an airplane and have to work on a nicotine rush to get their courage up. Once we're all settled in we dim the lights and leave a few candles placed strategically around, illuminating the room in long shadows. Kevin does some chakra toning and I ohm along, but it's too much for the others and they wait patiently for us to finish, puffing away furiously on their cigarettes.

Kevin is very open and takes time to give his cosmic download about ayahuasca and the hierarchy of the celestial realms, and answer any questions the group may have. "The brew is *cielo* ayahuasca—sky ayahuasca, very clean and light," he announces. "It also has a little *toé,* and *wambasi,* also known as *chagropanga,* which has the active DMT-content. It's often called the *grandmother spirit.* There's also some *mapacho* and a few other things."

Then we drink. As always, we go up one at a time to hold that little wooden cup, full of ayahuasca, the vine of souls. I'm conscious that this is my last ceremony, and of having held cups like this before in endless *malocas* and jungle huts across Peru. It is my intent tonight to talk to the spirit of ayahuasca, *la madre sagrade,* and to thank her for the journey I have gone on with her, the knowledge she has given me, and for the energy of all the beautiful people I have met. After all the ceremonies, and all the questions and things I had been asking, needing from the mother, this time I wanted to give back.

The brew itself is very gassy, but it goes down smooth and easy, and we sit back on the cushions and mattresses on the floor while Jane lies on the red velvet couch. Kevin begins to sing an *icaro* I recognize from Sachamama—*dun da da da da dah dun dunna dun dun duh da da dun*—and then suddenly fumbles and vomits prodigiously into one of the bowls on the ground. I instantly feel bad for him, my friend and my brother—I don't want him to look bad with the gringos, but as he convulses in wracking heaves on the floor, it's not looking good.

The dog is running around furiously overhead and barking as Kevin picks himself up and moves to the bathroom, breaking the circle and everyone's expectations. As he cleans himself up the thought flashes through my mind: *will he be able to conduct the ceremony?*

"Ah, I'm sorry, that was a bit unexpected, even for me," he apologizes as he returns and sits by the altar again, picking up his *shacapa* fan and rattle and starting a beat. He launches into another *icaro* to ease back into things, and then dowses the candles, letting a calm darkness descend. After he's tuned us in he comes round and blows *mapacho* smoke on us, singing individual *icaros* with healing vibrations unique to our energy fields. His song is as strong as any indigenous *curandero* and a flash of pride for my shaman-brother breaks through me.

After a while the ayahuasca becomes like a bridge to my past and I remember everyone I have drunk with—the *curanderos,* the *ayahuasqueros,* and the gringos—holding them all in my heart and thanking then. I remember all the drinkers bunkered down on the wooden floorboards and dirt floors of *malocas* across Peru, my seed-brothers and sisters. I know that we have drunk from the vine and we share the same tale, we who have unlocked the secret rooms in our hearts and connected with the spirit world within. These are not just words for us, they are valid experiences, places of being that once touched, can never be forgotten.

Time is endless in the dark, but after what seems about an hour Kevin's voice rings out, asking if anyone would like another cup, and Jack and I oblige. An age goes by and the medicine stews and brews, working on a deep, cellular level. I'm getting flash visions of snakes moving through me in multi-colored fractaling waves . . . The medicine is working on my DNA, showing me strands of myself, but everything feels healthy and there's no need to vomit as the medicine works its way down, down, down, deep into my core . . .

I'm curled up in a fetal state, enduring the visions and *holding on,* holding onto the seeker, the journalist, the identity construct which is narrating this story, all the pressures of "me". . . and having to learn the same old lesson once again:

Hold on. Let go. Don't hold on. Let go.

I hold onto so much all the time and because I've adapted I didn't even realize the holding was there, deep within me—until I have to purge. I rush to the bathroom and thank God—there's a porcelain toilet. I just manage to get on it as the purge moves down and through me like a colonic irrigation. Maybe I should try a little vomit, I think. I still don't really feel like it but—*bluuurrrgghhh* I spew into the sink, spraying wave after wave of ayahuasca purge out of me and leaving a foamy residual bubbling like carbonated water. Ah, the beauty of the medicine, that cleanses and relieves . . . and makes us fresh . . .

I'm in the bathroom with the door shut, on the toilet, when more visions come, shimmering and molding into my being . . . Throughout my Amazon trip the ayahuasca visions have consistently been jungle flavored, or swirling kaleidoscopic energy patterns . . . But this time they're very different: zigzag triangles and pyramids, squares and crosses, all the Incan designs I've seen throughout Cuzco on blankets and handicrafts . . . It's the energy of the Andes radiating from the hills and mountains and the *Apus,* carrying me into a giant clockwork Incan trip . . .

I just make it back to my mattress in the lounge room before I'm transported into the sky and suddenly a fully realized, three-dimensional color view of the Andes unfolds before me like a movie. I'm seeing cities, like Burroughs said one sees on *yagé,* but Andean cities, built from adobe tiles and mud, ancient civilizations that flash before my eyes all fresh and new. Overlaying them is this glistening light and energy coursing through, like a circuit.

I zoom in and out of the vista below me and soon find myself at Machu Picchu again, flying over the sacred city, which looks like a stone shaker-shaker in microcosm of the heavens above. My spirit hovers and I go into what some commentators have called the "prison complex," telescoping down into the chambers, heavy under the weight of the stones.

It's dark here, an almost total absence of light, but I can feel the spirits of two priests, dressed in black ponchos with black helmets or hoods. There are other people here, too, but it's all very dark and heavy, like I've just ghosted into a ritual sacrifice in action, and I will myself away.

And then I'm flying over Cuzco again and in the shape of it I glimpse the puma, and it's beautiful, the spirit totem is glistening and alive, purring at me.

Suddenly I'm pulled out of my fugue state when Kevin comes by for some one-on-one healing, and with my eyes open the visions subside . . .

"It's your time," Kevin says. "Your higher guardian angel is speaking to you, you heard it recently, yeah? Knowledge is coming through and *you're walking the path.* The spirits have told me it's time to give you a gift, a new crown," he says, cupping my face with his hands, tender in the dark. He works on my third eye then, rubbing ash over it and pressing down firmly with his thumb.

"The energy in your third eye is like a corkscrew," Kevin explains, "and as I was adjusting it the right way it kept winding back the other way, so set it was in its patterns. But now your third eye is attuned. The spirit gates are open." He sneaks me a warm smile. "It's not me doing this, it's the spirits that choose. I'm just the intermediary for them."

I close my eyes and fall back into the vision, picking up where I left off. Kevin keeps singing *icaros,* specially crafted sounds that hook my energetic body and pull me out of the baseline groove and plunge me into a higher dimensional state. As well as seeing visions my sound sense tunes in, and I can hear an underwater-accordion made of sea coral... It sounds like the eerie, squelchy, high-pitched vibrational angel-speak I heard at Machu Picchu echoing and reverberating inside me.

It's *my icaro* communicating with me, I realize, the song of the stone that was placed in my heart back at Love Creek... *muchas gracias*... I begin singing the song, humming it back and joining the *planetary icaro*...

And then suddenly the vision changes, and I'm in the presence of a grandmother spirit... She comes to me then, a little Shipiba woman, like all the Shipibo blanket hustlers I've seen on my travels in Pucallpa and Iquitos with their crazy ayahuasca vibrational pattern-maps sewn on their blankets and skirts.

She is withered and worn but her skin is so vibrant and her essence radiates from her... This body is all she has in the world, and the wind and the rain and the sun all beat down upon her and it makes her soul strong—and that's all any of us have, really, our soul-strength. We blanket ourselves in comfort and in Western ways, in all the material things, and they make our soul soft. But *Grandmother Aya,* she is old and worn, and strong.

She holds out her hand and invites me with her on a final journey, and without hesitation I take it. Together we climb up into some type of metal ship, or canoe—it has the same energy as the *collectivos* I've been on throughout Peru, coming back from Ollantaytambo and Urumbamba, on the way to the Sacred Valley, squeezing into tiny vans with twenty people and a goat, our energy fields overlapping, no pretense, just us being us in that space.

As we settle into the space *collectivo* she looks at me, and says, *Little niño, child of my heart, do not be afraid. You have gone to the jungle of your soul and faced your demons. And now it is time to meet the Maker . . .*

A violent wind picks us up and we lift off. Up. Up, into the stars, speeding towards a constellation I recognize as the Milky Way . . .

I glance back down and have a flash of the Nazca lines, the totems of the bird and the astronaut, and intimations that the whole Incan culture was pointed towards the stars because that was their destination. This is where all their spiritual journeys led them: Innerspace leads into an infinite vibrational sea of the Godhead, and all outerspace is like the outer edge of a wheel, connected to the central axis of the Source.

We're hurtling through the heavens and I can feel the dimensions passing and how each level has a role. I can see where the glossolalia of the throat chakra and the visions of third eye are stored as Aya reads me and visions feedback and the remembrance begins . . .

I pass through the evolutionary tunnel and I'm stripped raw, toggling between past and future states, opened up to multidimensional time to see all life as an unbroken thread, past-present-future all one hyperobject . . .

As I pass over to the other side, Aya looks at me, opens herself, and says, *Keep growing, little seed, and move towards the light . . .*

BIBLIOGRAPHY

Ascott, Roy. "The Bridge Is Not the Gap: Mapping New Territories of Media and Mind." An article on *btgjapan.org*, 2001.

Beech, Charlotte, and Rob Rachowiecki. *Lonely Planet Peru*, 5th edition. Lonely Planet Publications, January 2004.

Bingham, Hiram. *Lost City of the Incas*. Phoenix, 2003.

Bohm, David. *Wholeness and the Implicate Order*. Routledge, 1995.

Bucke, Richard Maurice. *Cosmic Consciousness: A Study in the Evolution of the Human Mind*. Arkana, 1991.

Burroughs, William, and Alan Ginsberg. *The Yagé Letters*. City Lights, 1963.

Callaway, J.C. "A Proposed Mechanism for the Visions of Dream Sleep." *Medical Hypotheses* 26 (1998): 119–124.

Callaway, J.C., G.S. Brito, and E.S. Neves. "Phytochemical Analyses of *Banisteriopsis caapi* and *Psychotria viridis*." *Journal of Psychoactive Drugs* 37, no. 2 (2005): 145–150.

Campbell, Joseph. *The Hero with a Thousand Faces*. Princeton University Press, 1968.

Castaneda, Carlos. *The Teachings of Don Juan: A Yaqui Way of Knowledge*. University of California Press, 1968.

Charing, Howard G. "Communion with the Infinite." *Sacred Hoop* magazine, 2005, 30–33.

Cobo, Father Bernabe, and Roland Hamilton. *Inca Religion and Customs*. University of Texas Press, 1990.

Copens, Philip. Viracocha Voyage. *Frontier Magazine* 10.5, October/November 2004.

Davis, Erik, and Michael Rauner. *The Visionary State: A Journey through California's Spiritual Landscape*. Chronicle Books, 2006.

Davis, Wade. *One River: Explorations and Discoveries in the Amazon Rain Forest*. Simon & Schuster, 1996.

Dobkin de Rios, Marlene. *Visionary Vine: Hallucinogenic Healing in the Peruvian Amazon*. Waveland Press, 1972.

Eliade, Mircea. *Shamanism: Archaic Techniques of Ecstasy*. Arkana, 1964.

Elorrieta Salazar, Edgar, and Fernando Elorrieta Salazar. *Cusco and the Sacred Valley of the Incas.* Tanpu S.R.L., 2001.

Fraser, Sylvia. *The Green Labyrinth: Exploring the Mysteries of the Amazon.* Thomas Allen & Son, 2003.

French, Hayley, and Helen Cline. "Biodiversity Prospecting, Trade, and Community Rights." *European Biopharmaceutical Review,* Spring 2003.

Frost, Peter, and Ben Box. *Footprints Cusco and the Inca Trail Handbook.* Footprint Handbooks, 2002.

Gimbutas, Marija, and Joseph Campbell. *The Language of the Goddess.* Thames & Hudson, 2001.

Gonzalez v. O Centro Espirita Beneficente União do Vegetal, 546 U.S. 2006.

Gorman, Peter. "Making Magic." *Omni Magazine,* July 1983.

Grob, C.S., D.J. McKenna, J.C. Callaway, G.S. Brito, E.S. Neves, G. Oberlander, O.L. Saide, E. Labigalini, C. Tacla, C.T. Miranda, R.J. Strassman, and K.B. Boone. "Human Psychopharmacology of Hoasca, A Plant Hallucinogen Used in Ritual Context in Brasil." *Journal of Nervous and Mental Disease* 184, no. 2 (1996): 86–94.

Grunwell, John N. "Ayahuasca Tourism in S.A." *Newsletter of the Multidisciplinary Association for Psychedelic Studies (MAPS)* 8, no. 3 (Autumn 1998): 59–62.

Gurdjieff, G.I. *Meetings with Remarkable Men (All and Everything).* Penguin, 1993.

Hancock, Graham. *Supernatural: Meetings with the Ancient Teachers of Mankind.* The Disinformation Company, 2007.

Harbrink-Numan, Paula (Tarzana). "A Female Shaman!!! Norma Panduro." *The Iquitos Times,* June/July 2006, 14.

Harner, Michael. "The Sound of Rushing Water." *Natural History Magazine,* June/July 1968.

Hofmann, Albert. *LSD: My Problem Child.* Houghton Mifflin, 1983.

James, William. "Subjective Effects of Nitrous Oxide." *Mind* 7 (1882).

Janes, Julian. *The Origin of Consciousness in the Breakdown of the Bicameral Mind.* Mariner Books, 2000.

Jenkins, John Major. *Galactic Alignment: The Transformation of Consciousness According to Mayan, Egyptian, and Vedic Traditions.* Bear & Company, 2002.

Jung, Carl. *The Archetypes and the Collective Unconscious.* Princeton, 1980.

Kaku, Michio. *Hyperspace: A Scientific Odyssey through Parallel Universes, Time Warps, and the 10th Dimension.* Anchor, 1994.

Knight, Danielle. "'An Enemy of Indigenous Peoples': The case of Loren Miller, COICA, the Inter-American…" *Multinational Monitor,* June 1998.

Lamb, Bruce F. *Wizard of the Upper Amazon: The Story of Manuel Cordova Rios.* Houghton Miffton, 1971.

Lane, John. *Iquitos: Gateway to Amazonia; The Alternative Travel Guide,* second edition. CETA, 2006.

Lee, Martin A., and Bruce Shlain. *Acid Dreams: The CIA, LSD and the Sixties Rebellion.* Grove Press, 1985.

Lovelock, James. *Gaia: A New Look at Life on Earth.* Oxford University Press, 2000.

Luna, Luis Eduardo, and Pablo Amaringo. *Ayahuasca Visions: The Religious Iconography of a Peruvian Shaman.* North Atlantic Books, 1991.

Luna, Luis Eduardo, and Steven F. White, eds. *Ayahuasca Reader: Encounters with the Amazon's Sacred Vine.* Synergetic, 2000.

McKenna, Dennis. *Ayahuasca: Human Consciousness and the Spirits of Nature,* edited by Ralph Metzner. Thunder's Mouth Press, 2000.

McKenna, D.J., J.C. Callaway, and C.S. Grob. "The Scientific Investigation of Ayahuasca: A Review of Past and Current Research." *The Heffter Review of Psychedelic Research* 1 (1998): 65–77.

McKenna, Terence. *The Archaic Revival: Speculations on Psychedelic Mushrooms, the Amazon, Virtual Reality, UFOs, Evolution, Shamanism, the Rebirth of the Goddess, and the End of History.* HarperCollins, 1991.

———. *Food of the Gods: The Search for the Original Tree of Knowledge.* Bantam, 1992.

———. *The Invisible Landscape: Mind, Hallucinogens, and the I-Ching.* HarperCollins, 1993.

———. *True Hallucinations: Being an Account of the Author's Extraordinary Adventures in the Devil's Paradise.* HarperCollins, 1994.

———. Time and Mind, *deoxy.org.* A Partial Transcription of A Taped Workshop, May 26/27, 1990.

Moffic, H. Steven. "What About the Bicameral Mind?" *American Journal of Psychiatry* (May 1987): 144.

Narby, Jeremy. *The Cosmic Serpent: DNA and the Origins of Knowledge.* Tarcher/Putnam, 1999.

Ott, Jonathan. *Ayahuasca Analogues: Pangaean Entheogens.* Natural Books, 1994.

Peet, Preston. *Under the Influence: The Disinformation Guide to Drugs.* The Disinformation Company, 2004.

Pinchbeck, Daniel. *Breaking Open the Head: A Psychedelic Journey into the Heart of Contemporary Shamanism.* Broadway, 2003.

Plato. *Republic,* third edition. Hackett Publishing Company, 2005.

Protzen, Jean-Pierre, and Robert Batson. *Inca Architecture and Construction at Ollantaytambo.* Oxford University Press, 1993.

Reinhard, Johan. *The Ice Maiden: Inca Mummies, Mountain Gods, and Sacred Sites in the Andes.* National Geographic, 2006.

Salak, Kira. Peru: Hell and Back. *National Geographic Adventure Magazine,* March 2006.

Sammarco, Francesco, and Dino Palazzolo. El Mundo Magico: Conversations with Sachamama. ... Amazonian Vegetalismo in the Words of Don Francisco Montes.

Shuna. *Re Nudo* (Italy), 2001; *Kindred Spirit Magazine* (England), 2001; *Altrove* (Italy), 2002.

Savinelli, Alfred, and John H. Halpern. MAOI Contraindications. *Newsletter of the Multidisciplinary Association for Psychedelic Studies (MAPS)* 6, no. 1 (Autumn 1995): 58.

Shannon, Benny. *The Antipodes of the Mind: Charting the Phenomenology of the Ayahuasca Experience.* Oxford University Press, 2003.

Sheldrake, Rupert. *A New Science of Life.* Park Street Press, 1995.

Shoemaker, Alan. "Medicinal Plants of the Amazon." *The Iquitos Times,* June/July 2006, 5

Shulgin, Alexander, and Ann Shulgin. *TIHKAL: Tryptamines I Have Known and Loved; The Continuation.* Transform Press, 1997.

Strassman, Rick. *DMT: The Spirit Molecule; A Doctor's Revolutionary Research into the Biology of Near-Death and Mystical Experience.* Park Street, 2001.

Sullivan, William. *The Secret of the Incas—Myth, Astronomy, and the War against Time.* Three Rivers Press, 1997.

Talbot, Michael. *The Holographic Universe.* HarperCollins, 1991.

Weiskopf, Jimmy. *Yajé: The New Purgatory, Encounters with Ayahuasca.* Villegas Editores, 2004.

Wilcox, Joan Parisi. *Keepers of the Ancient Knowledge: The Mystical World of the Q'ero Indians of Peru.* Vega, 2002.

PERMISSIONS

Chapter Three, "Jungle Fever," was originally published in truncated form in *Australian Penthouse* magazine; Chapter Four "Space Cadets," was excerpted in *High Times* magazine; parts of Chapter Five, "Cosmovision," were printed in *Filmmaker Magazine* online; the interview with Kevin Furnas in Chapter Six, "Hamburger Universe," was printed on *Undergrowth.org*; and Chapter Seven, "Surfing," was printed in full in the psychedelic anthology *The Journeybook: Travels on the Frontiers of Consciousness* by Undergrowth Inc (2009).

The author gratefully acknowledges the permission of all interviewees in the quotation of their work, especially:

Roy Ascott: Excerpts from the article "The Bridge Is Not the Gap: Mapping New Territories of Media and Mind" (*btgjapan.org*, 2001). Reprinted by permission of the author.

Howard G. Charing: Excerpts from the article "Communion with the Infinite" (*Sacred Hoop* magazine, 2005). Reprinted by permission of the author.

Peter Gorman: Excerpts from the article "Making Magic" (*Omni* magazine, 1983). Reprinted by permission of the author.

John N. Grunwell: Excerpts from the article "Ayahuasca Tourism in South America" (*Newsletter of the Multidisciplinary Association for Psychedelic Studies (MAPS)*, 1998). Reprinted by permission of the author.

Terence McKenna: Excerpt from "Tryptamine Consciousness" recorded talk from 1982 and "New Maps of Hyperspace" excerpt from a talk given at the Berkeley Institute for the Study of Consciousness, 1984, reprinted in *The Archaic Revival: Speculations on Psychedelic Mushrooms, the Amazon, Virtual Reality, UFOs, Evolution, Shamanism, the Rebirth of the Goddess, and the End of History* (HarperCollins, 1991). Reprinted by permission of his estate, Lux Natura.

Jeremy Narby: Excerpts from *The Cosmic Serpent: DNA and the Origins of Knowledge* (Tarcher/Putnam, 1999). Reprinted by permission of the author.

ACKNOWLEDGMENTS

Thanks to Brian M., who got there first and sent back the map; Flavia and Flami for being Argentinian angels on my trip; Danny for all the sugar; Tom Guise for printing "Jungle Fever" in *Australian Penthouse;* John Bowman for traveling with me to innerspace and recording the alien sounds; Vance Gellert for photographing the jaguarflutterbys; Mad Mick and the girls at the bunkhouse; the Gringo Girls; Gerald and the Yellow Rose for the best food this side of Texas; Alan and Mariella Shoemaker; Jan Kounen; Dennis McKenna; Percy Garcia and Chuck; Margaret and Shane; Theo; John Bernstein; Richard Grossman, Marty, and Rachel; Guillermo; Rama for being my guardian angel and for the pancakes; Norma and Tarzana; Juan and family; Carlos, Len, Julia, Carina, and Jolane for the study notes; Ron Wheelock—brother, I hope you get that roof fixed one day—and Queto for the unconditional love; Juan Acosta for the brainwaves; Sarah; Adele; Javier; Scott Petersen; Rolando for coming back from the madness; Hamilton for the talk; don Francisco for the brew; Rachel for the *icaros;* Pedro and Javier for the good vibes; the family Bardales for welcoming me in; Brian—good luck with the Prime Directive, brother; don Leonardo; don Augustine and family; Emilio for going the distance up the Amazon with a mad gringo; Joel Harris for the long walk to Damascus; Tessa—the whole world knows the blanket covers are down now, dear; Mira for the directions to Machu Picchu; Big K., Kenneth, Jungle, Phoebe, Phe, and Opoeia for the space and time to write this book; Rumi; Jewelli for loving me so well; Jennifer McMahon for the proof is in the pudding; and of course, those who were with me in spirit—Kerri, Foxy Afra, Mary, Tim, and all the ground crew past and present.

And to Kevin Furnas, who crossed over early to lead the way—because in the school of life you were a brother and a teacher. In La'kesh . . .

ABOUT THE AUTHOR

Rak Razam is a new wave entheogenic researcher and the cofounder of Undergrowth.org. A freelance journalist and editor, he specializes in underground and counterculture, spirituality and technology issues. He lives in Mullumbimby, in the far north of NSW, Australia. Contact him via his website: www.rakrazam.com.

Photo of Rak Razam by Tom McKinnon

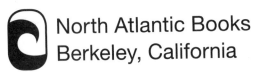

North Atlantic Books
Berkeley, California

Personal, spiritual, and planetary transformation

North Atlantic Books, a nonprofit publisher established in 1974, is dedicated to fostering community, education, and constructive dialogue. NABCommunities.com is a meeting place for an ever-growing membership of readers and authors to engage in the discussion of books and topics from North Atlantic's core publishing categories.

NAB Communities offer interactive social networks in these genres:

NOURISH: Raw Foods, Healthy Eating and Nutrition, All-Natural Recipes

WELLNESS: Holistic Health, Bodywork, Healing Therapies

WISDOM: New Consciousness, Spirituality, Self-Improvement

CULTURE: Literary Arts, Social Sciences, Lifestyle

BLUE SNAKE: Martial Arts History, Fighting Philosophy, Technique

Your free membership gives you access to:

Advance notice about new titles and exclusive giveaways

Podcasts, webinars, and events

Discussion forums

Polls, quizzes, and more!

Go to www.NABCommunities.com and join today.